ACCLAIM FOR LISA SEE's

ON GOLD MOUNTAIN

"Both serious social history and one family's version of realizing the California dream. . . . Fascinating."　　　*—Seattle Times*

"[See] proves to be a clever, conscientious, fair-minded biographer . . . . [She] has done a gallant job of fashioning anecdote, fable and fact into an engaging account."
　　　　　　　　　　　　　—The New York Times Book Review

"A matchless portrait not only of a remarkable family but of a century's changing attitudes. . . . The ambitions, fears, loves, and sorrows of See's huge cast are set forth with the storytelling skills of a novelist."　　　　　　　　　　　　　*—Publishers Weekly*

"Particular in its vivid characters, epic in its sweeping scope . . . compassionate and perceptive."
　　　　　　　　　　　—Michael Dorris, author of The Broken Cord

"Extraordinary! Every sentence pulsates with humor, muscle, meaning, and cool snappy music. . . . Wonderful."
　　　　　　　　　　　—Belle Yang, author of The Lost World of Baba:
　　　　　　　A Return to China Upon the Shoulders of My Father

LISA SEE

ON GOLD MOUNTAIN

Lisa See is the *New York Times* bestselling author of *Shanghai Girls*, *Peony in Love*, *Snow Flower and the Secret Fan*, *Flower Net* (an Edgar Award nominee), *The Interior*, and *Dragon Bones*. She wrote the libretto for the Los Angeles Opera adaptation of *On Gold Mountain* and served as curator for the Autry Museum of Western Heritage's exhibit *On Gold Mountain: A Chinese American Experience*, also featured at the Smithsonian Institute. The Organization of Chinese American Women named her the National Woman of the Year in 2001. She lives in Los Angeles.

Visit Lisa See's website at
www.LisaSee.com.

ON GOLD
MOUNTAIN

THE ONE-HUNDRED-YEAR ODYSSEY OF
MY CHINESE-AMERICAN FAMILY

LISA SEE

VINTAGE BOOKS
A DIVISION OF RANDOM HOUSE, INC.
NEW YORK

FIRST VINTAGE BOOKS EDITION, SEPTEMBER 1996

Copyright © 1995, 2012 by Lisa See

All rights reserved under International and Pan-American
Copyright Conventions. Published in the United States by Vintage Books,
a division of Random House, Inc., New York, and simultaneously in Canada
by Random House of Canada Limited, Toronto. Originally published
in hardcover by St. Martin's Press, New York, in 1995.

Photo credits: Title-page spread, Asian American Studies Library,
University of California at Berkeley, and page 1, Natural History Museum
of Los Angeles County.

Library of Congress Cataloging-in-Publication Data
See, Lisa.
On Gold Mountain/by Lisa See—1st Vintage Books ed.
p. cm.
Includes bibliographical references and index.
ISBN 978-0-307-95039-0
1. See, Lisa—Family.
2. Seay Family.
3. Chinese Americans-California—Biography.
4. California—Biography. I. Title.
F870.C5S44 1996
929'.2'0899510795—dc20 96-11821
CIP

www.vintagebooks.com

Printed in the United States of America
10 9

*For the great-great-grandsons of
Letticie and Fong See,*

*Alexander See Kendall
and
Christopher Copeland Kendall*

Fooling around in the papers my grandparents, especially my grandmother, left behind, I get glimpses of lives close to mine, related to mine in ways I recognize but don't completely comprehend. I'd like to live in their clothes a while. . . .

Wallace Stegner, *Angle of Repose*

CONTENTS

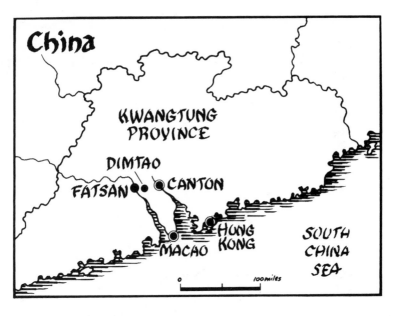

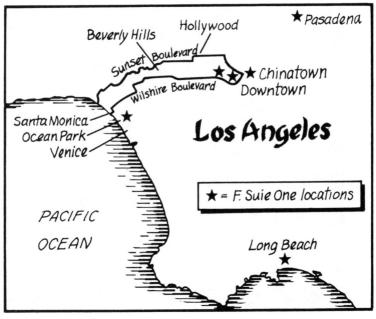

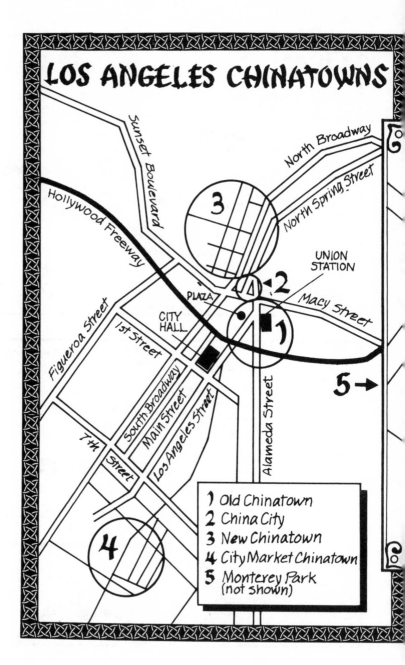

LOS ANGELES CHINATOWNS

Sunset Boulevard

North Broadway

North Spring Street

Hollywood Freeway

3

UNION STATION

PLAZA

△ 2

Macy Street

Figueroa Street

CITY HALL

1st Street

1

5 →

South Broadway

Main Street

Los Angeles Street

Alameda Street

7th Street

4

1 Old Chinatown
2 China City
3 New Chinatown
4 City Market Chinatown
5 Monterey Park
(not shown)

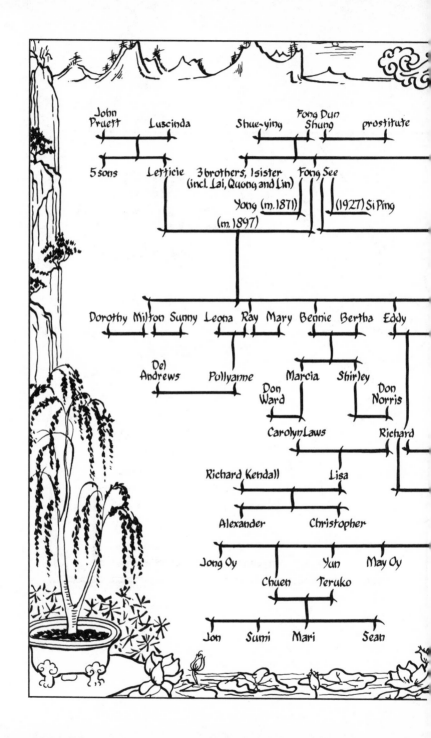

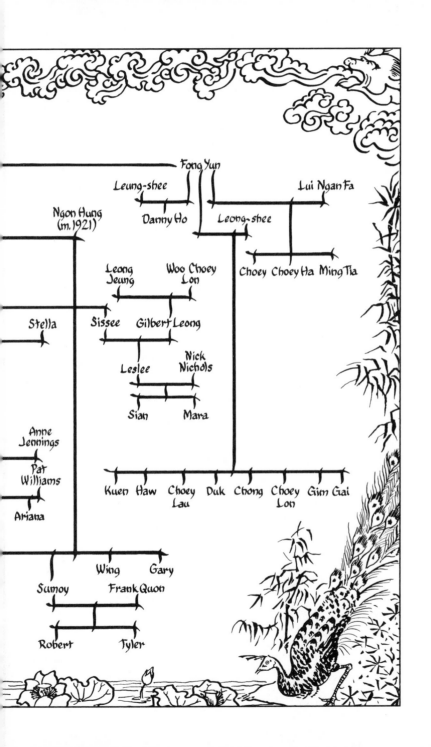

FOREWORD

$\mathbb{F}$ O N G See, my great-grandfather, left China in 1871 as a youngster, found prosperity on the Gold Mountain (the Chinese name for the United States), and lived to reach his hundredth birthday. Rising out of a mass of nameless Asian immigrants, he became one of the richest and most prominent Chinese in the country. He lured customers into his Asian art store by selling tickets to see a stuffed mermaid. He loved money, and had a childlike enthusiasm for fancy cars. He also had a way with women. My family always "knew" that Fong See had two wives. The marriage between Fong See and Letticie Pruett—my Caucasian great-grandmother—would go on to establish the See name. The second wife, a Chinese waif who had supported herself making firecrackers, was only sixteen when she married my great-grandfather, who was sixty-four at the time. This family always lived under the name of Fong. Altogether, Fong See sired twelve children—five Eurasian, seven Chinese—the last born when he was in his late eighties. This is the story of the Sees and the Fongs and how they assimilated into America.

As a girl, I spent frequent weekends and most of my summer vacations with my paternal grandparents in Chinatown. We would pass through a moon gate guarded by two huge stone lions and enter the dark, cool recesses of our family's Chinese antique store, the F. Suie One Company, a gigantic mercantile museum that contained, among other things, porcelains taken from the royal kiln and floated downriver on sampans; altars pillaged from provincial temples; and huge architectural carvings shipped in sections to be reconstructed by Fong See's sons in one of his many warehouses.

At lunchtime, Grandma Stella and I would walk up the street to a restaurant that must have had a real name but that we just called "the little place." Along the way we'd stop to chat with Blackie at the Sam Sing Butcher Shop, with its gold-leafed roast pig in the window. We'd stop in at Margaret's International Grocery and browse through the aisles with their salted plums, dried squid, and fermented tofu. At the restaurant, we'd go back to the kitchen to chat with the cook and watch as he packed up our order into cartons.

Once back at the store, I'd go upstairs to the workroom, with its huge machinery and its pinups of sedate Chinese maidens, where my grandfather and great-uncle Bennie would be engulfed by dense clouds of sawdust and the din of saws. Bennie would invariably look at me wild-eyed and shout, "I'm gonna put you in trash can." Terrified, I'd scramble back downstairs and my grandfather and uncle would wash up with Lava soap.

After lunch, if I got bored—perhaps after playing in the mountains of straw packing, or climbing into the arms of a gigantic Buddha, or making a fort underneath one of the large altars—Grandma Stella would let me "help" her while she worked on the restoration of a coromandel screen. I might clean brushes or mix ink; sometimes she let me use my fingertips to press clay into the chipped areas. Or I might help my great-aunt Sissee as she dusted and polished her way from the bronze room to the art room to the room for scrolls and fabrics, and from one end of the main hall—which held exquisitely carved furniture—to the other.

In the late afternoons, my grandmother and great-aunt Sissee would relax in wicker chairs in the back of the store over cups of strong tea. During that quiet and comfortable time they would reminisce about the past. They told intriguing and often silly stories about missionaries, prostitutes, tong wars, the all-girl drum corps, and the all-Chinese baseball team. They spoke about how the family had triumphed over racist laws and discrimination. Then, as inevitably as Uncle Bennie's threat of the trash can, would come my grandmother's assertion that, "Yes, during the war, the *lo fan* (white people) made all of us Chinese wear buttons so that they would know we weren't Japanese."

My grandmother taught me how to wash the rice until the water ran clear, then—without the aid of a measuring cup—pour water over the grains in the steamer up to the first knuckle of a hand. It didn't matter if it was her knuckle or mine, she explained; for five thousand years the system had worked perfectly. Finally she would place a few lengths of *lop cheung,* a delicious pork sausage, on top to cook as the rice steamed. Meanwhile, my grandfather would be chopping ingredients. Once the rice was on, I became my grandfather's second cook. "The best I ever had," he used to say. Together—although all these years later I can't remember a single thing I did—we would make up a dish of tomato beef for which he was remembered decades after his death.

At family weddings, we'd wait at our table for the bride to come by, and my grandmother would let me be the one in our group to hand over the *lai see*—"good-luck money" wrapped in a red envelope with gold characters of felicity and fortune limned on the outside. My grandmother would take me from table to table through huge banquet rooms, explaining who each and every person was and how they were related to me. "This is your first cousin once removed. This is your third cousin."

In 1989, Aunt Sissee celebrated her eightieth birthday with a traditional Chinese banquet. I will always remember how my cousins and I left our banquet room to spy on the wedding taking place in the main dining room, where at least five hundred guests kept tapping their chopsticks on their bowls or glasses, making an amazing racket. "Well, they must be from Taiwan," one of the cousins sneered. "You know, FOBs, fresh off the boat." Since Fong See's first voyage and his early dubious career selling crotchless underwear to brothels, the family had become the old line, the aristocracy. No longer FOBs, we were ABCs—American-born Chinese.

That evening I gave Sissee a copy of Ruthanne Lum McCunn's book, *Chinese American Portraits,* which, for all its tragedies, secrets, and illicit exploits, also conveys a powerful cultural and artistic ethos. Three days later my cousin Leslee called. She wanted me to know that Sissee, her mother as well as my great-aunt and the only living child of my great-grandfather's half-Chinese, half-Caucasian family, thought it was time for a book to be written about our family and that I was the person to write it. The following week I was over at the store with my tape recorder, listening to the stories Aunt Sissee, my grandmother, and my cousin had to tell. That first day I learned that Fong See was not the first family member to come to the Gold Mountain. His father—my great-great-grandfather—had worked as an herbalist during the building of the transcontinental railroad. I also found out that Fong See had not two but *four* wives. All through the years my relatives had kept these marriages a secret; bigamy was against the law and embarrassing to his children.

Two months later Sissee died suddenly, but Leslee encouraged me to continue with the book. Our friends and family were getting up into their eighties and nineties, she noted, and when they died their stories would be lost. At Leslee's urging, I pressed on. My relatives, including my father, who truly were not disposed to participate, did so—I believe—to honor my great-aunt's wishes.

During the last five years I have interviewed close to one hundred people, rich and poor, Chinese and Caucasian. I struggled with the difficulties posed by different names for the same person: Milton, Ming, Ming-ah, Ah-Ming for my great-uncle; Fong See, Suie On, and See-bok for my great-grandfather. I tried to decipher the heavily accented English of old men who confuse the words for *he* and *she, him* and *her,* in this time and in this town. I spoke with some who could no longer remember their own mothers' names. "It was a long time ago," one man told me.

Poring over documents in the National Archives, I discovered that immigration authorities had been after my relatives from the very beginning, but never really caught on to what they were doing. I received help from numerous libraries, historical societies, and academicians. I nagged relatives, friends, and customers to rummage through their attics, basements, and closets for photographs, papers, and other memorabilia from fairs, art shows, and family rites. I looked at films and videotapes, scrapbooks and letters, packing slips and tax records. In total ignorance, I struggled with the difficulties of the Chinese written language: Should I use Mandarin or Cantonese? And how should I romanize it: with the Wade-Giles or Pinyin system? (Ultimately I decided to use Cantonese with the old-fashioned Wade-Giles method, in keeping with the era of the book. However, medicinal words are more properly rendered in Mandarin/Pinyin.)

What has emerged is a story of melting—how people and cultures melt in all directions. What I haven't yet mentioned is that when my grandmother included herself among the Chinese who had to wear buttons during the war, she might be tucking loose strands of red hair into her bun. My grandmother—like my great-grandmother—was Caucasian, but she was Chinese in her heart. She had melted into that side. Over the years, she had packed away her eyelet dresses with their cinched waists, and had adopted black trousers and loose-fitting jackets, which she always wore with a beautiful piece of Chinese jewelry. She learned how to make lettuce soup, how to give those brides their *lai see,* how to be a proper Chinese daughter-in-law. My great-grandmother, grandmother, and mother were as Caucasian and "American" as they could be, yet they all chose to marry men whose culture was completely different from their own.

Many of the Chinese I interviewed talked about Caucasians as *lo fan* and *fan gway,* as white people, "white ghosts." Often someone would say, by way of explanation, "You know, she was a Caucasian like you." They never knew how startling it was for me to hear that, because all those years in the store and going to those wedding banquets, I thought I was Chinese. It stood to reason, as all those people were my relatives. I had never really paid much attention to the fact that I had red hair like my grandmother and that the rest of them had straight black hair. But I had other proof as well. All Chinese babies are born with a Mongolian spot—a temporary birthmark in the shape of a cabbage—at the small of their backs. I had a trace of that spot when I was born. Though I don't physically look Chinese, like my grandmother, I am Chinese in my heart.

Finally, it is hard to read any book on Chinese immigration or the Chinese experience that isn't critical of other books on the same material. All of them have their own views on racism, poverty, the role of women, language, politics, art, love, and beauty. I don't know who's right or wrong, or who's more historically accurate as opposed to more politically correct. All I can hope to do is tell *our* story. *On Gold Mountain* doesn't purport to be the whole truth—just *a* truth, one that has been filtered through my heart, my experience, and my research.

PART I

CHAPTER I

THE WONDER TIME

1866–71

FONG Dun Shung hoisted his Gold Mountain bag onto his shoulder and nodded one last time to his wife, daughter, and Number One and Number Four sons. He turned, and began the half-day's walk to Fatsan, where he would board a sampan and float east through the Pearl River delta to the big city of Canton, then south to Hong Kong, where he would board a ship for *Gam Saan,* the Gold Mountain. Fong Dun Shung and his second and third sons padded single file along the raised pathways that divided the pale green ricefields that lay just outside the protective wall of Dimtao. How long, he wondered, would it be before they returned home?

Fong Dun Shung had heard of other men who had made their fortunes as Gold Mountain men. Defying the powerful ties of family tradition and the more tangible threats by the Dowager Empress of death by decapitation for leaving China, many men had gone looking for gold. It was said of *Gam Saan* that a man could find pieces of gold as large as a firstborn son lying openly on the ground for anyone to pick up and keep. Now people talked about this railroad and jobs to be had for any man who was willing to work hard. In his village, the men guessed that even if you couldn't save one thousand American dollars, you would make at least eight hundred. Fong Dun Shung shifted the weight of his basket from his right shoulder to his left. He was lucky. He was being given a free trip to the Gold Mountain, and he and his sons had already been promised jobs.

These had been harsh years for his family. Dimtao was a poor village, and this branch of the Fong family was one of the poorest. Fong Dun Shung didn't own land, not even one miserable *mou* in a time when the whole world knew that at least three *mou* were required to sustain a single life. He couldn't rent land, for he was too poor even to buy rice seed.

He was an herbalist, trained in an art many thousands of years old. From his father he had learned that the most important thing in the universe was *qi*—the essential life force—and that the balancing of *qi* was imperative to maintaining good health. He had learned to envision the human body as a universe containing the five elements—wood, fire, earth, metal, and water—and that each of these elements governed a corresponding organ—liver, heart, spleen, lungs, or kidneys. If any of the six essences—wind, cold, summer heat, dampness, dryness, or fire— became overbalanced, then a body would weaken and fall prey to disease and illness. He had learned all this from his father, and in these past years Fong Dun Shung had been teaching his sons.

Fong Dun Shung was a traveling man who, with his older sons, wandered from village to village throughout the countryside. On good days, villagers clustered around as his sons beat gongs to announce their arrival. Then they laid out mats and blankets on the rough dirt outside a family association house inside of which the births and deaths of all of a village's ancestors were carved into stone and mounted on cool walls. Perhaps it was this close proximity to the thoughts of ancestors, or perhaps it was the *kung fu* that Fong and his sons performed to attract children and old people. He couldn't say now. But for many years—as he tossed a son through the air, or moved himself through the exercises based on the movements of the deer, bear, tiger, monkey, and crane, which would be restorative for rheumatism, arthritis, digestive disorders, and chronic fatigue—there had always been customers.

At the end of the exhibition, Fong displayed his herbs. Women clustered around. "What may I take to help make strong the son who grows in my belly?" a woman heavy with child might ask. He would give her a packet of ground peach pit, tiger thistle, and the leaf of the pagoda tree to facilitate blood circulation. "Healthy parents have healthy children," he liked to say. "If you keep your blood strong, then your children will go through life disease-free and have healthy children of their own." For women who would not stop bleeding after childbirth, he prescribed brews made from Japanese catnip, turmeric, and safflower.

He was ministering to a woman with boils when the railroad scout spotted him and asked if he would like to go to the Gold Mountain to help the Chinese laborers when they got sick. "The coolies don't trust our western doctors," the foreign devil rattled off in tones that Fong could not understand, but which were translated for him by a Chinese helper. Fong was told that the railroad company would pay for his passage, his herbs, and his knowledge. He didn't have to consider this proposal very long; he knew what his life had been like in the last few years.

As his family had grown, as his sons had asked for wives but could not afford to pay the bride-price for a proper wife, or even to buy an unwanted girl as a concubine from a family even more desperate than his own, Fong's business had become more difficult and customers harder to find. Some of the reasons for this he knew from gossip, but how could a grown man trust gossip? Fong Dun Shung was an unimportant man, who could neither read nor write. So he had to trust gossip, and what he saw with his own eyes.

These were times of terrible unrest in China. When he was a young man and just married, there had been the first Opium War of 1840. His country had paid six million taels of silver to Great Britain to redeem Canton, as well as a thirty-three-million-tael indemnity payment. Hong Kong had been given to the British, and other ports had been forced open. Opium had flooded the market. Over the years, Fong had seen what this did to rich and poor alike. The Second Opium War, which had ended only six years ago, in 1860, was even worse: another huge payment had been made to the British; missionaries had been permitted to come in and preach about their one god; more ports had been opened; and cheap, mass-produced items had begun to be imported, destroying his country's small industries. It was unfair, but China's weapons—spears, swords, arrows, and outdated cannons—were no match for British artillery, rifles, and ships.

The plunder of his homeland didn't stop with outsiders. Only thirteen years ago the Red Turbans—groups of clans and secret society members—had captured nearby Fatsan and tramped through the villages and fields toward Canton. Imperial troops and local militia had tried to combat these ruffians, and in the process entire villages had been burned to the ground. In the same period the Punti (the "Local People") and the Hakka (the "Guest People") had waged their own useless civil wars. If this were not enough, Hung Hsiu-ch'uan, who called himself the Second Son of Heaven, had led the T'ai P'ing Rebellion, capturing and holding Nanking as the capital of his own dynasty. Twenty-five million people had died in the countryside, from war and its resulting famine. Warlords, sensing that the ruling Manchus would do nothing to stop them, now mounted their own campaigns—ravaging, pillaging, extorting.

As Fong traveled through the countryside, he would often pass villages that had once given him good business. Sometimes he would not even have to enter through the gates to know that death had come; the heads of men to whom he had sold herbs in years past hung on stakes outside the village walls. He would walk on. Where in the past he had seen children calling out good-natured greetings from astride the backs of water buffalo, he might see a few half-starved, naked children hunkered down next to village streams, hoping wearily to catch a fish. Again, nothing to do but shrug and walk on. Nothing to help them now, and only trouble to find.

Now, as he followed the river south toward Canton, Fong Dun Shung hoped that he would become a successful Gold Mountain man and return in a few years with gold in his pockets. He imagined that he would become the headman of his village, and that everyone would look up to him. He would be rich. He would have many wives and many more sons. It was possible.

In 1862 the slave trade was banned internationally, so foreign men tricked, coerced, or "shanghaied" Chinese travelers into signing contracts for boat fare, which left them little better than slaves. Like the blacks who had been shipped to America from across the Atlantic, the Chinese, too, were loaded onto overcrowded ships where they lived belowdecks for the duration of their voyage across the Pacific. Conditions on shipboard were nightmarish. On some vessels, men found themselves stacked like cordwood in three-tiered bunks six feet long and thirteen and a half inches wide, with only seventeen to twenty-four inches of headroom. These holds reeked with the stench of humanity as hatches were battened down to prevent escape. The sojourners— men who promised to return to their home villages—were given a bucket of water a day for washing and drinking. Food was also scarce. The foreigners knew from past experience that the fastest thing to break a man's spirit was hunger.

No one knows exactly which ship bore Fong Dun Shung and his two sons to the Gold Mountain, but in earlier days, death rates were consistently high. On the *Exchange,* 85 of 613 coolies died. In 1854, after eighty days at sea, the *Libertad* reported 150 dead from scurvy and "ship's fever." On the *John L. Stevens,* which carried 550 immigrants, conditions were so bad that standees had to take turns on the too-few bunks. Conditions improved when the four massive ships that constituted the Pacific Mail Steamship Company's fleet began carrying as many as 1,200 passengers in steerage. Men brought their own bedding and slept on wooden frames. During the day these beds could be cleared for living space. Still, men suffered from seasickness and diarrhea, from bad food and tainted water, and often arrived in San Francisco after their thirty-odd-day journey in severely weakened condition.

By the time Fong Dun Shung arrived in San Francisco, in early 1867, the sight of hundreds of Chinese streaming down the gangplanks of these huge ships had become common. The laborers changed from their filthy traveling clothes to clean, blue cotton tunics and pants. Their queues, neatly braided, swung rhythmically behind them. Each carried with him rolled blankets, matting, and a basket filled with his meager possessions, all tied together with a length of rope.

Fong Dun Shung and his sons felt lost and confused in the hubbub of the wharf. There were no immigration procedures, no customs officials. He had been told he would be met by someone. But by whom? Above the sounds of the commotion along the wharf, Fong heard the strains of his dialect. He looked at his sons, who nodded their agreement.

"We must find the man who belongs to that voice," they seemed to say. Gently pushing through the crowd, they noticed that other men from the ship seemed to be grouping together around other Gold Mountain men who called out in various dialects: "I am from Nam Hoi. I look for all men from Nam Hoi." "I speak Sze Yup. All men who recognize this language of strong men, come to me now." Fong and his sons found the man who spoke the Fatsan dialect from the Nam Hoi district. The labor agent ordered Fong, his sons, and a handful of others into single file. They trotted away from the crowded dock and along the streets leading to the center of the city.

How strange it looked. Certainly, Fong Dun Shung thought, this must be a city with great *feng shui*—the propitious confluence of air and water. Buildings clung on hillsides catching the water, wind, and air. Some were brightly painted, like temples. Mostly they were far apart and seemingly unprotected. As much as he hoped never to see the sea again except to return home to his wife and other children, Fong couldn't help but glance back and down to the bay, which shimmered in the crisp, wintery sunlight.

On they trotted until they reached Chinatown. Bright red lanterns hung here and there. Three-cornered pieces of yellow silk swayed in the slight breeze before some buildings, telling these new visitors that here were restaurants. Signboards advertised herbs, clothing, jobs. He saw no sign of women except a few lonely, pale faces that peeked out from small barred windows. Prostitutes, his guide told them.

The family's time in San Francisco was destined to be short. Before leaving the city, Fong, with chits from the railroad office, procured satchels of cinnamon, hawthorn, gardenia, clove, licorice, and chrysanthemum in the form of leaves, blossoms, roots, rhizomes, and pods. He could not anticipate what lay ahead, but he knew from experience that men everywhere suffered from colds, cuts, and stomach troubles. With help from the Six Companies—a federation of benevolent societies representing districts and counties in China—his sons sought out and purchased heavy boots and black hats. At the end of the week the trio boarded another ship, this time a riverboat, which slowly carried them to Sacramento, where the Chinese travelers again divided into groups and were transported by wagon or train to worksites high in the Sierra.

The California that Fong Dun Shung entered was a peculiar place filled with nature's bounty—fertile soil, a wide variety of animal life, mountains, deserts, valleys, and rich mineral deposits. It was a land destined to be forever built on dreams. The same hopes for gold nuggets the size of babies that had originally enticed early Chinese sojourners had also enticed men to leave their town houses in Boston, farms in Ohio, ranches in Montana, and plantations in Georgia. These men had come alone, for the West was no place for womenfolk. Until 1869, when the transcontinental railroad would be completed, California was seventy percent male, and they were a lawless bunch—rowdy, rough, filthy. Few "good" women lived among them. One result of this lack was that there were no women to wash clothes. Wealthy men sent their clothes to Hong Kong to be laundered, starched, and ironed. A dozen shirts cost an outlandish twelve dollars and took two to four months to make the round trip. But for years people looked forward to "steamer day," when loads of clean wash would enter San Francisco Bay and be distributed to its owners. For at least one week, everyone would be smartly dressed and starched.

In 1850, two years after gold was discovered at Sutter's Mill, California became a state. Eleven years later, in 1862, the first anti-coolie club was formed. That same year, Leland Stanford became governor. In his inaugural address he said, "To my mind it is clear, that the settlement among us of an inferior race is to be discouraged by every legitimate means. Asia, with her numberless millions, sends to our shores the dregs of her population." Later that same year, Stanford became the president of the Central Pacific Railroad.

The Big Four—Stanford, Charles Crocker, Mark Hopkins, and C. P. Huntington—embraced the grandiose idea and the potential profits of a transcontinental railroad. Certainly the need was there. As construction began, three equally unpleasant choices awaited even the most hardy westward-seeking adventurers. They could spend six to nine months—depending on the weather—sailing down the east coast of South America and around Cape Horn. Or they could sail as far as the Isthmus of Panama, pole up the crocodile-infested Chagres River in small boats, then transfer to a mule team for a fifty-mile hike over the mountains to the Pacific. Although this method cut months off the trip, it carried with it the inherent risks of yellow fever, cholera, and death. Finally, adventurers could spend six months crossing the deserts, plains, and mountains from the Missouri River—a dangerous trip frequently ending in death from disease, Indian attack, or accident. A transcontinental railroad would reduce the travel time to one week and substantially improve the odds of a safe and healthy arrival. With a shorter, less arduous trip, more women might make their homes out West—the prospect not only of clean wash but of company in bed proved to be a powerful motivator for California's mostly male population.

The Central Pacific Railroad broke ground on January 8, 1863. Two years later, only fifty miles of track had been laid. Crocker became convinced that the Asian race that had built the Great Wall of China could also build his dream. It was also cheaper and faster to bring workers to San Francisco from Canton by boat—given good winds and fair seas—than to recruit Caucasian laborers from east of the Mississippi.

At first, Crocker met with tremendous resistance. Upon hearing the idea, the superintendent of construction exclaimed in distaste, "I will not boss Chinese." And Stanford, who had campaigned on an anti-Chinese platform just four years before, faced public embarrassment if he reversed himself. Still, Crocker pressed his case, relying on the simple fact that his partners were astute businessmen accustomed to considering the bottom line. At the beginning of 1865, fifty Chinese men—former miners who had experience with drills and explosives—were hired on an experimental basis. They proved so successful that six months later between two and three thousand Chinese worked on the railroad.

That first winter was the harshest on record. "Crocker's Pets," as they came to be known, lived like moles. They dug tunnels through forty-foot snowdrifts and continued to lay track. Avalanches whisked men away, tunnels collapsed. Still the work went on. When the spring thaws came, men were uncovered still standing and holding their tools, their faces frozen in death masks of horror.

By the summer of 1868, nine-tenths of the fourteen thousand railroad workers on the Central Pacific were Chinese—nearly one-quarter of the total population of Chinese in the country. They dynamited through 1,695 feet of solid rock to create the Donner Tunnels. While the workers on the Union Pacific rushed through the flatlands of Nebraska and the plains, the Chinese on the Central Pacific built a line that rose seven thousand feet in one hundred miles. Lowered by wicker baskets down sheer cliffs, they chiseled through granite and shale to carve out shelves on which to lay track. With hammers, crowbars, and dynamite they made the earth yield to the ambitions of the Big Four.

Each night, high in the mountains, Fong Dun Shung and the other Chinese laborers gathered around the campfire. One night there might be a game of *dow ngow,* the game of the battling bulls, with each man shaking the dice to determine who should throw the dominoes first. But mostly they played fan-tan. The dealer placed a small handful of buttons from a pan on the ground under a cup. After bets were laid down, the cup was lifted and the buttons counted out four at a time. The men who guessed how many buttons would be left—one, two, three, or none—would be winners depending on how they had placed their bets.

Occasionally they were entertained by fiddlers or flutists who had broken free of life on the railroad gang and now traveled from camp to camp. On some nights, professional storytellers regaled them with tales of the Monkey King Sun Wu Kung, or the Stories of the Manchus or of the Three Kingdoms. At regular intervals a civilized barber came into camp and the men waited their turns to have their foreheads shaved and their queues rebraided. On those evenings when no visitors came through, the tired laborers would ask Fong Dun Shung to tell them a story.

"Remind us of our home," someone might say, as he poked at a sweet potato cooking in the embers of the fire.

"Tell us the story of the snake again," another might request.

Fong Dun Shung looked out at the men sitting on their haunches, their faces worn and creased from the stifling heat of summer and the bitter cold of winter. "Many centuries ago," he began, "deep in the heart of the province of Yunnan, a farmer was pestered by a snake who refused to die. At daylight the farmer would leave his hut and see the reptile. At night when he came home from his ricefields the snake would still be there. He had been idle, sitting and warming himself on the big stone that lay near the farmer's well. This would make the farmer so angry that he would take a length of giant bamboo and beat that snake until even its death shivers had left him for good. The farmer would take the serpent's lifeless body and toss it carelessly into the weeds. But the next morning when the farmer emerged from his hut, the snake would once again be warming itself on the stone."

Fong Dun Shung paused to let this miracle sink in. A few of the men spat into the fire.

"Day after day," Fong Dun Shung continued, "the farmer killed that insolent snake and threw him away. Day after day the snake slithered out of the weeds and once again took its place by the well. One night the farmer decided to wait and see what spirit or god it was that revived his nemesis. As the moon rose and illuminated all below it, the farmer watched as the snake lifted its head and nibbled at the leaves of the weeds that were supposed to be its resting bier. In this way, through that canny farmer's observation of that wily snake, our ancestors discovered the curative powers of herbs, and thus our country's great healing art was invented."

"Tell us the rest," a young man called out.

"That lowly weed was *san qi*," Fong Dun Shung explained. "For centuries the most famous herbalists in China have used it to make *bai yao*, the white powder that binds the edges of wounds and causes them to heal swiftly. The soldiers in our country have always used this and bestowed upon it the special name of 'gold-no-trade.' I used it on you, Ah-yee, last spring when you drove the spike through your calf, and on you, Ah-sing, when you slipped down the cliff and we thought you had ended this life."

Unlike his sons and the other men who worked on the line, Fong Dun Shung spent most of his days in the camp. He attended to men who were sick, holding their heads up as they drank the bitter herbal teas that he brewed to relieve their symptoms. Sometimes he would be called out to the line to see a man who had been injured. Fong would speak to the head of the gang to confirm whether a man could go back to work or whether he needed to rest in camp.

Fong Dun Shung usually saw the men who hung from baskets down the sides of cliffs when they were already dead. Sometimes the rope holding a basket sheared off and a man's body was broken on the rocks hundreds of feet below. At other times the basket men would swing out away from the cliff for the detonation of dynamite, only to have the basket swing in again too soon. What good could Fong do for those men whose arms and legs had been torn away, whose faces were left a bloody mass of unidentifiable tissue, bone fragments, and blood? He and a few of his countrymen would see to the burial, noting the site so that eventually the bones could be dug up, cleaned, and sent back to China for proper burial.

In winter, Fong Dun Shung prepared tonics to stave off chills, fever, phlegm, coughs, nausea—symptoms that plagued his countrymen in these snowy mountains. In summer he mixed potions to cool a man's body when he had suffered heatstroke, or to soothe insect bites or sunburn. All year round he had on hand poultices for cuts, scrapes, abrasions, sprains, broken bones—all those things that endangered the men as they hammered and chiseled and dynamited their way sometimes around the mountains and sometimes straight through them. Creating these mixtures was time-consuming and required his total attention as he selected and ground ingredients, boiled them until they had reduced by half or more, then sealed them in earthenware jars.

When a man traveled to the Second City of Sacramento or to the Big City of San Francisco, or when a man left this land of hardship forever to return to his home village, he would come to Fong Dun Shung for a dose of spring tonic, for every man wished to be virile when he visited a prostitute or was reunited with his wife. If Fong had been a scholar herbalist instead of a peasant herbalist, he would have given those items that were most linked to male potency—the dried genitalia of male sea lions and seals, dried human placenta, the tail of the red spotted monkey, gum of tortoiseshell, and wild donkey hide. But simple herbs—ginseng, wolfberry, and horny goat weed—were more readily available to him and safer and gentler in action.

As he ground the ingredients for his spring tonic, he didn't think about his fate. He did not dwell on his hardships. He did not feel these things or any other emotions. He was an herbalist, trained to observe the world outside himself, and so he did.

The Chinese in his camp worked twenty-six days out of an American month, from before dawn to dusk. For this they earned twenty-eight or thirty American dollars a month; in their villages they might have earned the equivalent of three to five dollars a month. His countrymen would not eat the food provided by the *fan gway,* or "white ghosts," so they bought their own cooking utensils and food. Gang leaders made up orders for shipments from home, and eventually supplies of rice, sweet potatoes, noodles, dried fish and oysters, bamboo shoots, seaweed, salted cabbage, dried mushrooms, peanut oil, and dried fruit would reach them. Throughout the warmer months, traveling Chinese merchants passed through camp, and a man might treat himself to a luxury—a pipe and tobacco, a rice bowl and chopsticks, a toothbrush, an oil lamp.

He had heard his countrymen commended for their cleanliness and work habits, for the esteem in which they held their families and ancestors, and for their quiet and sedate pastimes. These things were all true. He had seen them with his own eyes. Tang Men were different from the white ghosts who ordered them around. Every day his countrymen took sponge baths. As long as he had been in this camp, Fong had not seen a white ghost take a bath; they smelled rank and putrid from their sweat and the cow meat they ate. Many of the white men indeed became ghosts when their souls left their bodies during the frequent fights they got into at night. Fong had only heard of one Tang Man who had died in a brawl. White men drank a lot and passed out in their own vomit. His countrymen did not drink at all—at least not the fiery liquid that turned the *fan gway* into fools.

His countrymen drank tea, boiling the water from mountain streams just as they had boiled the water from cisterns and wells in China for thousands of years. The white man drank straight from those same streams, and Fong often spent days scornfully watching the white doctor as he tried without success to provide relief to a man bent double with stomach cramps, weakening from malaria, or the *qi* seeping out of him as he died from cholera.

After Fong's story, his sons and the other laborers retired to their tents for the night, their bones weary from eating so much bitterness during the day, and with dawn only a few hours away. Fong lingered by the embers and allowed his mind to drift to his home, so far away. He knew that other men liked to talk about their villages—how theirs was the most beautiful or fruitful in the province, how a Sze Yup man was better than a Sam Yup man, how their plentiful sons would look after them when they became esteemed old men. Fong Dun Shung never participated in this banter. Instead he looked up at the stars, which seemed as close as an arm's reach this high in the mountains, and let his mind travel from light to light across the universe, until he was over his home village of Dimtao and in his old life as a traveling herbalist.

He dreamed of men who were matter-of-fact about sexual matters. There was no need for embarrassment, for often in these villages the peasants knew how strong a man was, and how happy his wife was, by the number of sons they produced. Those men who had no sons were often pushed forward by their friends. "I need something to make my penis as strong as that of an ox," a man might request. "My wife longs for the seed to make many healthy sons." Good-natured joking and teasing accompanied these times as Fong Dun Shung would pretend to ponder the dilemma, scrounging through his vials, jars, and cloth packets with much concerned determination, until he presented with a great flourish the ingredients that, brewed as a tonic, would make his customer's wife's visit to the temple at the next New Year's Festival joyous indeed.

He dreamed of poor grandmothers, toothless and wizened, who asked for something to cool them. "Cold foods—fruit, vegetables, sliced pork, crab, and fish—will reduce your body heat," he suggested to those who complained of too much sweat and parched mouths. Then he sold them cooling herbs—gardenia and white peony—to help purge their inner fire, which he knew had not come—as it often did in young men—from an overindulgence in sex, drink, and food. In winter, when the old women had too much interior cold and shivered from fever, headache, vomiting, and body pains, he would say, "Take hot foods—fried, spicy, or those soaked in wine—to heat up and invigorate your body." For their excessive belching, he gave them cloves.

Other grandmothers and wives, with bound feet, sent out servant girls or forlorn daughters-in-law to ask for help for their nervous disorders. These were "wood emotions" and would be cured by treating the liver. He ground together the root of Chinese licorice, the fruit of the jujube, and common wheat kernels. "Boil these with water until reduced by one-third. Take one dose, sipping gradually," he would recommend. He recognized that those red-faced wives who laughed too much and too shrilly had too much fire and their hearts needed to be cooled. These women and their children reminded him of how much he missed his own wife and children; they reminded him of traditions so earthly simple that even naming children was as easy as One, Two, Three.

He dreamed that he walked back to Dimtao, where the alleys were just wide enough for a wheelbarrow to pass through. He searched among the one-room huts that made up Dimtao for his wife and children. Was his wife well? Was Number One keeping the ancestors' graves cleaned and performing his other filial duties? And what of Number Four, Fong See?

In his mind's eye, Fong Dun Shung passed by older houses with bell-shaped roofs. He remembered telling his sons when they were young that these houses had roofs like a dragon's back so that when it rained the water would run off quickly, and when it was hot the warmest air would rise up into the roofpeak and keep inhabitants cool. He stepped into his house, which had no windows and no real door. The entrance had swinging bamboo doors—like those of saloons in the white devils' towns. In his dreams the bamboo was pushed aside, and only the large wooden dowels that slid from one doorjamb to the other, like crosswise jail bars, provided any protection. Fong knew that bad people would be kept out and that the good people of his family would be safe and cool inside. He relished the feel of the hard-packed dirt under the soles of his feet. Inside, the cool brick and high tiled roofs offered a respite from the stultifying heat and humidity.

On these dreamy nights in the Sierra, he thought of the rain that beat down on his roof on summer days. He could see his youngest son—in his mind still wearing the split pants of a toddler—perched on the high stone threshold of the front door as the rain came down. Each house had a high threshold to show the neighbors that a family was of high standing, and to protect the house from the muddy water that swirled over the riverbanks during the annual floods. But it didn't matter, because—and here Fong smiled to himself—the whole roof leaked and the threshold was the only place to stay dry during even the lightest rain.

Fong Dun Shung continued his dream walk outside the village to the ricefields—watery pools during planting season, a dull blanket of amber by harvest. Even in his dreaming, he was careful. The raised dirt paths that separated the paddies and the small roadways that led away from Dimtao were purposefully miserable and crooked—sometimes leading nowhere—so that evil spirits wandering the countryside would get lost and not find their wicked way to the village. Sometimes he saw a relative, and would nod his head in greeting. The very name of his village, Dimtao, meant to nod one's head in greeting. The peasants from his village, all of them Fongs, were good people.

But what a terrible man he was! Every night his reverie was cut short by this thought, because it was a truth as unchanging as the stars above his head. Each month, the boss doled out Fong's twenty-eight dollars— the same amount that his second and third sons earned for their back-breaking efforts. The other men in camp set aside a certain amount for gambling, then sent the rest by wire to their wives and families in their home villages. A lucky few gambled and won. Fong Dun Shung always felt sure that he would be one of them, but after each payday he discovered once again that he was not. So when the professional letter writers came through camp, Fong Dun Shung took that opportunity to stroll out to the far end of the line. When his friends gave their dollars to the bank men for an overseas wire, Fong retired to his herbs, saying that his spring tonic required his attention.

One year slipped into another. Shue-ying, Fong Dun Shung's wife, sometimes thought that the only way to tell the passing of time was when the monks in the temple to the north banged upon their huge bronze

bell in the morning and their deep sounding drum at night to call people
to prayer. Days passed, then weeks, months, and years. She thought
back to days long gone when acrobatic troupes, magicians, or poets who
stopped by the village would often recite a poem: "If you have a daughter, marry her quickly to a traveler to Gold Mountain, for when he gets
off the boat, he will bring hundreds of pieces of silver." But time had
drifted away and now that poem changed: "If you have a daughter, do
not marry her to a traveler to Gold Mountain, for he will leave her and
forget her." Surely this had happened to Shue-ying, because since her
husband and two sons had left, she had heard nothing from them. She
did not know whether they were dead or alive; all she knew was that
life had been difficult before they had gone to seek their fortunes and
now it was even worse.

She married off her daughter, Lin, to Jun Quak, a man from another
village, and would probably never see her again. Her eldest son was
wasting away in an old mud house down one of the alleys in the village.
He had given his life to the opium pipe, and his duties—caring for the
graves of their ancestors, going to the temple, performing the proper
rituals of New Year's—had all been spirited away in the drug's smoke.
He had also stopped selling herbs, and their pitiable income had dwindled to almost nothing.

Shue-ying. Her name meant "heroine of the snow," but she had never
felt much like a heroine. Her family had been poor, and she had been
sold as a small girl. The world knew that her life was not to be one of
oiled hair, lovely embroideries and silks, and delicacies laid out for each
meal. She had no mother to wrap her feet into "golden lilies." Instead,
Shue-ying had the big-boned feet of a peasant. She was small but strong.

Strong enough to carry people on her back from village to village.
Aiya, these people cackled at her to hurry, to stop bouncing, to walk
smoothly over the hard, rich earth as they traveled to make their New
Year's calls, or to attend a funeral or wedding. Sometimes they would
rap their knuckles on her shoulder to hurry her along. She would burn
with anger and embarrassment. They were peasants, just like she was!
But no one would walk if they could ride. For the people of Dimtao
she was a cheaper method of transportation than hiring a rickshaw or
a sedan chair. For her humiliation and hard work, she would earn a few
pieces of *cash,* enough money for a sack of rice.

This work—demeaning as it was—meant not only survival for herself,
but survival for Fong See, her Number Four son. He'd been nine years
old when his father and brothers left for *Gam Saan.* Shue-ying often
wondered what would become of the two of them. She was already
married, so no decent man would help her. She was too used-up to
become a prostitute in Fatsan or Canton. She hoped that the gods would

let her and Fong See slip by unnoticed. Any more bad fortune and they
would have to live on the street, living off the generosity of others,
passing from house to house with beggars' bowls in hand.

By 1870 the transcontinental railroad had been completed, and Fong
Dun Shung had opened an herbal emporium, Kwong Tsui Chang, in
Sacramento. On the wall of his shop, Fong Dun Shung posted a yel-
lowing newspaper photograph of the golden spike being driven to symbolize the completion of the railroad. He remembered when the bosses
had come around, pushing his countrymen aside so that the photograph
could be taken. The Men of Tang were not to be in the picture, nor
were they to be praised by most of the dignitaries who took the podium
that day. Only Crocker acknowledged them: "I wish to call to your
minds that the early completion of this railroad we have built has been
in large measure due to that poor, despised class of laborers called the
Chinese, to the fidelity and industry they have shown." Fong now knew
he should have paid more attention to those words and the lack of them
from others that day.

Fong Dun Shung often thought of those last few days on the railroad—
how the men had been filled with excitement as they rushed to be the
first team to finish, how once it was over no one knew quite what to
do. Some men went home, traveling back along the tracks they had
laid. They took with them little more than what they had come with—
their Gold Mountain baskets packed with padded jackets, a change of
clothes, leather boots. They had money, but many lost it gambling on
their ships—their years of toil lost when the button count didn't come
out in their favor too many times in a row.

Others from his camp went in the opposite direction—east. No one
really knew what was there, but, again, they had money in their pockets.
Perhaps they might start a laundry or find work on a farm. Still others,
hearing about rail projects in Washington and Oregon, went north. But
most, like himself, traveled back over the mountains to Sacramento,
where a huge land reclamation project offered jobs to men who would
work hard for little money.

There had been no rejoicing, no firecrackers to send these men whom
he had cared for over the years on happy, safe, prosperous journeys.
Most he never saw again. Some—so he had heard from those who
gossiped when they came into his shop on I Street—were truly never
heard from again. Some gangs had been taken up box canyons and shot,
or left to freeze or to wander until they weakened and were eaten by
wild animals. Fong Dun Shung didn't know that these stories were true,
but he didn't know that they were lies either. He had lived among these
white men long enough to know the depth of their hatred.

After the railroad was completed, he took the little money he had saved and came to Sacramento, where he opened the Kwong Tsui Chang, which meant roughly "Success Peacefully," down by the railway depot and wharf. Here he was able to continue his occupation as he had since his own father had died. For the first time in Fong Dun Shung's life, he was earning a good income. Still, he didn't send money home to Shue-ying and his two sons.

He used many excuses to explain his behavior to himself: Perhaps they had died. Perhaps they had forgotten him. Perhaps it was best that he spend his money on the sons who were on the Gold Mountain with him. These sons, Fong Lai and Fong Quong, had taken day-labor jobs and earned barely enough to feed, clothe, and house themselves. Fong Dun Shung regretted his lack of respect for his wife. He regretted even more that he had not properly taught his second and third sons the centuries-old art of Chinese medicine. If only he had taught them, he reasoned, they would be able to take full responsibility for themselves.

Just as he had during his years on the railroad, Fong Dun Shung tried not to think of these things, but focused instead on the practice of medicine. He still helped men who complained of too much cold or heat, too much dampness or dryness. The only difference between what he had done during the past few years and what he did now was that once again he administered to Chinese women—nearly all of them prostitutes.

As early as 1854, the Honorable Hy Ye Tung Company had shipped to San Francisco six hundred girls to work as prostitutes. In those early days, peasants worn down by famine, drought, and warfare could sell their daughters in Canton for as little as the equivalent of five U.S. dollars. By 1868 the newspapers referred to this practice as the "importation of females in bulk." Just as the coolie laborers had signed their lives over to men of little honor for passage to the Gold Mountain, many of these girls—aged twelve to sixteen years—did the same, pressing their thumbprints into contracts they could not read. Although the purchase of any human being had been declared illegal in the United States, this trade flourished virtually unchecked. By the time the railroad was completed, fair-faced girls of quality, bought in Canton for fifty dollars, could bring in as much as one thousand dollars in California; younger girls, or girls already diseased or unattractive, might still be bought for a few dollars and turn a profit of two hundred to eight hundred dollars each.

On the days when the steamers chugged upriver from San Francisco with a new supply of girls, a crowd always turned out for the auctions. Each girl could look forward to a different destiny. A few fortunates were purchased for marriage, just as they would have been in their home villages. Some might be purchased to be so-called high-class prostitutes. The least fortunate, the ones born with bad luck over their heads, would spend the rest of their short lives in tiny rooms called "cribs," with a bed as their only furniture and a barred window as their only light on the outside world.

Fong Dun Shung had a vested interest in these goings-on. He saw men before and after: those who first wanted sexual prowess, and then returned to get something to cure the disease that threatened to rot away their manhood. He saw the women too, when they suffered from those problems that could affect their lives and livelihoods—venereal disease, pregnancy, tuberculosis.

Fong Dun Shung prospered, for there was much business to be had. He still gambled, but now he won more frequently. He had only one problem. He was lonely for a woman's companionship. He did what he saw the prosperous men around him do. He married a *louh geui*—one who always holds her legs up—and tried not to think of his family in China.

Even to the tiny village of Dimtao, word eventually came that the Great Railroad had been completed. Still, Fong See's mother had not heard from his father. Every day she seemed to get older, but Fong See knew that life was not as hard for her as it had been after his father first left, and he had searched through the fields looking for grass to cut and sell to farmers who fed it to the fish kept in village ponds. It was a hard job, and he had received little money for his efforts. But because of this work, he knew where all the villages had their fishponds. When the rains came and the ponds overflowed their banks and flooded the rice-fields, Fong See waded out into the murky water and caught fish with his bare hands. On those occasions, he and his mother would have a good meal—whole fish steamed with spring onion, ginger, and soy sauce.

An old Chinese proverb says that when one family is without rice, a hundred families will come to its aid. Like many proverbs, this one expressed more wishful thinking than reality. But in the case of Fong See, one family did step forward to help. In 1871, an aunt and uncle—not true relatives, but good people from the village—saw Fong See working hard and not earning much money.

"Would you like to go to America?" the old uncle asked him.

"Of course," Fong See answered, knowing he had no money for such a trip.

"I will loan you the money and you can pay me back," said the uncle.

Everything began to move quickly for Fong See. His mother saw the wisdom in the old uncle's offer. Her youngest son had shown himself to be enterprising and responsible. She felt confident that if he went to the Gold Mountain, he would search out his father, earn money, *and* remember to send both home to her. In a few days, Fong See—the fourth son of Fong Dun Shung—would look one last time upon the small village of Dimtao. Then he would walk south toward Hong Kong and board a ship that would take him across the sea on a journey at the end of which he hoped he would find his father and brothers, and encourage them to retrace their steps and return to the home village. But first, Fong See had to complete his role as groom.

Marriage festivities were always something to look forward to in the village. This time, many of the usual traditions had been passed over or hurried along. Fong See's mother and the go-between, who arranged marriages for couples from neighboring villages, had selected and bought for him a girl, named Yong, from a family even poorer than his own. Fong See still had not seen Yong, though the go-between had promised that she had good health and was from sturdy country peasants who had always had male children to bless them until this one unfortunate daughter. Yong would work hard and know her place. Was she pretty? Fong See did not know.

His mother had gone to a fortune-teller, and a propitious day had been selected to accommodate his pending departure. Negotiations between the two families had followed the prescribed rules, but again were settled quickly. These were both poor families, so the only real bargaining had been over the bride-price. Shue-ying had sent only one basket of bride cakes and, instead of a whole roast pig, just a few slices.

The purpose of the marriage was to ensure filial ties to China and the home village of Dimtao. In his weeks, months, and possibly years away, Yong would beckon to her husband in his day thoughts and haunt him in his dreams. He would not forget her—or his mother—and would eventually return home. During his absence, Yong, aged ten when he left, would be little more than a servant girl.

Now, as Fong See waited for the bearers to bring his betrothed to Dimtao, he considered what she had been doing in these last days and hours at her home. She would have taken a bath in pomelo leaves gathered by a close female cousin, and sat in her family's rice-drying tray while her female relatives combed her hair and braided it into a style appropriate for a married woman. She would have prostrated herself before the family's ancestral tablets, then again before her mother and father, whom she would never see again. If she was lucky, a few of the peasants from her village might slip her some *lai see*—good-luck money that would always be hers and hers alone.

Fong See allowed his mind to consider what this evening might hold. There would be no banquet, for his mother did not have money for that kind of celebration. There would be no wedding chamber, just his straw-covered pallet in the corner of his mother's one-room house. There would be no consummation, for little Yong was just that—little.

Fong See tried to concentrate on the future, his journey, his search, but his thoughts kept drawing him to the past. He had been born in the auspicious month of August in 1857 in the village of Dimtao in the district of Nam Hoi in the Pearl River delta of Kwangtung Province of the Middle Kingdom. His village was located a half-day's walk from Fatsan, a commercial city to the north, and a full day's walk from Canton. He knew every corner of his village and everyone who lived there, for they were all related to him in one way or another.

Fong See was fourteen years old, certainly old enough to take a wife. Although he had no formal education, he was enterprising and clever. Before his tenth birthday he had gone to Canton, where he had sold peanuts—a symbol of prosperity—on the streets. Life in Canton was different from that in the village. Even time itself seemed more important there, as hour-callers walked the streets, calling out the time throughout the day. In Canton he saw thousands of people living on boats along the riverbanks. He had heard that some of them lived and died on those boats without ever setting foot on shore.

He had seen girls even younger than he was, going to silk factories before dawn and returning home after sunset. Sometimes, as he walked from his favorite streetcorner for selling his wares to his boardinghouse, he would peek inside the wooden slats covering factory windows to see the girls sitting before steaming woks, their hands in boiling water as they unwound the silk cocoons. Other girls in other factories lost their eyesight from days and nights spent embroidering phoenixes and dragons in the forbidden stitch.

He had witnessed many amazing things in the southern city—puppet shows, snake charmers, acrobats balancing bowls on long bamboo poles. He had seen professional beggars waiting in line outside the great compounds—how he longed to know what lay behind those heavily carved doors—hoping for a little rice or the leftovers from a banquet to fill the wooden bowls they held in their hands. Some were gaunt, barely more than skeletons; others—whole families of professional beggars—were a fright to the eye, with their self-inflicted wounds.

He had seen men punished for breaking the law by having their heads put in cangues—huge wooden platforms fastened around their necks like a collar. Fong See recognized this for the clever punishment that it was. A man could not sleep, for he could not rest his head. He could not eat, for he could not reach his hands to his mouth. He could not bat away a fly or a mosquito that tormented his ears or eyes, but he could continue to work with his hands. As a man struggled with the weight and the humiliation, characters written on the wooden frame told the world of the man's offense.

Fong See had seen other men sitting for days on end with their hands locked into wooden stocks. What better punishment for a robber than to lock his evil hands in wood for all his neighbors to see? In Fong See's village, the punishment was more severe. If someone stole a chicken, he would have to go before everyone in the village. The village guard would bang a gong, and everyone would take a turn to whip that robber one time. The physical punishment was bad, but the loss of face in front of the whole village was even worse.

Fong See stood as a crackling burst of firecrackers announced the arrival of the sedan chair. All around him villagers pushed forward to watch as the two bearers came to a stop and held steady the red-draped sedan chair. As little Yong stepped down she saw the red veil that covered her face quiver slightly. With his fan, he tapped Yong's head, raised the veil, and looked down into the pale face of his child bride.

Several months later, as his countrymen jostled past him and went belowdecks, Fong See gripped the railing of the riverboat that slowly glided from San Francisco Bay up the yellowish river toward Sacramento. He had heard that most of these trips went overnight, but since he had been on the Gold Mountain, he had tried to see and experience as much as possible. For months in the Big City of San Francisco, he had walked the streets of Chinatown, stopping at every herbal shop and visiting every acupuncturist's office, inquiring if anyone knew his father or brothers. When Fong See turned up nothing, he decided to try Sacramento, the Second City.

"Little Brother, you and I must be of the same mind."

At the sound of his dialect, Fong See turned to see an older man with baskets and rope-wrapped packages at his feet.

"You must be wise indeed to stay out here while our countrymen go belowdecks to possible death. Do they not think? Do they not remember?"

"Old Uncle," Fong See responded, using the customary honorific, "I am traveling to Yee Fow, the Second City. I do not understand."

The older man thrust his chin forward, pointing at the young man. "You are new here?"

At Fong See's nod, the older man explained. "The *fan gway* call these boats 'floating palaces.' I call them death houses. Do you remember your mother telling you never to lift the top off the rice pot? Not only will this ruin the rice, but you could get a bad burn. This boat is like that pot. It runs on steam. Below, there are great boilers that explode when the white devils forget to attend to them. When I was a young man, only a few years ago, a boat called *Yosemite* exploded just after leaving a place called Rio Vista. We will pass there later today. When the explosion came, bodies flew through the air. One hundred died in the first burst, another fifty died in the second. Only Tang Men perished from the explosion, or from drowning when the boat sank. I saw their bodies floating in the water. Their skin had scalded and split. The *fan gway* buried our countrymen in one grave. You could not blame them.

Our countrymen were nameless pieces of boiled flesh. The *fan gway,* what do they care about human beings? They saved the gold, not the people. Later they brought that death ship back to the surface. They cut it up and made it into a new boat that even today plies these waters. I saw these things, and they turned me into the old man you see before you."

By staying on the deck, instead of going down to the "China Hold," where hundreds of his countrymen paid a few cents to travel in steerage going up and down the river in search of work, Fong See learned much. As he spoke further with the old man, he learned that the drafts of these ships were so shallow it was said that they could run on land after a rain. He learned that at night or in the fog, the captain rang his bell and waited for an echo to bounce off a building so that he would know which way to go, which way to turn. He heard other stories about captains who didn't hear the echo or were lazy in their duties, ran aground, and splintered their vessels in the heavy fogs that blanketed the tule marshes.

Fong See stood by the old man for hours. Looking straight down, he saw turbid water that churned and swirled with each revolution of the paddlewheel. For most of the trip, mud banks kept the river within their gentle embrace, but sometimes they passed high levees like those he knew in China. They had been built by fellow sojourners, the old man told him. The boat chugged past flimsy wooden buildings that clung to the riverbank on stilts—again reminding Fong See of China. He had seen places like that in Canton when he sold peanuts on the street. The boat passed cultivated fields where he saw his countrymen bent in their labors.

"Come," the old man said. "I will show you something."

Fong See followed as the old man ducked behind a pile of cloth bags, then, checking to make sure that no one was looking, climbed the crew's stairs to the upper deck. They hunched down low and crept along the deck until they reached a window.

"Go ahead, Little Brother. Take a look."

Fong See raised his head and peered inside. He didn't care what the old man said—this *was* a floating palace. The room was huge, unlike anything he had ever seen in his life. It went up two stories, but where the second story should have been, a balcony clung to the walls. The moldings along the railings where white women in full-skirted silk gowns rested their gloved hands were elaborately carved. Other women sat on red plush chairs around marble-topped tables, and sipped from tall-stemmed glasses. A few of the people danced to the strange music that wafted through the window.

Looking at the floor-to-ceiling mirrors encased in gold frames, Fong See wondered if they could be real gold. He saw bearded men, in fine woolen suits and silk shirts, some with hats that stood straight up or were shaped like bowls, and women with red and gold demon-hair piled high and topped with hats covered in feathers—their images repeated over and over again in the mirrors' reflections until they nearly made him dizzy. He wanted to be in that room, be a part of that group with their fancy clothes, their effortless talk.

"Hey, you! Get down from there before I throw you overboard." Fong See didn't understand the words, but he understood the sound in the crewman's voice. His companion said something in the foreigner's language, grabbed Fong See's arm, and they went back down to the river level.

As they sat on their haunches by the railing, the old man said, "The white demon does not like us in his country. We are the ones who make it easy for them to come here. We are the ones who risk our lives and sometimes die to build the railroad that opened this land to them. Now they forget."

"But this cannot be," Fong See said. "There is fortune here for everyone."

"You are wrong. For the *fan gway* only."

"But we are Tang People. We are honorable people. Surely they treat us well."

"What brought you here, Little Brother?"

"I come in search of my father," Fong See said bravely, proudly. "He is an herbalist. I hope to find him in the Second City."

"Ah!" the old man spat, then looked at the boy shrewdly. "There is more?"

"I have come to make my fortune on the Gold Mountain. I have a wife in my home village. I want to make her proud. I wish one day to dress her in the finest silk and give her enough servants so that her feet may never touch the ground and her hands and face will never lose their luster."

"You come for money."

"Yes, Uncle, didn't you?"

"Of course I come with my dreams, but, Little Brother, so does the white demon. He comes across the country on tracks that I and my brothers laid with our own hands. Now he says *he* wants to work."

"But don't they all work?"

"In the old days, no. They stand. They talk. They tell us what to do. These new demons, they want our jobs and they want us to go away."

"But I just got here."

"Listen to me. Be careful. Be wary. If they do something to you, you take it. You don't let them see you mad. You hide your anger. You look blank, like this, so that they cannot see inside you."

Fong See looked at the older man's face as he seemed to pack away all that made him alive and human until he was as blank as a wall without paint, without posters, without notices. Then the man grinned and was himself again.

"People come from the other ocean and they become citizens," he continued. "But we cannot. If they hit you or steal from you or murder you, there is nothing to be done. They can cheat us out of our wages. They can rape our women. But we are like the Indian or the black man here. No power. No voice. No way to get retribution. It is not like in our home villages, where a man must accept the punishment of the villagers. On the Gold Mountain, a Chinese is not even allowed to testify against a white demon."

The old man turned away and looked out across the yellowed water, beyond the levee and fields to the cloudless sky. Fong See realized that the conversation was over. He still had many questions, but then he thought that the old uncle's words must be wrong. Surely his mind had grown bitter from years alone. It could not be right that his countrymen were not treated as guests in the foreigner's land.

In the life story of Fong See, the events surrounding his first wedding, his transition from boy to man, his voyage to the Gold Mountain, the search for his father, his birth, even his name, will always dwell in a nebulous world of fact mixed with mystery, fantasy, and apocrypha. This is purely American, for in what other country can a man—any man (or woman, for that matter)—reinvent himself over and over again? Fong See and his descendants created his history from a mosaic composed of perceptions, feelings, sometimes wishful thinking, and undeniable fact. Not surprisingly, not everyone agrees on the details.

More than a hundred years after these events, even Fong See's name is disputed. His granddaughter named her daughter Sian, after both the archaeological site in China and the name of endearment she believes her grandfather was called as a small boy, See-on. Some say his childhood name was Yong Yee. Others say that was the name of his Number One wife, with Yong as her clan name. In his government interrogations, Fong See said that his marriage name was Fong Ngai Jung, but it wasn't a name anyone in the family can remember him using. A large number believe that his name was always just plain Fong See: Fong as the clan name and See, literally meaning "four," as the fourth son.

Still others have said that, yes, he was plain Fong See, and that when he came to this country and gave his name—Fourth Son of Fong—to the immigration men, they heard "Fong See," and so See became his last name. A small handful say that no, the real story is that when he came to this country the immigration officials asked him where he was from and he answered, "I come from across the sea." Hence, his name became See, because, as everyone knows, immigration officials on both coasts took a certain malicious pride in renaming people. No matter what the "true" story, See was his last name for the next fifty years, after which he would once again take up the last name of Fong. But since the F. Suie One Company and later the F. See On Company were to be the names of his stores, his white customers would call him Mr. Suie, Mr. See, even Mr. On, but *never* Mr. Fong.

Sissee, Fong See's eldest daughter, said that her father was married for the first time when he was just seven years old, the very year that Fong Dun Shung left for the United States. He wasn't looking for his father; rather, his father had sent for him, since he would be the easiest of his children to bring to this country. Only later, after Fong Dun Shung had experienced success, did he return to China. Danny Ho Fong, Fong See's nephew, said that his grandfather was never "lost" at all. Fong Dun Shung went to the new *Gam Saan* of Alaska, forgot to send money home, and that's why Fong See and his mother were "super struggling" and lived in "super poverty." (Unfortunately, Danny Ho died before he could be questioned more fully on this story.)

Ming Chuen Fong, Fong See's eldest son from the third wife, has said that his father was a vegetable peddler in China who went to market with his wares carried in two baskets hung from a pole across his shoulders. Chuen agrees that his father was betrothed before he set sail, but says he was already seventeen years old; Fong See never found his father or his brothers, for they were already back in China, where Fong Dun Shung was a successful gambler. An entry in *The Stories of Chinese Americans,* published by *Foshan Wen Shih* magazine in China, states that Fong See was twenty years of age when he "followed his countrymen to the United States to make a living"; it was where he "struggled and had many bitter experiences," and where his father "did not do well and died in a foreign land without ever returning to China."

Of all the "lies" that Fong See told, perhaps none is more slippery and elusive than those regarding his age. One family story is that he was two weeks short of his hundredth birthday when he died. Aunt Sissee used to say that when her father got to a certain age he liked to tack an extra year onto his actual birthday—on Chinese New Year's or at the birth of a new child—so that by the time he died, he was telling customers that he was 120 years old. As for "hard" fact, in his immigration files Fong See states on several occasions that he was born in 1866 (not 1857) and landed in the United States in 1881, when he was fifteen. Then, beginning in 1917, he changed his story, telling immigration officials that he couldn't remember when he was born or when he came. But the immigration files are often unreliable, riddled as they are with tricky questions and equally tricky answers.

In his day-to-day life, Fong See told newspaper reporters and customers that he arrived in the United States in 1871 and moved to Los

Angeles in 1874. This was partly true. Fong See incorporated his store in Sacramento in 1874, but didn't settle in Los Angeles until 1897.

It might be well to consider what one of his grandchildren has said: "If you tell a lie, then you must have a motive for telling that lie." So perhaps in this wonder time we can give Fong See his invented history with all its exaggerated truths and concrete fantasy. Since Fong See saw himself—publicly advertised himself—as a man who had his feet on Gold Mountain soil in 1871, then perhaps that is when he arrived: after crossing the ocean not on a Pacific Mail steamship (the preferred method of travel) but on a clipper ship, "carried over by the wind," as his fellow countrymen called it—at the age of fourteen, already a married man.

CHAPTER 2

EXCLUSION

1872–93

N o t long after Fong See caught the riverboat to take him up the Sacramento River, John Milton Pruett and his family were packing their belongings into the prairie schooner that they'd bought to transport themselves and all their possessions from Pennsylvania to Independence, Missouri. From there they planned to join a wagon train and continue west along the Oregon Trail to what they hoped would be a better life.

Back in 1803, the Louisiana Purchase had legally extended the boundary of the United States' territories to the Rockies in the Northwest. But, boundary or no, trappers and hunters were already penetrating into the area beyond, while along the Pacific Coast, ships actively explored rivers and harbors, seeking places to pick up sea otter pelts to trade with China. The United States wasn't the only country interested in this land so rich in natural resources. The British also wanted a share, as did the French, Russians, and Spanish. The idea of physical occupation had long been the basis for claims of sovereignty, and here that principle was at work again. Even as Britain's Hudson's Bay Company became increasingly entrenched, American settlers in the Willamette Valley in northwest Oregon argued for recognition by the United States government.

In 1845, President Polk notified the British Foreign Office that the United States planned on assuming complete sovereignty over the Oregon country. The following year, Great Britain agreed on condition that the forty-ninth parallel become the boundary. Even so, the U.S. government needed homesteaders in the territory to continue to establish sovereignty. Lured by a vision of almost unlimited agricultural opportunities and the promise of up to 160 acres of free land if single and 320 acres if married, provided that they built a house on that property within twelve months, settlers began their trek west.

The first pioneers along the Oregon Trail had the luxury of open land with plenty of grass and good water for the horses, oxen, and other livestock that accompanied families on their journey to their new homes.

Still, there were hardships aplenty. Children too young to walk some-times fell off their family wagons to be crushed by the wheels. Most died instantly; others lingered, dying awful deaths as their lives literally jostled out of them as their parents continued their arduous westward march. There was no time to stop, no time to linger, no time to mourn. They had to cross the mountains before winter set in.

By May 1872, when John Pruett, his wife, and four sons left Penn-sylvania for new opportunities, the Oregon Trail had been much trav-eled. In some places the relentless passing of wagon wheels had ground ruts deep into solid rock. The four-hundred-mile stretch from the Platte River in Nebraska to Fort Laramie in Wyoming averaged twelve graves to the mile. Indians, who had been relatively solicitous in the early days, now saw clearly what lay ahead. Although many of the Indian nations signed treaties, others resisted forcibly. Along the trail, the Pruetts passed through Pawnee, Cheyenne, Sioux, and Shoshone territories. In Oregon the native population had been pacified to a great extent, but during the last twenty years there had been several uprisings where settlers saw their homes burned, and lives on both sides were lost.

Perhaps even worse, the land along the trail had been totally stripped of vegetation. Whatever livestock this last wave of pioneers brought with them, they would have to pack along feed for it. Fortunately, the Pruetts were Pennsylvania Dutch and not given to concerns over worldly possessions. With no tears, Luscinda Pruett gave away her embroidered tablecloths, all her china but the most durable, and whatever else the family thought they could live without, to make more room in the wagon for grain and water. Thus prepared, the Pruetts began the dusty two-thousand-mile trek—from Independence to Fort Kearney, from which point they followed the Platte River to Fort Laramie, past Independence Rock, and across Sublette's Cutoff to Soda Springs. From there they went south along the California Trail, then north again along the Ap-plegate Trail, past Klamath Lake to the Rogue River Valley. After five months the Pruetts arrived in Oregon.

Since the best land in the Willamette Valley had already been home-steaded, the Rogue River Valley was the final destination for the Pruetts and other pioneers throughout this decade. Even along the Rogue, the only plots left were in the Big Sticky, a name coined by the Indians for the soil that clung in gluey clumps to wagon wheels, moccasins, and horses' hooves. The Pruetts searched until they found the abandoned homestead of Samuel M. Hall, equidistant between Central Point and an area that would one day become Medford.

On October 12, 1872, John Milton Pruett went to the office of land patents and registered for the property. He now had his farm as well as four strong sons, another son on the way, and a wife who, in fourteen years of marriage, had proved herself a hard worker, faithful, and trusting in the Lord. Together they began the backbreaking work of clearing the manzanita, chaparral, and grass that grew on the valley floor as high as a horse's shoulder. God willing, they would make a good life for themselves.

Until his Number Four son appeared on the doorstep of the Kwong Tsui Chang Company after searching the few herbal emporiums in Sacramento, Fong Dun Shung had thought he would never see his home village again. But with his son's arrival and after hearing about Shueying's hard life, he decided to go home. Within months of his reunion with Fong See, Fong Dun Shung left his three sons in California to take care of the shop, and returned to Dimtao a rich man with plenty of gold pieces to show for his years away. How the peasants stared at him! How rich he looked in his western clothes! How prosperous he appeared when his bearers set down not only his original Gold Mountain basket, but other baskets as well, filled with strange items from the foreign land. And how cowed his Number One wife was when she saw her husband's Number Two wife step down from her sedan chair swathed in embroidered pale blue silk.

During his first days home, Fong Dun Shung hosted a banquet to show off his new wife, his wealth, his booty to all the neighbors who had thought him dead or lost forever among the white demons. He paid his respects to the ancestral graves—pulling weeds, laying out offerings, lighting incense, performing every prescribed custom to atone for his long absence. Only Fong Dun Shung, who had been to the Gold Mountain and had seen real riches, knew that he was not the big man the villagers thought he was. Keeping that knowledge to himself, he built a two-room brick house with an attached kitchen shed and settled back for what he thought would be his indolent years—a little gambling, sex with his wives, the birth of grandsons and sons.

It was not to be. Every day for a year or so he listened to his wives argue, but he found he was not strong enough to scold them into silence. What could he say to them? He had deserted his first wife; after what seemed a lifetime in the civilization of Sacramento, he had brought his second to what he now recognized as a backward village. During those nights he spent at her side, she whimpered and cried to go back to the Gold Mountain.

"This is your home now," he whispered in her ear. "You are a China girl. You belong here with me, your husband." But he knew it had been a mistake to bring her back to Dimtao. His Number Two wife had been born in China, but had been sold and shipped to the Gold Mountain as a child. She had grown used to the ways of the white ghosts—their sounds, their bodies, their dress, their food. She could not remember the ways of village life—the poverty, the crudeness, the gossiping.

From the cock's first crowing until the stars rose in the heavens, he listened to the arguing of the two women.

"Scum of a snail," Shue-ying might hiss, as she heated the wok for the evening meal.

"Red-faced peasant," his Number Two wife might retort.

"Barren wife of one thousand men," Shue-ying would shout, then comfort her infant son, Fong Yun, with gentle caresses and cooing words.

"Turtle's-egg abortion," the California wife might snort back as her chopsticks clicked rudely on the side of her rice bowl.

"Concubine who is as diseased as the leper who begs on the streetcorner."

In this battle of wives, which was as old as China itself, he knew that his second wife would lose. Although she had proved to be barren— and none of his herbs or potions had helped her—she had kept him content for many years. But she was certainly no match for a wife whose name meant "heroine of the snow."

One day during Fong Dun Shung's second spring home, he ate his *jook*—rice gruel—belched to show his satisfaction, perfunctorily scolded his Number One wife for her laziness, then walked out to see if there was a man in the village willing to leave his fields to indulge in a gamble. At noon he returned for lunch. He slurped his noodles and lay down on his pallet to sleep through the enervating heat of the afternoon. Later, Shue-ying awakened him, shaking his shoulder and whispering, "Come quick, husband. The sow who calls herself your wife will not move."

When he reached his Number Two wife's bedside, he found her staring unseeing at the ceiling. The lines of worry and sadness that had clouded her face in this last year had smoothed again into the porcelain planes that he remembered from their years together in California. Only her open mouth, with its piece of gold on her tongue, showed the cause of death. Like the leader of the T'ai P'ing Rebellion, whose own dreams had been dashed, Number Two wife had committed suicide by swallowing gold.

How long had this wife suffered? Number Two wife could have called out, could have changed her mind, but for the only time in her life she had chosen her fate. Her determination was so great that they found her lying peacefully in death with her hands held rigidly at her sides, her clothes unwrinkled.

So it was that Fong Dun Shung's Number Two wife passed from birth to death with no one to remember or record her name. She was a disgrace, a secret. To forget her name might mean that she had never existed. Over months and years, people would begin to forget, only to be reminded by a village gossip, an unhappy wife, or an unfortunate nephew whose life in the Gold Mountain had been shrouded in poverty and unhappiness. In later generations there would still be one or two who would remember, sneer, and lewdly whisper, "You know, she was a prostitute."

Perhaps in despair, perhaps dulled by boredom, Fong Dun Shung went back to his old ways and gambled away the rest of his Gold Mountain gold.

Between 1871 and 1874, Fong See witnessed incredible changes in the land and in the quality of life of Sacramento's citizens. Many of the "civilizing" changes were the direct result of the efforts of his countrymen. He watched as the tule marshes, peat bogs and silty waterways that made up the Sacramento delta had been reclaimed by the Chinese. Draft animals couldn't do the work, since their hooves sank in the mud; whites wouldn't do the work because it was too hard and unhealthy. Toiling in water up to their waists, Chinese laborers built miles of levees, ditches, dikes, canals, and irrigation channels to drain the swampy land. By the time they were done, 500 million acres in the Sacramento area were reclaimed and land values rose from one dollar to one hundred dollars an acre. But the Chinese owned none of it, since the Alien Land Act of 1870 forbade the ownership of American land by Chinese.

As the land was reclaimed, Chinese laborers plowed and planted. They spent their waking hours packing peaches, apples, and pears, harvesting hay, digging asparagus, and picking beans, strawberries, and cherries. Every day they looked forward to the same stooped labor, except for rainy days, when the landowners required them to make bushel baskets. As on the railroad, a dollar a day seemed adequate wages for either reclamation or farm work—ten to twenty dollars a month less than the going rate for white workers in California, but more than for workers of any color in other states.

Other Chinese laborers worked in woolen factories or in paper and knitting mills. They built highways and railroad lines to crisscross the state. They cut wood and cleared land. Some worked in borax beds or salt works. In the hops fields, they gathered, cured, and sacked the crop, which then went to breweries where other Chinese saw to fermentation and bottling. They helped raise and slaughter pigs and poultry. They rolled cigars and cigarettes. They manufactured slippers, pantaloons, vests, skirts, drawers, overalls, and shoes. A few went south to Monterey, where they fished, not just for the usual fare eaten by Caucasians, but also for abalone and shrimp. Since most Americans found these odd ocean tidbits not only unpalatable but also conclusive evidence that the Chinese were subhuman and had the tastes of animals, the shellfish were salted and shipped back to China. Along the way a sub-industry was invented: abalone shells could be polished and used in all manner of decorative arts.

From San Francisco, some Chinese went to sea as coal heavers, deck-hands, cabin servants, and sailors. Others tried making harnesses or bricks. Still others became coachmen or house servants. A few started their own businesses, opening small laundries, keeping a few whores in cribs, or running little chop suey joints, grocery stores, or butcher shops—all catering to the same clientele—the people of Fong See's home country.

His countrymen were popular among landowners and factory owners. The Chinese, it was said, were always at their work stations on time. They didn't lag or loiter; they didn't gossip like American factory girls. But, to the public at large, these jobs were invisible. No man ever considered who rolled his cigar, cut the wood for his fireplace, or made his underwear. So the importance of the Chinese in supporting the whites' rising standard of living went largely unappreciated. Still, a few believed that any sudden expulsion of the Chinese would throw the entire state into confusion.

Fong See had done many of these jobs himself. He constantly tried to improve himself—with work first, then with language, dress, and attitude. When he first arrived, he worked in the potato fields, earning a dollar a day, where he pulled weeds, hoed, then later dug up the tubers. He had never done farm work before, not even in his home village, and it seemed interminable and hot. He decided that he was more suited for indoor work and did whatever jobs he could find for a boy still in his teens. For a short time he worked as a helper in a laundry. Sweeping floors and washing dishes in a restaurant, he learned how to cook, which prepared him for a job as a cook in a brewery and later at a ranch.

In time he found that the best job was to walk from door to door, selling merchandise. He sold hats, brushes, curtain rods—whatever he thought someone might buy. The white women who answered the door were mostly kind and gracious. Emboldened, he engaged them in con-versation beyond his sales pitch. Amazingly, they listened and re-sponded. His English improved and his opportunities expanded. He was only seventeen years old, but he already knew that to get ahead in this country he would have to be his own boss.

On June 24, 1874, Fong See walked into the office of Sacramento's city clerk. Although the people with whom he had worked during these past few years had always told him to beware of the white ghosts, Fong See was not afraid. He stepped up to the high counter and carefully said the words, "I want to sign paper to make business." After just three years in the Gold Mountain, Fong See's English was still rudimentary; the man behind the counter could easily have made fun of him, mocking his hesitant English in the quacking tones of the vaudeville Chinaman: "I wantee signee paper makee work-work." But the clerk had not seen many Chinese pass through this office, and chose to be helpful. He opened the registry of partnerships and wrote in what little information he could ascertain—a name, a date. The columns listing the type of business and the names of the business partners were left blank.

In celebration of his official papers, Fong See walked to the Conrad Young Photography Studio on J Street. The photographer positioned him and ordered him, "Don't move. Don't move," then disappeared behind his black fabric-draped box. Fong See looked directly into the camera lens. At seventeen years, his skin was smooth and hairless. His mouth was full, his nose flat and wide. His face was fuller than it would be in later years, when its angularity and high planes would seem to drop decades from his years. As usual, his bowler hat was tipped back on his head, his queue rolled up and tucked inside it.

His clothes were western. Ever since he had observed the Victorian opulence on his first trip upriver, he had sensed that his place was in there among those white men and women in their finery, and not down in the dark, cramped quarters of the "China Hold," with his countrymen and their fears. Today he wore a three-piece suit and a starched white shirt with a wing-tip collar. A tie pin, with a stone looking much like a diamond, punctured the knot of the western-style white tie that bulged just a bit between neck and vest.

Fong See left the photographer's studio and walked along Sacramento's Front Street toward the intersection of Third and I streets, where Chinatown nestled on the south shore of what had once been called Sutter Lake but was now called China Slough. Front Street bustled with merchants, peddlers, and con men—all those people who catered to weary and susceptible travelers as they stepped off the train. Dust whipped up under the hooves of horses and the wheels of wagons that came to this intersection to pick up or unload goods—barrels of syrup and whiskey, bales of hay and cotton, crates of peaches and plums, burlap bags of wheat and barley. On streetcorners, young boys called out news headlines—the more gruesome the better. Saloons and hotels offered varied entertainments—operas, plays, and balls. It all presented a lively scene, but Fong See knew that the annual floods here were as bad as those in his home village, if not worse, for they not only destroyed buildings and ruined businesses but also brought cholera.

He reached I Street and turned right, keeping to the south side of the street. An odd combination of smells rose up to meet him as he neared Chinatown between Second and Fourth streets. The air carried the familiar and sweetly pleasing scents of ginger, opium, and incense, mingled with the foul odors that drifted from nearby dairies and slaughterhouses. The air wasn't the only unpleasant aspect of this place. The water in the China Slough was also foul. From the south, laundries emptied their filthy water and other refuse into the lake. On the north bank, the railroad company dumped its oily debris into the water. The lake was so polluted that on more than one occasion it had caught fire.

As much as he longed for acceptance in the world outside the confines of I and Third streets, Fong See always felt a wave of relief as he entered this familiar enclave. At this corner stood a wall that had become the center of Chinese life in the city. The five thousand Chinese who lived in Sacramento County came here to peruse the personal messages affixed to the wall: "I am looking for my son, Quan Lee. If you see him, please ask him to contact his father through the Hop Sing Tong." "Do not work for Farmer Smith. He does not pay his wages and the food is not fit to eat." Tongs hung notices, written in gaudy calligraphy, of upcoming meetings. Old men, sitting on upturned fruit crates, read the news to those who were illiterate.

Farther down the street stood a pawnshop where sojourners returning to China might trade their belongings—their matted bedding, a pair of blankets, a sheet, a wooden pillow—for a few dollars. If a traveler returned to the Gold Mountain, he could redeem his belongings. If not, they would be sold to another unfortunate beginning his life of bitter loneliness.

Chinatown. It was familiar yet unique. It offered Fong See and his fellow sojourners pleasures and diversions unlike anything they had seen in their home villages or in the big city of Canton. In gambling dens, men could of course play the usual fan-tan, but it was not uncommon to see two merchants dressed as wealthy mandarins, carrying miniature bamboo cages containing beetles or grasshoppers, step down into an underground arena where the insects would battle, and spectators would wager on the outcome.

There were also opium dens. In the Big City of San Francisco, the dens had long been a tourist attraction for the picturesque tableaux that they presented. Recently, white men and women of means and social standing could be seen in these places, lounging on carved wooden pallets, drawing in smoke from the pipe's stem, and letting their minds drift away in release. In Sacramento, this white incursion into the dens had caused considerable scandal. Although Fong See scorned opium, there was no escaping its aroma on Chinatown's streets.

Fong See walked past shops that had scrolls on either side of their doorways affirming the good wishes of the owners: "Ten thousand customers constantly arriving." "Profit coming in like rushing waters." "Customers coming like clouds." But for most of his countrymen there had been no customers, no rushing waters, no clouds. They lived in poverty, away from their families and ancestors, too poor to save enough money for the return passage, too heartbroken to walk into their home villages old men with empty pockets.

Forgoing the transitory pleasures of opium and gambling, Fong See saved his money. Each month he went to the bank and cabled money to his mother and wife in the home village. He also treated himself— sometimes buying a western-style hat, tie, jacket, or shoes. In just these few short years he had already transformed himself from a brave little peasant boy, who worked for his mother on the streets of Canton, into a young man who eschewed the dress of the poor whites for the elegance of the wealthy ones he had seen on the riverboat. He was training himself not to be a peasant—not just through his clothes and job, but in his mind. He was always thinking, observing, trying to create for himself a context so that he could become a part of the larger world.

In early April of 1877, Luscinda Pruett lay dying. Her mind wandered over her life in Oregon, her children, her husband, and God, whom she knew she'd be meeting soon. She'd had fever for weeks, and now the pneumonia had grabbed hold of her body and wouldn't let go. Not that it wasn't peaceful lying here, as Mrs. Peterson sponged her forehead with cool cloths and the Reverend Peterson gave a discourse on the second commission of Christ to his Apostles. Or was he reading from the tenth chapter of First Corinthians? Maybe that wasn't it at all. She knew she'd heard him give these sermons before, at their Sunday meetings. No matter. The Petersons lived a few farms over. Reverend Peterson had made quite a name for himself in these parts—working all day on his farm, then rewarding himself by riding on horseback throughout the county to preach the Word to small congregations and gatherings in the valley. When he wasn't preaching, he was ministering to the sick and dying. Why, nearly every week he had a burial to attend to in this county alone.

Luscinda tried to focus her mind to track the course of her illness. She had five sons—Irvin, Loren, Charles, Rodelwin, and little John. The last had been born their first season out here. They had all survived, and all were strapping. A year ago, in 1876, the same year that the Lord had decided in His wisdom to let Custer die at the Little Big Horn, He had finally blessed the Pruetts with the birth of a daughter, Letticie.

This sixth pregnancy and birth had been particularly hard on Luscinda. She was forty-one and sometimes so tired her bones ached and her mind ached until she couldn't stand it anymore. Her days were full of chores punctuated by breakfast, lunch, and dinner for the eight people in her household. She baked all her own bread, pies, and cakes. In summer she put up all her own preserves and vegetables to see the family through the winter. Sometimes she wished that she could stop scrubbing and washing and cleaning and scalding, that she could put off milking the cows and feeding the chickens and minding the kitchen garden.

Luscinda had been taken ill at the end of February. At first she worked through it, because a farm didn't wait for people to be well and strong. A farm went on, no matter what. Finally she'd gone to bed, and even in her delirium she'd been aware of the consternation around her when a neighbor's demented son fell in a tub of boiling soap and died. She remembered another boy who'd fallen into the chaparral and cut himself so badly that he'd bled to death as his parents watched. Women died of consumption or in childbirth or of cancer. Men were run over by plows or trampled by horses, or accidentally shot themselves with the guns they always carried. It wasn't that life was necessarily harder here. Even back in Pennsylvania, Luscinda had borne babies and worked the farm. But she'd been younger then, stronger maybe, and not so worn-out lonely.

March had been corn-planting season. John had plowed; the boys had planted. Letticie had played near Luscinda's bedside. As she lay there, she'd thought about their time in the valley. Central Point marked the actual center of the valley; from their farm the Pruetts could see in every direction across vast fields to the surrounding pine-covered mountains. In the foothills, homesteaders who had come to this land twenty years before the Pruetts had planted orchards. In summer, under blazing heat, the fruit ripened and brought in plentiful crops. Sometimes John traded a pig or a few sides of bacon for so many lugs of peaches, which she, in turn, peeled by evening and put up by sundown the next day.

From her kitchen window, if the fog that plagued the Big Sticky lifted, Luscinda could see Table Rock and McLoughlin Peak. Somewhere up there in the mountains lay Crater Lake. She had hoped that one day the boys would be able to manage the farm while she and John traveled the eighty miles for a vacation. Now she thought that that possibility was about as likely as their soil turning into fertile loam overnight.

In late March she'd taken a bad turn. John had sent Irvin over to the Petersons' house for dried beef and a bottle of the Reverend's home-made cough syrup, for which Irvin paid one dollar. Even with her fever she'd been pretty mad. "No point in wasting money on me," she'd said. But John wouldn't listen to "that nonsense," as he called it.

Luscinda often worried about money. They owed Magruder's over in Central Point for syrup, starch, candles, matches, castor oil, and salt, and W. C. Leever's Hardware for washtubs, chamber pots, watering cans, and washboards. The family tried to barter goods and services as much as possible, trading three cans of lard for three gallons of black-berries, or lard for dried fruit, or lard for envelopes, or equal trades of lard for butter. Sometimes the older boys, Irvin and Loren, did hauling for neighbors, and had once been paid the grand sum of seventy dollars for hauling freight for the Emaline Mining Company. This year the Pruetts' oats had sold at fifty cents a bushel. When these good times came, they'd go into town and get the horses and themselves shod. If there was money left over, Luscinda might splurge—fifty cents at Magruder's for coffee or tea, or for half a pound of tobacco for her husband, or maybe even a dollar for twelve yards of printed cotton and some hairpins.

This last week, it had stormed. She had listened to the rain hit the roof and trickle down the windows, knowing in her heart that she might never hear it again, never live to see another spring. Of course, after five years living on the Sticky, she thought she'd seen all there was to see. All year long, John battled the soil using Reverend Peterson's clod masher when he could, or just going out with the boys and tilling by hand, trying to make some sense of the land. They'd put in corn and squash, alfalfa and wheat. They raised a few cows and chickens, and always tried a few shoats come spring. Sheep were tricky, since eagles like to swoop down and disembowel the lambs, but they kept a few anyway.

These last two days she'd been fighting the pneumonia hard. But the fight was so peaceful somehow, just lying here and listening to the voices around her, all the people she loved. Once she'd heard someone say, "We've been trying to catch that counterfeiter who's been running around somewhere between here and Bear Creek." But then she thought that couldn't be what they were talking about, because then she heard someone say, "On the point of death . . ." Only it didn't worry her, because Reverend Peterson and his wife were there with their soothing words about the Hereafter and Faith and Jesus and God. No, that wasn't it at all, he was whispering in a soothing voice, "Yea, though I walk through the valley of the shadow of death . . ."

Then it was very quiet and it seemed that all the neighbors had gone home. Now only John sat by her bedside, holding her hand. He had always been a good man—a good father and husband. She wanted him to say something, to say he loved her, but she knew that wasn't his way, wasn't their way.

The time is here, she thought. What about my baby girl? Who will show her how to be a good woman? Who will love her like a mother? Who will teach her about duty, hard work, religion? Who will make sure she finds a proper husband? If only I could keep Letticie with me.

The next morning a light dusting of snow lay on the surrounding mountains, and the ground was sticky from the rain of the previous evening. John Pruett paid six dollars for a coffin, two dollars to a man to dig the grave, and another couple of dollars to have his wife carried to her final resting place on McHenry's land, down the road from the farm, about halfway to Central Point. In the late morning, all of the neighbors on both sides of the Sticky flat attended the funeral of Luscinda Pruett, who had lived not quite five years in Oregon. As Mrs. Peterson tried to calm baby Letticie, John thought of the words he would have chiseled on the gravestone:

LUSCINDA J. PRUETT

DIED

APRIL 9, 1877

AGED

41 YEARS, 6 MONTHS

Jesus loves the pure and holy

"Sister Pruett died in full assurance of Faith," Reverend Peterson began. Soon it was over and the neighbors went home. That night Martin Peterson wrote in his diary, "Morning cloudy, day sunny at times then cool and cloudy with a little sprinkle of rain. We with near all the neighbors on both sides of the Sticky flat attended Sister Pruett's funeral this forenoon. I preached a short Discourse at the grave, according to her request which she made before she died. The family are very much afflicted over her leaving them." For his final entry, he added, "W. W. Gage and Gilbert and others arrested the counterfeiter over on that side of the flat yesterday evening."

The next morning was clear, frosty, and a little hazy. The newest widower along the Sticky spent the day harrowing. Irvin sheared a few sheep. Loren mucked out the barn and fixed a fence. Charles and Rodelwin walked into Central Point to go to school, came home, and did their chores. Little John, who was just four, fed the chickens, gathered the eggs, and watched over his baby sister.

By the late 1870s, Fong See officially ran his father's Kwong Tsui Chang Company, which now stood at 609 K Street between Sixth and Seventh. When he moved out of Chinatown, he changed the name of the store to the Curiosity Bazaar. His neighbors were Mr. Luce, a marble cutter and tombstone maker, T. L. Acock, who made his living in real estate, and R. S. Davis, a dry-goods merchant.

Instead of herbs, Fong See and his brothers manufactured underwear for brothels. Fong Lai and Fong Quong had tried to continue the herb business, but they had no experience. Their father had never taught them how to choose ingredients or brew tonics, or how to match herbs with a patient's symptoms. Customers had quickly found other herbalists to treat them, and the Fongs had been left with an empty storefront.

Although they knew next to nothing about herbology, they did know about clothing manufacturing from working in clothing factories themselves. Lai and Quong had worked first as apprentices at six dollars a month, then as journeymen at twenty dollars a month. Once they had learned enough, they felt ready to open their own factory. Although Fong Lai and Fong Quong had the experience, they worked for their younger brother, who acted as the front man and manager of the Curiosity Bazaar. It was not the Chinese way, in which age was revered, but the American way, in which the smartest and wiliest took charge. They were all members of the Gwing Yee Hong, the Guild of Bright-Colored Clothing, which served the needs of those who sewed shirts and ladies' garments and undergarments.

While his brothers and a few other men sewed in the back room, Fong See traveled up, down, and across the state, selling the factory's merchandise to Chinese and white prostitutes. He didn't go to San Francisco, where more than sixty women's underwear factories kept up with the trade of both good and fallen women. Instead he went to mountain camps, railroad camps, farms along the delta, and as far south as Los Angeles. Everywhere a train stopped, there were bound to be men who wanted to satisfy their bodily desires and women who were willing to slake that lust.

In Fong See's father's day, almost all the Chinese women in the state had been prostitutes. Later, when Fong See had first come to Sacramento, nine out of ten Chinese women were prostitutes. Now, as he traveled through cities and towns, he saw how they lived. They tended to reside in groups of two to six, and were kept by a man or sometimes by a madam. Only a few tried to make it on their own.

Some were swathed in silk, satin, and lace, and lounged in beautiful houses, waiting for customers to come in and make their selection. These lucky women ate good-health meals to stimulate their desires—rice, pork, eggs, liver, and kidneys. Other, less fortunate women peered out from the barred windows of their cribs and wore the meager clothes of farm peasants. "Lookee two bits, feelee floor bits, doee six bits," they would call out to white men in their broken English. No strong-sex meals for these women—just rice, a few slivers of vegetable, and doses of opium to assuage their loneliness. But even they made money for their owners. Seven customers a day for the lowest-grade prostitute could bring an owner $850 a year. No matter which kind they were—silk or cotton, healthy or diseased—all prostitutes needed Fong See's stock.

He carried with him lacy drawers split at the crotch like a baby's pants in his home village—only these were made of fine China silk and edged in ribbon and lace. "No need to undress completely," he would say as he laid out his wares. "You open your legs, the man goes in, he comes out, it's all done. No need to take off all clothes. The man likes to see his prize wrapped like a present. White, lacy, beautiful, no matter how many men you have today. You buy extra pairs, your private parts always look clean and new." For the lower-class prostitutes he brought ribbon-edged muslin underwear and camisoles.

Once he sold his wares, he returned to the factory. Besides his brothers, the men who worked for him were mostly from the Chungshan district near Macao, and were known for their dexterity with a needle. As true craftsmen they earned more than the customary dollar a day. His workers might make two or three dollars a day for twenty-two to thirty weeks of work, averaging $364 a year—not as much as the tailors and seamstresses in the Big City, or as much as white workers in other factories. But here they had companionship, craft, and the knowledge that they were working for a Chinese, not a foreign devil.

Fong See worked hard to be independent. He didn't want to be a laborer. He didn't want to be at another man's mercy—not a white man, not a Chinese man. He wanted to build an empire. He wanted to have men work for him, be beholden to him, look up to him. He felt that in some ways this was already happening. He hired extra men, knowing that as soon as they had honed their skills and earned enough money, they—like Fong See's older brothers—would leave to open their own small factories. There was always turnover, but the men were cheap and the factory kept going.

Fong See sold his goods and brought back a profit—enough to provide them all with food, lodging, entertainment, and money to send back home to wives and mothers. He was the one who went next door to Israel Luce, the tombstone cutter, to pay the rent. His brothers couldn't do it; they didn't have enough wits, courage, or English.

Fong See learned not only how to sell but how to stand up to those foreign devils who wished him out of the country. "He took it from me by violence." "He cheated me out of my wages." "They were lying in ambush." "The immigration will soon be stopped." He practiced these phrases as much as he practiced "Buy one dozen, get one pair free." Fong See was brave; he wasn't afraid to travel where he wasn't wanted, he wasn't afraid to talk to white or Chinese women. They liked him, often offering to trade their wares for his.

On this day, as on every day, the men in the factory sat around a large table, concentrating on their needlework. Bolts of ribbon and lace and stacks of ladies' undergarments in various states of completion lay about in haphazard piles. The men meticulously stitched tucks and pleats into the thin fabric, which then fanned out into voluminous bloomers. Fong See had discovered that neither the prostitutes nor their customers were all that interested in the embroidery. They preferred the flamboyant. The more tucks, the more pleats, the more ruffles, the better.

The silk had been his idea. He'd remembered it from his years in Canton, and had gone to Charles Solomon to learn how to navigate the treacherous waters of importing. Mr. Solomon ran a Japanese bazaar and had also encouraged Fong See to go into curios—baskets, fans, and cheap porcelains. For now, he stuck with underwear. The importing costs had been slight, but his profits had jumped in ways he couldn't have imagined. The American girls especially loved the new merchandise, and it made him think. Most of his countrymen imported things like ginseng, bamboo shoots, and soy sauce—items that made for a civilized life on foreign soil—but no one had yet found the Chinese product that Americans would buy. His success with China silk proved there was a market, but he needed something with broader appeal, something that he could buy cheap in China and sell for more in the United States. Perhaps Mr. Solomon was right after all.

Along one wall of the factory, two hired men pumped at sewing-machine pedals with their bare, hardened feet. As usual, the men who ran the machines and the men who did the handwork kept up a continuous stream of conversation about the exclusion law that the white men were planning in Washington.

"They say that what we have suffered is only the beginning," said Fong Quong.

"Since we have been here, they have cut our freedom," added Fong Lai. "They have tried to make our lives even worse than those we suffered in our home villages."

The men grunted their acquiescence. Every day it got worse in Sacramento. White men, taking advantage of railroad price wars, streamed into the state like rice grains running out of a punctured sack. These men were always angry. They tripped, slapped, beat, and spat on Chinamen. The foreign devils threw eggs and tomatoes. They took their filthy clothes to the Chinese to be cleaned and, when they came back for them, refused to pay, sometimes taking a day's work and throwing it on the ground so that a hapless laundryman would have to begin all over again. These white men pulled queues, jerking a man's head back till he fell on the ground. Oh, how they laughed.

The Chinese had endured many hardships since coming to the Gold Mountain. Now they were treated worse than the village dogs whose purpose in life was to eat the shit and lap the piss that fell from a baby with split pants. They had thought they had eaten bitterness in the past, but it was sweet cake compared to what they now endured silently and with no inkling of revolt. They swallowed their anger. They learned to *bai hoi*—stand aside, avoid conflict.

White-demon newsboys on streetcorners still called out their news. They shouted out when Black Bart robbed another stagecoach. They hooted out the exploits of the good Earp brothers and the evil James brothers. But recently their hollering was of a different sort. As they held their newspapers aloft, Fong See saw drawings of Chinese men with their features exaggerated—queues becoming poisonous snakes, beautiful eyes transformed into elongated deformities, teeth rendered as blood-sucking fangs. At night, when he went for noodles, he sat with men who read aloud from the American newspapers in which his countrymen were described as heathens and barbarians—savage, lustful, impure, diseased.

The threat to "racial purity" seemed to inflame white Americans most of all. "Were the Chinese to amalgamate at all with our people," said John F. Miller, a speaker at the state's constitutional convention, "it would be [with] the lowest, most vile and degraded of our race, and the result of that amalgamation would be a hybrid of the most despicable, a mongrel of the most detestable that has ever afflicted the earth." Soon afterward, California enacted legislation to prohibit the issuance of a marriage license between a white person and a "negro, mulatto or Mongolian."

But this was just one of many unfair laws enacted in the past decade. A fifteen-dollar tax every three months was levied on laundrymen who carried their livelihoods on poles; the tax was only two dollars every quarter for those prosperous enough to own a horse and wagon—a law that clearly favored white men and hurt the Chinese. There had been laws against firecrackers and gongs, although no one had been able to enforce these. In San Francisco, if a man was arrested, his queue would be shaved—a deep humiliation and loss of face. That same city passed a law requiring five hundred cubic feet of air per person in rooming houses, when few sojourners could afford the luxuries of either space or air. In some cities, Chinese children couldn't attend schools with white children. The Chinese couldn't buy land. Some laws even punished white businesses for hiring Chinese laborers.

It seemed that whenever the Chinese began making a profit, the Caucasians took it from them by enacting laws—laws limiting the size of shrimping nets, laws forbidding ironing after dark, laws banning the importation of prostitutes, laws banning any paraphernalia connected to the lottery or even allowing Chinese to visit lotteries, laws requiring that laundries be built of brick or stone and have metal roofs, laws forbidding the hiring of Chinese for public works. The laws not only acted as a constant, niggling persecution, but denied this specific race the very things that brought most European immigrants to American shores. Although some of those laws were overturned by the Supreme Court, many were not.

"Perhaps this is just the gossip of the old men who sit on the street-corners," offered one of the young apprentices.

Fong Quong snorted, then said, "I have seen many things since I came to the Gold Mountain, and I know that there is no future for us here. The railroad is finished, and every time it travels west it brings a thousand more devils. You tell me who is going to get the jobs."

"But what can we do?" another apprentice cried out.

"What we have always done," answered Quong. "We will keep working. We will continue to send money home to our wives and mothers. Most important, we will keep to ourselves."

"They say the Chinese must go. I am not stupid. I will go back to my home village. I will spend my days with my wife and sons."

"That is not for me," said Fong Lai. "They may want us out, but I am going to stay."

"I agree, and I'm sending money to my home village to bring my younger brother before the law is passed. If you don't get in now, you never will."

"I'm sending for my good-for-nothing son," said another worker. "Perhaps here he will learn the meaning of hard work."

The winds of politics and money had shifted the sands of the Chinese immigrant's life. Certainly the depression of the 1870s, in which 30 percent of the people of California lost their jobs, had contributed greatly to the antagonism between Caucasians and Chinese. A job was a job, and whites, who represented a 90-percent majority, felt they were entitled to it first. But there were other factors as well. Gold production had dropped to one-third of what it was in 1869. The tourist trade to the state had diminished as visitors opted instead to travel to the Centennial Exposition in Philadelphia. Then Mother Nature conspired against everyone, especially the Chinese. During the winter of 1876–77, rainfall was one-quarter the normal amount of the previous twenty-five years; this had dire effects on the wheat, cattle, and citrus industries. Chinese who worked on ranches and farms lost their jobs; later they were replaced by white laborers.

With the state in turmoil, politicians stepped in—not to help, but to take advantage for their own personal gain. The "Chinese issue"— beginning with Governor Stanford, before he realized the money he would make from the Chinese on his railroad—had been a sure-fire winner in elections. The issue became so hot that even on the national level "the Chinese question" could make or break a politician. In the 1876 presidential election, swing votes were tied to the Chinese exclusion issue. Rutherford Hayes endorsed exclusion and won the election. Once in office, he reiterated his stance, saying the "present Chinese invasion" was "pernicious and should be discouraged. Our experience in dealing with weaker races—the Negroes and Indians . . . is not encouraging. . . . I would consider with favor any suitable measures to discourage the Chinese from coming to our shores." In the next election, James Garfield carried the anti-Chinese torch into office.

Eventually, all anti-Chinese legislation would be enacted on the eve of national elections. To get the labor vote, a candidate had to be anti-Chinese. No one was more so than Denis Kearney, the president of the Workingmen's Party, who took to speaking in vacant city lots, where he began and ended each speech with the proclamation, "The Chinese must go! They are stealing our jobs." In the crowds that came to hear him, men carried placards that read WE WILL NOT GIVE UP OUR COUNTRY TO THE CHINESE, and OUR RIGHTS WE WILL MAINTAIN, and WHITE LABOR MUST TRIUMPH.

In Congress, the arguments for exclusion were purely racist. Many of them were the same ones that had been used against the Irish decades earlier. The Chinese took jobs from "real" Americans. The Chinese were dirty, drank too much, and lived on too little money. They didn't spend their money in this country, preferring to save it and send it home. The Chinese worshiped their ancestors; wasn't that something like worshiping an idol? They worked too cheaply, and when they were out of work—unlike Americans—they became hoodlums. The Chinese carried disease; they were clannish; when they died they sent their bones back to China, as if American soil wasn't good enough for them. In other words, the Chinese were totally unassimilable.

Some of this rhetoric was not only inflammatory but downright false. Accusations that the Chinese spread "loathsome diseases," for example, were a dime a dozen. When the *Grass Valley National* wrote that any Chinatown in California was "but a synonym for a row of brothels, a collection of stinks, and the dwelling places of thieves and prostitutes," it failed to note that the same was true of just about *any* California town at that time. Visiting brothels, gambling, and smoking opium were activities common to Chinese and whites of all economic levels. The Chinese *did* send their meager earnings back to China, but the fact that American China traders made millions in the opium trade each year, and sent their money back to their homes in Boston and San Francisco, aroused virtually no criticism.

Ironically, many of the attributes that Americans found distasteful about the Chinese were the very things the Chinese found equally repellent in Caucasians. The *fan gway* spoke an unintelligible language. They had peculiar vices. They didn't understand the ways of the universe. Their religious beliefs and practices were incomprehensible. They followed a strange calendar. Additionally, whites didn't welcome the New Year properly by cleaning the house, preparing foods to bring good luck in the coming months, settling old debts, or honoring their ancestors. They had absolutely no sense of family. In sum, Caucasians were barbarians and there seemed to be an unending supply of them perfectly willing to take the jobs that the Chinese had fought so hard to develop.

The Exclusion Act of 1882 was devastating. Under this law, Chinese laborers wouldn't be allowed to enter the United States for ten years. The wives of current resident laborers were also barred from entry. All Chinese needed to be registered and carry their residency papers at all times. Finally, they were declared totally ineligible for citizenship. (This clause alone allowed the United States to join Nazi Germany and South Africa as the only nations ever to withhold naturalization on purely racial grounds.) Only Chinese who were teachers, merchants, students, tourists, and diplomats would still be permitted entry.

The men who worked in Fong See's garment factory were not alone in their fears. In 1881, 11,890 Chinese entered the country. The following year, 39,579 Chinese—only 136 of them women—slipped in before the Exclusion Act went into effect. Although it took a while for immigration officials to gear up, the law would prove to be extremely effective. Just six years later, only twenty-six Chinese came to the Gold Mountain. In 1892 the Geary Act went into effect, extending and toughening the original law, and putting the burden on immigrants to prove they had a right to be in the United States. If a Chinese was found to be in the country unlawfully, he could expect imprisonment of up to one year, followed by deportation with the denial of bail in habeas corpus proceedings. As a result, not one single Chinese came to American shores that year.

In his worst imaginings, Fong See couldn't have envisioned what would happen to the Chinese in the years to come. The Exclusion Law permitted—even encouraged—the basest elements of men to boil over and explode into violence and cruelty. The Driving Out began. In the Cherry Creek district of Denver, white ruffians ravaged Chinatown, looting homes and businesses, and beating unfortunate residents. One Chinese was saved when his white friends nailed him inside a packing case and carried him through the mob. The only white man to take a public stand was a gambler and gunslinger, who held back the rioters with a gun in each hand, demanding, "If you kill Wong, who in the hell will do my laundry?"

In Tacoma, Washington, seven hundred laborers were herded into railroad cars and driven from town. Eventually all Chinese would be forced to leave that city, and for decades not a single Chinese would live within its environs. In fear, Chinese in Seattle boarded steamships for San Francisco. In Tombstone, Arizona, cowpokes cut cards to determine to which points of the compass the Chinese would be sent. In Tucson, a Chinese was tied to the back of a steer and sent out across the desert. In Rock Springs, Wyoming, twenty-eight Chinese were killed, eleven of them burned alive in their homes; others were shot in the back as they tried to escape. On the Snake River in eastern Washington, thirty-one Chinese were massacred. In Alaska, Chinese miners were crowded onto small boats and set adrift. In Redlands, California—

after years of planting, pruning, harvesting, sorting, and packing citrus—Chinese were barricaded in sheds as white roughnecks raided orange groves. Despite assistance from the National Guard, houses were burned and buildings looted. By the end of the century, the Chinese were completely driven out of California's citrus industry.

Caucasians—even if they supported Exclusion—would acknowledge the injustice of what happened to the Chinese in a popular expression of the day: "He doesn't stand a Chinaman's chance." But Fong See would not be bowed. There had to be ways to get around the laws, and he would find them.

CHAPTER 3

LOVE

1894–97

S INCE Exclusion, the government had begun tracking all Chinese-owned businesses throughout the country as a way of keeping tabs on merchants, the one permitted class of Chinese immigrant that could easily be faked. Every Chinese business had to report twice yearly on the status of the company and the number of partners or "merchants" involved. Immigration officials cross-checked dates and names for possible shenanigans, using the files as the basis for interrogations of Chinese residents wishing to travel in or out of the country. In 1894, twelve years after the Exclusion Law went into effect, Fong See once again filed a business application. But he was involved in manufacturing, a category not covered by the new immigration laws.

In a practical move, Fong See decided to change the name of the Curiosity Bazaar back to Kwong Tsui Chang, the original name of his father's herb store. He hoped this would help establish the fact that the Fong family had been merchants for more than two decades. Fong See was Americanized enough to know that Kwong Tsui Chang sounded foreign. He changed *Kwong* to *Fong, Tsui* to *Suie,* and *Chang* to *On.* Legitimately or not, Fong Suie On represented a significant change to Fong See's ears. For his immediate purposes, he listed the store as the Suie On Company. The original meaning of Kwong Tsui Chang—Success Peacefully—was abandoned.

Like many Chinese of this time, Fong See formed a *hui,* a partnership of up to ten men designed to let them claim status as "merchants." The first partnership pact for the Suie On Company stated that the members of the firm were "dealers and manufacturers of Ladies' Underwear, and General Japanese Bazaar, doing business at No. 609 K Street in Sacramento City." The eight members who made up the firm were Fong See, Fong Jung, Fong Lai, Fong Dong (Fong Dun Shung), Jun Sik, Fong Yun, Kang Sun and Fong Ken. Fong Dun Shung and his fifth son, Fong Yun, Fong See's nine-year-old brother, had partnerships though they were in China. Fong Lai was listed as a partner, while Fong Quong's name was left off, even though he was in Sacramento at the time. As for the others, they are lost to history, although the business file notes that Fong Ken was on board a steamer in port on April 18, 1894, the day the agreement was drawn up.

Each member had an interest of five hundred dollars in the firm, bringing the total capital to four thousand dollars, but these amounts were fictitious. Certainly Fong Ken, who languished on the steamer awaiting entry based on the establishment of his merchant status, could not have had such a magnificent sum in his possession. One thing is certain: although the company was listed as a partnership, Fong See was clearly the owner and mastermind behind this official document. His photograph is the only one that appears on this agreement, as well as on all subsequent business documents until the government decided to stop keeping track of Chinese-owned businesses. Fong See was the sole proprietor; the others were merely partners on paper as a means of establishing their merchant status.

In other *huis*, partners drew lots to see who would get to use the money, but Fong See had convinced his brothers and the others in the firm that he was the boss. He had "bamboo in his chest"; that is, he was a man confident in his work and skill. Fong See's older brothers, cousins, father, and friends saw that he was the only one among them who had the confidence and courage to go forward. He had a vision of how things should be and he pursued it.

On May 3, 1894, with his merchant status now affirmed, Fong See applied to the Collector of Internal Revenue for the Fourth District of California, and was granted a certificate of legal residency, number 130020, issued to a "person other than a laborer." Soon after, the Suie On Company—or the Curiosity Bazaar, as it was still known by its customers—moved to 723 K Street, in the Oshner Building. Fong See owned four sewing machines and had as many as ten men working for him. Business was thriving.

"Letticie, take Donna and Georgia outside for a while. They're bored and I need to rest a spell. Come back in an hour to start dinner."

"But I have homework," Ticie Pruett said to her sister-in-law, Jennie, who was already slipping off her high-button boots and lying back on the bed. Ticie shrugged. She wanted so badly to have an education. She was good at arithmetic. Her teacher at the school in Central Point— perhaps realizing that Ticie would one day have to support herself— had taught her simple bookkeeping. The problem was that, with all her housework, Ticie couldn't get her homework done and was always late for school. The boys teased her about it—"Ooooh! Look who's late again!" She hated it when they made fun of her.

Ticie took the children outside as she was told. They sat down in the cool shade of the cottonwoods that lined the drive. It was early June and already hot as a blister. At five and three years of age, Donna and Georgia didn't mind playing with each other and soon occupied themselves looking for rocks and building little piles with them. Toying with a strand of her auburn hair, Ticie glanced back at the house, where a tobacco plant climbed over the cook shed. She sighed. There was no point in making a fuss. It had been this way since Jennie had married Ticie's older brother, Irvin, after their father died.

Ten years ago, when she was eight, the family had gone to the county races. There wasn't much to do out here except work, so the family had always enjoyed these diversions. Their religion did not forbid racing so long as no wagering was involved, so John Pruett, an avid horseman, entered a one-horse buggy race. It had been raining, and when they got home her father complained of cold. Within the week, he contracted pneumonia and died. Everyone said it was just like what happened to her mother, but Letticie couldn't remember anything about it. All she knew was that she'd loved her father. He'd nicknamed her Ticie. She was still called that at school, but never at home. Her father was the only one who had truly loved her.

Ticie hadn't been old enough to take care of a house full of men, so Irvin had married Jennie Garrett, who'd been born in Montana. The Garrett family had thought they'd find luck out west, but it hadn't worked out that way. The Garretts had been poor, and Jennie had brought nothing to the marriage except her ability to run a household, which she did until Ticie was old enough.

A year later, Ticie's third brother, Charles, got married. Melinda Cox's family had come out early from Tennessee and homesteaded good land. Upon their marriage, Charles was given 286 choice acres abutting the foothills where they raised grain, alfalfa, and fruit. The couple had two children, Mabel, now aged six, and Guy, aged three. Melinda wasn't nearly as awful as Jennie. Letticie figured that Melinda knew how to be gracious because she'd had to be kind to the farmhands when she was growing up. Jennie, on the other hand, was as poor as a church mouse and as mean as a rattlesnake.

After Ticie's nieces and nephews had been born, she'd been shuttled from one farm to the other. With each baby they expected her to do more work. "Change baby." "Feed baby." "Wash out these diapers. Scrub them good." She didn't mind doing chores. She was used to it, in fact; the problem was *how* they asked her. No, they didn't ask her, they ordered her. Churn the butter! Make the beds! Do the wash! Feed the chickens! Mend the clothes!

Her closest brother, John William, had just married Effie Caster. Ticie had been the witness. She'd always loved John best, but now he had someone to love him, and he no longer paid Ticie any attention. She couldn't blame him for it. The point was none of them loved her or cared for her. She was alone in this family. An outcast.

She wasn't a bit like any of them. She remembered how enraged her brothers and the neighbors had been when the railroad was being built. "I hate those chinks they've got coming around here," Irvin used to say after Sunday dinner, even though everyone at the table knew that the Chinese had panned for gold along the Rogue River long before any of *them* came to Oregon.

"You coming with us tomorrow night?" Charles might ask, when a gang of farmers got together at night to pull up the rails that were laid during the day.

In her dim memory—or maybe it was just that she'd heard her brothers talk about it—she remembered when the miners on Jackass Creek had stoned the Chinese, burned their cabins, and jumped their claims. John Miller had shot one of the Chinese in the back, but he'd gotten clean away with it because "it served that Chinaman right. He got what was coming to him." She thought of the Chinese men she'd seen working on the railroad or on neighboring farms. She wasn't afraid to look right into their faces, many of them scarred either from birth or from the hardships they'd found here. In their eyes she saw a mirror of the same loneliness she'd felt for so many years.

At school, the teacher let her look through *The Democratic Times*—just one large sheet of paper folded in the middle which gave the news of the valley and the world. Ticie always skipped the "Central Point Pointers" section, because what news could be there that she cared about? She turned instead to "Foreign News" and "News Nuggets Picked up West of the Sierras," and read the reports of the rail extensions connecting county to county, state to state.

There was a world out there, and Ticie Pruett longed to be a part of it. She'd been saving whatever she could from her allowance and from the occasional odd job she did for neighbors. She knew it wasn't much, but it would get her as far as Sacramento. (She'd dreamed of San Francisco, but she'd read it was too expensive.) Her one bag of clothes was packed. Tonight, while the others slept, she'd leave the farm and all the people who'd been callous toward her, walk into Central Point, and board the morning train. It was 1894, and Ticie was eighteen years old.

A few weeks later, as the bell announced the arrival of a customer, Fong See looked up to see not a Chinese or American whore, but a young woman with her hair pulled up into a knot on the top of her head. Her hair had frizzed in the damp air, and small tendrils hung down, framing her face in wisps of rosewood-colored strands. The girl paused momentarily, then asked, "Do you have any openings for employment?"

"You want job?" Fong See asked.

"Yes," she said, stepping farther into the shop.

"You no work here. This not a place for you."

"Well, I don't know what this place is," she said, "but I've been all over the city and nobody wants to hire me." She seemed on the verge of tears.

"This not a place for you."

"Why?"

"This business for whores," Fong See answered.

"Oh," the girl said, her voice quieting in disappointment.

"Make underwear for prostitute."

The girl's face brightened. "This isn't a house of ill repute?"

"*Aiya!* You stupid girl! This a factory. I own."

"I can sew."

"I no need that. I got plenty man help me. You go now. This no place for you."

The girl stared at him for a moment, then lowered her eyes. She sighed, shook her head, mumbled her thanks, and went back outside. From his place at the counter, Fong See watched the girl—her hair burning deep auburn in the sunlight—as she paused, looked first to her right, then to her left, shook her head again, then walked left down K Street. Fong See shrugged and went back to his work.

Several times over the next few days, Fong See's thoughts were drawn back to the girl. He had come in contact with more Caucasian women on the Gold Mountain than had most Chinese men, so he shouldn't have given the girl a thought. But he did. He remembered her fresh skin, her pretty hands, her small waist, her slight overbite. He recalled her manner—straightforward, with an underlying somberness. A few times he thought he saw her pass by the plate-glass windows of his shop—her rich, thick hair always catching his eye. Keep your mind on business, he told himself.

Then, one morning, while he was in the back of the shop, giving the day's orders to the men, he heard the chime of the Chinese bells hanging from the front door, and went out to see her standing at the counter again.

"Hello," she said. "Do you remember me? I'm Letticie Pruett."

He nodded.

"I could still use a job," she said. He watched as she tried to smile.

"No job here for girl like you. No job for girl."

Letticie was about to leave when the bell once again sounded. Madame Matilde, one of Fong See's oldest customers, stepped inside. "I need some more of that underwear," she said. "I don't know what my girls do with it."

"Madame Matilde, good see you today. You want to buy?"

"That's what I said," the glittering woman replied. "I'm needing some new merchandise. Now, chop-chop."

"One pair? Two pair?" Fong See asked, the words rolling together as he struggled with the *r* sounds.

"Jesus!" Madame Matilde spat out. "Now listen, Fong. I come in here every month. And every month I order the same thing. A dozen pairs in silk, a dozen pairs in muslin, and a couple of those camisoles. Now, like I said, chop-chop."

Fong See stared at Madame Matilde. She had spoken so fast that he hadn't understood her words. As he opened a cabinet, he overheard Madame Matilde say to Letticie, "You have as much trouble with him as I do? I can't understand a word he says."

"He asked how many pairs you need."

"Jesus, I already said that!" The older woman snorted in frustration. She tapped her fan impatiently. "Ah, hell. I just don't have time for this today." With that, Madame Matilde walked to the door, calling over her shoulder, "I'll be back another day, Fong."

After Madame Matilde left, the girl watched as he put away the merchandise.

"You could use someone like me, you know," Letticie said.

"No job!" Fong See said firmly.

The girl smiled shyly at him again and left. *Aiya!* So much activity in the store, Fong See thought, and no money changing hands. This was not the way it was supposed to be.

The next day, Fong See opened the shop and set the men to work. Business was slow, slow enough that he had time to stand at the window, gaze out into the street, and see the girl sitting on the wood-plank sidewalk across the street. She was staring at the Suie On Company. After lunch, he had the opportunity to pass by the window again, and he saw her still sitting there. All afternoon, Fong See was aware that the girl—what did she call herself? Letticie?—was watching him, watching who came in and who went out. He smiled to himself when someone left the shop with a large order, and cursed himself when someone walked out empty-handed. But what was he thinking? he asked himself. Keep your mind on business, he lectured himself time and time again. When the men went home and he locked up the shop, he made it a point not to look across the street in Letticie's direction.

The next morning she was waiting across the street when he arrived. He promised himself he would ignore her completely, which he did until Madame Matilde came into the shop. "Ready for a business transaction today?" she asked.

Just as he was about to speak, he heard the bells on the door and looked up to see the girl with the rosewood-colored hair step into the shop.

"Good morning, Madame Matilde," Letticie said. "What can we do for you today?"

"I'm thinking maybe two dozen," the woman said, looking first to Fong, then back at the girl. "But only if I can get a good price. Bulk discount."

Letticie turned to the Chinese man, looked him square in the eye, considered, then stepped behind the counter. "Now let's see what we have . . ."

Fong See stood aside as the girl took over, pulling open drawers until she found what she wanted. He watched as her neck and cheeks turned red as she displayed the garments. But she was nothing if not determined. "I hope you'll notice this fine needlework, ma'am," she said. "Just look at these pleats. Why, we both know there aren't many seamstresses in the world who can compete with this fine craftsmanship."

A half hour later, as the madam left with her brown-paper-wrapped parcel, the girl turned and gazed at him in her intent and somber way. "As I said before, I've been all over this city. I can't get a job, because I don't have experience. And I'm not about to join Madame Matilde's establishment, although I've certainly received enough offers of that kind since I arrived. But you can see I'm not like that."

"You still want job?" Fong asked.

"I've been watching your shop," she continued. "I've watched you lose customers."

"I no lose customers. They just don't want to buy."

"You're wrong. People come to your shop because you have a . . ." She groped for the words. "You have a unique product. People come here because they *want* to buy. That's why you need someone like me. I'm a woman. I can help you with those . . ." Again she stumbled around for the right words. She straightened her shoulders, and said, "I can help you with those special women. I speak good English, so I can help you with English-speaking customers. If you pay me a decent wage, you won't be sorry."

Fong See stared at the girl. Didn't she realize that he was Chinese?

"You could get in trouble working here," he said.

For the first time, he heard her laugh. "Don't you think I could get in more trouble working for Madame Matilde?"

He wasn't worried about *that*. He was worried about what would happen if someone decided to take offense that he had hired a white woman. This girl didn't seem to care.

The young woman stepped forward and extended her hand. "I told you before, my name is Letticie Pruett. You'll be happy you hired me."

*

In the following weeks and months, Fong See continued to be amazed by the auburn-haired apparition who appeared at his front door each morning. She was so different from the other Caucasian women that he had met in his years on the Gold Mountain. She didn't wear feathers or satin or lace. She was practically and simply dressed—maybe a cotton ruffle here or there. She didn't stink of perfume or men. Instead, she exuded an intoxicating odor of soap, powder, and lavender water. And while she was in no way like the prostitutes who came to him for their underwear, she was always kind to them, almost respectful.

"That is not a job I would want to have," she once said. "But I can understand how circumstances could lead a person into becoming a fancy lady."

See, it was things like that. "If you don't mind," she'd said tentatively one day, "I think we should say we're selling fancy underwear for fancy ladies. It sounds so much nicer. Our ladies will appreciate it too."

Half the time he didn't know what she was talking about, but in this she'd been right. At first the girls had laughed. "Fancy underwear for fancy ladies. That's us! You bet." But they'd grown to like it. Where just a few months ago they'd have come in and said, "Give me some of that crotchless underwear," now they asked for "fancy underwear." And it was selling. Selling so well that Letticie had begun keeping the books. He smiled to himself as he recalled the look on her face when she'd realized that he didn't keep real books, just the fake ones for the immigration inspectors.

"You keep books to know how much you have—what's selling, what's not, your profits, your losses," she'd explained.

"I keep those in here," he'd said, pointing to his temple.

She'd shaken her head. "No, the business is too big now."

"You want, you do," he'd answered, not knowing how to tell her that he could neither read nor write in Chinese, let alone English.

A few months later she'd come to Fong See again. "I hope it doesn't sound like I'm interfering, but I think you should ask the men to make up some regular underwear. Plenty of women would buy it if that certain part was just sewed shut."

He had put the men to work on it immediately. They were happy with Ticie's presence. Since she'd arrived, their good luck had blossomed. Each of them sent home more money each month. But it was more than just money. Ticie showed them a respect such as many of them had not felt since leaving their home villages. She communicated as best she could—using sign language, gesturing, smiling at them, sometimes patting their shoulders. For many, it was the first time they had been touched by a white woman. She didn't seem afraid to sit down at the work table and companionably sip a cup of tea. Lately she'd even begun to share their pot of noodles, sometimes looking over Fong Lai's shoulder to watch how he cooked them.

She helped them with their English, stressing how to pronounce words, make sentences. She'd grown serious when one of the workers had called her a *fan gway*. When she'd asked what the words meant, and been told that they meant "white ghost," she'd asked, "Now, why would you want to call me that? I'm not a ghost. I'm flesh and blood, just like you. Surely there is another word you could use." The men had discussed it heatedly, then finally settled on *lo fan,* which meant simply "white person."

Fong See was probably nineteen years older than Ticie, but tradition said that at least ten years' difference was good and proper for marriage. He didn't know why he even allowed himself to think along these lines. He had a wife in China to whom he continued to send a monthly allowance. More important, it was against the law for a Chinese to marry a Caucasian. Still, his mind raced with reasons why marriage was a good idea. Indeed, he did have a wife in China, but he had only seen her once, and they had never consummated their marriage. In his mind— and he realized this was a peculiarly western thought—he and Yong weren't married at all. Besides, tradition also suggested that a man might have a country wife to care for aged parents and a city wife for home and companionship.

Ticie didn't need to know about his first wife in the home village. The men in the factory would never mention her. Instead, they would respect him for having climbed another step on his ladder of importance, for there were few Chinese who had either the courage or the charisma to pursue a white woman. Finally, marriage to Ticie would change him from a sojourner to a resident. If he married her, he would not leave her. He would honor her as his true wife. He loved her.

Fong See and Ticie Pruett made good partners and that was important in this country. For years he had thought, If only I had an American partner who could see the opportunities that I see. Letticie wasn't a man, but she was much like him. She had bamboo in her heart. She, too, had a vision of how life should be.

Letticie Pruett See thought it was funny how things turned out. When she'd left Central Point, she'd been just a girl full of girlish dreams. She'd thought how easy it would be for her to become a city girl with a job and beaux and finally a husband. In her first flush of excitement, she'd marveled at the electric lights, the crowds, the theaters, but it hadn't taken her long to discover that no one wanted her. Well, some had wanted her, but she wasn't going to use her body to muck about with smelly old men.

Desperate, she'd gone into the Suie On Company. How could she have done such a crazy thing? What had possessed her? Desperation, she thought again. No one—not her teachers, brothers, or sisters-in-law—would have believed how she'd acted. Against all reason, against everything she had ever learned, against her own common sense, Letticie persisted. She pretended to be brave and industrious, knowing that if she didn't get a job she would have to return to Oregon. Besides, she knew she could help Fong See. He needed her, which was more than she could say for anyone else. Still, she was probably more surprised than Fong See when he hired her.

She loved the way the boss listened to her ideas. The men made up the new underwear, and she'd been able to sell it to good, honest women like Mrs. Acock, the wife of the real-estate man. It had taken some persuasion on Letticie's part even to get Mrs. Acock into the store, but now she was a regular customer. If Mrs. Acock didn't like what they had on hand, Letticie asked the workers to make up something special for her. Mrs. Acock had told her friends, and now several of the merchants' wives along K Street came in to buy from Letticie.

She didn't stop with changes in the underwear. Mr. Solomon, the importer, had been trying to sell Fong See other types of merchandise for years. "Try it," she told him. "Try it and see if it works. Start with cheap things. If they don't sell, you won't be out much." The next time Mr. Solomon made his quarterly stop at the Suie On Company, Fong See ordered baskets, fans, and some inexpensive porcelain. For an hour they bickered over price and quantity. After the curios sold, Letticie encouraged Fong See to order more from Solomon, and also from Mr. Snedegar at Hale Brothers. Now Mr. Snedegar came in once or twice a week just to write up orders. And the women customers who had begun to come in with Mrs. Acock now bought other things as well. Even Mr. Luce, the landlord, had become a customer, buying all of his Christmas presents in the store this past December.

Letticie supposed it was natural that one thing would lead to another. Hard work to success. Loneliness to happiness. Friendship to love. On January 15, 1897, Letticie Pruett of Central Point, Oregon, and Fong See, the fourth son of a Chinese herbalist, were wed. They went to a lawyer to draw up the papers for a contract marriage. Their union would be recognized by the state as a contract between two individuals, since California forbade interracial marriages.

But when Letticie looked at the contract, with its fancy calligraphy and heavy embossing, she thought, What difference does it make, between one piece of paper and another? Fong See had promised allegiance to her for all time; she had promised likewise. She loved him. Who could say why? She knew nothing of the ways of love, except that it defied all logic.

Letticie wrote her brothers of her marriage, and received a terse letter back, in which her family disowned her. How could she marry a Chinese? It was disgusting, they wrote, and she was no longer their sister. She knew she would never see or hear from any of them ever again.

But Suie, as she called her husband, was kind, smart, a hard worker. Oh, she knew how popular he was with the ladies. She blushed to think of the practice he'd had! He knew how to butter up women with his sweet words and twinkling eyes. But it didn't matter, because he treated her like a lady.

He'd had trouble saying her name, Letticie, because of the *L*. She suggested he call her Ticie, as her father had done. She'd also had trouble with his name. Fong was his last name and See was his first, except that Fong was actually his first name and See was his last. She didn't want to call her husband See. That didn't make any sense at all. "It's a tricky business, trying to settle your name legally," she cautioned. "We don't want to attract attention from the authorities. We don't want them to point a finger at you. They might think you aren't telling the truth. So we'll always be Sees." He agreed, and she'd taken to calling him Suie or Suie On. It was the name of the store, but it seemed more personal somehow—just between the two of them. Besides, it was easier for the customers. They couldn't be expected to remember so many different things. Let them think the store was named for him. It would place him one more notch above the workers.

They had only one problem now: this damned underwear business. She sniffed. Fancy underwear for fancy ladies! In a pig's eye! Even with the addition of curios and undergarments for decent women, Suie was still in the crotchless underwear business. It seemed to Ticie, as a married woman, that it offered simply too many opportunities for straying.

"Business is drying up," she told Suie. "We should get out of here before the authorities crack down so hard there won't be a single bawdy house left in the city." She hammered away at his pocketbook. "Not enough margin anymore in fancy underwear. Pretty soon we won't make any money."

When he scoffed at her concerns, she retorted, "You've spoken of the Driving Out. One day that could happen to us. We might as well go now, while we can plan our own future."

"Where?" he asked, jutting his chin at her.

"Only two Chinatowns remain intact—San Francisco and Los Angeles."

"More Chinese in San Francisco," he said. "Maybe safer for us."

"Maybe, maybe not. No place will ever be completely safe for us, Suie. Besides, too many have already gone to San Francisco. Everything's been grabbed up."

"*Lo Sang,*" her husband said, mulling over the Chinese name for Los

Angeles. He had made plenty of money there during his traveling-salesman days.

"I'll place my bets on Los Angeles if you will. The City of Angels. We'll like it there. Not too many Chinese. The people are tolerant. We'll find more opportunity. We might even become rich."

"I am husband. I make decision."

"I *want* you to make the decision. It's just that Los Angeles is a more progressive city. Sacramento is a pit."

Letticie was at least partly right. Despite observations made to the Chinese Bureau by Messrs. Acock, Solomon, Snedegar, and Davis, as well as by Mr. Luce's son, that the Suie On Company was "well thought of in Sacramento," the underwear business was indeed dwindling. By the end of the century, the Guild of Bright Colored Clothing would fade into oblivion, while Los Angeles would present a picture of opportunity. No matter what, the Sees were well out of Sacramento. In February of the following year, a fire would sweep through the Oshner Building, wiping out the remains of the Sacramento branch of the Suie On Company.

PART II

CHAPTER 4

LO SANG

1897–1902

THE Chinese began trickling into the little pueblo of Los Angeles as early as 1850, settling along the Calle de Los Negros, more popularly known as Nigger Alley. But it wasn't until the 1870s, when the Southern Pacific began constructing a line to Southern California—a project rife with heavy losses from accidents and injuries—that the Chinese came and stayed. They began leasing land from the old estate of Juan Apablasa, an adventurer from Chile, and Benjamin Wilson, who would later become part of the permanent landscape when a mountain was named in his honor. For the first time on the Gold Mountain, the Chinese had found an area that replicated their South China climate.

Still, the Chinese continued to suffer. Here, again, they were stoned, vegetable carts were upset, queues pulled. One newspaperman conjured up "a hundred vile opium dens, where Chinese, white prostitutes and fast young men spend night and day smoking opium." Other reporters kept would-be restaurant patrons at bay by reminding wary readers that the Chinese liked to eat abalone and squirrel, that their chefs roasted chickens alive to remove their feathers. Laws—such as the one forbidding laundrymen "to sprinkle clothes by squirting water from their mouths"—were put into effect to harass and humiliate.

These smoldering conflicts had raged to the surface on October 23, 1871, twenty-six years before Fong See and Letticie arrived in Los Angeles, when hostilities erupted in Nigger Alley between two rival tongs—the Nin Yung Company and the Hong Chow Company—over the ownership/marriage of Ya Hit, a girl whose comeliness was only equaled by the profits that both companies hoped to make from her flesh. Attempting to calm things down, a white policeman intervened, and was shot. Shortly thereafter, another white man—a saloonkeeper turned rancher—fired randomly at Chinese houses along Nigger Alley. When his volleys weren't returned, the rancher strode onto a porch and boldly walked to the door, where he was met by a barrage of bullets. He staggered back, muttering, "I am killed."

News quickly traveled through the city that the Chinese were "killing whites wholesale." A mob of vigilantes, composed of Mexicans and Anglos, descended on the area. Using pickaxes, they chopped holes into the Coronel Building, where many Chinese were hiding; others simply shot at it. Emboldened, men stormed inside, where they found not tong thugs, but respectable Chinese men and women, cowering in fear. Two dead Chinese were dragged outside, where they were kicked, pummeled, and finally hanged for good measure.

The alley disintegrated into chaos. A city councilman picked up a loose plank from the sidewalk and batted a Chinese over the head with it. Another officer helped things along by handing Chinese over to the mob to "take them to the jail." Most never made it. Among the latter was a Chinese doctor who was robbed, shot in the mouth, then hanged. Men ransacked apartments and businesses for the gold that the Chinese purportedly hoarded in their dens. Others ran through the streets with stolen sacks of rice, bolts of silk, bottles of wine, even roast geese.

By the end of the night, the bodies of seventeen Chinese men and boys swung from a wooden awning in front of a carriage shop, from the sides of two prairie schooners, and from the crossbeam of a gate in a nearby lumberyard. Within days, another two Chinese died from complications of gunshot wounds. At least five hundred Angelenos—approximately eight percent of the city's total population—participated in the "night of horrors," as the popular press dubbed it.

But the riot became an odd boon to the Chinese. During the troubling later years of the Driving Out and the enactment of the exclusion policy, Angelenos maintained a certain cool distance from the hot tempers of the rest of the country. The city's racists had a difficult time generating enthusiasm for their anti-Chinese clubs, while across the state such clubs flourished. Boycotts against the Chinese and Chinese-employing businesses customarily failed in Los Angeles. In 1877, when the Labor Organization of Los Angeles called for the "peaceful and legal" removal of the Chinese, local papers reminded residents of the "disgrace" of the riot.

So Chinatown grew, paralleling the growth of the larger metropolis. Gold may have been what first brought people to California, but it was the golden warmth of the sun that kept them coming in a steady stream. Railroad wars encouraged this influx, with ticket prices reaching an all-time low in March of 1886, when it was possible for a brief time to buy a cross-country fare for one dollar. What had once been acre upon acre of orchards, vineyards, and grazing land was sucked into urbanization by the great flood of immigrants.

As in other cities around the country, immigrants sought out their own kind. Mexicans, who had been on the scene seemingly forever, had Sonoratown. Italians settled a few blocks away in Little Italy, while the French established another colony nearby. For now the Chinese carved out a small place for themselves bordered on the south by slaughter-houses, on the east by railroad yards and a gas plant, on the north by the fading glory of the old Spanish Plaza, and on the west by the burgeoning Caucasian metropolis.

By 1897, when Fong See and Letticie moved to Los Angeles, Nigger Alley had passed into history. In its place, Los Angeles Street was extended through to the Plaza. Apablasa and Marchessault streets bisected Los Angeles Street. Where they crossed Alameda Street marked the main entrance to Chinatown. Other unpaved streets and alleyways—named for the children and grandchildren of Juan Apablasa—were jammed chockablock with western-style brick buildings and crumbling Spanish adobes painted in brilliant hues of red, yellow, and green.

The interiors presented a different sight altogether. More than half of the rooms had no windows; many others were concealed behind false doors. Some white social workers believed that the interiors had evolved according to Chinese custom, based on the belief that evil spirits didn't like the darkness or to turn corners, but others knew the secret rooms were a Gold Mountain necessity: they provided a means of hiding illegal residents or facilitating escape from gambling dens. Few buildings had heat or electricty. Bachelors lived in boardinghouses, sleeping in bunks with small ovens wedged between them. In these rooms could be found every type of vermin known to man—ants, fleas, cockroaches, rats. Residents trapped the rats in wire cages and killed them with boiling water.

The city fathers frequently complained about Chinatown's filth, saying that it created a health hazard for the city at large. The politicians had a point. By 1880, nearly all of the fruits and vegetables consumed by Caucasians were grown by Chinese who had leased small plots of land along Adams, Pico, and West Washington. But the corrals in Chinatown, which housed the vegetable peddlers' horses, swarmed with insects. A state commission also found seven privies in the corrals. All this wouldn't have been such a problem if the peddlers didn't sleep alongside their horses, if the wagons—loaded with the city's fresh produce—weren't kept there all night, and if the produce weren't washed in the horse troughs in the morning. But as easily as city fathers could get upset, they could also calm down—especially at the thought of having to pay for any improvements—and life would go on as usual.

Upon their arrival in the city, Fong See and Ticie first went to Chinatown, where they saw sights reminiscent of Sacramento's Chinese quarter. Street vendors offered sugared coconut shavings, rice cakes, and roasted melon seeds. Signboards beckoned customers with tantalizing promises. Men might find a cure at an apothecary with a sign that read BENEVOLENCE AND LONGEVITY HALL, or HALL OF HARMONY AND APRICOT FORESTS. Restaurants along Marchessault Street promised both nourishment and enchantment with their names—Fragrant Tea Chambers, All Fragrance Saloon, Balcony of Joy and Delight. The air itself seemed to beckon with the aromatic odors of roast pork, duck eggs preserved in oil, dried abalone, and cuttlefish.

By then, Chinatown had a weekly newspaper, three temples, and a theater. The ghetto had district associations, family associations, and tongs—which provided arbitration of disputes, helped residents thread their way through the immigration bureaucracy, and offered protection. Eight missionary groups insistently courted converts. The Methodist, Congregational, and Presbyterian missionaries were by far the most successful, as they tried to meet the worldly needs of immigrants by teaching English and providing job placement.

As in Sacramento, Fong See saw that here again the Chinese preferred to look after themselves. They took care of each other when they were dying. And when they died, relatives or the Chinese Consolidated Benevolent Association would see to their burial at the Evergreen Cemetery, the only graveyard in Los Angeles willing to take "Orientals." Later they saw to the digging up and sending back of the bones to China, since the Chinese believed that the only pathway to the spirit world was through the soil of China. As in most things, the white press embellished the more gruesome aspects of this custom, reporting on the rotting human flesh, the scraping clean of fleshy remnants, the open and smelly coffins, and queues left lying about the gravesites with bits of scalp still attached.

Neither Fong See nor Ticie wanted to live in Chinatown. To settle there would have been a step backward. Instead they opened their first store on First Street, between Spring and Broadway, right in the heart of the Caucasian business center near City Hall. Once more they altered the name of the store to the F. Suie One Company, adding the initial *F* for Fong and an *e* on the end of *On* to make the name appear more "American."

Although several blocks from Chinatown, the Sees lived above the store like most Chinese merchants. They continued to sell curios purchased from Charles Solomon, began to trade in baskets, and, against Ticie's frequent objections, continued in the underwear business. The F. Suie One Company still had eight partners, but with a smaller number in the United States. Just before Fong See and Ticie had left Sacramento, Fong Quong had returned to China. Within months of settling in Los Angeles, Fong Lai had also decided to go home. Four of the partners were relatives in China; the other four worked in the store. None of them was a true partner, just employees who paid a price—either in money or in labor—to maintain their merchant status.

During these early days, Ticie—now pregnant—often felt lonely. She longed for advice and encouragement, but no Caucasian women would speak to her, and in Chinatown, men outnumbered women twenty to one. The majority of Chinese women were prostitutes living sad lives in cribs along Alameda Street. The few others were kept behind locked doors, protected like precious gems by husbands afraid to let their wives risk exposure on the street.

On May 22, 1898, within five months of moving to Los Angeles and less than two years after their marriage, Fong See went out into the night and brought back Anna Mueller, a German midwife who catered to Chinese women. The baby squalled at the indignities of his birth. Ignoring Mrs. Mueller's protestations, Fong See peeled away the baby's swaddling and turned him over on his belly. There at the base of his spine was his Mongolian spot. The baby may have been half-Caucasian, but to his father's mind he was full-blooded Chinese. Fong See wanted to name his son for the great Ming Dynasty, which at its zenith had been responsible for the flowering of China's great cultural traditions. As a name, Ming would imply brightness and intelligence.

"But I'd like to name him Milton, for my father," Ticie said when Mrs. Mueller had rewrapped the infant.

As the child began to nuzzle at his mother's breast, Fong See felt proud. His wife had given him a son. He could reward her.

"Milton," he said in agreement, then added, "But his Chinese name will be Ming Fook."

Shortly after Ming's birth, the Sees moved to 328 South Spring Street, where the F. Suie One Company still advertised itself as dealers and manufacturers of ladies' underwear and as a Japanese bazaar. A second son, Ray—or Ming Hong—was born on June 2, 1900. One year later the family moved to 414 North Main Street, another Caucasian neighborhood just a few blocks off what is now called Pershing Square.

The new store had three rooms. Merchandise was displayed in the front, where Ray, now a toddler, like to rest his head on the cool surface of a ceramic water buffalo that served as a doorstop during the long, hot days of late summer. From here, Ray could look out onto the street, where the scorching light seemed to bleach everything a ghostly, ashen white. In the back, the family shared a room. Across the hall, four men—"partners"—kept up the rhythmic pumping of four sewing machines.

Although the inspector for the Collector of Customs appraised the stock—Chinese and Japanese goods, as well as undergarments—at $4,000, Fong See estimated the value at closer to $25,000. Obviously the inspector didn't know what he was looking at. By 1901, the contents of the store had evolved. By now customers could also choose from a large selection of silks and embroideries, screens, bronzes, furniture made from teak and the China nut tree, finer Chinese and Japanese porcelains, and a few high-quality antiques.

The Sees owed this change to Richard White, a former soldier of fortune, who had retired at the age of forty-five to take a job in the plumbing department of Holbrook, Merrill & Stetson. A dapper man, he carried an ivory-headed cane, and his hair had already turned white. He was more than a little smitten with Ticie. Since he couldn't give her love, he gave her the gift of business. One day he walked in with some antiques he had bought in China years before, during his soldier-of-fortune days. "This is the kind of merchandise you should carry," he told her. "This is what will make you different from other merchants." Against her husband's objections, Ticie placed the antiques in the window. Within days they were gone, and for good money.

Mr. White brought in more antiques. Once again, Ticie sold them. Still, Fong See hesitated. Curios were enough, he said. "There's no risk in curios. We've always done well with them."

"But our customers seem to want quality," Ticie insisted. "They're willing to pay more for something better."

As the store's profits increased, Fong See realized that Ticie was right. Caucasians would buy antiques, often agreeing to pay an outlandish price for something Ticie had purchased from Richard White for very little. Once Fong See and Ticie realized that they couldn't rely on one source, they began going to auctions. Slowly the farmer's daughter and the herbalist's son learned how to recognize good pieces. Within a couple of years they were conducting auctions themselves, sometimes selling thousands of dollars' worth of merchandise in a single afternoon.

Ticie made herself essential to the business. She kept the books, and researched the limited sources for Chinese antiques in the country. She was in the store every day—first with just her husband, then with Milton and Ray. Fong See was a good businessman, but Ticie had heart. There was a kindness about her that attracted people—both Chinese and American. She listened to the Chinese bachelors who worked in the store when they spoke of their wins or losses at the gaming tables. When they were sick, she sent for the doctor. When they needed someone to help them with English words, they asked her. They sought her advice when it came time to sign rental contracts for their rooms. As they prospered, they came with lease agreements for their new businesses. She helped them write letters in English, and fill out forms for their residency certificates, taxes, or fines. They depended on her judgment, and she was never too busy to help them. Although they never spoke of their loneliness, often it seemed that they just wanted to be near a woman who was both a wife and mother.

Gradually, Ticie attracted others who would become lifelong friends. Some, like Richard White, helped change the course of her fortunes as well as those of her family's for generations to come. Besides Richard White, whose affections would always go unrequited, there was Florence

Morgan, the wife of a California oyster king. Although they were still rich by Chinese standards, the best of the Morgans' good times had passed.

Even though the Sees prospered, even though they brought in merchandise from China and sold it quickly, even though Ticie had given birth to two sons, there was one matter on which Fong See would not budge. "I would like to live in a house," Ticie begged repeatedly. "I would like to buy property so that we can live as a real family and not just as merchants above the store." But Fong See was only interested in what was showy, and to him nothing was more showy than an automobile.

So while Ticie worked in the store, cooked the meals, and changed and washed the diapers, her husband was being driven around town in the first automobile to be owned by a Chinese anywhere in the country. Ever the businessman, he used this car to promote a new herbalist in town. With advertisements hung on the sides and a uniformed chauffeur to drive, Fong See and the herbalist tooled along the streets of Chinatown, inviting a crowd of awestruck citizens to visit the new herb shop. Fong See would never learn how to drive, but he would maintain a consuming interest in automobiles. Cars showed the world how he, an outsider, was more innovative and open to ideas than the insiders of the city.

In 1901, after the quelling of the anti-foreign uprising known as the Boxer Rebellion, Fong See packed up his young family and took them to China for a year. He hoped to buy antiques and other goods at deeply reduced rates from people still reeling from the upheaval. To Fong See, it seemed far more difficult to leave the Gold Mountain than it had been to come here. As a boy, he had simply boarded a clipper ship and set sail. Now he needed a plethora of documents—stating who he was, who his wife was, and verifying that his children were American-born—to show that he and his family had a right to return to the United States under the merchant-class exemption.

Fong See hadn't foreseen how tedious the process would be. He had two American-born sons and an American wife. He was recognized as a merchant by the state. Still, the way the immigration officials examined him made him feel like a coolie. He listened while his friends and associates—his insurance agent, the auctioneer, and Richard White— were questioned on his own truthfulness. None of these queries was as awkward as those surrounding Ticie.

"Is Fong See a married man?" the inspector asked Mr. Conant, the insurance agent.

"I understand that he is," Conant replied, "but I never saw a marriage license."

"Is he living with this woman as his wife?" the inspector asked.

"Yes, sir."

The inspector persisted. How long had Conant known this woman? Had he seen her about the store? The inspector asked, "Have you been introduced to her as his wife?"

"No," Conant answered. "But she has told me she is his wife."

"Has Suie One told you that she is his wife?"

"I cannot remember that he has."

The inspector didn't fare much better with Richard White regarding the status of Ticie, but he painted a convincing picture of Fong See, the merchant. "Is there a laundry, lodging house, restaurant, or pawnshop connected with this place of business?" the inspector asked.

"No, sir," White answered.

"Has this man whom you have recognized as Fong See been engaged as a huckster, peddler, fisherman, laundryman, or servant, or performed manual labor of any kind since you have known him?"

"No, sir."

When the inspector asked how much merchandise was manufactured in the store, White answered gruffly, "Manufacturing cuts very little figure there."

"Have you ever seen Fong See engaged in the act of making goods?"

"He has men to do that work," White answered.

On July 23, 1901, Fong See and his family received written permission from the U.S. government to travel to—and later return from—China. During their final preparations before departing Los Angeles, Fong See and Ticie had ample opportunity to go over the in-depth interrogations—the first either of them had experienced. For several years now, Ticie had been wanting her husband to get out of the underwear business. "I was right about starting the curios in Sacramento and I was right about going into antiques," she said. "I think I'm right about this. After our interviews, I think you can see that it's dangerous for us to continue to manufacture. We—you—would be in real trouble if the government decided you were a laborer and not a merchant."

Finally, after all these years, Fong See agreed to give up the underwear business. The risk was simply too great. Since he no longer needed the sewing machines, he had them packed in crates to be shipped to China with the rest of the family's luggage. He would give the sewing machines to his mother and the people of Dimtao, who would benefit from the ease of the invention, which required no electricity to operate and little training to use. The former operators, who had for so long made the underwear, stayed in the store. While Fong See was gone, they would look after things as best they could.

In September 1901, the Sees left for San Francisco, where they boarded the SS *China*. Ticie was filled with excitement. As a girl back in Oregon, she had never imagined that she would have the opportunity to travel to a foreign country. And China! Yet Ticie anticipated feelings of homecoming and familiarity, for she had been living as the wife of a Chinese man for four years. She wanted to explore the village of her husband's birth, watch her children experience new sights and sounds, and meet her in-laws and her husband's other relatives.

In October the family arrived in Hong Kong. They traveled first to Fatsan, then to Fong See's home village. It had been thirty years since he left Dimtao. Now he stood before his parents, seeing them together for the first time since his father had left for the Gold Mountain. Shue-ying wept. Fong Dun Shung immediately turned his attention to Ticie, speaking a few halting words of English called up from memories dusty and worn. Fong See's youngest brother, Fong Yun, stared open-mouthed. Villagers clustered around the bearers, who had carried the family from the thriving little city of Fatsan through the ricefields to Dimtao, and watched as they unloaded the pedal-powered sewing machines.

With Fong Dun Shung leading the way, Fong See, Ticie, Ming, and Ray walked through the narrow passageways of the village. The house that Fong See had grown up in no longer existed. In its place stood a new house far grander than any of the buildings other than the ancestral temple in the village. As he stepped over the high threshold, Fong See saw that his parents' home consisted of a large room with no windows. Outside, in the small courtyard, an open-air lean-to served as the kitchen. Almost as reflex, Fong See and Ticie picked their children up off the hard-packed dirt floor. During the coming months, they would not live here, but in another house even more primitive than this one.

"Don't worry," he said quietly to his wife. "Don't worry."

"I'm not worried, Suie," she answered, smiling. "It's life in the country. We'll be fine."

The following weeks and months bustled with all manner of activity. Ticie's in-laws took her and the children to the ancestral temple, where she paid her respects to the ancestors of her husband's family. Fong See had stone plaques carved with her name and those of the children, which were then hung alongside those of the many generations of Fongs from the village of Dimtao.

They each made courtesy calls: Ticie to her husband's first wife, Fong See to his extended family. Ticie had been aware within the first week in the Sacramento factory that Suie was loyal to his family, and that each month he sent home a stipend. However, he'd never mentioned a wife. Only in preparation for this trip had he even told her about the woman. "I have been married to Yong since before I left for the Gold Mountain," he'd said. "But you have given me sons. You are my true wife. You are my American wife." Ticie had chosen to believe him.

Out of respect for a foreigner's strange customs and feelings, Yong had been sent to a neighbor's house. Stepping into the cool gloom of the house, Ticie was greeted by a shrunken old woman who peered up at her, tilting her head like a bird and looking sideways out of the corner of her eye. It took Ticie a moment to realize that this old grandmother was not a grandmother at all, but her husband's wife.

Yong and Ticie could not communicate through words, but as they sipped their tea, the women came to understand each other. Yong, who had left her village as a young girl, had spent her life as a servant to her mother-in-law. Yong only knew the drudgery of the village, and had aged far beyond her forty years. Her face had wrinkled, her hands and feet had hardened, her spine had curled, her womb had never received the seed to create sons. Although her natural inclination was to reach out to the woman, Ticie remained uncharacteristically cool. While only a concubine by tradition, Ticie was the first wife in station. Had she not provided her husband with two sons? She sat ramrod-straight. She ran her hands over her nicely tailored gown. She was the real wife here. Ticie promised that Yong's monthly stipend would continue until her death.

Fong See was having experiences of a different sort. To return to the village of his youth was not at all what he had expected. Number One brother had died from opium. Numbers Two and Three had returned to the village after their brother's marriage to Ticie. Number Two, Fong Lai, had married a no-name girl, and had a son and two daughters. Number Three, Fong Quong, had also married a no-name girl—this one from the neighboring village of Low—and had a son. Fong See's sister, Lin, had married Jun Quak, from Tee Chin village. Number Five, Fong Yun—who had been born after Fong Dun Shung's return—was young, ambitious, eager. Fong See had plans for him, but they needed time to unfold.

Fong See looked for the couple who had helped send him to the Gold Mountain so many years ago, only to find that the old man had died and his wife was ailing. All these years, as the Chinese New Year came and went and others followed the custom of paying back debts, Fong See had not repaid the loan. Overcome by guilt and remorse, he promised to take care of the widow as if she were his own mother. Village gossips would discuss this event for years to come—the good deed, the amount of money that traded hands, the largesse, the honesty. In time it would seem that the whole countryside knew how Fong See had helped the old woman with—could it be true?—a gift of two thousand American dollars. The small kindness to an ailing woman would be the seed of a legend that would be tended and watered with loving care and wishful thinking. It would grow like the giant bamboo—fast and strong—the legend of Gold Mountain See.

*

Every precaution was taken to ensure the children's health, but Ticie fell ill. She had gone to China with smooth white skin. She would go home with the scars of smallpox, or "the flowering-out disease," as her in-laws called it. When Fong See realized the severity of his wife's illness, he became distracted with worry. Since their marriage, he had grown to love her in a way that he could only describe as "western." She was not a no-name girl like the wives of his brothers; he did not view Ticie as a servant or a piece of property. Over the years she had impressed him with her spirit, her independence, her strength. He hoped that these very attributes would help her as she struggled against the disease.

Yet for all of his anxiety, Fong See could only offer his wife comforting words. He had to trust his father to save her from death. Ticie was vaguely aware of Fong Dun Shung as he hovered over her, murmuring soothing words in a language she didn't understand. He fought for her life when she herself had ceased to care.

She was riveted by the sensation of burning followed by numbness as Fong Dun Shung placed a cloth soaked in herbs across her chest and another across her face. She experienced a brief sensation of coolness as her skin met the open air, followed immediately by the crazy, incessant itching of the smallpox, followed by the taming poultice. Time and time again, she thought she would fly out of her skin even as he held on to her hands and spoke softly.

Fong Dun Shung prepared different medicines for each stage of her illness: *sheng ma geng tang* to release the muscles during the fever stage; *sheng ji da biao tang* for the rash; *xin xue zhu jiang tang,* with its active ingredient of silkworms, for the suppurant stage; *hui jiang tang* for crust forming; and *gu ben xioa du tang* for crust loosening. He also brewed teas to restore her overall well-being, including *xi jiao di huang tang* with rhinoceros horn—which was known to clear heat, relieve fire toxins, cool the blood, nourish the yin, dispel blood stasis, and stop bleeding—and *bao yuan tang,* the oldest smallpox remedy, which strengthened the *qi,* her life energy.

Ticie gradually recovered but remained shaky. Every day Fong Dun Shung and Shue-ying walked her to the outskirts of the village and back to build up her strength.

"You are our true daughter-in-law," Fong Dun Shung said in his halting English. Shue-ying rattled something in her cackling voice. Fong Dun Shung nodded, then translated, "She say you are Number One wife, not Number Two. She tell Number Four—only one wife, you. He listen. Do what mother say."

"Thank you for everything you've done." They were such formal words for what she felt. Her in-laws had embraced her and the boys.

They had harangued their son about this wife thing. They had given her back life itself.

Her father-in-law smiled. "Be careful. Go slow. You still weak."

With Ticie well, Fong See—perhaps realizing how close he had come to losing her—insisted on having a formal photographic portrait taken of his family. Ticie thought she was strong enough to get herself and the children ready, but once she had them dressed in long gowns and embroidered caps and shoes, fatigue settled over her. She was too weak to put up her hair in her customary style, so Shue-ying pulled the auburn tresses back into a severe Chinese bun at the nape of her neck. Then her mother-in-law helped Ticie into an embroidered skirt with thousands of miniature pleats, and fastened the frogs of the silk jacket.

Fong See, attired in a mandarin robe, already posed regally in a carved chair before the photographer. Ticie sat nearby, her hand resting on a decorative table that stood between them. The photographer placed the children next to them. Ticie tried to focus on the table's mother-of-pearl inlay and the incongruous objects that lay upon it—the covered teacup, the opium pipe with the tassel hanging from its stem, the stack of joss paper, the western-style clock—but the effort seemed too great for her. It seemed, in that captured moment, that she was hardly in her body at all.

Fong Yun, Number Five, understood that he was fortunate. Fong See had been sending money home for years, always saying that he wanted Fong Yun to have a good education. "Every family should have a scholar," his brother often wrote through the letter writer. "This will bring us honor." No one ever spoke of Imperial examinations or the life of a true scholar. They just wanted Fong Yun to be able to read, write, and do sums.

But even with education, what opportunity did he have? In 1895, when he was twenty, he married a no-name girl from Low Tin village. She assumed the name Leung-shee—simply meaning that she was a married woman from the Leung clan. The following year, Fong Yun went to Guilin to work for a cousin who owned a distillery. He did paperwork and managing. He met the mayor. He thought he was doing well. Then one day he was told to go to a certain mountain to pray to Buddha. People said, "That is a great place to go," and so he went.

As Yun traveled by sedan chair, he watched laborers gathering mountain grass to stoke the fire in the distillery. He traveled a long way, up and up, but no matter how far he went, people still cut the grass and carried their oversized loads back down the mountain. "This is a hard life," Fong Yun said, his voice surprising him in the confines of the sedan chair. He stared at those people and felt pity for them. He said,

"I cannot stay here any longer. I will go to the Gold Mountain." But he was alone and no one heard him.

When Number Four first returned to the village, Fong Yun said, "Take me with you to Lo Sang."

His brother shook his head. "The Gold Mountain is a very bad place. It has bad gambling. It has bad women. It is very wicked."

Fong Yun asked many times, but always his brother refused him. "I am worried that if I bring you to the Gold Mountain you will do all those bad things."

During the following weeks, Fong Yun watched as his brother met with families and walked away with his stomach full of teas and sweetmeats and his hands full of family heirlooms. Fong Yun wondered at the people who lived in the Gold Mountain. What could they want with these peasant goods—the ceramic pieces, the wooden carts, the musical instruments? Yun followed his brother to Fatsan and watched as he negotiated to export baskets, paper goods, fireworks, pottery, and furniture.

Yun was young but not stupid. He realized that the way to go to the Gold Mountain was to make himself indispensable. He bought a manual for traders. He could not read the English words, but in one column the editors had placed Chinese characters that phonetically duplicated the English. He started at lesson one: *An ox. My ox. Is it an ox? Is it? Is it an ox? No ox. Is so. Is it so? No.* Fong Yun practiced phrases: *He is a man of his word. That is just what I want. Cock-fighting is mean and cruel.* Other things he couldn't understand. *Don't swallow stones.* What did this mean? Was it some foreign-devil habit? Was it a proverb? He couldn't tell. He also pondered at great length the eighty-three entries under "female." *Adjutrix, administrix, adulteress, amazon, authoress, baroness, begum, belle, bridesmaid, canoness, chaste woman, concubine, countess, cully-lady, dame, damsel, daughter, dignified woman, dissolute woman, doctoress.* The list made his head swim. *Washerwoman, wench, whore.*

He mastered commercial words for *annual income, assets, auction, treaties, tariffs.* He learned the rules relating to passengers, luggage, and duty-free goods. He scanned the duty lists for bamboo ware, tin bangles, baskets, clothing, and confectioneries. He memorized duties reported from the U.S. Custom House: chinaware, 55 percent; jewelry, 25 percent; silk, 25 percent. Each of these he reported to his brother. Together they worked out amounts on the abacus to see if these items could still be profitable after packing and shipping costs.

Fong See said he admired Ming furniture. Yun accompanied his brother to furniture factories and antique shops. Yun watched as Fong See bargained for items for the store, as well as big rosewood armoires and a long, rectangular table in *hung-mou* wood—both in the Ming style—as belated wedding presents for Ticie.

Eventually, Ticie joined them on these excursions. Fong Yun listened as Fong See and his wife learned about ceramics and porcelains. Together they looked at ceramic monochromes, *ding yao*s and powder-blues from the north. From the Ming Dynasty, they studied the brush-strokes of the blue-and-whites—the quality, the refinement, the depth of the cobalt blue in contrast to the white clay. In the south, they bought polychromes—the overglazed enamels of the Ch'ing period. From the T'ang Dynasty, they bought figurines of camels, horses, acrobats, female courtesans, and sages. (When the originals seemed too expensive, they bought reproductions, which Fong See said could be artificially aged without difficulty.) In time they learned to seek out grave robbers who could provide them with tomb figures, porcelains, and ritual bronzes.

At every stop Ticie asked questions. "How do I know this bowl is good? What should I look for?" Because she was asking, a merchant would answer and they would all learn. "You look at the whiteness of the paste, the whiteness of the clay, the thickness of the sides of the bowl. The thinner the clay, the better the quality of the piece. We use the finest kaolin clay—pure white, with particles that are very fine. A piece made from clay of this quality will have much strength." The merchant might escort them outside, then say, "Hold this bowl up to the light. See how it has a perfect silhouette? See how the light glows through the porcelain? These elements show you that the piece is good."

Ticie made inquiries even when they visited peasant factories. At each place she was respectful, and the men answered as though she were the Empress herself. "There is no tensile strength in these pieces," a crafts-man might venture. "They are of common clay." Or, "Some people say our work is clumsy and thick. But this is an inspired piece. Yes, it is true this jar is only used for oil, but when the potter held his hands to the clay, it came up to greet him."

They learned how glazes were applied, how a craftsman achieved the finest results in his powder-blues from sprinkling a thin dusting of powder onto a clear glaze. They learned what to look for in *sang de boeuf* pieces, and about all the accidents that would happen when a large draft of air was forced into the kiln and the flares caused drips to oxidize in blazes of purple and blue. That happenstance, that intentional accident, was highly prized. It created art, made value.

At the end of his year-long visit, Fong See told his younger brother, "I need a person who is educated to work for me. I will not depend on a stranger. You are family. If you are willing to be honest and loyal, I will bring you to Lo Sang."

"Of course, brother," Fong Yun said.

In September 1902, Fong See and his family left China on the SS

Korea for the month-long voyage to San Francisco. Yun said good-bye to his wife, Leung-shee, and traveled to Hong Kong, where his father set him up in a temporary "branch" of Kwong Tsui Shang, Fong Dun Shung's old business, selling ginseng and herbs. This, combined with a fictional interest in the F. Suie One Company dating from 1896, established Fong Yun's merchant status.

CHAPTER 5

IMMIGRATION

1902–13

T H E See family arrived in San Francisco in late 1902. Fong See stood out from the mass of Chinese immigrants; his wife was a white woman, and their children were American citizens. This, combined with the family's obvious wealth, meant that their interrogations were perfunctory. Within hours the family was processed and on its way to Los Angeles. Once again they settled into the store on Main Street, where each day new merchandise arrived from the Far East. Fong See's workers occupied themselves prying open crates and removing excelsior and rice-scrap wrappings to reveal new surprises. With so much stock on hand, Fong See began to think of ways to expand to meet the needs of an ever-changing and growing city.

Downtown Los Angeles may have still been rough-and-tumble, but all around the outskirts, residents were beginning to bask in their wondrous luck. Contented farmers watched as heavy bunches of grapes strained at the vines. Row after row of lemon, lime, and the ubiquitous orange trees filled the air with their intoxicating scents, and served as the most eloquent advertisement for Southern California. The land was so rich, it was said, that farmers grew cabbages as large as toddlers and watermelons heavier than men.

At the seashore, bathing beauties basked in long woolen costumes. To the east lay the dreamy town of Pasadena, where wealthy easterners came to winter. They loved to have fun. They formed their own riding club and rode to hounds. For New Year's, they raided each other's yards and thrashed through the Arroyo, where they swooped up armfuls of roses, geraniums, poinsettias, bougainvillaea, pampas grass plumes, and the feathery branches of the California pepper tree. They decorated every carriage, ranch wagon, buggy, and tallyho in garlands, wreaths, bunting and a profusion of flowers for the annual New Year's Day parade.

Fong See and Ticie saw Pasadena as the logical place for another branch of the F. Suie One Company. The town's citizens had the three things that the Sees needed to be successful. They were rich. They were sophisticated. And, since most of them had come from the East, they weren't leery of doing business with a Chinese.

In December 1903, just two months after the birth of their third son, Bennie (Ming Loy), the Sees opened a store in Pasadena, on South Raymond Avenue across from the Green Hotel. At first, customers may have been set at ease by Ticie's white, matronly presence. As time went on, they came back to see Fong See. To spend an afternoon with him was an adventure.

With three children, two stores, and an active auction business on the side, Fong See required more help. On January 3, 1904, Fong Yun and his older brother Quong arrived in San Francisco Bay on the *Coptic*. Unlike Fong See and his family, the brothers were detained and treated as common immigrants—just two members of a nameless "horde" of Chinese that the United States was determined to keep out. The inspectors made thorough physical examinations of both men, matching Quong to his original exit file and noting that Fong Yun had a small mole on his forehead, small pockmarks on his neck, and a large amount of hair on his legs.

Two days later, Yun's interrogation began aboard ship. Yun, through an interpreter, described his education, how his father had bought stock for him in the F. Suie One Company when he was just a boy, and how he had worked in Hong Kong in a business, the Kwong Tsui Chang, that was "virtually" his. After just thirty-four questions, Inspector Ward Thompson wrote, "I have the honor to report that this applicant in no way controverts the statements set forth in his certificate and that his appearance and conduct are consistent with his claims."

Things didn't go as smoothly for Fong Quong, who, like Fong See, arrived with the status of "returning merchant." Over the next several weeks, immigration officials would use money, intimidation, and time to elicit the information they wanted. Quong's first interview also took place aboard the *Coptic* before Inspector J. Lynch, interpreter H. Eca Da Silva, and a stenographer. Fong Quong was as much of a human being—with desires, dreams, and weaknesses—as the men who sat across from him, yet they toyed with his future as though they were gods on Mount Olympus.

Inspector Lynch was suspicious from the start. He began with easy questions—What is your name? How old are you? Where were you born?—then quickly progressed to Quong's alleged business interests in this country, querying him on his status at the Suie On firm in Sacramento.

"In what Chinese year did you first become a member of that firm?"

"I think it was my seventeenth year," Quong answered nervously.

"How much stock is carried in your Los Angeles store?"

Fong Quong, who had never been to Los Angeles, answered, "About twelve thousand dollars."

"Did your firm manufacture anything at the Sacramento store before you went to China?"

"No," he lied.

"Do you know if they manufacture anything in Los Angeles?"

"No."

"Isn't it a fact that your firm manufactured ladies' underwear in your store in Sacramento?"

"I misunderstood," Quong said. "We employ people to do the work on the underwear. The partners do not take a hand in it."

Inspector Lynch was far from satisfied. He asked Quong to give the names of "white men" who could vouch for him. Quong—frightened and humiliated—dredged through his memory and came up with the names of Luce, Acock, and Davis. After giving this information, Quong was transferred to the dilapidated warehouse on the Pacific Mail steamship line's wharf, which had been turned into a processing station after Exclusion. Every morning Fong Quong awoke to increasing feelings of fear, frustration, and uncertainty. But he could only wait.

A week later, Mr. Lynch wrote to Charles Mehan, the Chinese Inspector in Charge, that he had traveled to Sacramento and personally examined the white witnesses, except for Mr. Luce, who had died some three years before. Mr. Lynch deemed these interviews "worthless." Mr. Mehan, in turn, wrote Mr. Putnam, the Los Angeles Chinese Inspector in Charge, to "please cause an investigation to be made in the case."

On January 16, the very day that Yun arrived in Los Angeles, Fong See was sworn in to testify in the matter of Quong. Fong See described his own past—his birth, the housework and peddling he had done in Sacramento, the partners in his firm, the location of each of his stores. At this last bit, Inspector Putnam seemed to brighten.

"Have you an interest in any other store?" he asked smoothly.

"Yes, I got one at Pasadena just opened," Fong See responded.

"Didn't you have a store last summer on Fourth Street in this city?"

"Yes, I had one there where I auctioned goods every day."

"Didn't you have a store in Long Beach last summer?"

"Yes."

Finally, Mr. Putnam got to the crux of the matter. "What white men are there who know Fong Quong owned an interest in the firm of Suie On while at Sacramento?"

"That is a long time ago. The old fellows nearly all died, and I don't know," Fong See shrugged.

Putnam queried Fong See on the dry goods man, Mr. Davis, the tombstone man, Mr. Luce, and finally Mr. Acock. "What is his business?"

Even Fong See was unnerved by this relentless questioning about people whom he hadn't seen in six years. "I don't know if he did any business at all," Fong See answered, his English faltering. "Don't know what he did, but sometimes real estate, and something else. I did not see enough; he old man."

Despite this one momentary lapse, Mr. Putnam wrote a flattering letter back to San Francisco, stating that he had visited the Main Street store—noting that it was in the American part of the city and not in Chinatown—and found it to be a legitimate mercantile establishment.

Meanwhile, on January 23, Inspector Thompson reported that he had interviewed Mr. Davis and found his testimony unsatisfactory. Three days later, Thompson once again interviewed Fong Quong in the detention shed. This time the questioning was short and to the point. Was there any other white man in Sacramento who Quong thought might remember him? "There are many that I know," he answered, "but I cannot recall their names. I do not know of any particular names now, but there are people in firms there who would know me if they saw my photograph or saw me in person."

A full month later, Israel Luce's son was located in Sacramento and interviewed. The inspector asked him to identify a photograph. "That is the brother of Suie On," Luce answered.

"Do you know this man's Chinese name?"

Mr. Luce hesitated. There were three or four of those Fongs, and he never could match them up with their names, except that Suie On was the man in charge and the one who paid the rent. The inspector asked if he was sure that this was a photograph of his father's neighbor. "Yes," Mr. Luce assured him. "I could go and pick him out among ten thousand Chinamen now."

On February 25, after fifty-four days in custody either on board the *Coptic* or in the Immigration Services detention shed, Fong Quong was released. But his problems were far from over. In Los Angeles he had to obey his two younger brothers. Fong See had been running things forever. Now he had chosen Fong Yun, who was educated, to be the bookkeeper and assistant manager. After a little over a year in Los Angeles, Fong Quong finally understood—just as the inspectors knew from experience—that not every man could rise above the mass of Chinese laborers. Fong See had done it. Fong Yun might do it. Fong Quong didn't have a chance. He packed his Gold Mountain basket and returned to China, where he died a few years later, leaving his "share" in the F. Suie One Company to his son.

Throughout this period, the See family continued to reside above the Main Street store. In 1905, Letticie found out she was expecting another child. It seemed a logical time to move. But where? Letticie wanted a house. Her husband refused. Although both of them liked Pasadena, they felt that the city wasn't ready for a Chinese family to move there.

At the beginning of 1906, the family moved to 510 North Los Angeles Street, in Chinatown. Fong See felt—correctly, as it turned out—that with his reputation his customers would follow him anywhere, even to Chinatown. One month later, on February 19, 1906, the German midwife delivered Leo, whose Chinese was Ming Quan. Neither of these names would take hold. Instead, Ticie called her fourth son Eddy, for Mary Baker Eddy, the founder of the Christian Science Church.

If there was a high-class part of Chinatown, Los Angeles Street had to be it, distanced as it was from the filth east of Alameda Street. Directly in front of the store lay the old Spanish Plaza, and beyond that the city's first church. Next door to the F. Suie One Company stood the Lugo House—the homestead of a Spanish land-grant family long disappeared from the area. Now it housed the Hop Sing Tong, where bachelors rented rooms. This block of Los Angeles Street sloped down toward Alameda, giving the stores deep basements, some of which ran all the way through to Alameda. For some entrepreneurs, this expansive underground area provided an ideal location for gambling dens. For Fong See, it became one long, dark warehouse.

The family still lived above the store, but most days they could be found down in the cool, musty confines of the F. Suie One Company. With the new merchandise from China, the store settled into what it would always be. Inspectors would no longer find men bent over sewing machines and needlework. (Ticie, never one to let things go to waste, used the leftover silk for making lampshades.) By now the family had found its primary product in Chinese antiques.

The store was long and narrow, measuring 26 by 150 feet. Oil lamps were kept low to cast shadows and hide dust. The farther customers walked into the store, the better the merchandise—or "stuff," as it was called by the family. If the customers were obnoxious or just tourists, they wouldn't get past the first few feet of curios. If customers knew what they were looking at, they might be invited in a few more steps. Enticed by section after section of new surprises, they would travel back to areas redolent of teak and age. Finally, Fong See might say, "You are a very special customer. Come with me. I show you something very special." By this time a customer would be so dizzy with titillation that the deepest, darkest warehouse became the ultimate treasure trove. No customer, if he or she ever wished to be invited again, would leave this final warehouse empty-handed.

The success of the branch stores in Los Angeles and Pasadena, followed by a third in Long Beach, cemented Fong See's reputation among the Chinese. He was the only one among them who had the courage and strength to deal with Caucasians. The white devils looked up to him, they listened to him, they *bought* from him. Fong See was able to hold his own as a *man* with them.

In 1905 construction began on a new immigrant-processing station on Angel Island, on the Sausalito side of San Francisco Bay. After the 1906 earthquake, builders were temporarily diverted to more pressing needs, but on January 21, 1910, Angel Island finally opened. Immigration officials hailed Angel Island—which, like Alcatraz, was escape-proof—as "the Ellis Island of the West." The Chinese immigrants who lingered there—from two days to as much as two years—called it by the more lyrical name "Isle of the Immortals."

Across the country, at Ellis Island, the period between 1900 and 1920 marked the peak years of immigration, with 14 million immigrants entering the United States. Immigrants to the West Coast were far fewer, and a much higher percentage were turned away. Each Chinese who came to the United States for the first time, and any Chinese returning to the United States from a visit home, went through interrogations.

As immigration rules tightened, many Chinese took advantage of the few loopholes in restrictions for entrance to the Gold Mountain. Forming their own *hui* or partnership, cooks, houseboys, laundrymen, and gardeners became "merchants" and were permitted to bring in a relative or, with any luck, a wife. But the greatest boon to Chinese immigrants came with the San Francisco earthquake, which destroyed most of the city's records, including birth certificates. Suddenly a Chinese laborer could say that he had been born here and was an American citizen by birth. (It was said that every Chinese woman living in San Francisco would have had to have borne eight hundred sons if each Chinese claiming American citizenship by birth were honest.)

As "citizens," men could bring in their wives. In 1910, Chinese women numbered only five percent of the total Chinese population in the United States. From 1910 to 1924, one in four Chinese entering the country would be a woman. As "citizens," the Chinese could also bring over their sons. The law stated that children of Americans were U.S. citizens no matter where in the world they were born. A new and effective scam developed in which an American citizen of Chinese descent falsely reported the birth of a son in the home village. Such "paper sons" were guaranteed entry into the United States, with automatic citizenship. In China, the market in false birth documents skyrocketed.

False papers, however, didn't guarantee entry. Immigrants still faced the ever tougher questions of interrogators, who were relentless in their efforts to bar common laborers from entering the country: How many trees grow in your home village? Who are your neighbors? How many children do you have? Do you keep a dog? How many steps are there before your doorway? What is the location of the ancestral temple? Each question was designed to induce an immigrant to make a mistake, proving that he was not the son of an American citizen, that he did not come from the village he said he came from, that he wasn't a merchant, student, teacher, minister, or diplomat. The interrogation process was effective and unforgiving. From 1910 to 1935, only one in four Chinese immigrants was allowed to remain in the United States.

Where was Fong See during all this? He had formed his partnership long ago, and the names of his "partners" were listed in his business file with the California branch of the Immigration Service. When men died, they left their "partnerships" to their sons. Others sold their partnerships to an uncle or nephew. The fact that Fong See was the sole owner of the business didn't matter. The partnership established an immigrant's right to enter the United States.

Fong See was dedicated to helping his relatives *and* making a profit. The people who came to the United States as partners in the F. Suie One Company worked as clerks and salesmen in his various enterprises. He bankrolled at least two—an herbalist and a butcher. But only one man, Wing Ho, became a real partner. He ran, and eventually owned, the Long Beach branch of the F. Suie One Company. No matter how the "partners" were employed, all of them were beholden to their benefactor, sometimes throughout their lives and the lives of their children.

On the partnership lists, some names fell off, only to be replaced by a roster of new ones: from Kang Sun in 1894 to Kum To in 1919 to Louie Chong as late at 1933. Fong See was hardly alone in his efforts. The Sun Wing Wo Company on Los Angeles Street—which sold goods wholesale to the F. Suie One Company—had twenty "partners" on paper, with each one bringing in his relatives.

Inspectors were diligent and zealous, writing back and forth for additional files to support an immigrant's case. Some files, such as Fong See's or Fong Yun's, were hundreds of pages in length. How closely inspectors read those documents and acted on them is open to question. Certainly some immigrants were harassed relentlessly. But Fong See had few problems bringing in people, as evidenced by the case of Fong Lai.

The Sacramento business record lists "Fong Lie" as an original member of the Suie On Company dating from 1894. In early interrogations, Fong See stated that this person, Fong Lai, was his brother. The next set of business papers lists a Fong Lai, but indicates that he didn't acquire his partnership until 1896. Subsequent interviews present a very different picture.

On July 20, 1912, Fong See told an inspector that his brother, Fong Lai, had died eighteen years earlier, in 1894, leaving behind a widow (a foot-bound woman), a boy, and no girls. On this same date, Richard

White testified that Fong Lai was an active partner in the Los Angeles store. It wasn't until May 1917, however, that "Fong Lai" applied for lawfully domiciled Chinese merchant status so that he might return to China for a visit. He based his request on the partnership records of the F. Suie One Company.

On May 11, 1917, in an interview on Fong Lai's behalf, Fong See said that Fong Lai would have been fifty-six, but died "a long time ago in China," and was never in the United States. Realizing his error, he later interrupted the pattern of the questioning: "I want to make a correction," he said. "My brother, Fong Lai, used to be my partner in my store here in Los Angeles, and went back to China about twenty years ago." Later he added that Fong Lai was fifty-two years old. If he was fifty-two, then Fong Lai would have been a toddler when he accompanied his father, Fong Dun Shung, to work on the railroad, never mind that he would have been younger than his so-called "younger" brother, even with all the complexities of *that* date. "Fong Lai's" own testimony muddies the waters further; in it he states that he was fifty years old, born in Wah Hong village in the Sun Ning district. He also said that he returned to China not in 1897, as earlier reported, but in April 1908, for a year-long visit.

With Fong Lai, the family participated in a clever shell game. Fong Lai, the brother, certainly existed. But this new Fong Lai was really Ing Lai, more commonly referred to as Dai-Dai by the family. This Fong Lai was a friend from China who'd entered the country on the original Fong Lai's papers. The first Fong Lai went back to China in 1897, apparently returned to the United States, and went back to China again in 1908, where he died. Although the photograph of the Fong Lai of 1917 showed a very different-looking man, immigration officials paid no attention. By this time, Fong See had enough respect in the white community that the officials of the Immigration Service didn't look very hard.

"There is no doubt that this applicant is now and has been for a number of years a merchant, member of the F. Suie One Co., of this city, which has three separate stores each of which is well stocked with Chinese and Japanese curios and art goods," wrote Inspector W. A. Brazie. "The testimony of the witnesses shows that he is a bona fide merchant and he is well known to this office as a member of the firm above noted."

For a man who sometimes aged merchandise in horse manure or coaxed Pasadena matrons into paying more than they should, this scam was easy. Paper sons proved to be trickier, as both Fong See and Fong Yun learned when they tried to establish the existence of new "sons." In 1910, after a visit to Dimtao, Fong Yun, during the usual holdover at Angel Island, suddenly announced that he had two sons in China—

Fong Ming Gong (aged thirteen) and Fong Ming Lung (aged eight). Two years later, Fong See told an inpsector that his first wife, Yong, whom Ticie had met in China, had died—a truth. He went on to say that she had two children—a baby girl who died when she was a few days old, and a son, Fong Hong, who was born in 1881, the very year that Fong See maintained to authorities that he arrived in the United States. Next to the questions and answers regarding Fong See's so-called children the immigration officer marked each line with a dramatic slash. Realizing his mistake, Fong See never mentioned Hong again. And, by 1917, records show that Yun's "sons," Ming Gong and Ming Lung, had "died."

For many, these post-earthquake interviews served as a means to change life stories. Both Fong See and Fong Yun reported that their Chinese wives, as well as their mother, Shue-ying, had bound feet. If Fong See and his brother could have wives with bound feet, why not give all the partners' wives bound feet? Poor as they were, the "partners" hoped that one day the Immigration Service might make allowances and let them bring in these wives of good birth. A small transgression, surely, but one that was telling. Family history and social standing could change with just a few carefully placed words.

By 1910 the F. Suie One Company was the largest store in Chinatown, and Fong See himself was, as Richard White said, "about as near an Americanized Chinaman as can be." Fong See told officials that he took home seventy-five dollars a month, but this was part of a larger immigration game to give validity to the fact that he paid Fong Yun fifty dollars and the lesser partners only thirty-five dollars a month. All this was as it should be. Fong See was the one who was responsible for the rent—one hundred dollars a month in Pasadena and sixty-five dollars a month paid to the Gee Ning Tong in Chinatown. He was the one ultimately responsible for the partners' needs: food, lodging, clothes, wives, pastimes.

Fong See had become a man of property, owning three houses in Dimtao. In America, he traded Chinese rugs for forty-four undeveloped acres east of Los Angeles in La Habra. He also bartered merchandise in exchange for property near Signal Hill in Long Beach, named optimistically Athens on the Hill. For years this property would captivate the family with unfulfilled promises of oil riches. These deals showed just how smart Fong See was—to have outflanked and outsmarted the Caucasians yet again. Let them enact their law forbidding any Chinese ineligible for citizenship from buying land in California. He'd "traded" for his, and placed the properties in his American wife's name.

The world as Fong See knew it was slowly changing. Fong See, who scrupulously avoided the many associations in Chinatown, was always interested in the larger goings-on affecting the Chinese in the country and listened each afternoon as Fong Yun—Uncle, as he was called by the children—read from *Chung Sai Yat Po*, the Chinese Daily Paper. Mostly the paper reported news of humiliations: An immigration officer had shot a Chinese sailor for spitting at authority; a Chinese man and a Greek man had gotten into a fight when the latter decided not to pay the former for his meal; a cook, who hadn't been paid his wages, was shot and killed by his white employer. It also reported on new laws: A health ordinance required the inspection of all Chinese businesses that sold food, including restaurants and grocery stores; anyone caught without their resident papers would be jailed, then deported. The paper reported, as well, on new trends in immigration, as it did in 1908, when Mexico temporarily became a new steppingstone on the path to opportunity; Chinese crossed the border on foot and by small boat and horse cart. To reverse this flow, the Los Angeles police were accepting any tips on new faces in Chinatown. New immigrants could be assured of arrest and search. Indeed, a Los Angeles mechanic had recently turned in seven Chinese who were just passing through.

Opium arrests, tong wars, prostitution, and gambling got big play in the Chinese press. In a series of articles, a family association reached out to opium smokers: If you feel bad when you're quitting, come and get special medicine from us to help you through your pains. Gambling had come under increasing pressure by the whites. The trouble was, *Chung Sai Yat Po* reported, the Chinese liked gambling the way Americans liked movies. Could the government grant the Chinese a special right to gamble in exchange for their help in arresting those involved in the opium trade?

Fong See always listened to his brother's readings about interracial marriages with heightened interest. In 1907, Uncle read a news story in *Chung Sai Yat Po* about a certain Chiu Si Ho who eloped with a Caucasian, much to the consternation of the girl's parents. That same year, a Chinese man married a Negro woman. No one knew if it was legal, but the pastor decided to go along with it anyway. But for every "success" like these, there were men like Samuel Gompers, who declared that "the Caucasians are not going to let their standard of living be destroyed by negroes, Chinese, Japs, or any others," and that "the offspring of miscegenation between Americans and Asiatics are invariably degenerate." These assertions proved so persuasive that California, Arizona, Georgia, Idaho, Louisiana, Mississippi, Missouri, Nebraska, Nevada, South Dakota, Virginia, Utah, and Wyoming all passed laws forbidding intermarriage between Chinese and Caucasians.

In Fong See's own home, the world also continued to change. In 1909 the German midwife was called one last time, to attend the birth of Florence, named in honor of Mrs. Morgan, Ticie's only woman friend.

Florence's Chinese name was Jun Oy—true love. With five children, two stores, and forty-four acres she wished to develop, Ticie had little time for herself. She knew how lucky she was compared to the Chinese wives of laborers, who never had a midwife to see to them. Instead, her neighbors worked until the last minute, then squatted in a corner, groaned, and there would be a new baby son or daughter. After the birth, the woman got up again, cut the cord, washed the baby, and resumed working—doing piecework, rolling cigars, tying onions and scallions into bunches.

The laborers' wives had hard lives, while the wives of merchants led stultifying, sheltered ones. Merchants' wives rarely stepped outside their upstairs apartments for fear they would be kidnapped. Like Ticie, many of them had lesser cousins and nephews to do housework, cook, and shop. Some women never left the house except for a *moon yuet,* the one-month celebration of the birth of their children. Days stretched out with embroidery as their only activity.

Ticie knew all this because she reached out to some of the Chinese mothers in Los Angeles. When a neighbor gave birth to a son, Ticie was usually one of the first to arrive with the traditional Chinese "baby soup" of peanuts, pork, whiskey, and ginger. After Florence's birth, many of the women returned the kindness, promising that the soup would painlessly bring in Ticie's milk and help coagulate her blood.

With each new child, Ticie gained in status. With each year that the business prospered, she gained in power. One day she said to her husband, "You're not under the rule of the Manchus anymore. You live here." He listened and cut off his queue.

CHAPTER 6

FAMILY DAYS

1914–18

O NE day in 1914, Fong See closed his shop at 50 South Raymond Avenue in Pasadena and boarded the streetcar to take him back to Chinatown. He was a handsome man who looked far younger than his fifty-seven years. Today, as usual, he wore an elegant, tailor-made suit. The only incongruity in his appearance of cultivated refinement was the sack of fruit he carried. No one on the car knew that the day's earnings nestled among the oranges.

Business in Pasadena was more than he could have hoped for. His customers came to the resort for the winter season—December through May—with suitcases full of cash. They had a love of beauty. They embraced culture. And they had an eye for things Oriental. Fong See knew that when they returned to their eastern homes they talked about the adventures they had coming into his store. In his mind he could even hear them: "You've just got to go to the F. Suie One Company. That's the place to go, all right."

In Pasadena, he only had non-Chinese customers—most knowledgeable, a few ignorant. The brothers Charles and Henry Greene—among the founders of the California Craftsman architectural movement—understood what he had. They appreciated the simplicity of line, the quality of the wood, the restrained motif. When they came in, they liked to bend over a table or cabinet and examine the skillful tongue-and-groove joinery.

Grace Nicholson was another good customer. She had come to California in 1901 with a few hundred dollars and her skills as a stenographer. She'd quickly abandoned clerical work to open a shop on South Raymond, where she sold American Indian baskets and jewelry. After Fong See moved in next door, she'd taken an interest in Far Eastern merchandise—not just Chinese, but also Korean, Japanese, and Indian. Now, like Fong See, she also sold Asian art to collectors and museums. Fong See didn't worry about the competition—though Victor Marsh, John C. Benz, and W. W. Gerlach also sold Asian merchandise in Pasadena—because the way Fong See saw it, there were plenty of customers for all of them, with the big hotels so close by. And he was the only one to hold auctions at the Green and Maryland hotels, where he served tea and entertained the tourists with far-fetched tales of kingdoms, warlords, and pirated antiques.

Besides, he had his two other branches in Long Beach and Chinatown. He didn't concern himself too much with Long Beach. Wing Ho did a wonderful job, with only an occasional visit from Fong See, which usually ended up as a family excursion to the amusement park on the Pike. Fong See was much more involved with the Chinatown store, where Letticie saw to the day-to-day business and looked after the family upstairs. This division of labor made good business sense. Fong See, as a Chinese man, was a novelty in Pasadena. Letticie, as a white woman, offered a sense of security to Caucasians who wanted to venture down to Chinatown, which still had a reputation in Los Angeles as a dangerous place.

Fong See was the most respected businessman in Chinatown, and the only importer of any consequence. That was why, when a sojourner returned to China, he brought his most precious belongings to Fong See in hopes of getting extra cash. What cultured Chinese would have perceived as junk—usually simple household goods such as everyday porcelain or an incense burner—was intriguing to white customers. Fong See could sell these items for ten times what he'd paid.

Fong See still loved money and automobiles. He loved to look through magazines and brochures on cars. In time he would buy his elder sons—Milton and Ray—new cars, a Packard, a Hudson, a Stutz, a Willys-Knight, a Cadillac, a Lafayette—all beautiful, with long, sleek lines and rich colors. If that meant hiring a chauffeur/mechanic to keep the things going, that's what Fong See would do. From his first days in this country he had realized that only money could protect a man—not a family association or a tong. If you had money, whether it was here or in China, you had protection. And he was a man very well protected.

As far as Fong See was concerned, he had a façade that needed to be maintained, and his wife would not cooperate. She refused to do as she was told. He had said many times, "No roller-skating. I do not want to see children in skates. Waste of time!" Yet he knew from his brother, and from others who kept him informed, what his wife and children were doing in Chinatown. As he came home from Pasadena, Ticie would call out, "Pa's coming," and the younger children—Eddy, Bennie, and Florence—would take off their skates and hide them. No one said a thing as he came in, but he knew just the same.

He was irritated about the boys and furious about Florence. He'd seen to it that Florence was the most photographed Chinese girl in the entire city, and perhaps in the country. She had a unique look about her—solemn, quiet, pensive—that he was always trying to capture. At least once a year, but often every few months, he took her to different photographers—first the Elite Studios, then Hartsook, then Edwin Williams, over on Bonnie Brae. Fong See had photographs of his daughter in Chinese clothes. He had others of her dressed like a princess in organza and lace, with a big ribbon in her hair. She posed on carpets, on piano stools, and holding an armful of paper flowers. She was dainty and perfect. She was not the kind of girl who should be out roller-skating!

He tried to be stern with his wife. He *was* stern. But in some things Ticie was adamant. When the boys started introducing his Florence as "Sissee," he was angry. "She has this name for a reason. Am I now to have another child who does not go by the proper name? If you want to call her something else, then call her by her Chinese name, Jun Oy. Not this Sissee." But his wife just laughed, patted him on the arm, and said, "Now, Pa, what would we say to the boys? That's their name for her. When customers come in the store and ask who our daughter is, Milton answers, 'That's Sister See.' It's sweet, don't you see? Sister See is Sissee."

They argued constantly about how to raise their daughter. "She is an American girl, Suie. Let her be," his wife said.

"No, she is Chinese daughter. She needs to be . . . " He struggled over the Chinese words and concepts. His daughter needed to be trained to be virtuous, graceful, courteous, polite, and obedient. "No dancing. No games. Stay home. Learn to sew. Take care of house. This is good daughter."

"But, Suie, that's no fun. She's just a girl."

"Girl will grow up. She must learn the Three Obediences. When at home, obey father. When in home of husband, obey husband. When she becomes a mother, obey son."

Ticie had laughed at that. "That's downright silly."

How could he make Ticie understand? "No good husband for Jun Oy if not good daughter. She must learn."

It made no difference to Ticie how often Fong See put his foot down. She simply wouldn't obey him in matters concerning their daughter. He could trace Ticie's independent streak to his one big mistake. He should never have given in on the issue of his queue. Well, of course she was right. He would have cut it by now anyway. No one had a queue anymore, since Dr. Sun Yat-sen and his Republic. But that wasn't the point. First the antiques, then the queue, then his daughter's name, that's how it went. Now Ticie was running the Los Angeles Street store. Always she nagged him. "We need to improve. We *must* improve. No more curios. We're in the antique business." When they were in China, he had wanted to buy baskets and fans, and Ticie had said, "Well, of course you should, dear. We'll always have walk-in trade that won't be able to spend much money. They'll just want a little remembrance of their visit to Chinatown. But those are just curios, don't you see?" She'd wanted to buy architectural wood carvings, clay idols, handicrafts, and embroideries, including shoes for bound feet and children's caps. Those things he bought, but he'd also gone ahead and shipped crates of fans, baskets, and wickerware.

The profits on antiques were clearly better. "You see, Suie," Ticie said, "Americans aren't that familiar with old Chinese things, but when they see them they want them." Ticie knew the merchandise. She knew how to talk to the customers. What was it Mr. White had said? "Your wife has a nice personality, and people want to buy from her." This was no way for a proper Chinese wife to act. But Fong See just couldn't seem to win an argument with her, because her logic was too clever.

When he wanted the children to go to the Methodist Chinese-language school run by Mrs. Leong, Ticie said, "Absolutely not! We're in America. We should do as Americans. Our children are American. They must learn the ways of our country." Ticie saw no reason for her children to learn Chinese. In fact, she thought that all the children in Chinatown would be better off spending their time learning English rather than losing their few free childhood hours to the study of calligraphy and classics.

He couldn't completely fault his wife. The children were half Caucasian, after all, but he was angry nevertheless. A man should be the boss. A man is the king, and he was the king of Chinatown. He wanted to rule "with an iron hand." Marriage should be a simple thing: the wife makes requests and the husband either grants them or doesn't.

Last week his wife had said, "The children need shoes again."

He answered, "All they do is drag their toes on the ground."

"Suie, the streets aren't paved in Chinatown. Shoes are going to wear out faster than if we *lived in a house* in a neighborhood that had sidewalks."

That made him mad. He wasn't going to build a house in La Habra or Long Beach. Those properties were too far away, and they were in Letticie's name. He loved and trusted his wife, but why should he take the risk? But whenever he sent money back to Dimtao to help the villagers, or whenever he purchased another *mou* of land, she started again. "What good will land or houses in Dimtao do us? You help everyone in *your* family, but you won't help *our* family. Why is that, Suie? Why?"

He could have said, "The people in the village have no opportunity for education, so I started a school. When they have famine, I send money to buy food."

Instead he said, "I don't want grass. I don't want flowers. I don't want trees. That's crap." What he meant was that white neighborhoods could be unpredictable.

"Suie, it's not right to have all the boys and Sissee in one room. Besides, we should have a place where people can visit, not just the store. . . ."

He thought of an old saying from his village: "Waste no time quarreling with a woman." Ticie made him so crazy that his mind looped and looped in all this nonsense. Finally, he had gone back to her original question. "No shoes, final word," he said sternly.

He did triumph in other matters. He insisted that all the boys come home from school to work. He could control them that way, keep track of them, make sure they did as he said. Sissee, on the other hand, was not allowed to work, except to help her mother decorate baskets and do her embroidery. "You stay in the store," he told his daughter. "You be quiet. A girl must do needlework. Go do your embroidery! That's women's work. That's girl's work." He checked his daughter's progress daily. He knew that sometimes she cried over her needlework, but in this matter he would not yield. No man would marry a Chinese girl if she didn't master the womanly arts.

All this thinking had put him in a foul mood by the time he disembarked from the streetcar and climbed the stairs to his family's apartment above the store at 510 Los Angeles Street. When he walked in, he immediately questioned the two older boys about their day. By not sending his sons to Chinese school, he was able to send them door to door selling curtain rods, tassels, and jade rings. The ladies in Los Angeles's finer homes like to tie the rings with silk ribbon or cord and use them as handles or pulls on draperies, or on bells to call their houseboys.

"You do good selling today?" he asked, knowing what their answers would be. Milton would have come home with a pocket full of money and Ray would be empty-handed.

"No," Ray answered sullenly.

"What you do? Go for sleep? You no good boy. You good for nothing." When Ray didn't bother to answer or even look at him, Fong See spat out, "Phaa! No good."

He turned his attention to the others. Fong See noticed the rosy cheeks of his two youngest children and realized grimly that they had been out roller-skating. Knowing he wouldn't get anywhere if he mentioned that, he asked, "Where did you get those new shoes? Did your mother buy those for you?"

At that moment his wife walked into the room, briefly threw her arms around him, took his sack of oranges, and said, "Of course not, Suie. Mrs. Morgan bought all of the children new shoes. Isn't she a dear?"

He looked into the faces of Eddy and Sissee and knew that his wife was lying.

At fourteen, Ray, like most boys his age, had nothing but contempt for his parents and family. He hated Chinatown. He hated seeing poverty every day. He hated the smell. He hated his father's idea of child-rearing: "If you love your boy, apply a stick. If not, stuff him with candy." He hated the way his father rapped the kids on the knuckles with his chopsticks for not using proper table manners. Most of all, he hated how his father kept them all under his iron fist, as though he were the boss of them all, as though he knew everything there was to know in the world, when all he was was an immigrant who could barely speak English.

Ray hated his brother, Milton, who got everything—all the love, all the treasures, all the best clothes—just because he was the firstborn. A *Chinese* custom, when they were all *American*. For as long as Ray could remember, he had wanted to grow taller than Milton. One day he couldn't stand it anymore, and he burst out, "I'm going to grow to be six feet tall!" Everyone laughed at him. No Chinese ever grew that tall, they said. So far, at least part of that wish was answered. He grew taller than anyone else in the family, and was still convinced that he would eventually reach six feet because their laughing logic didn't make any sense. He wasn't Chinese, couldn't they *see* that? Now he was the one who should have been getting clothes first, then passing them on to Milton. Of course, it didn't happen that way. Milton still got his clothes first, because he was due them as first son.

Ray was only fourteen, but he had pride. He didn't like to be *some sort of object* to be paraded out as a way of getting a sale. He remembered as a tiny boy that whenever the man from the Mission Inn, out in Riverside, came to the store, his father would get all the kids dressed in Chinese getups, like a bunch of Manchu princes. After hours of negotiation, with the deal finally closed, the man from the Mission Inn would ask to take a few snapshots. Milton and Ray would have to stand outside the store with the man's daughter and have their pictures taken. She would always be placed in front because *she* was the important one. Milton and Ray were decoration. He hated that. He hated that girl, and once kicked her so hard she cried.

Sometimes he tried to think if there was anything, just one thing, that he had liked growing up. But there were only stupid memories. He could remember how they'd all walk with his mother to the streetcar and his little brother, Bennie, would be raising Cain. His mother would be soothing and comforting. Then she'd start licking her finger and wiping their faces as the streetcar came rumbling down the street. He *hated* that. He remembered how when he was really little he'd rested his head on the ceramic water buffalo with the large glass eyes when it was hot. He must have been awfully young, because he knew he'd sometimes napped there. But his father had sold it to the man at the Mission Inn, and that was that.

He hated them all. (With one exception. He loved his mother, not that he could ever say it. He was too old for that kind of stuff.) He hated the gamblers in the next basement over. He hated that his father was a partner in one of the lotteries. He hated how his father made everyone work hard every day: first uncrate, then straighten the nails. He hated the idea that his father wanted to expand to one store per son—Chinatown, Pasadena, Ocean Park, Long Beach. He hated it when his father went to China after the revolution of 1911 to scoop up belongings from the fleeing and desperate, just as he had after the Boxer Rebellion.

Ray hated the damned basket trade. He knew all the vices in Chinatown—the gambling, the opium, the women—but his father had only one vice, baskets. They were like a drug to him. How many could a person use, after all? His father bought them in groups of three, nestled together. First they had to be pulled apart. And the bugs! Ray and the other kids had to pick them out. The fine white dust of bug-shit filled the air, getting in their mouths and nostrils. The biggest baskets were sold off to laundrymen. The medium-sized ones went to merchants for storage. The little ones were, quite simply, the bane of his existence.

The kids took turns staining the small baskets with asphalt. It killed the bug eggs and gave the baskets a rich, aged brown color. (The asphalt mixture—a stew of gasoline and pitch—had been so successful that his father now had them "aging" coins and beads too.) Then his mother decided that the baskets still looked too plain. They'd begun attaching beads, tassels, and Peking glass rings. Ma—who'd learned how to do fancy knotting from the neighbor women—and the other kids would sit around the kitchen table and pull big needles through those baskets until their fingers were numb with fatigue. When Ma said, "This is a darn good business," Ray cringed.

It was all so embarrassing, he thought. But nothing was as bad as his father. He sometimes heard customers talking about his father: "Oh, he's such a character." "Oh, he's such a charmer." "Oh, Charlie, I just love the glint in that Chinaman's eye. He's so different from the rest." He saw his father as—he didn't know exactly—a barker in a sideshow? "Step right this way, ladies and gentlemen." The way he'd draw them farther and farther into the store, like they'd get to a naked lady in the last room. Most weren't that lucky. His father had a way of sizing people up. Often a customer would come in, and he'd say, as clear as a bell, in perfect English, "You can't afford this. If you want something, go down that way. Mr. Kwok has what you want." Only there wasn't a store down that way for miles, and there certainly wasn't any Mr. Kwok.

Ray wanted out of the family and out of Chinatown.

In the summer of 1916, approximately a thousand miles north of Los Angeles, in the Big Bend area of Washington State, an eleven-year-old girl, Stella Adele Copeland, looked out across sloping hills covered in golden wheat to where a huge combine harvester with its thirty-two horses and mules slowly mauled its way across the earth. She listened to the rhythmic sounds of the slicing of the wheat by the header, the ripping and trickling of the separator, and the *shush-shush* as the straw blew back out into the stubble of the field. It was another hot, dry harvest day.

Stella wiggled her toes in the warm earth, enjoying the feel of the dirt and kicking at it until little motes of dust blossomed up around her ankles. Dust was everywhere this time of year. During the wheat harvest, the horses, threshing machines, and binders tossed dust straight up into the air, creating huge brown clouds that drifted across the fields. For miles in every direction along the roads, dust billowed behind the endless stream of wheat haulers.

For years, Stella—an only child—and her parents had followed Charlie Slusser's machines from farm to farm. First he'd only had a McCormick header, but then he'd gotten the combine harvester. No one else in the county could afford to buy one of his own, so, when fields turned golden with ripe wheat, Slusser's machines were called to service. Itinerant workers—mostly men, but some women—followed in the combine's wake to do the manual labor. But Stella's mama, Jessie, was a good cook, and everyone knew that farmhands stayed where the food was decent. So for the last couple of summers Stella and her parents had stayed at this place.

Stella glanced over to the cook wagon where her mother prepared the afternoon meal. Mama looked so beautiful, with her copper-colored hair, that Stella always felt like an abandoned cat next to her. Stella had red hair too—but it was fiery red, cropped short, and always straggly after these days out in the sun and wind. And, while Mama had skin as smooth as satin, freckles sprinkled Stella's face and arms.

Soon she and Mama would pack up the sandwiches and walk out to the big machine to deliver lunch. Stella never liked to get too close to the combine. Some kids, who also accompanied their parents to the local farms during harvest time, liked to drop mice or kittens down into the separator. But Stella had heard the story about the boy who kept bothering the header tender until the man dangled the boy over the separator. The boy had somehow slipped from his grasp and gone clean through. The men on that farm had been so angry that they didn't wait for the law. They hanged that header tender right from his machine.

Still, Stella loved being out on this farm. Town worries drifted away, and the earth, the sun, and the seas of wheat soothed her feelings of hurt, abandonment, and shame. Out here, life was pretty simple. She went barefoot the whole time, and didn't have to worry about wearing out her shoes so badly that Grandma Copeland would have to take them to the shoemaker for steel toe guards. She hated how the town children made fun of her for those, hated how poor they all knew she was.

Everyone in town—well, at least every kid in Waterville—knew Stella was a toughie. Try anything with her, and you could get in a real bad fight. Stella didn't like it when people said snotty things to her, when they tried to act better than she was. She knew how the kids gossiped about her, but their parents were even worse. She remembered the day the butcher's wife had grabbed her daughter's arm and said, "Oh, don't play with her. She's the washerwoman's granddaughter." As if being a butcher was so great? Stella couldn't do anything about the parents, but she could beat the bejesus out of the kids. Anyway, she had red hair, and a quick temper was her birthright.

Stella didn't care what the townspeople said; she was proud of her family. On her father's side, the Copelands had come out to Waterville—which wasn't too far from Wenatchee—from Ohio. Stella's grandfather had deserted the family as soon as they reached Washington, and Grandma Copeland had been left alone to take care of her family of seven. She'd bought a little house on the outskirts of town—with its own well, a woodshed, barn, chicken coop, and horse and buggy shed—and then had become the town's washerwoman and midwife. Her boys took turns pulling water up from the well, which she heated on the stove or over an open fire in the yard—depending on the season. Using Fels Naphtha soap and a washboard, she scrubbed the garments and linens of Waterville's more prosperous residents until her knuckles were red, cracked, and gnarled. With her sadirons—eight- and nine-pounders from the Sears, Roebuck catalog—Grandma pressed out wrinkles and made perfect pleats. Stella loved Grandma Copeland.

Harvey, Grandma Copeland's son and Stella's father, was "a handsome son of a gun." Papa had started a dray business with his brothers, but he said, "Hauling a cord of wood ten miles for a dollar seventy-five doesn't interest me much." He dreamed of better things. "I've got to keep my eyes open for the main chance," he often said. Stella knew Papa wanted to have adventures, but he was stuck—married and with a kid.

Stella's mother, Jessie, was a Huggins. The family had originally lived in Vermont, tried homesteading in South Dakota, then come out to Waterville. Grandpa Huggins had died just as the train crossed the state border, so Grandma Huggins, like Grandma Copeland, had raised her kids alone. Stella wasn't close to Grandma Huggins. For one thing, the old woman was pretty well-to-do and didn't think Stella's dad was good enough for Mama. For another, Grandma Huggins had moved to Los Angeles, and none of them saw her that much.

Stella didn't know why Grandma Huggins had gone down south, because Waterville was really a wonderful place, even if the townsfolk weren't that nice. Surrounded by fields of undulating wheat, Waterville—with its population of one thousand—boasted public schools, a bank, seven churches, a feed mill (with rollers for making both graham and whole wheat flour), four saloons, an electrical plant, a "cozy little jail," two five-hose fire carts, a dentist, and two physicians. It also had general merchandise emporiums, wallpaper stores, a furniture manufacturer, a watchmaker, two blacksmiths, and a musical instrument maker. Citizens encountered no hot winds and no cyclones, and though they had to face a four-month winter, they knew that temperatures seldom fell below zero. (During one cold snap, however, Rogers & Howe sold twenty-five fur coats—in cowhide, dog, bear, and calf skin— in just two weeks.) A few Indians inhabited the area, but they were of the peaceful, drunken variety, only occasionally swarming through town to gamble over their stick games or trade a cayuse.

Out on this farm, Stella was with Mama and Papa only, instead of being left with one relative or other. Her parents always seemed to be putting her on a train to stay with Aunt Eva in Everett, Grandma Copeland in Waterville, or Grandmother Huggins down in Los Angeles. Not that Stella minded making those trips alone. She was pretty big now, so she could go anywhere by herself. When she traveled home and the train conductor asked her where she was headed, Stella invariably chanted in a loud, clear voice, "Waterville, Washington, Douglas County." The conductor always smiled and made sure she made the right transfers.

Stella wasn't afraid of much. Well, once, when they'd gone on the ferry to Vancouver, British Columbia, and Mama and Papa hadn't wanted to spend the money for a full fare, she'd been pretty scared when the captain asked how old she was and she forgot to lie. She'd thought for sure he'd throw her overboard, but he didn't. She remembered that trip vividly because it was the first time she'd eaten bananas and cream, and she'd thrown them up. Even though she'd been as sick as a dog, she'd always thought those bananas had tasted pretty neat. They'd had a nice time in Vancouver. A lot better than when they'd stayed in the central valley, where it had been as hot as the dickens and Mama had hung wet blankets in the cook tent to cool it off.

When Stella was eleven, her first menstrual period came, and Mama showed her how to fold the rags and pin them to her underwear. Later, Mama told her to soak them in a pan under the clawfoot tub in the bathroom: "Now you wash them out and don't you dare leave them there too long." Yes, Stella was a woman now, and of strong constitution. When she was four, and Papa had had a job in the mountains—she couldn't remember where exactly, because she was too young back then—she'd had rheumatic fever, or maybe measles. Maybe both at the same time. That seemed like something that could have happened, because she almost died. They'd lived in a one-room cabin, and she remembered Mama taping newspapers to the window to keep out the light, then taking more newspaper, lighting it, and waving it around the room to kill the germs. Mama had concocted a homemade remedy, a mixture of onions and sugar, cooked down to a thick marmalade, for Stella to eat.

To pass the time, Stella had cut out paper dolls from the Sears, Roebuck catalog. Every morning when Mama went to work, she'd say, "No matter what happens today, I want you to clean up. If you take sick, I don't want to have to send for the doctor and have him see your mess." Stella thought that was a good lesson, because you never knew when something bad might happen and people would see how you lived.

Last year, when she was staying with Aunt Eva in Everett, Stella had come down with smallpox. She'd had sores in her ears, nose, and mouth, but she'd been pretty lucky because she didn't have any bad scars, as did some of the kids she'd seen. Then, while staying with Grandma Copeland, Stella had had whooping cough. They'd thought she was a goner that time for sure, but Grandma had dosed her every couple of hours with a teaspoon of sugar and a few drops of turpentine to clear the air passages.

She didn't get sick once in Los Angeles. She'd visited there last year, when she was ten. It seemed that the healthy climate was the reason Grandma Huggins had moved there in the first place; she had a brother who was a doctor, and he'd come west from Kansas to Los Angeles, where he'd bought land in the Wolfskill Orchard tract—land that had once held orange groves but was now being converted to housing. One day Grandma had told Stella, "My brother says that the real gold in California isn't nuggets and it isn't oranges, either. The real gold is the sunshine. People will get well if they go there. He says there's money to be made from consumptives." Soon after that, Grandma Huggins and her sons—Stella's uncles—had packed up and moved down south. With money they'd saved, they had opened the Huggins Hotel, right across from the Santa Monica Pier. Stella knew all about it because she'd seen it with her own eyes—the roller coaster, the caressing ocean, the beckoning breezes. Still, she was happy to get home. She missed Mama and Papa.

The best thing about harvest time was that Stella wasn't sent off somewhere. Summers were for being with Mama and Papa—whether they were traveling and looking for jobs, or staying at a farm like this one for something more permanent. During the day, Stella's dad helped out in the fields, hefting the 140-pound sacks of wheat onto the flatbed wagons. Papa didn't make much money, maybe forty dollars a month for the farm work, plus whatever he made from barbering. "It's a lot better than some farmers make," he liked to say. "I don't want to spend my life fighting ground squirrels for my livelihood." Since Mama worked the cook wagon, they also got her salary.

The cook wagon was a boxlike house on wheels, with benches and tables along either side and steps at the back, with a door. It was hotter than hell inside. Even Mama's wet blankets didn't help. The burners and ovens blazed continually. Mama made griddle cakes, biscuits, and thick slabs of bacon for breakfast. During the rest of the morning, she kneaded dough for bread, beat batter for cakes, sliced fruit for pies, while keeping an eye on the stew over the fire. Every day there were twenty or thirty men for breakfast, lunch, dinner, and midday meals in the forenoon and afternoon. The men were always hungry. Mama earned three dollars a day; sometimes, if she was lucky, a girl would be hired to come out from town and do the dishes for three dollars a week.

Stella liked it on the farm, where she had no grandmothers, no aunts, no uncles, no town kids, no bossing, no teasing. Here, Mama and Papa worked during the day. At night, Mama read to Papa from *The Adventures of Livingstone*. He couldn't read it himself, but he loved the story and Mama had read it to him many times. So it was nice—just the three of them these few weeks out of the year. And—best of all—there weren't any saloons.

That was it—the one bad thing. The Saturday-night dances. Every farmer had them—it was kind of like hiring a good cook. This is how they worked: They'd all take baths. Mama would wash Stella's hair. Then Mama brushed out her own long, copper-colored hair until it shone. After that, she rolled it into a loose bun at the top of her head, making sure to leave plenty of strands hanging down, which she wrapped around her fingers until they curled just so. The three of them would then put on their Sunday best for Saturday and walk over to the barn, with Papa mumbling promises to Mama.

Inside, a fiddler played. There'd be punch for the ladies and children. The men would also take cups of the pink liquid and step outside for a few minutes. Stella knew what that meant. It mean that in an hour or so—after Papa had thrown back more than a few cups of this special brew—he would come back in and be as drunk as a skunk. She'd be able to tell by the way he looked at Mama.

Because this was what always happened. Mama would get bored and lonely when Papa was out behind the barn with the men. Some handsome buck would ask her to dance. Why not? Mama was the prettiest one there. No farmer's daughter or field hand's wife was as pretty as she was. No one else had the beautiful hair, the smooth, pale skin, the small waist. Some man would dance Mama around and around. They'd get awful close, too close, even Stella could see that. Just about the time Stella would be wondering if Mama could feel that man's thing, the way they were dancing, Papa would step out on the dance floor, grab Mama's arm, shove her to the ground, then haul off and belt that bounder in the jaw. Her dad was the most jealous man Stella had ever seen, but Mama was partly at fault. Any fool could see she shouldn't be dancing like that if she was a married woman—even if she *wasn't* a married woman! One thing Stella knew for sure. She was never going to dance with a man, ever, as long as she lived. You could get in trouble that way.

Eddy was Sissee's protector. Eddy, who was almost three years older than Sissee, laughed when Ma called to warn them of Pa's approach. He laughed when he helped Sissee take off her skates and hide them before Pa rounded the corner. Eddy teased her and cajoled her and kept her company during the long hours that she sat doing her cross-stitch. At night he talked to her, whispering while she listened. Mostly their conversation revolved around how unjust their father was, and how Eddy was going to break the rules. Sometimes Pa would come in and start to yell. "What are you talking about? Are you talking about me? Be quiet! No talking!" Eddy would listen to Pa's footsteps as he walked away, then whisper, "He's jealous of us, Sissee. He doesn't want us to have fun. He doesn't want us to be happy. He doesn't understand us, but we can be our own way." Eddy gave her courage. He was her ally.

Jennie Chan was Sissee's best friend. Jennie lived down on Alameda Street. The Chan and See apartments were connected by a concrete bridge that went from rooftop to rooftop. Jennie and Sissee met out there every day. Often they just sat and talked and looked down into the courtyard below, where several restaurants kept their live chickens in crates. No, it wasn't a bridge—more like a rooftop courtyard or something. Sissee didn't know and didn't care. What she cared about was that she finally had a friend.

Her father sometimes complained that Jennie's father was just a vegetable peddler, that he kept his horses down at the stable, and stuff like that. But then he would turn around and ask Mr. Chan about his business. Sissee couldn't figure Pa out, but Eddy always had an explanation. "If Pa's so smart," he might ask, "why doesn't he know that Ma bought our shoes, not Mrs. Morgan? If he's so rich and important, why doesn't he want us to have good shoes? Ma has money and does what she wants. She can listen to him, but she doesn't have to do what he says." Sissee thought her brother was the smartest one in the whole family.

Most parents in Chinatown wouldn't spend money on luxuries for themselves, but they always tried to give something to their children. Like most girls in Chinatown, Jennie and Sissee had porcelain dolls and jacks. Their brothers had marbles and cast-iron trains and fire engines pulled by iron horses. But unlike the other neighborhood children, Sissee could splurge on special treats. Once Sissee had bought two tennis rackets, and she and Jennie had gone over to the USC campus to play. The balls had gone all over the place, and they'd never played again.

Sometimes the girls did errands for their mothers. Sissee's mother often sent them down to buy a whole meal from the Sam Yuen or See Yuen Restaurant. The girls especially loved See Yuen, which served American food—brisket of beef, pie, and the best bread any of them had ever tasted. They would stand behind the counter and giggle as the old man swatted at the flies that tried to land on the meat. Since Jennie's family didn't have much money, the girls also frequented the little market between the two restaurants, which sold buns stuffed with meat or soybeans.

Once Pa had traded some merchandise for a pair of Shetland ponies, and for a while the girls had gone down to the stables every day. Men hitched up the ponies to a little wicker cart and led the girls around the corral. Some of those men, Sissee thought, would do anything for her father. But those ponies went the way of the tennis rackets. They were a nice idea, but they were the meanest darn things. They were dirty too, and someone had to brush them and take care of them. Pa had finally traded them away. "For glue, I hope," Jennie had said, and the two girls had laughed some more.

Jennie knew about fun, and wasn't afraid of anything; Sissee was afraid of almost everything, but she had money. Between them they always had a good time. First they would walk into her father's store, weaving through the clutter, taking care not to bump anything. Then Pa would give Sissee money. Jennie said it was because Sissee was his little pet. Then they'd walk over to Jennie's apartment. The whole way— as they walked back upstairs, through the apartment heavy with the smells of roasting meat and potatoes, across the bridge, and into the other apartment, where Mrs. Chan peeled garlic and ginger for the Chans' evening meal—Jennie made Sissee repeat Chinese phrases over and over again.

"May we go to the movies?" Sissee would ask Mrs. Chan in awkward Chinese. "My father gave us the money."

Sissee knew that Mrs. Chan couldn't say no, so off she and Jennie went every Saturday afternoon. First they'd see the movie, then they'd walk over to See's Candies and buy a one-pound box. (They always chuckled over that name.) After they'd eaten it all, Jennie would muse, "It's a wonder we have teeth." That made Sissee giggle because it was such a grown-up thing to say.

Most of their adventures happened on Saturday, because during the week Jennie went to the elementary school for Chinese kids, while Sissee went to California Street School with Eddy, where they were the only Chinese. Ma said she wanted the children in American schools, so that's where Sissee and her brothers went. Bennie was going to Custer Avenue Intermediate School. Ray and Milton—who were in the same grade—attended Lincoln High School. Like their older brothers, Sissee and Eddy had learned to keep to themselves. It wasn't that the other kids were mean, exactly—well, there was *some* of that, but mostly she and her brother were just ignored. Every day after school, Sissee and Eddy came straight home. They were never invited to play with the other kids—either from school or in Chinatown. And Jennie couldn't play then because she had to go to Mrs. Leong's Chinese-language class at the mission.

Before summer, the two girls had joined the Girl Reserves at Jennie's urging. "We're pals," she'd said. "It'll be fun." But it hadn't been fun. Sissee knew she was pleasant and could get along, but she was too shy to pick up with those girls. When vacation came, Jennie had begged Sissee to go to camp. "Mother won't hold me back," Jennie stated boldly. "I do what I want." Sissee had been swept up in her enthusiasm. If her friend could do it, so could she. But when they'd gotten to the camp, Sissee had been so homesick that her brothers had to come and get her.

Nevertheless, Jennie encouraged Sissee. "We're not shy when we're together, huh?"

But Sissee always felt shy, even when she was with Jennie.

Sissee's other brothers made fun of the threesome—Sissee, Eddy, and Jennie. Some days when Bennie walked in from school, he'd say, "I saw that highbinder friend of yours." Sissee never got mad. It wasn't proper for her to show anger at an older brother, even if he did call her best friend a tong thug. But Eddy would hoot and holler: "Highbinder? Did you say 'highbinder'? That's an insult, Ben. Why do you talk like that?" But Bennie didn't care what he said. Everyone in the family accepted it. Bennie dressed however he liked, ate what he liked, talked how he wanted to—and if they didn't like it, too bad.

Today Jennie and Sissee met out on the bridge between their two buildings. Eddy joined them, and soon they were involved in a game of post office. Eddy went back inside to the bathroom, stood up on the toilet, and peered at the girls through the bars of the window. "Come on, you two," he said in mock impatience. "I don't have all day."

Jennie and Sissee took turns being customers. "I'd like to purchase two stamps," Jennie said, slipping a few scraps of pretend paper money through the window. Eddy frowned, said, "Yes, ma'am," and passed back the stamps that Ma had given them to use for their game.

Sissee stepped forward. "This package needs to go to Macao. How much will that cost?"

Eddy balanced the invisible package in his hands. "Well, let me see," he said. "Do you have anything to declare in here? Do I need to collect for customs?"

"Oh, I don't know," Sissee replied. "It's a gift." She smiled as she had seen her father do with customs inspectors.

Later they clambered back through the See apartment, yelling that they were going for a walk and promising to be home for dinner. Even without watches, the kids knew exactly when that would be. Around dinnertime, the vegetable peddlers with their lumbering horse-drawn carts would come rolling back into Chinatown. As soon as the teams hit Alameda, the drivers would loosen the reins and the horses would gallop pell-mell to the stable.

The kids knew every inch of Chinatown. For the past few years people had been talking about how Chinatown was going to be torn down to make way for a big train terminal. With that possibility, conditions had declined. Landlords refused to do repairs, and tenants were too scared to ask. Any mention of Chinatown to white society only brought a sigh, a shrug of the shoulders, and a breezy, "Yes, conditions are bad, but they are Chinese!" So broken windows were boarded up, keeping out rain and cold winds in winter, flies and dust in summer, and light and fresh air all year. If a sink or a toilet became disconnected, then whatever went down the drain ran out on kitchen floors or under houses. In many buildings, standing water and rubbish filled cellars. The kids saw all of this and could smell it, too. They knew which places to avoid. They knew which restaurant owners threw dead chickens and leftover food into their cellars and smelled up half of Marchessault Street.

The kids were always running into gruesome things, like the time they'd seen that man run over by the streetcar. He was already dead, but that car had rolled back over him and forward again too. Eddy said the driver must have panicked. The three of them stared at that body. They saw funny things, too—like the time Uncle Yun bought a horse and buggy and it ran away with him. The kids decided Uncle was too kind to beat a horse into obedience. By the next week he'd sold the horse and had begun walking to work again.

Today, when the kids went east across Alameda and down into the oldest part of Chinatown, they noticed a group of people standing at the entrance to one of the alleys. Sissee followed as Jennie and Eddy sidled into the crowd. It was another dead body—a casualty of a tong war. Again, they stared and stared, knowing that neither set of parents would let them out again if rumors were circulating about rivalries heating up.

"I guess that does it for us," Eddy said. "All we'll be doing is playing post office for a while."

"Eye for an eye," said Jennie.

"Two-for-one revenge," Sissee added.

"No matter who you are, the tongs will get you if you cross them," Eddy concluded.

Fong Yun, "Uncle," was, like Fong See, born poor. But unlike his older brother, he was destined to die poor. Between 1904 and 1918, Uncle, a kind, warm-hearted man, worked as a virtual slave for his illiterate but wealthy brother. Earning a paltry fifty dollars a month, Fong Yun wrote letters in Chinese, read documents, perused packing slips, kept the Chinese books, researched the antiques his brother brought over, and went to China himself every couple of years to buy merchandise for the store.

Fong Yun was a family man in his heart, but it was hard for him to be a family man when his wife and children were thousands of miles away. So he always saved his money, scrimping until he had enough to go home to see his growing family. In the last nine years he had made four trips to China—in 1909, 1913, 1915, and 1917—each of them lasting more than a year. Uncle would rather see his money disappear in time spent with his wife and sons than buy another carving or altar table.

Uncle was the first person in the family to stay on Angel Island. Returning in 1910 from a buying trip to China, Fong Yun had been detained at Angel Island for a week with hookworm. He would always remember the wave of panic he felt before the board of special inquiry upon hearing their final pronouncement: "Inasmuch as the medical examiner of aliens at this port has certified that this alien is afflicted with uncinariasis, a dangerous contagious disease, it is the unanimous opinion of the board that he be excluded and ordered deported. From this decision there is no appeal, and he is so informed, and he is further notified that if deported his return trip shall be at the expense of the steamship company that brought him here. However, if hospital treatment is applied and granted in this case, and a cure effected, he will be admissible under the immigration law. Whom do you wish to notify?"

"My brother," Fong Yun had answered, and within two weeks—with his brother footing the medical bill of seven dollars and fifty cents—Uncle was on his way south to Los Angeles. But he would never forget the fear of that day, or the fact that he owed yet another debt of obligation to his brother.

While Fong Yun stayed loyal to his family in China, his time spent with them only elicited excess household worry. Uncle's wife, Leung-shee, from Low Tin village, was a foot-bound woman, high class, but very weak from a coughing disease no one could cure. When she deteriorated, Fong Yun found a no-name girl of the Leong clan from the neighboring village of Shuck Kew Tow to help out. Hired as a servant, the Leong girl understood that she would also be a concubine, for although Uncle was a poor man in Los Angeles, he was a prosperous man in Dimtao.

Was it his fault that when he went back to Dimtao in 1913 and found Leung-shee too weak to perform her wifely duties, he turned to the servant girl with the wide feet of a peasant? Was it his fault that the servant girl gave him a son first? Was it his fault that Leung-shee only accepted him *after* the servant girl was pregnant, so that the child who should have been the first son turned out to be the second son? No matter. Leung-shee died and the servant girl became the Number One wife, acquired the proper married name of Leong-shee, hired a wet nurse to care for her stepson, Ming Ho, and bought a new no-name girl from a poor family to take over the chores. Relieved of her workload, the new Leong-shee devoted herself to her son, Ming Kuen.

On Thanksgiving Day in 1918, Ticie busied herself in the kitchen. She had shooed out Dai-Dai, the fake Fong Lai, who ordinarily served as family cook. Her husband and children were two floors down in the basement warehouse "staying out of Ma's way" as she prepared the meal. Enjoying the quiet and solitude, Ticie peeled sweet potatoes, scraping away the rust-colored skin to reveal the bright orange flesh. As she worked, she ran down a mental list of what still needed to be done. The turkey was stuffed and roasting in the oven. The cranberry sauce was cooling on top of the stove. She still had to make soda biscuits, mashed potatoes, and gravy—all last-minute tasks. She wanted the meal and the day to be as traditional as possible.

Ticie understood that the more her Chinese neighbors knew about Thanksgiving, the more they thought all this work for one meal was unnecessary. No Chinese liked turkey; to them it was almost indigestible. Despite this, local missionaries pressed would-be converts into celebrating Thanksgiving—as well as Christmas and Easter. These were American holidays. If the Chinese were going to accept God and Jesus into their lives, they should also try to become American—in their dress, eating habits, and holiday traditions.

Ticie considered this kind of thinking ridiculous. If you were Chinese, you should be able to meld Chinese and American traditions in whatever form you wanted. As an American who lived in Chinatown, she would celebrate this day with her family in her own way. In a nod to her Chinese husband and his workers, she added special ingredients—water chestnuts to the stuffing and fresh ginger to the pumpkin pies—to make the food slightly more familiar. She had chosen these sweet potatoes, though they were thoroughly American, because they were a common food in the Chinese countryside.

During American holidays, Ticie often yearned for the company of other Caucasian women. Even though her family had disowned her— perhaps *because* they had disowned her—she often thought back on the holiday traditions her family had observed on the farm. In her memory, Christmas was a time filled with the scent of baking gingerbread. She remembered her brothers coming in with a fresh-cut tree, and her sisters-in-law putting aside their petty quarrels to work companionably in the kitchen, making dinner and wrapping modest gifts. On Easter morning they had all met at church and, in the late afternoon, sat down together for baked ham. She recalled the chill in the air on Thanksgiving Day, the promise of snow to come, and, again, the gathering of the family.

In twenty-one years of marriage, Ticie had tried to make all holidays— both American and Chinese—joyous. When Chinese New Year approached, Ticie made sure that the children sent the kitchen god to heaven in a burst of firecrackers. Suie pasted up door gods outside the apartment and the various stores to keep evil spirits from entering during the festivities. Uncle, the only one among them who could read Chinese, decorated the walls with red paper scrolls filled with good thoughts: "May everything be according to your wishes." "Wealth, high rank, and good salary." "May we receive the hundred blessings of Heaven."

Suie took charge of planting narcissus bulbs in low-sided celadon dishes, knowing that if they bloomed in time for New Year's the family would be rich in the coming year. He adorned the family altar with oranges to bring future wealth and good luck, tangerines to symbolize good fortune, and apples for peace. During Chinese New Year, Ticie stepped aside and let Dai-Dai take full charge in the kitchen. He cooked dishes that would bring the family good luck, paying special attention to good-luck-word foods. *San choy,* lettuce, sounded like the Chinese word for prosperity; *ho yau,* oyster sauce, sounded like "good moments." The words for sticky rice cakes mimed the tones for "getting higher." The bachelors who came by to pay their respects sampled Ticie's rice cakes with gusto, for they implied possible promotion. They nibbled at her tray of togetherness, each octagonal dish filled with a different treat: candy, so that everyone might say good words, candied lotus seed to have sons, candied melon for growth and good health, coconut for companionship, and watermelon seeds to "have plenty," a salute to male sexual prowess.

As a family, the Sees participated in the ritual events of the neighborhood. At night the younger children—Bennie, Eddy, and Sissee— helped their father hide money inside cabbage and lettuce. The next day, lion dancers pranced and writhed down the street from storefront to storefront, snapping at the lettuce that hung before each business. The dancers knew ahead of time that the lettuce in front of the F. Suie One Company would be generous. Another year's good fortune assured, both for the See enterprises and for the charitable organizations of Chinatown.

This year, as the heat of September and October finally ebbed and the younger children began coming home with construction-paper pumpkins, drawings of cornucopias, and stories of the Thanksgiving fathers, Ticie knew that she and her family had a lot to be thankful for. They'd made fifty thousand dollars in sales last year, and would top that this year. The stock was holding steady—$15,000 in Chinatown, $25,000 in Pasadena, and $15,000 at a new store on Ninth Street. It was a measure of her husband's trust in his one real partner, Wing Ho, that he didn't worry about the Long Beach store.

In fact, Suie had been away for most of the year and had left her in charge of both the business and the family. He'd been traveling around the country, exhibiting and selling goods, then coming home for a few days or weeks, then going back out on the road again. When the influenza epidemic broke out, Suie was home just long enough to hire Mary Louie, the eighteen-year-old daughter of a produce man. She'd just started college when the epidemic started. When the school closed—as did all the schools in the city—she needed a job.

Alone except for the workers—the old "partners" and Mary—Ticie confronted her fears and appeared brave before the children during the epidemic. It seemed she didn't know a family that hadn't lost a son or daughter to the illness that swept through the community. Her daughter's friend Jennie had almost died. At night, Ticie had stayed awake listening to the ambulances as they screamed through Chinatown, taking the dead and sick to the hospital.

Ticie turned to her neighbors to ask what she could do to protect her children. "Western medicine won't help the fever," a neighbor woman told her. "Chinese won't get better if they take it. You should try herbs." Remembering how she'd been healed of her smallpox by her father-in-law, she took the children to an herbalist. During the rest of the epidemic, they'd all worn bags of herbs around their necks. Fortunately, none of them had gotten sick. And finally, Suie had come home.

As Ticie began slicing the sweet potatoes into wedges, she reflected that her children were doing well considering that their place in Los Angeles society was awkward. Last year, in 1917, Ming and Ray had graduated from Lincoln High School as the only Chinese in the class. Ming and Ray were handsome young men. Both were quiet, cautious, and sometimes unsure of their places. Like their younger siblings, they'd

Left: Workers on the railroad. (*Asian American Studies Library, University of California at Berkeley*)

Right: Work on the railroad continued, even in snow drifts. (*Asian American Studies Library, University of California at Berkeley*)

Bottom left: Chinese laborer in a garment factory.
(*Asian American Studies Library, University of California at Berkeley*)
Bottom right: Anti-Chinese cartoons such as this one were prevalent during the years leading up to the Exclusion Act of 1882.
(*Asian American Studies Library, University of California at Berkeley*)

Above: Marchessault Street in Los Angeles, 1896.
(*Los Angeles County Museum of Natural History*)
Right: Fong See as a young man, c. 1880s.

Ming, Fong See, Ray, Ticie, in China, 1901.

Left: Immigration photo of Fong Yun, 1903.
(*National Archives, Pacific Sierra Region*)
Right: This 1908 immigration photo of Fong Yun
shows how much he changed in five years.
(*National Archives, Pacific Sierra Region*)

Merchandise set up for an auction, sometime between 1910 and 1915.

Ming and Ray in the F. Suie One Company, c. 1904.

Early photo of an F. Suie One Company location,
possibly Long Beach.

Fong See outside the longtime location of the F. Suie One Company
at 510 Los Angeles Street, c. 1906.

Left: Fong See
decorates
a car show,
date unknown.

Right: Ray and
Ming pose with
the daughter of a
customer outside
the store, c. 1905.

Family portrait, 1914.
Top row: Ray and Ming.
Bottom row: Eddy, Fong See, Sissee, Ticie, and Bennie.

Above left: Sissee, 1914.
Above right: Stella Copeland, as a "city girl," 1912.

Right: Stella
and her mother,
Jessie, by a
cook wagon, c. 1913.

Right: Photo of four generations, 1905: Stella Copeland as a baby, with her mother, Jessie Huggins Copeland; her grandmother Flora Elizabeth Lewis Huggins; and her great-grandfather Chauncy August Lewis.

Left: Mrs. Leong's Chinese language class at the Methodist Mission in Los Angeles. Jennie Chan (Sissee's friend) is the girl standing just to Mrs. Leong's left. June 1919. (*El Pueblo de Los Angeles Historical Monument*)

Right: The Leong family in China, 1919. *Middle row*: Mrs. Leong, her sister, her father, her mother, and Leong Jeung. *Front row*: Elmer, Gilbert, and Margie. Ed Leong is on the left in the back row.

Left: Eddy, 1919.
(*National Archives,*
Pacific Sierra Region)

Right: Bennie, 1919.
(*National Archives,*
Pacific Sierra Region)

Left: Fong See, 1919.
(*National Archives,*
Sierra Region)

often been excluded. How many parties had Ray and Milton missed? How many dances? How many girls had said no, they couldn't possibly go out with them? Ming and Ray each had their own cars, the best money could buy, but only each other to drive with. Ticie worried about her elder sons' isolation, but she knew there was nothing she could do about it.

The Sees certainly had the money to send Ming and Ray to college, but none of them had considered this option. Ticie had finished high school. Her husband hadn't even gone to school. But they had found success as businesspeople. In turn, they expected Ming and Ray—and the younger children when their time came—to work in the store. In addition, few Chinese sons attended colleges or universities. Those that did usually came from China as already accomplished students, or from American Chinese families where the rarefied tradition of Chinese scholarship was valued.

As Ticie finished putting the sweet potatoes in a baking dish and topping them with maple syrup and dollops of butter, Sissee come into the kitchen. "Ma, Ma, come quick. Pa's about to open the surprise."

"Okay," Ticie said. "Let me do a couple of things and I'll come down with you."

Ticie basted the turkey, checked its temperature, and edged the pan over to make room for the sweet potatoes. She washed her hands and wiped them on her apron.

"Pa made us unpack everything else first," Sissee said as she pulled her mother toward the back stairs. "Eddy and I have been pounding the nails to make them straight. What do you think is in the crate, Ma? What?"

As Ticie walked down the stairs to street level, where the store was, and down another flight to the basement, she thought about how her husband liked to pick up odds and ends wherever he traveled. What better place to pick up these oddities than at exhibitions, shows, and world's fairs? "It's your love of curiosities," she said once after he brought home a mermaid—some sort of petrified fish—from one of the side-shows at a fair he'd been to. The owner couldn't give it away, but Suie had said, "I'll take it." Ticie thought it was the ugliest thing she'd ever seen, but it might be a draw if they ever opened a branch of the F. Suie One Company on the Boardwalk in Ocean Park.

Down in the basement, Sissee pulled her mother through the narrow aisles to where the boys rested, balancing on top of several unopened crates. Rice straw and excelsior lay about in fluffy piles. The wooden slates of the other packing crates had already been stacked in the corner. As Sissee had mentioned, the nails had been removed. Both wood and nails would be kept for some future use.

"Pa, we're here," Sissee said. "Can we see it now?"

Suie nodded at the two older boys, who pried open the remaining boxes. The excelsior fell away to reveal several bronze objects.

"But what is it?" Ticie asked.

"You'll see," Suie said. Bennie stepped forward, and with Eddy's help they put the object together, stacking tier upon tier to a height of six feet. Once it was assembled, they saw a *hu,* a ritualistic vase, used to decorate the entrance to a temple. On its surface was a dragon rendered in bronze, with brass alloy highlighting the scales. The rest was a mishmash of Chinese and Japanese motifs. The waves drew directly from the Japanese, while the clouds and the dragon's feet were obviously Chinese. There wasn't a person on earth besides Suie who would have brought the vase home. To Ticie's eyes, the *hu* was not a "pure" piece of art. It was just another curiosity.

"I was next to a booth where they had things from Japan," Suie said. "From the first day I see this bronze, I say to myself, 'I want it.' "

"Who do you think is going to buy it?" Ticie asked slowly.

"I don't care about that!" he responded. "We keep it. No one else has anything like this."

"Oh, Ma," Ray groaned. Immediately recognizing his tone, Ticie braced herself for the complaint. "I don't understand how Pa can spend money on this kind of extravagance, then make the rest of us pound nails. Why, Ma?"

"You be quiet!" Suie snapped. "You straighten nails or no dinner for you."

"Come on," Ticie said placatingly. "Let's not quarrel. Today's Thanksgiving."

Ray glared at his father, then picked up the nail straightener and got to work. Why did Ray have to act this way, Ticie wondered. They gave him everything he could possibly want, and he still wasn't satisfied. Ticie glanced at her husband and said, "I like the piece, Suie, and I'm sure we'll be able to use it for something. Now, why don't we go back upstairs and leave the children to finish up."

On the stairwell, Suie spoke for the first time since his momentary outburst. "I am a far-ahead thinker," he said. "That's why I go to shows and fairs."

"I know, dear. I know."

Downstairs, Ming gazed at the *hu* pensively and murmured quietly to his brothers and sister, "Another of Dad's follies." What none of them knew at that moment was that the vase would never be sold and would always be called Dad's Folly, a name that would make all of them laugh ruefully until every single one of them was dead.

Several hours later, the flaring tempers in the basement were forgotten as the family gathered around the dining table. Ticie saw the boys focus their attention on the platters of food—all the dishes that she'd eaten for every Thanksgiving since her birth. Eddy and Bennie fairly wiggled in anticipation. Although Sissee sat quietly with her hands folded in her lap, she, too, looked eagerly at the banquet before her.

The "partners"—the many bachelor "cousins" who'd been brought over—also crowded around the table. They came to dinner in sleeveless undershirts, as though this were any other dinner in the year. They gaped at the food, the plates, the prayers, the words spoken. This evening, one young man stared at the spread as though it were something from another planet. In her heart, Ticie knew that the worker *should* feel that way. Thanksgiving made no sense to him, just as many things she'd seen in China seemed strange to her.

In so many ways this was not the life that Ticie had envisioned for herself. Sometimes she wondered, What if Suie hadn't hired me? Would I have gone to work for Madame Matilde? Would I have gone home to Central Point? Would I have married some farm boy and spent my life worrying about drought, frost, and locusts? Would my children have known nothing more of the world than what they could learn in a one-room schoolhouse? Would my older sons right now be thinking about how they would ever be able to go out on their own, how they might support a wife and children, how they—like their parents—would ever be able to make ends meet?

On this Thanksgiving evening, surrounded by her family, Ticie knew how incredibly fortunate she was. Ticie Pruett had been an orphan; Ticie See was the mother of five children. Her family had abandoned her emotionally long before they had actually disowned her; now she had an extended family—her few white friends, all these men sitting around her table in their undershirts, even her kindly neighbors. Her family had been poor and hardworking; she still worked hard, very hard, but she and Suie had made a good life for themselves. At this moment, Ticie couldn't have asked for anything more, except maybe a house.

CHAPTER 7

THE HOME VILLAGE

1919–20

W̶HEN World War I ended, thoughts of travel, luxury, and frivolous fun filled the minds of many Americans. The Sees joined in this preamble to the Roaring Twenties by planning a trip back to the home village of Dimtao. As always, Ticie saw to family arrangements while her husband focused on those involving business. At Ticie's request, Anna Mueller filled out affidavits saying that she had delivered all of the children and that they were indeed Americans. With these in hand, the family set about getting their merchant-status permits from the U.S. Department of Labor Immigration Service.

Perhaps because the case presented seven people of varying status, the Sees went through a more difficult time than usual. First, immigration officials had to decide what to do about Letticie. The Consulate General of the Republic of China wrote a letter claiming her as "a citizen of the Republic of China, age 43 years . . . " Yet, looking at her enclosed photograph, U.S. immigration officials were confused. Mrs. Fong appeared American and said she was American-born, but this defied all logic. Searching back through their records to a trip Fong See had made alone in 1912, they found that he had testified to having an American-born wife. On further investigation, immigration officials discovered the "usual Chinese papers" for Fong See and his children from the 1901 trip, but no papers on file for anyone calling herself Mrs. Fong See. The only mention was found on the manifest of the steamer *Korea*: "Mrs. Fong See, age 24, American, no other data, no papers, wife of Fong See."

In a letter from the Angel Island station, Inspector W. G. Becktell wrote: "There appears to be some conflict of opinion as to whether an American-born white woman married to a domiciled Chinese merchant should be given Form 431 (for the wife of a lawfully domiciled Chinese merchant), or should be handled directly under the Immigration Law." Inspector Becktell later added that since the Los Angeles office had made no mention of the race of Fong See, "it might be assumed that in the opinion of the examining officers she is at least part Chinese."

After a flurry of letters and telegrams, the Immigration Service opted for simplicity by omitting Letticie's race entirely and issuing her a Form 431.

On June 9, a round of interrogations began. Inspector Harry Blee questioned Ticie on her marriage, her children, and the nature of her husband's business, then notified her that upon her return to the United States, she would be required to submit to the requirements of a literacy test. "I can meet the requirements, all right," she answered tartly. Blee then questioned Richard White, who had recently retired from the hardware business to a ranch outside Los Angeles, but who still visited the Sees every Saturday for lunch or dinner; Thomas Clark, a curio dealer who bought and sold goods for Fong See at auction; and police detective Clarence Shy, who stopped by the store as often as once a day. After these inquiries were completed, Blee moved on to the See children, beginning with Milton. After establishing twenty-one-year-old Milton's American and Chinese names, the inspector asked him to identify photographs of his parents, which he did correctly. "Can you speak Chinese?" Inspector Blee asked.

"No," Ming replied.

"Have you ever voted?"

"No."

"Did you register for military service during the war?"

"Yes," Milton answered, producing his papers.

"Do you know any Chinese persons born in the U.S.?" the inspector queried.

"Besides my brothers and sisters, none that I can testify to," Milton lied.

Moving on to Ray, who had just turned nineteen, the inspector asked him to state his name. "Ray See is my English name. I think my Chinese name is Fong Ming Fook, but I never use it." Again, photographs were produced and identified.

Bennie, aged sixteen, and Eddy, aged 13, answered promptly and also identified the photographs. Finally, Inspector Blee escorted Sissee, who was just short of her tenth birthday, into the room. As the youngest child, she was the most frightened. Like the rest, she was cautioned to tell the truth.

"What is your papa's name?" Blee began.

"Mr. Fong See."

"Do you know whose photo this is?" Blee asked, setting Fong See's Form 430 application and photograph on the table.

"That is my papa," she answered in a quavering voice.

Blee presented Ticie's Form 431 application and again queried the girl.

"This is my mama's picture," she told him. He showed her photographs of her brothers and asked her to identify them by name. Finally, Blee asked Sissee what she did. "I am going to the California Street School," she answered. "I am in the B4 grade."

Unsatisfied, Blee gathered the children together. "I show you here two other photographs, one marked 'Exhibit G' and the other marked 'Exhibit H,' which I will attach to the record. I will ask you each separately if you can identify these photographs." The children were again sent out of the room. Then, going by age, Blee called them in one by one. Each of the boys found and identified the pictures of their parents. As the youngest, Sissee was the last to be called. Presented with the photographs, she pointed, "This is Mr. Fong See, with the *G,* and my mama is the one with the *H.*"

As the interrogations dragged on, Fong See contacted the Chinese consul in San Francisco, which then wired the passport division of the State Department in Washington, D.C., to please forward the passports for the five native-born children without waiting for the arrival of their 430 forms. On June 18, the passport office wired back that this would be impossible. On July 1, based on evidence submitted and adduced during the investigation, the See children were found to "reasonably establish their American citizenship by reason of birth in the United States." The Department of State concluded that they could be regarded as citizens. The passports—heavy with extra documentation stating the race for each See sibling as "Mongolian"—arrived two weeks later, three days before the family's scheduled departure.

While Ticie handled immigration matters, Fong See focused his attentions on what would happen to the business while he was away. In February he had filed a revised partner list. Wing Ho still manned the Long Beach store. Fong Yun was managing a new store at 800 West Seventh Street, downtown. (Fong See closed the Pasadena branch, because only he had the expertise to deal with those customers.) The rest of the old names were removed from the partnership list, and a dozen new ones took their place. Ming Kuen and Ming Ho—Uncle's sons in China—were awarded "partnerships." As a precaution against unforeseen difficulties from future immigration inspectors, Milton, Ray, Bennie, and Eddy were also given "partnerships" under their Chinese names.

In the final hectic days before setting sail, Fong See drilled his workers on their duties during his absence. With instructions in hand, Uncle would oversee recalcitrant helpers and clerks, deal with customs officials when Fong See sent merchandise back to the States, supervise the uncrating of each piece, and provide testimony on behalf of the "false" Fong Lai for a return trip to China. At last, on July 17, 1919, Fong See and his family boarded the SS *Nanking* for the twenty-nine-day trip to Hong Kong via Honolulu, Yokohama, Tokyo, and Shanghai. They planned to stay in China for a year.

*

By the end of the first day out of San Francisco, Fong See had checked on everything of importance he needed to know, as far as this leg of the trip was concerned. He laughed when his children complained that the vessel was small and rocked miserably. Compared to the clipper ship he'd first taken to America, the *Nanking,* a steamer, was civilized and safe. It offered reasonable fares, decent cuisine, and accommodations for all classes. He had appraised his fellow passengers, noting which seating they were called for, and to which deck they retired after dinner. He'd seen only a few Caucasian passengers—missionaries with religious zeal in their hearts, and a handful of businessmen, their eyes glistening with the possibilities of the Far East—who took cabins in first and second class.

Most of the passengers were sojourners who'd come to the Gold Mountain, worked as laborers, saved their money, and were now retiring to their home villages with one or two thousand dollars in their pockets. Watching them hunker down on the open-air third-class deck for what they surely hoped would be a month-long game of fan-tan, Fong See thought of something his father used to say. Put one and a half Chinese together and you will find gambling. Already a dealer was counting out buttons in sets of four from a metal cup, while other men placed their bets.

Part of Fong See's mystique was his ability to make both the Chinese and Caucasians around him believe that he had more and lived better than they did. This trip was no exception. The Chinese aboard—whether in second class or steerage—believed that Mr. See and his family traveled as first-class passengers. "Fong See is the only Tang Man among us who has climbed to such heights," the gamblers might mumble in admiration, looking up from their fan-tan buttons.

In second class, Leong Jeung, who owned a produce stall at the Los Angeles Central Market, was not acquainted with Fong See. His wife, however, knew him well. For if Fong See lived as a merchant prince, then Mrs. Leong ruled as a despotic warlord over Chinatown's Methodist Mission, and ran the language school with dedication and uncompromising energy. Although the two rarely spoke, Mrs. Leong was not unaware of Fong See's importance. She could threaten the wives of her other countrymen with damnation if their children didn't attend Sunday school, but she would never succeed in these tactics with Fong See or his family.

"He is *the* importer," she lectured her husband. "He is a successful businessman. He is on his way to hell, but he is articulate in the language of the Gold Mountain. How fortunate we are as a family to have our staterooms on the same level as his."

Mrs. Leong was a poor judge of Fong See's speaking ability. She may have been an empress of her own language who devoted her life to teaching the children of Chinatown the eloquent strokes of Chinese calligraphy and drilling them for hours each weekday afternoon on passages from the classics, but her English was forever meager. Fong See's English was neither Hong Kong English nor Oxford English, but, as his American customers and immigration officials knew, he "got along."

For all the rumors that drifted among the Chinese and Americans on this voyage, none but Fong See's own family knew that they traveled Special Second Class. They ate with the first-class passengers and slept in beautifully outfitted cabins, but paid only a token amount over the ordinary second-class fare. Still, what a conundrum the Sees posed to those around them. Fong See—whatever age he was, from fifty-three to sixty-two, depending on who was asking—still looked youthful, his face unlined, his body slim. Dressed immaculately in a western suit, he entertained the Caucasian wayfarers with tales of Sung Dynasty landscape scrolls, Ming vases, and T'ang horses. For him, this trans-Pacific passage was just another way of luring potential customers to the F. Suie One Company; any location would do.

Where Fong See sometimes seemed too showy with his brash pinstripes and diamond tie tacks, his wife appeared quietly elegant in wellcut silk gowns of classic design and little artifice. Ticie, her auburn hair crimped and swept up into an elaborate bun, exchanged appropriate pleasantries with the Caucasian wives, but, in her effort to be a correct Chinese wife, she was subdued, self-contained. She had little in common with these women.

The two sets of sons, left to their own devices, prowled the ship. Ming and Ray—both gallant and debonair—found no young ladies with whom they could try to establish reputations as irresistible playboys. For diversion, Ming and Ray mercilessly teased Gilbert Leong—the eightyear-old pride of the rigid and strict Leong family. Gilbert was born "lucky," slipping from his mother's womb in the first year of Dr. Sun Yat-sen's Chinese Republic. The Leong family believed Gilbert was destined for a special, fortunate life. Ming and Ray, however, thought he was a little squirt. Each afternoon they took turns grabbing Gilbert by his belt, hoisting him above their heads, and shaking him like a pompom at a football game.

"Hey! Hey!" Gilbert screamed and yelled. "Put me down! Put me down, *please*."

He cried out in English. He tried Chinese. But Ming and Ray never listened, preferring the raucous encouragement they got from Bennie and Eddy. The gamblers in steerage looked up from their games of fantan and shook their heads. What could they do? These boys were from the See family. They were moneyed. They were spoiled. They were untouchable.

Sissee stayed at her mother's side. The stringent rules that applied to the only daughter of Chinatown's most prominent importer were followed to the letter, even away from home. Every night after dinner, Ticie tied up her daughter's black hair in rags. Each morning before breakfast, passengers and crew marveled at the little girl's pristine ringlets. (By the end of a day in the damp sea air, Sissee's curls loosened once again to the naturally straight hair of a young Chinese girl.) Needlework every day. No wandering off to explore the ship. The schedule varied only when seasickness felled the adults. Then Sissee kept her ailing mother company in their stateroom, serving her tea or bouillon.

The long days centered around the ship's meals. In steerage, surrounded by mounds of baskets, trunks, and boxes, men squatted around a communal dinner of rice and a single dish of stir-fried vegetables and meat. In the main dining room—with its white table linens, crystal, and silver—heavy American meals prevailed. Each night at the table for the few second-class Chinese travelers, some joker would regale his dinner companions with stories of his first trip to the United States.

"The peasants in my home village all helped to pay for my voyage, so I sailed not as a coolie but as a young man seeking his fortune," a traveler might tell his neighbors over beef Wellington, potatoes au gratin, and green beans almondine. "I spoke no English. I could read no English. Each mealtime, I would go to the dining room and look at the menu. The waiter would come. I would point to three things." Here, his companions would begin to laugh. They knew this story. They had lived it themselves. "The waiter would bring my dinner. A soup, a soup, and another soup."

After many days at sea, the *Nanking* chugged into Honolulu harbor. Standing at the railing, the children watched as laborers hauled up blocks of ice for the refrigeration unit and brought new stores aboard. The kids, as well as the adults, learned to appreciate this pattern. With ice refrigeration, each day out of port altered the quality of the meat. As the ice melted, sauces became heavier to cover the rank flavor of the putrefying flesh.

At Yokohama and Tokyo, most passengers contented themselves by staying on the ship and looking across the rain-swept pier to where Japanese ran to and fro, their heads protected by paper umbrellas, the clack-clack of their wooden sandals muted by the persistent deluge. The See boys ogled the scantily clad Japanese women who, from barges up against the *Nanking,* passed baskets of coal hand to hand up long ladders and into its belly. Their bodies—draped in only a few swatches of cotton—were streaked black and white with coal dust and rivulets of warm rain. But prurient interests had their time and place, and Fong See had other ideas for his sons. While Ticie took the younger children on sightseeing excursions through pelting rain, Fong See insisted that Ming and

Ray accompany him on social calls to local antique dealers to buy lacquerware, bronzes, and porcelains.

One merchant taught the boys what to look for in Imari pieces. "Do you see this color?" he asked. "You want to find the deepest cobalt blue or the deepest iron red. Look at the detail. Tell me what you see."

And Ming answered promptly, "It is a pattern based on woven brocade."

Fong See praised his son for the correct answer. He was pleased at how quickly they learned to recognize the differences between the Satsuma ware of the last century and the cheaper product made for curios. During the short layover, they bought goods worth thousands of dollars. Then they were back aboard the ship, pushing on toward China.

As the *Nanking* neared the coast of China, a shadowy shape flying past the railing, followed by a scream and a splash swept away by the ocean breeze, signaled to the crew that someone had fallen or jumped overboard. From first class down to steerage, the call went out in Chinese and English, "Man overboard! Man overboard!" Parents quickly checked on their children. Mr. and Mrs. Leong located Ed and Gilbert, Elmer and little Margie. Mr. and Mrs. See spotted Ming and Ray and Eddy on deck. Sissee, naturally, was at her mother's side. Bennie, however, was nowhere to be found. At Fong See's insistence, the captain piloted the ship in narrowing, then widening, circles through the churning water. First- and second-class passengers and all available crew members gaped over the sides of the ship, hoping to catch a glimpse of the boy, while the gamblers on the third-class deck seemed sullen and unperturbed. Ticie grew increasingly worried. Then, as the sun dropped behind the horizon, Bennie emerged groggily from a nap. He had dozed off in his own berth, but no one had thought to look for him there. The captain immediately called off the search, turned the ship around, and got back on course.

"Where have you been?" Ticie scolded. "We've been frightened to death."

"You a bad boy," his father chastised. "Put you in garbage can."

Even more reprehensible than being just absentminded and inconsiderate to the family, Bennie was accused of making everyone sick. "We've been going in circles—up and down through the waves," Ticie said. "Everyone has had to visit the doctor. This is your fault and yours alone."

The family's first flush of anger soon turned to the merciless teasing that would continue for a lifetime. How he'd slept through the shouts. How he'd slept through the grinding of the engine as it throbbed through the swells. How he'd made everyone seasick.

By journey's end, the gamblers provided a solution to the mystery: One of their party had lost everything—all his money earned from his long years on the Gold Mountain. He could not live with the loss of face. Everyone agreed he had followed the only course open to him.

At long last, the *Nanking* sailed up the Whangpoo, anchored, and waited for the tenders to ferry passengers to the Bund of Shanghai. For now, this was just a port visit. Months later the family would make Shanghai a major stop during their travels. But as the Sees gathered to look out at the western-style buildings that lined the Bund, the country enveloped them with its scents: the coal smoke; the cooking odors of garlic, ginger, and five-spice; the underlying stench of rotting fish.

For Fong See, this wasn't just a pleasure cruise. Nothing for him was ever that simple. Duty, pride, and business all played important roles in his schemes. As for duty, during Fong See's years away from the village, his father, Fong Dun Shung, had died, as well as his sister, Lin, his first wife, Yong, and his older brothers. They were buried on hilltops not far from Dimtao. Though Fong See lived thousands of miles away, all the proper burial traditions had been carried out to his specifications. As they lay dying, each was placed on a pallet by the door so that his or her spirit might find free air. A piece of paper had been placed over each of their faces so that they couldn't count the roof tiles, cursing the family always to live in a small house. From America, Fong See had enlisted a *feng shui* man to test the wind and water signs for burial sites. If all signs were auspicious, then the dead would be able to use these cosmic currents to benefit the living. Tables were set with food for the dead and other spirits. Firecrackers, gongs, and cymbals hurried the spirits along their processionals. Neighbors had been prevailed upon to make buildings, clothes, and people (especially servants) from bamboo and paper. Others cut brown paper into "road money," which was thrown into the air along the paths of the processions to purchase the right-of-way from evil spirits. All these artifacts of worldly life were burned at the graves so that the dead would have plenty in the afterlife.

Although all of the ceremonies had been properly attended to, Fong See knew that they had missed one key presence. That he had not been in Dimtao for the funerals of his first wife and father disturbed him. Now Shue-ying, his mother, was ill and not expected to survive another winter. Filial responsibility demanded that he pay his respects. Custom dictated that he present his children to their grandmother; that his wife show gratitude to her mother-in-law. He had been absent for the others, but he couldn't allow himself to neglect his mother. She had provided for him during the desperate years after his father went to work on the railroad.

As for pride, this trip gave Fong See the opportunity to show the people of Dimtao what a big man he had become. He was their benefactor. They owed him tribute.

Business required that he take this time to train Ming and Ray in the intricacies of selecting genuine antiques from fakes, or an interesting piece of folk art from an obvious tourist trifle. He would show them by example how to distinguish a cheat from a trustworthy opponent in the fine art of bargaining.

Ticie let her mind drift back to her last trip to China, nineteen years before. Then, China and the Chinese had still been foreign and new to her. Now she felt that she was—like the sojourners in steerage—going back to her own home country. Except for special American holidays, she rarely thought of herself as Caucasian anymore. She was Chinese, like her husband and her children. She was part of their world now. Yet something must have been troubling her, for she traveled with her own cache of twenty-dollar gold pieces, hidden away from her husband's watchful eyes.

Each of the See boys—Ming and Ray already young men, Bennie and Eddy still children—pondered what this trip would hold for them. Will I find riches? Will I find a beautiful girl to marry? Will I have fun? Will I be lost and forgotten? All of them wondered if they would be accepted. In America they were not Americans; in Chinatown they were not Chinese. What would they be in China?

Eddy remembered his friend Eddie Lee's story of going back to his home village to attend an uncle's wedding. "Every family had a water buffalo, a pig for sure," Eddie had recalled as the two boys sat on crates in the alley behind the store. "Every time I went outside, my cousins picked up dried manure and threw it at me. When it hit, that dung scattered like sawdust." The boys had called him names. He was full Chinese, no half-breed, and still they taunted him with the familiar epithets: "foreign devil," "white ghost."

Eddie Lee went back to his auntie's house to sort through the soap and the boxes of dried fruit given to him as farewell gifts before he left for China. Rifling through his belongings, he found some raisins in a shallow wooden box. He took the box outside, pried open the lid, and offered its contents to the bullies. "In five seconds, every raisin was gone. From then on, they were all my friends. They showed me where to steal sweet potatoes." Then Eddie explained the difference between orange sweet potatoes—how to pick them, start a fire with kindling, and cook them in the smoldering ashes—and the red-skinned sweet potato with the snow white meat that you could eat raw. "Boy, they were good," Eddie had said, but then he was Chinese and always said he had a Chinese stomach.

Now, looking out across the water to the Bund, Eddy, like his brothers and sister, considered that his own reception in the home village of his father, the home village of his ancestors, might be as chilly as those he'd sometimes encountered in Chinatown.

Sissee, her ringlets falling down her back, worried. If one of them was kidnapped, she would be the likely choice. Her skin was pale, her countenance sweet and innocent, her father rich. More important, kidnappers would view her as an American, and Americans—the world knew—valued their daughters. They would smell that she was *lo fan*. These thoughts were soon overcome by Sissee's curiosity as she listened to a strange music. She moved closer to her mother and whispered, "What is that song? What is that singing?"

"It is the sound of the Orient," Ticie answered. It was the voices of thousands of Chinese, as they spoke their native language, floating through the air to fill the hearts of her children.

After a brief rest in Hong Kong, the family traveled to the teeming city of Canton, then were carried a day's journey west by sedan chair to the home village. Dimtao was still modest—with no electricity, no running water, no glass windows. In recent years the people of Dimtao had built a twenty-foot brick wall around the village to protect themselves from the ravages of warlords, marauders, and bandits. (Over the last few years a million peasants had been conscripted into China's army. By the time their duty to their country was over, many had lost their ricefields, and they became ruffians, raiding villages, stealing pigs and chickens, and kidnapping the sons of wealthy landowners.) Now villagers entered Dimtao through specially guarded watchtowers. Still, no direct route led to the village; travelers had to know the right set of raised paths to follow.

The See family's entrance into Dimtao produced an effect similar to a circus arriving in a small American town. There were nine sedan chairs—one for each person in the family and another two for the interpreters that Fong See had hired to translate for his wife and children. (He would hire many others as he traveled up the China coast, and later inland to Peking and the Great Wall. His Cantonese, by this time, was only passing. His Mandarin was nil. He himself would need interpreters for every place he went in China except for this one small county.) The sedan chairs for the younger children each had two bearers. The adults had a total of six bearers apiece—four to carry them, two more to switch off when they got tired. In addition, Fong See had employed extra coolies to transport luggage, gifts for the people of Dimtao, and any merchandise he purchased along the way.

While many old-timers could remember back to the time, almost two decades before, when Fong See, his wife, and two infant sons had made their first trip back to the village, most of the people of Dimtao had never seen a Caucasian before. As Ticie stepped down from her chair, the villagers crowded around her. They were intrigued, fascinated. Before them stood a woman with pale white skin and hair that seemed aflame when caught in the sun's rays. And all of them—even Fong

See—had the smell of foreigners on them. Eddy, overexuberant, jumped down from his sedan chair, raced around, climbed up on a low railing by a pigpen, held up his arms, and declared, "I'm the king." When the interpreters relayed this to the curious crowd, they shook their heads. This boy was the king? King of what? They snickered behind their hands, careful not to show their teeth.

Even from his home on a distant continent, Fong See functioned as the headman of the village. He owned one hundred *mou,* approximately twelve American acres. He had a direct effect on almost all of the villagers' lives. Thanks to Fong See, children's stomachs would no longer bloat, and old women would no longer die from want of a bowl of rice. A few fortunate sons worked for Fong See back in Los Angeles, while the less adept members of his clan toiled in Dimtao's ricefields, wading through the paddies, planting seedlings, pulling weeds, guaranteeing a good harvest. Others worked the vegetable patches. The shoulders and backs of these farmers and their wives were bent from years of carrying buckets hung from a pole slung across their shoulders coolie-style to bring water to the rows upon rows of fresh green sprouts. At night these families returned to houses owned by Fong See. His wealth and power were greater than any they had ever seen. The villagers relied on him for their survival. Now they gathered around Fong See, knowing he would have brought gifts for them all.

He handed out *lai see* to the village children. To family members he brought special gifts. Leong-shee, Uncle's wife, exclaimed over a gold coin and a lacquer box concealing a bottle of perfume. Kuen, her five-year-old son, received a little boat with a propeller. He had never before seen a toy like this, and Eddy, with his usual enthusiasm, showed his cousin how to wind the rubber band and set the boat on a wobbly course through a shallow water puddle.

With gifts in hand, everyone followed closely as this well-dressed parade made its way down a narrow alley toward where Shue-ying was waiting in the house she had prepared for them. The dull gray brick had been whitewashed. Earthenware pots planted with miniature tangerine trees and blooming flowers had been festooned with red ribbons and set about her small courtyard. According to her son's instructions, impromptu mattresses had been made from hay stuffed into loose cloth bundles and laid across the rough wooden planks that ordinarily made up the beds. Lacquered wood pillows had been bought in nearby Fatsan. Each bed had been hung with mosquito netting. "Honey buckets" had been placed under the beds on the assumption that the children would be too western to run out along the raised paths between the rice paddies and do their business.

Under Shue-ying's watchful eyes, the servants had thoroughly cleaned the inside water system that ran from the roof to the outdoor kitchen area. One servant had gone for fresh water, carrying each bucket up to the rooftop storage tank, while another had cleaned each of the bamboo pipes that led back down to the kitchen. New gravel had been purchased and stuffed into each cleaned pipe. The water would filter through several levels of bamboo and gravel, and by the time it reached the kitchen holding pot, it would be clean. But even with these efforts, these foreigners—her son included—would not have the stomach strength to take the water straight. Everything would have to be boiled.

When they arrived at the house, there were no hugs, no kisses. Shue-ying's grandchildren saw her as she was—a frail Chinese woman nearing her nineties. She was not precious to them; they seemed strangers to her. Sissee and Eddy watched—not with pangs of jealousy, for they had never known what it was like to have a grandparent, but with a kind of detached interest—as she took her gifts of tinned cakes and cookies, stashed them on a high shelf in her room, and assured her grandson Kuen that, if he were a good boy, she would give him a treat.

Later that first afternoon, Fong See—sitting at a low table set with a pot of tea and porcelain dishes of sweetmeats—received villagers who had complaints. A cousin had hoarded rice; a second cousin argued that his family had not been paid the proper bride-price for his only daughter; someone else requested a better house. Another cousin, Fong Suey Ming, pointed out that most villagers had no capital to start their own farms, and that sending relief funds—as Fong See had done so generously during famine years—could not solve the basic problem. Suey Ming suggested that his honorable Gold Mountain cousin make a large donation to help the villagers start a real farming business. To everyone's surprise, Fong See promised to provide ten thousand American dollars.

That evening, Fong See hosted a banquet for the entire village. Each dish was filled with special ingredients that promised to bring long life, prosperity, and many sons. Fong See walked out among the tables, handing out more *lai see* to the children, the single girls of marriageable age, and a few relatives deserving of special attention and recognition. As Fong See passed from table to table, one of the old-timers spoke up. "Is our Gold Mountain See not like the woodcutter of legend?" A few mumbled their agreement and settled in for a postprandial story.

"The parents of the woodcutter were poor, and came from as poor a village as our Dimtao," the old-timer began. "The woodcutter learned to love the forest, and each morning as he worked there, he wondered if he could do something for his parents. One day he heard the rushing of a waterfall. As he drank from it, he discovered that it ran with sweet wine. He filled his gourd and took it back to his father. Just as in our village, news traveled quickly. The next day when the woodcutter went to the forest, he found his neighbors at the waterfall. Oh, how angry they were, for they found only water in the glistening depths. The neighbors were so jealous that they threw the woodcutter into the waterfall, leaving him there to drown. In despair, he filled his gourd with the water and went home to his father. Again the gourd was filled with wine. You see, many can go to the source, but only our Gold Mountain See can get the wine."

As the reunion ended, the evening turned dark and evil. Word passed that a spy in the village had informed local kidnappers of the whereabouts of the children. Fong See knew that he could not allow his family to stay in the village for any length of time. Even this one night posed many hazards. The children were quickly gathered up and locked into a stifling one-room house with no windows. Guards were hired and posted around the perimeter. Fong See questioned villagers to no avail.

After a restless and claustrophobic night, the family left Dimtao as quickly as they had arrived, but with far less fanfare. For the first and only time on this trip, they took the train. Kuen, Uncle's son, traveled with them. Fong See thought Kuen could entertain Sissee and Eddy in the weeks to come.

For Kuen, the following weeks in Canton were both amazing and bewildering. No longer did Kuen have to attend school, bowing to his teacher each morning and afternoon. No longer did he have to memorize the four books of Confucius or the classics of the great poets. No longer did he have to study from the traditional Chinese primer, the *Trimetrical Classic*, or, as it was more widely known, *Learning by Three Sounds*. No longer did he play on the backs of the village water buffalo. No longer did Kuen join his brothers and other boys of Dimtao as they mounted an army and spent afternoons in the ricefields fighting the boys from neighboring villages.

Kuen had never been outside Dimtao except to make the annual New Year's visit to the graves of his ancestors. As a result, Canton was far more frightening to him than to his foreign-born cousins. Kuen marveled at the wall twenty feet thick and close to forty feet high which protected Canton. He was astonished by a pagoda five stories high, the Temple of Five Hundred Gods, and the eight-hundred-year-old water clock. He was tantalized by the idea of the Island of Shameen with its lovely promenade shaded by banyan and camphor trees, but none of them was allowed to enjoy this, since only Caucasians were permitted on the island.

Kuen's uncle, unable to find a hotel or inn in Canton suitable for his western family, had rented a mansion from a wealthy mandarin. It was a fine place, a regular Chinese compound with a large garden, a series of interior courtyards, a private temple for meditation, and many, many rooms. Kuen's uncle said he wanted Ticie and the children to feel comfortable, and he made the house as European, as Caucasian, as he could. He commissioned a craftsman to make chamber pots topped with western-style toilet lids, which were then placed in a special room where they were lined up according to the size and age of each person. The bedrooms came with their own carved beds enclosed like small rooms by panels of carved teak and painted glass.

All of this was as unfathomable to Kuen as the way his ghost relatives spent their time. During the day, Auntie Ticie and Sissee might stroll past immense godowns, the warehouses where exports such as tea, silk, and cassia were stored to be shipped out of the country, and imports such as cotton, wool, opium, and kerosene were stored upon their arrival. Fong See and the older boys went to the bazaars where quaint curios and native articles of every kind might be bargained for and obtained. Jade sellers hawked decorative ornaments in varying shades of stone, in varying quality, and in prices from a few cents to several thousand U.S. dollars. Other kiosks carried rare porcelains, bronzes, ivory, and teak. In the furniture stalls, Fong See bargained hard for carved pieces, some of them inlaid with mother-of-pearl. He sought out idols, knowing they always sold well in his stores.

Kuen's uncle—so rich, so powerful—was secretive and clever. No one knew when he would go out or where he was going. Some days Fong See appeared in the downstairs entry dressed as little more than a peasant. Even though bad people wanted to get him, they couldn't, for Kuen's uncle was too elusive, too tricky to wear either his western clothes or the fancy robes of a mandarin out on the streets. Just as Fong See sought out oddities in his trips to fairs and expositions, he also sought out the strange and bizarre in China. He went to pawnshops and second-hand stores and bought them out lock, stock, and barrel. From antique dealers he bought huge lots, sometimes room upon room of merchandise. He risked buying pallets filled with this and that, not quite knowing if they would also include a piece of Han, T'ang, or Sung. It didn't really matter, he explained, because he knew he could sell it all, marking everything up at least three times its cost to him.

Years later there would be those who wondered if, when Fong See opened his pallets back in Los Angeles, he would pull out a Sung Dynasty bowl and say to himself, "This is Sung. This is not worth only three times the amount I paid. This is worth twenty thousand dollars." What is known is that some of the biggest collectors in the country went to Fong See, and that many of their collections ended up in museums. But Kuen comprehended little of this.

Everyone in the village said Kuen was lucky and he tried to feel lucky. He had heard tales of prosperous landlords and rich mandarins, so he had an idea of what to expect, but Fong See and his family didn't live according to those expectations. They didn't keep a cook in the house. They had no servants except for an old man who maintained the grounds.

The mother was beautiful, kind, and gentle. When they had first come to Canton, she went with Fong See to buy. Lately, Kuen had overheard them arguing in the courtyard when she arrived ready to join Fong See on his excursions. Kuen didn't understand their English words, but he noticed that now she elected to stay home, sit on what everyone called the veranda, and do her sewing.

The family treated Kuen well. He had a good time. He didn't make trouble. He spoke only a little, letting the others do the talking. If Eddy or Sissee or one of the others said he was wrong, he agreed that he was. If they said that he didn't play fair, he admitted it, even when he knew and they knew he was in the right. No matter what happened—even the time when his cousin Ming lifted him up by his pants and shook him like an old rag, and they both slipped on the wet stones and Kuen twisted his ankle—he did not complain.

Most of the time Kuen played with Eddy and Sissee. Eddy *liked* Canton. Bennie didn't. Like Kuen, Bennie didn't like to venture out of the compound, and acted nervous about what he was seeing, hearing, smelling. But Eddy liked hanging out with the people who would show him things. Those people turned out to be his interpreters, his rickshaw boys, the house coolies, and his sedan-chair bearers. After much pleading, his interpreter and a rickshaw boy might take him down to the Temple of Horrors, with its great crowds of fortune-tellers, jugglers, gamblers, peddlers, beggars, and children selling peanuts and matches, much as Eddy's father had done fifty years before.

Encouraged by Eddy's adventurism, his quick learning of colloquial Cantonese, and his irrepressible naughty streak, the interpreter and the kitchen coolie took him to Canton's bawdy houses—not the high-class places where Ming and Ray might be, and not the places where a dreadful disease was nearly as certain a reward as a night's pleasure, but places suitable for a fourteen-year-old foreign boy, where the girls were as young as he. For a few yuan, Eddy said, he could look, even touch. The girls—their faces powdered white, slashes of red painted across their lips—wore loose black coats and pants. Eddy had slipped his hand inside their jackets and run his fingers over their breasts. At least this was what he told Kuen.

Some afternoons, Ticie asked Kuen to teach Eddy and Sissee games that he liked, so he showed his rich cousins what they could do without money or store-bought toys. He taught them how to throw up a stone, then swipe up another stone off the ground, or throw up a stone and catch it on the back of his hand. Eddy would have nothing to do with this. "A girl's game," Eddy said in disgust. "Jacks." Eddy preferred the stick game called *gat*. Any boy would like *gat*—so named because the game made a *gat* sound. Kuen found two bricks and laid a short stick across them. He then used a longer stick to flip the shorter stick into the air. *Gat.* Sometimes Eddy would catch the stick, sometimes not. If he did, Kuen would then lay his long stick down on the bricks. Eddy had one chance to throw his short stick to try to knock Kuen's stick out of position. If he did—with a resounding *gat*—then he won the point. Sometimes they flew kites from the roof. Kuen taught Eddy how to attach shards of glass to his kite string and use it to try to cut the other person's string. Pretty soon, Eddy was good enough to "pirate" Kuen's kite all the time. The younger boy never complained.

In the afternoons, if Fong See had a visitor, tea was served accompanied by dishes of peanuts, watermelon seeds, salted plums, and preserved olives. As soon as Fong See had moved on, Eddy and Kuen snatched up the olive and plum pits and took them outside for their ongoing game of improvised marbles. Each took a turn tossing a piece of shattered roof tile to knock the olive pits out of a circle drawn in the dust. Sometimes they used the larger plum pits to knock out the smaller olives. Each boy's collection of pits waxed and waned with an afternoon's win or defeat.

Finally, Kuen's uncle and his family once again packed their trunks and prepared for a northward journey. Kuen was sent back to the village. He tried to tell his family and friends about his adventures, about how strange it had been to see first-hand how these foreigners lived. "We don't want to hear your bragging," his friends said. "I don't have time to listen to your nonsense," his mother chided. Kuen learned to keep his memories to himself.

Travel in China was difficult at best. Officials and the common peasantry had long fought the introduction of railroads into the country. The opposition was the result of old customs and a well-founded distrust of foreigners. Poorly educated people—cart drivers, wheelbarrow pushers, and boatmen—believed that the railroads would irritate evil spirits who would then seek revenge upon the populace. (A railroad would also deprive these common workers of their livelihoods.) The educated class, on the other hand, had discovered that when a foreign entrepreneur— from England, Germany, France, Russia, or the United States—built a road, that road was then used by that particular nation's government to extend its power in China, to gain some new piece of territory or trade advantage. Chinese officials realized that railroads—just like paved roads—would make travel easier for missionaries and other foreigners who wanted to exploit the country. The opposition had been so great that, back in 1875, the first railroad line from Shanghai to Wusung was bought by the Chinese authorities and destroyed. By 1919, however, there had been some progress, as fifty-four railroad lines tentatively webbed across China's great expanse.

So, except for their hasty retreat from Dimtao, the Sees never traveled by rail. Instead they went by sedan chair, river steamer, *hakka* (a wooden boat for small canals), junk, sampan, horseback, or by the steamers that plied the China coast. Outside the major cities, the Sees packed their own food and bedding, and brought along their own servants. Sometimes, after a long day's travel by sedan chair, the family would settle into a country inn furnished only with simple beds and a stove built into the wall to serve cooking and heating needs.

Pleasant days drifted by on river steamers. The younger boys made up games. Ticie read or did needlework, encouraging Sissee to sit by her side and practice her stitches. Fong See often disembarked and walked along the shore as coolies pulled and hauled the ropes attached to the boat. Sometimes these laborers would know of a local family in dire straits, a family so poor that the landlord was about to shoo them off his land for late payment of rent or the bad quality of their crops. To these families Fong See made side trips. Did this esteemed farmer have anything he wanted to sell? Perhaps an ancestral altar for New Year's worship? Perhaps some trinket from his honorable wife's dowry?

Travel by sedan chair was far more arduous. Four coolies carried Letticie's chair, two ran behind. When any two got tired, the new ones took over, never missing a step or upsetting the rhythm of their steady dog trot. The Sees had hired the best bearers, ones who promised always to stay out of step, which reduced the risk of motion sickness for the passenger. This type of transportation necessitated that Letticie and Sissee be separated. Sissee wore a white sailor hat to keep the sun off her fair skin. Letticie constantly looked back—shifting her weight, much to the coolies' annoyance—to check whether her daughter was still in sight. At each rest stop, Ma said, "When I see your white hat coming, I know you are safe."

During the next few months, Fong See fulfilled his third goal for this trip—business and the education of his sons. He and Ticie took separate approaches. Usually, Fong See focused on how to deal, while Ticie showed the boys what to look for. Just as artisans had taught Ticie how to appraise a piece of porcelain for its purity of design, she now taught her children. Ming and Ray—and, by osmosis, the younger children—learned to recognize the traditional shapes for Chinese porcelain—the ginger jar, rice bowl, and *mei-ping* vase.

At a kiln specializing in celadon ware, Ticie knelt in a dusty warehouse and ran her hands over the grayish green surface of a porcelain ginger pot. "You need to establish whether a piece is real or a fake," she explained. "Pa and I have three things that we look for when buying authentic pieces. First, the shape must *never* stray from the norm. If you have trouble determining this, look at the silhouette." Here she pulled the jar out to the center of the room. "Do you see that it is narrow at the bottom and bulges only at the top third? Next, we consider the color of the glaze."

"Like we did with the Imari in Japan?" Ming asked.

"Exactly," Ticie answered. "Over time you will learn to differentiate glazes by the quality and types of minerals used this year, ten years ago, or in the last century."

The last criterion—the quality of the brushwork—didn't apply as much to celadon ware as to the overglazed enamels of which Fong See was particularly fond. Still, it fell to Ticie to point out the painterly quality of the faces, landscapes, and flowers that adorned a work. "The fewer the strokes an artist uses, the more telling," she explained when they stopped at another kiln. "When you look at these enamels—or even scrolls—think about what type of brush an artist used, the amount of paint he allowed on the brush, the angle at which he held that brush. All of these things will help you decide whether a piece is worth the asking price."

At this, Fong See took over, telling the children that they must buy only what they felt confident they could sell. They should also keep in mind that a business profited by appealing to a variety of customers.

"We purchase good antiques for collectors and museums," Ticie went on. "We buy curios and copies for tourists. Sometimes we pick up cheap imitations that we can age for people who can't afford a real antique. We buy decorative pieces for people to put in their houses in Hancock Park and Pasadena."

From village to village, and city to city, the family traveled, stopping at kilns specializing in oxblood, blue-and-white, famille rose, and famille vert porcelains. They looked for scrolls, furniture, carvings, and embroideries. Ticie took special care with the embroideries, recognizing how the matrons in Hancock Park and Pasadena really *did* love the purely decorative. "These embroideries are popular with our customers who use them as doilies or runners on their dining tables. They like to drape the larger ones over their couches or pianos. Some use them for costumes at balls or masquerade parties." She taught Sissee how to examine the sheen of the silk and told her the story behind the "forbidden stitch"—outlawed because young girls went blind doing the intricate needlework.

Only occasionally did the family halt their peripatetic touring to enjoy the scenery. In Soochow, the family found the lotus in bloom and a lake lying still with hardly a ripple. These quiet and beautiful surroundings offered a respite from the hubbub of Canton. They traveled onward to Nanking, the old southern capital, to see the tomb of the "beggar king," the founder of the Ming Dynasty. Weeds grew with abandon, giving the place a desolate air, but the boys were especially excited to be here, for each of them carried the name of Ming in their Chinese given names. They found no other tourists, just a few barren women who made the pilgrimage to the tomb to toss coins onto the backs of the stone elephants which lined the royal pathway. If a coin stayed on the elephant, it was seen as a propitious omen for fertility.

In Tsingtao they discovered a German town intent on its brewery. The town was clean, the houses European. Everyone in the party sampled the German beer made for export, but all agreed that the pear wine made from the local fruit was far better. From here, they boarded a steamer and went north to Tientsin. After a short visit there, they traveled inland to Peking—the beautiful imperial city of wide boulevards. Ticie and the younger children went on day excursions to the Great Wall, the northern Ming tombs, the ruins of the Old Summer Palace, and the Fragrant Hills. Fong See, Ming, and Ray went out to buy. Eventually, Fong See left the older boys in Peking to continue learning about Chinese art and how to buy it, while the rest of the family went back south to Fatsan and Canton.

Ensconced in a nineteen-room mansion with nineteen servants, Ming and Ray quickly adjusted, applying their charm to young ladies of both good and bad family. The brothers felt sorry for the White Russian girls from Vladivostok, and spent many evenings with these lovely refugees. On other nights, the boys lingered in the city's more decadent "pillow houses."

In Peking the camaraderie between Ming and Ray, only one and a half years apart in age, began to show strains. Ming dedicated himself to the rarefied life of a Chinese gentleman. Each morning, a private tutor drilled him on his Mandarin. Each afternoon, he called for a sedan chair and set off to the commercial district. Inside the darkened den of an antiques dealer, Ming relaxed in a low-slung chair, sipping tea and bantering good-naturedly with a crafty rug merchant. Day after day, Ming returned. He turned carpets over and examined the quality of the knotting. He patiently counted those knots, knowing that the greater the number of knots per square inch, the thicker the pile. He queried the dealer on the silk content. He was unyielding about color.

"Yes, I know that the Chinese find the combination of yellow and blue or mauve and gray attractive, but I am buying for American tastes," he explained. "The people in my city won't appreciate these colors together. I would like to see more of the two-tone rugs of light and dark blue."

Ming had learned from his father that time would always win out in this game. After several days, Ming might complete a deal and a dozen rugs would be rolled and packed for shipping. That merchant would grumblingly write up two sets of documents: one for customs with a false, low price, and another, true set, which would be hidden away by Ming.

The more fluent Ming became in his Mandarin, the more Ray chafed at his own lessons. "Why should I spend my time learning a language, only to travel twenty miles and find that no one can understand me and I can't understand them?" Ray asked his brother. Ray never received a satisfactory answer. As for the buying excursions, Ray raved at Ming, "How can you can sit in some dugout, hour after hour, nursing a cup of tea and pause between sentences and never arrive at a price and go back two days later and go through the whole thing again? This drives me crazy! I want no part of it."

No matter what he said, Ray couldn't get his older brother to rebel. The pattern of their relationship had been established at an early age. Ming, as the firstborn, was entitled to the very best the family had to offer. Pa even plucked out the choice cheeks from steamed fish to give to his eldest son. Ming was being groomed to take over the store; Ray could only look forward to being a paper partner—all work, little pay, no respect.

Ray knew that his parents had expected him to grow out of the malaise of his early teens, but how he could he? Memories of his childhood burned in his brain—his father's raging, his mother's quiet disapproval, his brothers' mocking. In the store, his father would only let Ray wait on tourists—never the good customers. "Always some woman who wants to buy a pair of silk pajamas for her chauffeur!" he railed, but his complaints always fell on deaf ears.

Just as Ming and Ray had begun to drift apart, so too had Fong See and Ticie. Fong See—after acting the powerful patriarch in the village and traveling as a man of respect and wealth—no longer listened to Ticie's advice. She watched helplessly as, despite her objections, he bought property in the home village of Dimtao and in Fatsan, the commercial city west of Canton.

When she questioned him about these purchases, he shrugged and answered sullenly, "I want a hotel in Fatsan. And I'm going to build a house in the village. It will be grand. It will be a mansion."

"Suie! We don't *live* here! Why do we need a *mansion* in Dimtao when we live above the store in Los Angeles?"

This particular disagreement was nearly as old as their marriage. In the past he might have argued with her. But now he only looked at her blankly. It seemed that every morning he left their compound and came back in the evening with another new property. "What are you going to do with a basket factory?" she asked. "It's true we do a good business in baskets. Importing them has always worked just fine. But why do we need the headache of a factory?"

"I'm the man. I do the buying," he shot back.

He was right, of course. He had always done the buying, but *she* had always done the selecting. She felt powerless against him. In China—where she was a foreigner who barely spoke the language—she had no power. She could only wait and see what would happen next.

He came back from one excursion and announced that he had bought a factory to make fireworks. The younger children had been excited by this, but Ticie was angry. "Fireworks?" she fumed. "We're in the antiques business."

"I can sell fireworks," he responded hotly.

"Suie, fireworks will lower the tone of the store."

But he didn't care about her opinion. After all these years, he felt he knew as much as, or more than, she. In China he was a big man. He didn't need her. Ticie took his new-found independence and self-confidence as an insult to her. The more he tied himself physically to China, the more she began to examine her own life. Questions that for years she had repressed raged to the surface of her consciousness.

Why did he want to build a mansion in Dimtao? Why did he insist on appearing so grand before the villagers, exhibiting his deep pockets, bragging how he had made his fortune in the Gold Mountain? Most bothersome of all, why did he feel he needed to do all these things in China, while in Los Angeles she and the children still lived above the store? She tried to rationalize his excuses. Of course he felt indebted to the people of Dimtao for giving him the money to go to America. Of course he could make money, as he always had, importing both handicrafts and antiques. But with each passing day she saw him slipping away from her and into the arms of his mother country.

Then, when she thought that her husband could no longer surprise her, he announced, "Eddy will stay in Dimtao when we go home. He take care of Grandma."

"Eddy?" she laughed. "He's only fourteen."

"Fourteen a good age. I go to California when I am fourteen."

Nothing in her life had prepared her for the idea that Suie would consider abandoning a child to the backward village of Dimtao. Stunned, devastated, she found she couldn't frame an argument, but could only say, "We can't leave Eddy here."

"Eddy is the one." Fong See explained that Eddy, as the youngest son, was the logical choice. According to tradition, he was responsible for the care of the old people—in this case, Shue-ying—as well as for the annual upkeep of the graves of the family's ancestors. Ticie couldn't dispute the importance of the Chinese tradition, but the idea of this separation pained her nonetheless.

Eddy didn't help. He said he wanted to stay behind in China. He loved it here. From their first days in Canton, she'd seen how quickly he'd picked up the language, how kind he was to the sedan-chair bearers, how he was always ready—when the rest of the family was exhausted and took naps during the enervating heat of the late afternoons—to go out and see "just one more thing." She knew that he'd gone to bawdy houses. He was his father's son, after all, and at fourteen he was old enough. The problem was, she didn't want to lose him for what she recognized was a business deal.

When Fong See said he wanted Eddy to stay behind to take care of Shue-ying, she knew that he intended her son to manage the new ventures and property. Again, she couldn't win an argument with Suie about this, because *he* had come to America at the same age, worked hard, supported himself, gotten ahead. Eddy—with his father's blood running in his veins—could do whatever job or duty was required of him.

Her conversations with Suie took on a tone new to their marriage. They spoke in low, controlled, angry voices. "I want my son with me. I don't want him here to take care of properties that we don't need anyway."

"I can trust a relative," Fong See replied, as though he had not heard her. "I can trust Eddy."

"I've helped you bring many of your relatives to Los Angeles," she continued. "Why would I want to leave my son here when Wing and Dai-Dai and the others have done everything humanly possible to get out of China?"

"Eddy stay here. Go school. Learn Chinese," Fong See continued.

"Never," she responded. "One thing will lead to another. First he'll be in school, then a go-between will suggest a betrothal, and we'll lose Eddy forever. I'll never get him back."

When Fong See insisted, she said, "Family's family. I won't allow us to be separated. We're going back." She told Fong See of her private cache of gold. "You can either come with us or stay behind. If necessary, I'll pay our fares home."

In January 1920, after six months abroad, Ticie decided to cut short the trip and return home. She wired for Ray and Milton to come quickly to Canton. As soon as they arrived, Ticie and all of the children boarded a ferry bound from Canton to Hong Kong, where they would catch the *Nanking* back to the United States. Fong See chose to remain in China, ostensibly to oversee his business ventures.

Amazingly, a time would come when Ray would exaggerate and embellish upon his time in China—that he had spent two "memorable" years in Peking, "collecting antiques and designing carpets for the family import business," and that he was "completely fascinated by the incomparable beauty and ageless simplicity" of the antique furnishings he found in the homes of cultivated Chinese. In China, Ray would later tell reporters, he decided to "incorporate the venerable Oriental qualities into contemporary furniture geared to Occidental living."

Eddy would spend the rest of his relatively short life regretting that he hadn't stayed in China. In future years, his imagination would magnify his lost opportunities. But even as his professional disappointments and resentments increased, he would evolve into the most "Chinese" of all the brothers. For Bennie, by contrast, his time in China would be an aberration in a life that would otherwise be simple and defined by American convention. Ming would return to Los Angeles with a hands-on education in Chinese art, which he would use for the rest of his life.

On this trip, after twenty-two years of marriage, Ticie had distanced herself from Fong See. Still, as she stood at the ferry's railing on that day in 1920, she refused to worry about the future. She reassured herself that her disagreements with Suie were only temporary, and that when he came home their marriage would go on as before.

PART III

CHAPTER 8

PLAYBOYS

1920–24

B Y 1920, the population of Los Angeles had risen to one-half million, and that number increased daily. In August of 1919, while the See family was in China, 21,000 people had come by train, automobile, and steamship to reside in Los Angeles. In the same month of the following year, the city doubled this number. During the 1920s, slightly more than 350 new immigrants—some longtime Americans, some fresh off the boat—would take up residence in the county each day. Intoxicated by their good fortune, they would help Los Angeles grow from a mere thirty-two square miles at the turn of the century to a languid sprawl of more than 390 square miles by 1925. This development would catapult Los Angeles from the tenth largest to the fifth largest city in population in the country, considerably irritating residents of San Francisco, who had long held that theirs was the most important city on the Pacific Coast.

In this decade, average life expectancy in America would climb to fifty-five years. One out of every four American families would buy or sell an automobile, and the Ford Motor Company would go to market with a car that sold for as little as $290. Radio would become all the rage. Women would ponder the meaning of the first Miss America Pageant, and would take pride in the first woman senator, the first woman governor, Amelia Earhart's adventures, and the ratification of the Nineteenth Amendment.

Despite these sweeping changes, the two thousand Chinese who called Los Angeles home still weren't encouraged to pass beyond Chinatown's borders. They weren't allowed in the Bimini or Brookside pools. (A Chinese would have needed a doctor's prescription, and even that would have been a dicey proposition.) But distrust and suspicion worked both ways. To most Chinese, Caucasians were still considered foreign devils who could bring evil upon the neighborhood. During a school census, for example, residents of every apartment in China Alley had lit candles and hung prayers in front of their doors to ward off any evil the investigating teachers might bring with them.

Ming and Ray had no interest in the superstitions and limitations of Chinatown. China, especially the luxuries of Peking, had expanded their horizons. When Ming and Ray returned to Los Angeles, they had exotic stories to tell. The boys were rich. They were sophisticated. And they were extremely handsome. Ming's face was narrow and smooth like his father's, while his hair curled in small waves like his mother's. But everyone in the family thought that Ray was the more handsome. Ray's lips were full. He had a tendency to tilt his head down, then look up through thick lashes. The effect was sexual, sultry, and irresistible.

As the boys had changed, so had Los Angeles. When they were in high school, they had been ignored, shunned, excluded. With the release of each new Rudolph Valentino film—*The Four Horsemen of the Apocalypse, The Sheik,* or *Blood and Sand*—exotic sensuality became the epitome of male attractiveness, and Ming and Ray, with their Eurasian blood, found themselves increasingly popular. They looked for and found "Beverly Hills People," "American Friends," and "Jewish People." (Although it could just as easily be said that those groups looked for and found Ming and Ray.) They were asked to clubs and dances. Women brazenly invited them out to dinner and to bed.

Ray abandoned his resolution to "get the hell out of Chinatown." In the first place, neither Ray nor Ming had occasion to socialize with what they perceived to be their backward Chinese neighbors. More important, Fong See was still in China. As a result, the entire family was freed from his tyrannical presence. The boys now had the luxury to spend their father's money—drive fancy cars, buy expensive clothes and gifts, treat their new-found friends to evenings out—without having to justify a penny, listen to lectures, or obey any commands. They could, quite simply, do as they pleased.

Still, shouldn't Ray, with his dislike for his father, have broken away from Chinatown completely? He certainly could have looked for a job, and perhaps he may have, in a halfhearted fashion. But neither of the older boys *had* to work; all of their needs were provided for, all of their bills were paid. Why should Ray worry about "living in Chinatown" when he spent most nights sleeping between cream-colored satin sheets in the arms of some lovely woman who willingly accepted him into her bed?

It was the twenties. Ray and Ming didn't *worry* about a thing. What little work they did do became just another way to play and have fun. While their mother managed the downtown store, Ming and Ray spent most of their days out in Ocean Park, where they auctioned goods on the boardwalk. In this carnival atmosphere, the elder scions of the F. Suie One Company competed for attention with the roller coaster, dance halls, bath houses, and the splendor of Abbot Kinney's Venice, just a few blocks away, where crowds clustered to view the curiosities:

the charms of Madame Fatima, the snake charmer, and the man who "eats 'em alive!" Along the boardwalk, with its Italian deco buildings, Fong See's sons set up a tent. To attract passersby, they kicked things off with a vaudeville show, or sold tickets to see the stuffed mermaid. Then they took turns standing on a platform and auctioning off antiques and curios. Customers paid with hundred-dollar bills. Money was coming in so fast the boys could hardly count it.

Their take, considerable in the early years of this cash-crazy decade, was collected in a glass jar during the day, and spent in speakeasies, roadhouses, country clubs, and honkytonks at night. Since Prohibition was in effect, the boys hung out in Venice to the west and Vernon to the east, where "dry" laws were relatively relaxed. Sometimes they'd drive out to the Cotton Club, on West Washington in Culver City, and take over the whole place for a private party. But nowhere were Milton and Ray better known than at the Vernon Country Club, where the swankiest of the swank went to socialize and imbibe the best hooch. They liked to host big parties, hire Gus Arnheim's band, and generally have a wild old time. Unlike the poor Chinese, who eked out their livings in Chinatown under constant fear from unfair laws and harassment, Ming and Ray encountered no racism. Instead they were accepted for their looks, their money, and their never-ending desire to have a good time.

Ming and Ray cut a wide swath. They looked resplendent in their tuxedoes of exquisite cut. They wore their hair slicked back with bandoline. They could shimmy and tango from one end of the dance floor to the other with every girl in the place and have enough energy (and gall) to start again before the evening's end. Unlike some of the other young men about town, who babbled silly nothings like "bee's knees," "suffering cats," and "flea's whiskers"—Ming and Ray could regale ruby-lipped maidens with tales of Peking and Shanghai, of opium dens and Russian princesses.

Young women—their shoulders powdered, their rolled garters showing just above their knees—could tell that these men were rolling in big bucks. They drove the fastest, most beautiful, most expensive cars. They knew the best bootleggers in and out of town. They talked constantly of their plans for making their millions. They had dreams of becoming big land developers, owning penthouses, buying buildings, opening their own nightclub. As most of the young ladies must have noted, to dream such dreams didn't require any real work. These boys had a rich daddy who, it seemed, would buy them anything. Besides, what girl didn't like it when a man talked oil? When Milton and Ray mentioned the family property on Signal Hill, there wasn't a young woman in the county who didn't know that gushers were blowing in out there almost every day.

Milton's days as a playboy were destined to be short. On June 11,

1921, in a civil ceremony in Tijuana, he married Dorothy Hayes, a contract player at Paramount. Dorothy, like many who interpreted the federal law against alcohol as all the more reason to drink as much as possible, drank far too much. Ming didn't hold back either. Their early married years were one long, glorious party.

Still in China and secure in the knowledge that Ticie was taking care of business in Los Angeles, Fong See settled into the routine of a landed Chinese gentleman. After years of curbing his impulse to buy land, he embarked on this enterprise with a vengeance. In the village, people happily traded their mud or brick shacks for American dollars that they could exchange for huge amounts of Chinese money. Buying property in Fatsan for his hotel proved to be more difficult, for on the site that Fong See had chosen stood Bu Sing Huei Kwan, a family association temple that housed records for the Bu Sing clan dating back hundreds of years. Eventually the patriarchs of the Bu Sing fell victim to their own avarice, agreeing not only to sell the property but also the thousand clay statues that had been part of the temple's religious decoration for as long as anyone could remember. Once the patriarchs had parted with these, Fong See encouraged them to sell the rest: a large, multi-armed Shiva with the sun and moon in each hand, and a set of carved, gessoed, gold-leafed, and painted male and female Ming Dynasty tribute figures.

He purchased all of the temple's carvings, including an arch that stood twenty feet high behind the main altar. The arch, of carved, gilded wood, portrayed the Eight Treasures: the pearl, the lozenge, the pair of sacred scrolls, the cups made from rhino horn, the coins, the stone chime, the mirror, and the artemisia leaf. Also carved on it were bats, the symbol of long life (Fong See recalled how his father had used dried bat to ensure longevity, good sight, and a general feeling of well-being and happiness); a rendering of a gourd, to remind pilgrims of Li T'ieh-kuai, one of the Eight Immortals, as well as necromancy and mystery. There were phoenixes, deer, doves, two-faced dragon bats—all symbols of good luck, longevity, and immortality. All of these purchases were packed and shipped to Los Angeles.

In early 1921 the construction of the Fatsan Grand Hotel—a modern, four-story structure in a city that had never before had a hotel, let alone one with western-style toilets and bathtubs—neared completion. Fong See conducted daily inspections of the property. As he walked through the main courtyard to the wooden steps that led upstairs to the main entry for the hotel, he could see that work still needed to be done, but it was already evident that the lobby would be very grand. A large front desk of carved mahogany had been installed, which curved from the top of the stairs across the length of the room. At each end of the lobby, floor-to-ceiling stained-glass windows cast a glow of Peking rose, celadon green, and imperial yellow. The window at the front of the hotel looked down to the bustling street below. The rear window opened onto a courtyard that would one day be cooled by the shade of large plants and dotted with tables and chairs for the weary traveler. Across the courtyard he observed workmen painting the building that would serve as his town house.

Wandering through the first three floors of the hotel, examining the heavy wooden guest-room doors with their frosted-glass windows, he conjured up in his mind's eye the Bradbury Building in Los Angeles, and instructed the architect to have numbers stenciled on each transom. On the fourth floor, Fong See saw, though he didn't fully understand, how modern the kitchen would be when completed.

A small army of laborers was on their hands and knees, laying tile. He had found a ceramics factory in nearby Shiwan to re-create the intricate designs he had grown to admire in the mansions and great public buildings of Los Angeles. Now, on each floor of the hotel, he found tilework in geometric patterns—some in a star of red, black, and white, others in ribbonlike designs that unraveled down the long hallways in magenta, puce, and aquamarine.

One sunny morning late in January, sedan-chair bearers, trotting along the raised walkways between the rice paddies, carried Fong See from Fatsan to Dimtao. As he neared the village, he saw the high roof of his nearly completed villa towering over Dimtao's protective wall. When he reached the gatehouse at the main entrance of his new compound, he was met by his architect, who guided him into a spacious courtyard. Now the courtyard was just rough dirt strewn with the detritus of construction, but in time it would become an arboretum of exotic plants and trees.

Fong See was nothing if not a man with an opulent imagination. Just as the Fatsan Grand Hotel paid equal homage to the art deco sensibilities of Southern California and the famed ceramic works of Kwangtung Province, so too did the mansion in the village. Craftsmen from across the country had been hired and brought to this small village to make stained glass, to chisel teak room dividers inset with glass etched in cloud and dragon motifs, and to draw up exquisite ceramic designs that would then be manufactured in Shiwan, as they had been for the hotel.

He paid attention to every detail. Sewer pipes—a mystery to both the architect and the laborers, and therefore exposed throughout the house—were embellished with glazed ceramic floral garlands in yellow, green, white, and pink. Above each of the windows were delicately rendered three-dimensional glazed birds reminiscent of those found in the thousand-year-old Temple of Ancestors in Fatsan. Decorative carved and enameled landscapes graced the second-story veranda. On the more practical side, this would be the first house in the history of the village to have glass windows and western-style toilets.

Fong See climbed to the spacious sheltered pavilion on the roof to survey his domain—the fields afar, the brick and mud huts of his cousins and the peasants who worked in his fields below. It only pained him that his mother would not live to see the completion of these efforts—the culmination of her own hard work and sacrifice. In recent days, Fong See had hired four men to lift her onto a long rattan chair and carry her through the village to view the house. He promised himself that he would stay in China until Shue-ying died. When she joined her ancestors, he would personally see to the professional mourners and the banquet.

For all of these efforts, the villagers praised Fong See. People liked to tell the story of the time the noodle peddler came through Dimtao while Fong See was taking a walk, and Gold Mountain See had bought noodles for each of the villagers who had gathered together to chat under a banyan tree. Because of this and his other charitable deeds, the villagers protected their Gold Mountain See during his time in Dimtao. "He is a very important person from the Nam Hoi District," they told each other. "Whenever people ask if he is Gold Mountain See, we must deny it." Every time they denied his identity—and another gang of potential kidnappers was thwarted—Fong See would host another banquet. He relished their approbation, which made him feel strong and powerful.

Today, before leaving the village, he ordered a stone carver to inscribe a piece of marble with the blessing "Happiness Is Coming Through the Gate," to be inset above the porticoed entrance to the house. Fong See also instructed an artist to paint the characters of two Confucian couplets—one stressing family harmony, the other divining family prosperity—to hang on either side of the front door. Of course, there was just one problem. Whom could he trust to take care of it all when he went home?

Fong See had the mansion, the Fatsan Grand Hotel, and the ongoing export business for the F. Suie One Company. He also owned factories that made paper goods, firecrackers, baskets, and kites. He had built his empire on the sweat, blood, and trust of his family members. It would have been inconceivable for Fong See to bring in an outside person to manage things. Uncle was a logical choice, but recently he'd shown signs of dissatisfaction with his position within the F. Suie One Company. Fong See had then settled on Eddy, but Ticie wouldn't hear of it.

A year had passed since Ticie had returned to Los Angeles, and Fong

See still hadn't completely forgiven her. He still didn't understand why Eddy couldn't have stayed in China, when Fong See himself had been on his own, selling matches in Canton when he was only seven, and had married and gone to the Gold Mountain when he was Eddy's age. But Fong See also knew that his disagreement with his wife went far beyond whether or not Eddy should take care of business in China.

The way Fong See saw it, Ticie wouldn't obey him, didn't respect him, and refused to see him as the person he had become. He was no longer a young Chinese man striving to get ahead in a foreign land; after years of struggle in Los Angeles, he realized that he could only achieve limited success. In China he could reach as high as he wished; he could use his money and influence in any way he chose. All of the things he had dreamed about in Los Angeles were actually possible for him in China. Here he was Gold Mountain See—landowner, exporter, headman of the village. But he couldn't maintain this position without help.

Without a blood relative in China on whom he could rely, Fong See decided that Ming should marry a local Chinese girl with a competent family. Through a go-between, Fong See found sixteen-year-old Ngon Hung, whose name meant "Red Face," from Nam Bin village in Fong See's own Nam Hoi District. Ngon Hung supported herself by making firecrackers. Each week she went to a factory where she picked up thick red paper, took it home, and, with the grace that came from countless repetitions, rolled the paper into red casings. Next she hammered the bottom to close each firecracker, leaving the top open, and finally she packed them upright into huge rounds to be returned to the factory where other workers would insert wicks and powder.

Ngon Hung was the only child of a widow, Fong Guai King, who was rumored to be business-minded, level-headed, and organized. Indeed she must have been, for when Fong See met Guai King, even though she was a foot-bound woman, he decided to entrust his many interests to her. They negotiated a bride-price for Ngon Hung. All that was needed was a groom.

No one living today remembers exactly what transpired, and, as is often the case with deceptions, the record is shadowy. One story is that Milton was sent for, and when he arrived in China, his father reminded him of the plight of Chinese bachelors in Los Angeles and what they wouldn't do for a wife. But Milton balked at marrying the peasant girl. He was a playboy, after all, used to fast women and fast cars. Unwilling to lose face, Fong See married the girl himself and, in traditional fashion, the bride didn't see her husband-to-be until the wedding night. Instead of a young and handsome groom, she discovered a man with graying hair who was already shrinking with age and complained constantly of scratchy skin.

In this scenario, the fact that no one mentions that Milton had already married Dorothy Hayes presumably shows that the city-wife/village-wife tradition was an accepted pattern in the family. Nevertheless, immigration records show that Milton didn't go back to China in 1921 or 1922. However, he did return in 1925, and it's possible, though highly unlikely, that even at this late date (after Ngon Hung had already given birth to a daughter), Fong See still wanted him to marry the girl. In fact, there is another story that Milton *wanted* to take a second wife during his 1925 trip to China, but that the bride-price couldn't be resolved.

The most reliable version is that Ticie was in the store and noticed Uncle acting strangely after receiving one of her husband's letters. She asked Uncle to translate the whole letter, but he refused. For years they had worked side by side, Ticie doing the books in English while Uncle did them in Chinese. "You're a good woman," Uncle is reputed to have said. "You've slaved alongside him and helped him make money." Then he wrote his brother to suggest that he renounce this new marriage: "Ticie has been a good wife to you. You promised our mother that Ticie would be your Number One wife. You can't have a better person than Ticie." All this may be true, but Uncle still couldn't bring himself to tell Ticie what his brother had done.

And yet somehow word got out in Chinatown about what Fong See was up to. Rumors passed from mouth to mouth, from store to store, with the fury and speed of those who wish harm on the mighty. Jennie Chan, Sissee's old friend, must have experienced a certain malicious glee in confronting the girl who had shown off her wealth with movie tickets and boxes of candy. "I hear your father has another wife," Jennie said. "Everyone in Chinatown knows about it." It was news to Sissee, just as it was news to the rest of the family. Finally, Ticie stole the letter Fong See had written Uncle, took it to a professional letter reader, and discovered positive proof that her husband had married again. As Ticie railed against Suie, Uncle tried to intervene. "Don't be so hardheaded," he told her. "Don't close your heart. Don't be stubborn." Like her husband, Ticie didn't listen to Fong Yun's advice.

For years the family maintained that this third marriage was simply a business arrangement. But as relatives have died and morals have changed, the family has loosened its view. "My grandfather had no reason other than his own whim," says Richard, my father. "He was just a horny old man." Sumoy, the youngest daughter of Fong See and Ngon Hung, believes that her mother was brought to the United States as a young "cousin" or "niece," and not as a wife at all. "My mother was beautiful, and this was a chance for her to come to America," Sumoy says. "She was surprised to be marrying my father, but she wasn't shocked. She had been told that this person would take care of her. She wouldn't starve, and her mother would be taken care of, too."

Sumoy believes her father regarded the marriage as a way of showing his status. "My father was successful, and he was telling the world he could have a teeny-bopper. He could say that he was still able to produce children and could provide for them. To have a wife from China and to keep her in the Chinese tradition made him feel stronger." Of the marriage between Fong See and Letticie Pruett, Sumoy adds, "She had four boys, and for a Chinese family to have that many sons is a feat in itself. But to surmount the odds"—the miscegenation laws and the racist attitudes of Chinese and Caucasians—"they must have had a great love."

And so it was that early in 1921, Fong See, a man in his mid-sixties, married Ngon Hung, a beautiful sixteen-year-old with high cheekbones and fine skin. Within the prescribed time, Ngon Hung gave birth to a daughter whose name, Jong Oy (Deep Love), was eerily close to Sissee's of Jun Oy (True Love). Shortly thereafter, Ticie filed for a legal separation from her husband.

After Shue-ying's death and burial in the spring of 1922, Fong See left China. Upon his arrival in Los Angeles in May 1922, Fong See sought the advice of the former soldier of fortune Richard White, who, in turn, directed him to the services of Mr. Ogden, an attorney. By 1924, the contract marriage to Ticie was made null and void, with no formal divorce, for it had never been a state-recognized marriage. The couple divided the La Habra and Long Beach properties, with Ticie getting the better half. In exchange, Ticie relinquished her claim on all properties in China. For child support, Fong See promised to pay twenty-five dollars a month for Sissee alone.

Fong See kept the store at 510 Los Angeles Street, changing the name to the Fong See On Company. From now on, he would go by his true last name, Fong. Ticie closed a new Pasadena store. She also took the majority of the good merchandise—including all of the best antiques from the Pasadena and Chinatown stores—leaving her husband between $50,000 and $80,000 worth of stock. She moved her family out of Chinatown to the store at Seventh and Kip streets, one block west of Figueroa, in downtown. This store retained the name F. Suie One Company.

Ngon Hung would have to wait several years to take her rightful place at the side of her husband on the Gold Mountain, although he traveled frequently to China to see her. In 1924, the United States government passed a new immigration law, colloquially called the "Second Exclusion Act." Designed to prohibit the immigration of Japanese, the law also allowed the practically unlimited entry of immigrants from Ireland, Italy, and Poland, but only 105 annually from China. While the law encouraged European immigrant men to bring their wives, who had non-quota status, it completely barred the entry of women from Japan, China, Korea, and India. Even the wives of U.S. citizens were excluded. (In addition, any American who married a Chinese national lost his or her citizenship.) Over the next five years, virtually no women left China to come to California. As a result of the new law, the male-female ratio in Chinatowns across the country once again dropped. In Los Angeles the ratio hovered at ten men for every woman.

On December 20, 1927, the American consulate in Canton finally granted Ngon Hung permission to travel to the United States. On January 3, 1927, she boarded the SS *President McKinley*. The U.S. Department of Labor's Immigration Service recorded her arrival in San Francisco on February 28, 1928. Fong Ming Chuen, Ngon Hung's infant son, accompanied her. Acquiring permission for Jong Oy to come to the United States would take several more years, as her 1921 birth gave the immigration inspectors pause. After posing as a legally married man for so long, Fong See had a hard time explaining this new family to immigration interrogators. If Fong See wasn't "divorced" from his American wife until 1924, how could he have a daughter with another woman? If Jong Oy was an adopted child, as Fong See maintained, then what legitimate reason could there be for her to come to the United States? Jong Oy and her parents would not be together in Los Angeles until October 22, 1932.

Statistics, transit dates, and immigration records would have meant nothing to Ticie in the devastating weeks and months following her discovery of her husband's marriage to a sixteen-year-old girl. Ticie had been apart from her husband before. He had gone to China without her. He had traveled around the United States, going to shows and fairs for weeks and months at a time. It never occurred to her that Suie would take another wife. Of course there had been Yong, her husband's first virgin wife, but she had meant absolutely nothing to Suie. So Ticie hadn't worried when Suie's absence turned into months, and the months became a year. Suie was just doing business, she assured herself. As soon as the hotel was completed, he would come home and everything would go on as before.

Ticie hadn't believed it when Sissee had come home, teary-eyed and scared, and relayed the gossip on the street. Even when she'd heard her husband's own words spoken through the mouth of the letter reader, she hadn't truly believed. Walking back up Marchessault Street and into the store, she kept her head up, refusing to acknowledge neighbors who called out greetings along the way.

Of course, she could just ignore the new wife. Ticie even told Sissee, "What can I do about it? It's a part of Chinese life. Multiple marriages for wealthy Chinese men are considered proper." She had certainly dismissed Yong, but when Ngon Hung had Jong Oy, the possibility of ignoring the marriage evaporated. Ticie's only choice at that point was to pack up the children and as much of the contents of the two stores as possible, and move on.

That first night, as she lay in bed in her room above the new store on Seventh Street, staring at the ceiling, the reality began to sink in. Her whole body burned—with embarrassment (how could she face her neighbors and her friends?), with shame (how could she be married to a bigamist?), and, ultimately, with anger (*how could he?*). The heat of her feelings invaded her body, and she threw off her quilts. She tossed uncomfortably. Finally she got up and wandered aimlessly through the upstairs rooms of the private quarters, then downstairs through the cluttered aisles filled with antiques. All the while her mind raced. What should she do now? What *could* she do? Was there anything she could have done differently?

With few answers to these questions, Ticie submerged herself in work. She was so busy—unpacking and putting away personal belongings, unwrapping merchandise and setting up displays—that she managed to ignore her feelings. Eventually the initial burning of her heart cooled to a sorrowful aching that would never leave her. And still she had to persist, working harder than ever.

With her keen business sense, Ticie understood that she had not only suffered a deep personal loss—she had no hope of ever being loved by a man again—but a professional one as well. People had come to the F. Suie One Company to see Fong See, because he always gave them a memorable performance. She had recognized the innate racism in their fascination. Fong See was a charming Chinaman. Customers were entertained by his wisecracks and abrupt temperament. They were enthralled by the way he stood up to them as a real man, knowing full well that he must be perfectly "safe" since he had a white wife and half-white children. Now this aspect of the business was gone forever. She couldn't do it alone, and Ming and Ray had too much dignity to perform.

With only twenty-five guaranteed dollars a month to support five people, Ticie had to focus on selling the antiques that filled the new store. Ironically, she had been given the opportunity to realize her dream of making the F. Suie One Company a success purely on the quality of her merchandise. She reined in Ming and Ray, curtailing their bonvivant lifestyle. She needed them at her side, paying their own way, helping her make sure they didn't all end up in the poorhouse. Most important, she had to act brave in front of the younger children.

After the separation, the children tried to shut their minds to their father. Without Fong See's clout and money, they fell from their comfortable positions as the privileged children of the wealthiest man in Chinatown to just kids with better-than-average looks, trying to make their own way in the larger city.

Sissee, twelve years old in 1921, was only four years younger than her new stepmother, and she tried to keep in contact with her father. She often went to Chinatown by herself to visit him. One day she walked in and he snapped, "What'd you come in here for?"

"Well, Pa, I just came in to see you," Sissee said.

"What do you want?" he pressed.

"I don't want anything from you," Sissee said, tossing her long ringlets back over her shoulder. "Shucks, I'm not coming in here for a handout." With that, the normally shy and quiet girl turned and walked out. As she left, she thought to herself, Why should I come down here just so he can kick me in the butt? In the past she might have had Jennie Chan to talk to, but as her old friend put it some years later, "Out of sight, out of mind. We didn't know how to talk or share things anymore."

Out from under their father's iron fist, the four boys expanded their boundaries. The two youngest, Eddy and Bennie, were finishing up at Polytechnic High School. Eddy was goofy and good-humored, with high energy. Bennie was taller and stronger than Eddy. The two boys had an active rivalry. Nowhere was this more evident than in their cars. From down in Chinatown, Fong See sent word: "Don't give everything just to the two older boys. You've got to divide it." Unfortunately, he wasn't willing to back it up with any more than the twenty-five dollars a month already allotted to Sissee. So, instead of the elegant models that their father and older brothers loved, the younger boys opted for speed and practicality with souped-up Model Ts. The cars were relatively simple, and Eddy and Bennie—with help from local German mechanics who built racing engines—learned how to take out heavy metal parts and mill them down to a lighter weight.

The boys loved to race. Bennie could go faster on a straightaway, but Eddy could beat his brother on a hill. Eddy especially like to outpace the police. After he'd given them a good run for their money, he'd stop and chat with them. "What'd you put in this car?" they might ask. All thoughts of tickets were forgotten as Eddy opened the hood and spent the next half hour explaining what he'd done to the engine.

While the younger boys were out racing cars, the older boys maintained strained contact with their father by helping him decorate the tents where auto shows were held. Fong See's love of the automobile had evolved over the years. He now collected brochures from manufacturers, and was well versed on all the latest models. In turn, the manufacturers had become well acquainted with Fong See. By decorating the car shows, Fong See was able to get a rare first look at the new models and then buy them for Ming and Ray. Fong See and his older sons hung tapestries, draped fringed Spanish shawls, and hauled out Dad's Folly and other bronze pieces. They hired tea-time girls in drop-waist flapper dresses, with ribbons around their foreheads, to dance the afternoons away.

Even though the financial break with their father had been abrupt, Ray and Ming continued to fly with Roaring Twenties optimism. The boys felt sure they could make it on their own. Convinced that Seventh Street was going to be the city's main artery, Ray talked his mother and Ming into taking a long-term lease for land on the corner of Seventh and Bixel, just a few blocks west of where they were now, where a twelve-story building (the legal height limit) would be constructed. The lease, which was for eighty-nine years, was to have an aggregate rental of $3,655,000. The building would cost $500,000 to construct. Ray and the architect discussed how the building would incorporate Oriental elements along the ground floor, where the F. Suie One Company would have its main branch, with forty-five feet of frontage along Seventh Street. The store's exteriors would utilize a carved marble entrance shipped from a Lamaist temple in Peking. Inside would be a miniature temple and a special room for Chinese antiques. A private patio would be designed to display garden furniture and exterior decorative appointments. The family also planned to take the entire basement and another two floors for their penthouse suites. Despite all this planning, and the fact that the news of the lease made the front page of the Sunday *Los Angeles Times,* the deal never went through.

Ming and Ticie opened a new store in Pasadena at the corner of Los Robles and Green, while Ray managed the branch downtown. Of all the children, Ray—while still accepting gifts from his father—was the bitterest about the separation. Now, for the first time in his life, Ray had a goal: he wanted to help his mother keep the family together. He would do whatever it took to make that happen. He especially liked working with the movie studios.

Renting props for auto shows, as well as costumes and props to theatrical companies, naturally led to doing business with Hollywood. Sometimes the store at Seventh and Kip would be practically empty of merchandise—everything from tiny hair ornaments to rugs to the big temple carvings from the Bu Sing temple. The first week of a rental, the boys charged ten percent of the cost of a particular item. After that, the price jumped to fifty percent of the estimated value. Often the studios kept merchandise for a month or two. Although the F. See On Company and Tom Gubbins's Asiatic Costume Company, which was in the same block as Fong See's store in Chinatown, siphoned off some of the rentals, almost every movie with a Chinese theme that would be made during the twenties and on through the nineties would profit the F. Suie One Company.

Mary Louie, the girl who'd been hired to work in the store during the influenza epidemic, witnessed many of these goings-on. She saw how Milton and Ray hung out with their gang of fast livers; how glamorous women customers came in and propositioned the boys, Milton in particular; and how Ray took the women up on it, until he found and married Leona Blade, taking her to Mexico to make it "legal." As handsome as Ray was, Mary observed, Leona was plain, so plain that she rarely allowed her picture to be taken.

It seemed that despite the trauma of the separation, the family was not only surviving but succeeding. The older boys continued their wild Roaring Twenties ways. They drove fast. They had affairs. They defied Prohibition. Often, when Mary Louie arrived at the Seventh Street store and went into the locked treasure room to put away her hat, gloves, and purse, she'd stumble over Ray's passed-out body. Mary would call Ticie in Pasadena. An hour later, Ticie would enter the store absolutely livid. While Ray held his head and promised never to do it again, Ticie took his bottles—at fifteen dollars a pint from his bootlegger—and poured them down the toilet. But sometimes, if Ray and Mary weren't paying attention, Ticie would take a bottle and tuck it into her purse. As well as things were going on the surface, she needed relief for the lonely aching of her heart.

As one year folded into another—with Stella Copeland following her parents as they looked for work, or as she was shuttled from relative to relative—she couldn't have guessed that one day she might marry into a Chinese family. She had heard about Chinamen in Waterville. There'd been rumors that some of them ran a restaurant right in town, although the curtains were always drawn and Stella had never heard of *one single person* who'd gone inside. So when the restaurant went bust, she didn't know for sure if they'd been real Chinamen or if that had just been a bunch of gossip. And of course she'd heard about the Chinamen who'd panned for gold down along the Columbia River near Wenatchee until they'd been run out of town. She remembered one old-timer who'd said, "By the time those Chinamen left, there wasn't enough gold left to fill a bedbug's tooth." She supposed that meant they were thorough.

The first time Stella actually saw a Chinaman, she was six years old and traveling around British Columbia with Mama and Papa as they looked for work. Stella could remember looking out the second-story window of the boardinghouse down to the street below, where two white men helped an old Chinese woman across the street. The woman had feet as tiny as a baby's, and tottered like one, too. "All the heathen Chinee women have their feet that way," Mama explained later. "The men bind up the feet of their wives and daughters to crush their bones and their minds. Then they always obey." Stella hadn't seen another Chinaman until she moved to Los Angeles.

When Grandma Copeland died, Stella knew that it was just a matter of time before people couldn't figure out what to do with her. She couldn't follow Mama and Papa everywhere—and the truth was that even staying out on the farm in the summer no longer appealed to Stella—and it seemed as if every relative in town had taken her in at least once. So there she was, just fifteen, and getting shipped off to stay with her aunt Cora, Papa's sister, down in Los Angeles.

It had looked as though Aunt Cora was going to have a nice life. She'd married and had a son, and they'd all moved to Denver. Then her husband got pneumonia and died. Six months later the baby was gone too. After that, Aunt Cora went to Los Angeles and took a job at Cawston's Ostrich Farm, selecting the best plumes and styling them into hats. Eventually she opened her own millinery shop. The only problem was that Aunt Cora had TB and there was no sure cure. The way Stella figured it, everyone had gotten together and said, "Why not send Stella to Cora?"

Why not indeed? Stella had been to Los Angeles when she was ten, and all she could remember was missing Waterville. So now everyone kept telling her why Los Angeles was great. She'd heard that out at Cawston's they not only raised ostriches, but people rode around on them as well. And there was this other place—some lion farm or something—where a crazy man rode around on those beasts and people paid to see it. In Los Angeles, Aunt Cora wrote, there were flowers all year round. It was so sunny that in some place called Pasadena—Cora promised to take her there—the residents went out on New Year's Eve, picked all the flowers they could find, and held a Rose Parade that was unlike anything else on earth. It all sounded made up to Stella, like some trick to get her excited about Los Angeles so that she wouldn't notice what was really happening.

In late 1920, when Stella moved to Los Angeles, she couldn't understand why she'd been so upset. She'd loved Waterville, but the biggest thing that had ever happened there was the war, and even that wasn't a big deal. Everyone had gone down to the train station to see the boys off. All the girls had knitted washrags for them. Some of the boys had come back, some hadn't. So what? Every year when school started, some kids came back and some were plain dead. Fifteen years old, and this is what had happened on her last birthday in Waterville: A delegation had traveled to Ephrata to see Rainmaker Hatfield. A leaf-roller pest was troubling the apple orchards down in Wenatchee. The wheat still looked fine but needed rain. Nazimova was starring in *Eye for Eye* over at the Nifty. That was it.

Stella'd been wrong about Los Angeles. Everything Aunt Cora and the others had said was true—the ostrich farm, the lion place, the bathhouses, the flowers. For a while it all seemed magical, and some of that magic rubbed off on Stella. When she turned sixteen, Aunt Cora gave her a patent-leather purse and a two-pearl ring, the most extravagant presents Stella had ever received. Then she won a contest for her drawing of Sarah Bernhardt, and it was all in the papers.

Stella experienced new things every day. She saw all kinds of different people—rich and poor, brown and black, and everyone kind of mixing together on the street. Every day, Stella and Aunt Cora got on the Yellow Car to take them from their rooming house for single ladies down Wilshire Boulevard to the Rose Millinery Shop. Every day, Stella looked out the window to watch for that white woman—the one with the auburn hair that was crimped and ratted up to give it height—and the Chinese girl—the one with the ringlets and perfectly ordinary big feet—as they walked down the street. Every day, Stella wondered about them. Who were they? Why were they always together? And why didn't the girl have bound feet?

Later on, she saw some other Chinese, only then it was kind of scary. On Sundays, Stella and Cora went to the Bimini Bathhouse with Bess Mayland and Ann Annette Hagen. Aunt Cora knew Bess and Ann Annette from the early days when they'd worked at Cawston's. Now they all owned their own specialty shops for hats, gloves, and dresses. They were young women on their own—widowed, or unmarried to stay independent. After a swim, they'd get on the streetcar and go back downtown. Usually they went into Chinatown, where they knew they could get a cheap meal.

"Stay close and don't get separated," Aunt Cora instructed her friends as they crossed the Plaza and picked their way down Marchessault Street. "We don't want anyone kidnapped by white slavers." And because Stella had read all those romance books up in Waterville, she knew this was a real possibility.

As they went down one of the unpaved roads into the darkest part of Chinatown, where they'd found a place to get a bowl of those funny noodles for a dime, Bess Mayland said, "This is a bad place, all right. It's full of bad girls who do bad things. I don't want to tell you, Stella, but if you touched one of them, you'd get a disease so bad your privates would rot away."

Nothing like that ever happened. They got their dinner, then poked around. They never knew what they were going to find. One time they stumbled across a festival and bought some knickknacks—a fan and a paper lantern. Once they saw a funeral, but it wasn't like any Stella had ever seen before. It was more like a parade. People carried big photographs of the dead man. Everyone was dressed in white. People

moaned and groaned like nobody's business, and the firecrackers made
Ann Annette and Bess jump in surprise.

Of course, things had to change. Aunt Cora had TB, and it was awful.
Stella did the best she could. She helped in the shop and tried to make
things easier for Cora as she became increasingly bedridden. Pretty soon,
Aunt Cora got so weak that her doctor came by and drained her lung
into a bucket right at the house. When Stella rinsed the bucket with
water, the contents bubbled up like some living thing. Cora continued
to weaken and lose weight; by the time she died, she weighed only fifty
pounds.

The next thing Stella knew, it was 1922 and she was bouncing from
house to house again, just like when she'd lived in Waterville. First she
went to stay with Grandma Huggins at her new place over on Towne
Avenue. Then Mama and Papa moved down to Redlands, east of Los
Angeles, and Stella stayed with them for a while. Then she went to live
with her cousin Vernon and his new wife, Ida, who were fifteen and
sixteen, and had set up housekeeping in Glassell Park, a stone's throw
from downtown. Stella shared a room with their baby, Dorothy. Stella
went to Polytechnic High School, and paid for her upkeep by baby-
sitting Dorothy, working as a nanny, and designing rugs.

Stella loved art; Aunt Cora had recognized that. Before her death,
she'd instructed her brother to make provisions for Stella to attend art
school. Stella applied to Otis and Chouinard. In the meantime she went
to the Potboiler's Club, which had been founded by Sigurd Russell, the
son of actor Edmund Russell. The newspaper called the place a "hotbed
of enthusiasm, cooperation and genius." Stella thought that was true.
People painted and drank coffee to all hours of the night. On Saturday
nights they held dances—not that she'd ever join in, but it was fun to
be there anyway. On Sundays, Mr. Russell had lecture programs. Once
a month, people got together and put on a play. The Potboilers had an
employment agency for artists, a swap bureau, even a newspaper called
Art for Art's Sake. She met plenty of interesting people there—all of
them artists and bohemians. Stella figured she could count herself among
them now, too.

Then, before she knew what hit her, Stella fell in love. She knew the
exact moment: Polytechnic High Graduation Day, 1924.

Of course, she'd noticed him in Mrs. Stonier's commercial art class,
and anyone could tell that Eddy See was a Chinaman, except that his
black hair was just a little bit brown, and instead of hanging down
straight, it went every which way. He didn't seem like those other ones
down in Chinatown, with their faces cast down, too nervous to look at
you straight on. Eddy didn't seem to be afraid of anything. When he
talked to the other kids, they all listened and laughed. And there were
rumors around the school that Eddy and the principal were good friends.

People said that when Eddy didn't want to be in class, he would go down to Mr. Preston's office and the two of them would sneak out the window and be gone for the rest of the day. Anyway, she was surprised when Eddy asked her out for his graduation-day picnic, because what on earth would he want with a kid like her? Hell, she couldn't even dance.

Eddy picked her up in his car. She'd seen Model T's before, she'd even been in one, but never one like this. The interior had been stripped and redone in some woven straw material that looked like basket weaving. He said it came from the Philippines. But the most amazing thing was that the car jumped with life.

"I hopped it up," Eddy explained, as the car roared up a hill. "My third brother has one too. It's faster than mine but not as beautiful."

Stella didn't understand what he was talking about.

"My older brothers, they go for the flash," Eddy continued. "You know, a Packard, a Stutz, cars like that. I can't keep track. Pa buys them new ones every year. But Bennie and I would rather see what we can do with our cars. With a little more work, I'll beat them all."

Stella and Eddy were supposed to join the rest of the class at the beach, but they never made it. Eddy said he'd made a wrong turn—east instead of west. And maybe he had, but Stella could hardly believe it, if he'd lived here all his life. Even *she* knew which way the ocean was. All you had to do was head into the breeze and the cooler air.

But Stella didn't mind, because soon the ramshackle buildings on the eastern edge of the city became fewer and she and Eddy were on a dirt road heading out to the desert. The wildflowers were out, and they were surrounded by acres and acres of bright orange poppies dotted here and there with bursts of lavender lupine. Finding a cluster of palm trees, they pulled over and laid out a blanket and opened the picnic basket Eddy's mother had packed. She'd made sandwiches with the crusts cut off. Best of all, she'd put in a thousand-layer cake from the Elite Bakery. When Aunt Cora was still alive, she used to stop sometimes and pick up petit-fours at the Elite, and they were all right, just too small. On Stella's birthday, Cora had brought home one of these big cakes, and it had been like taking a bite out of heaven—a thousand little creamy layers and just so much pastry. Now Stella and Eddy had their own cake, and it seemed to mean something, although Stella wasn't sure exactly what.

They spent the afternoon there, eating, laughing, watching the dry wind shiver through the palm fronds overhead. Mostly Stella listened. She liked the sound of Eddy's voice, and he didn't seem to mind that she didn't say much. And it was true! He said he really did climb out the window with Mr. Preston.

"I don't have much time for school," Eddy said. "I've been to China. I've been to the Great Wall. Stella, life isn't like school."

Stella said she understood. She also knew what it was like out of this city with its streetcars, tall buildings, and honking automobiles. She longed to tell him about summers spent on ranches in the cook tent with Mama, how Papa got drunk and got in fights, how people she loved seemed to die in the most awful ways. Instead, Stella kept her mouth shut and listened to Eddy's tales of Chinese girls losing their eyesight from spending their days doing the forbidden stitch, of big brothers bargaining for woven rugs just outside the red walls of the Forbidden City, of men and women who did forbidden things—thank God he didn't tell her what they were—for just a few American cents.

A few days later, Eddy asked her over to his house for dinner. Ida helped Stella wrap bandages around her breasts, tightening them flapper-flat. While Stella brushed out the pincurls in her bob, Vernon gave her a pep talk. He was that way, always encouraging her. She knew her cousins had a special sympathy for her and everything she'd told them about Eddy, since they'd married against their parents' objections.

"Things can go either way," Vernon said as Eddy's car pulled up. "But Ida and I are for you, no matter what anyone else says."

Eddy drove her down the dirt roads of Glassell Park, across the Los Angeles River, and onto pavement. Stella was surprised when they passed Chinatown and went out along Figueroa. They pulled up at the corner of Seventh and Kip, in front of a place called the F. Suie One Company. It didn't look like a house to her, and she wondered for a moment if maybe she'd made a big mistake. What if this family was a bunch of white slavers, like the ones Aunt Cora always talked about? The loud buzzing of an alarm greeted them as they entered the store, and Eddy called out, "It's only me."

Stella trailed behind Eddy and stepped into another world. The smell here was musky, heady. She felt for a moment that she might faint. Darkness cast a gloom through the long room, and she blinked for what seemed an eternity, waiting for her eyes to adjust. When they did, she was afraid to move, everything was so cluttered. What she was looking at moved her in some strange way. The rich wood of the carved chests seemed to invite her to run her hands over their surfaces. Her eyes danced over floor-to-ceiling carvings attached to the walls. Statues of gods and goddesses—many taller than she was—stared at her, some welcoming, others stern and condemning.

"I'd like you to meet my sister—everyone calls her Sissee—and my mother," Eddy said.

The girl with the ringlets! Behind her, that woman with the face as kind as you could ever hope to see.

"So this is the little girl that my son has been talking about," Eddy's mother said, extending her hand and smiling. Her words washed over Stella, so cool, so calm, so gentle. Ticie put a hand on the small of Stella's back and guided her through the narrow, uneven aisles to the back of the store and upstairs to the family quarters.

Soon other people began to arrive. Bennie with his girlfriend, Bertha Weheimer. Ray with Leona. Dorothy came alone because Ming was out of town on a business trip. Eddy had said Dorothy was a knockout. "She has to be," he'd said. "She works over at Paramount. Ming met her in a nightclub." Stella had only read about people like that in magazines.

Stella wanted to like Ray. He appeared big and sure of himself. He was handsome like a movie star, with dreamy eyes and swollen lips. But Stella had learned long ago how to recognize someone who didn't like her. "We want Brother to go to medical school," he said. "You'd better understand that right now." Eddy had never mentioned anything about medical school, but that wasn't the point. Stella and Ray just didn't take to each other.

While Ticie cooked, the family perched on straight-backed chairs set about a long wooden table in the brightly lit kitchen. On the table Stella noticed chopsticks but no forks. When Stella began to finger them nervously, Bennie explained their purpose. "We use them like this," he said, taking up the sticks and putting them in his mouth like straws, "to drink our soup." When Ticie ladled soup into Stella's bowl, she picked up the chopsticks and tried to drink her soup, but nothing came through. Everyone laughed, Bennie the loudest.

Stella felt her cheeks redden and she thought she might cry, but then Ticie said, "You boys stop kidding the life out of this girl." Stella couldn't believe it, but they stopped, at least for a while. Once the dinner was laid out on the table, Ticie sat down next to Stella and showed her how to hold the chopsticks.

The dinner was strange, no getting around that. Every so often Eddy or his mother expertly reached their chopsticks into the main dishes, plucked out a morsel, and plopped it into Stella's bowl. What could she do but eat them? No one told her what they were, and she thought it was a good idea not to ask. She liked the food, sort of. The green stuff tasted like soap, but tasty soap, and those spongy white cubes and wrinkled black things floating in a brown sauce were oddly comforting. And by the end of the meal, she'd learned how to eat rice by holding the bowl up to her lips and shoveling the kernels into her mouth with her chopsticks.

She learned other things too. They weren't "Chinamen," but Chinese. "When people call us that," Ticie said, "it's like calling a colored person a nigger." Stella wondered why Eddy's mother said "us," as if she were

Chinese too, but again, she wasn't about to ask. Stella found out that those tiny feet were called "golden lilies." Chinese women's feet weren't bound in an effort to subdue them to their husbands, Ticie explained, but because it was an old Chinese belief that they were graceful and pleasing to the eye. Ever since the new Republic, though, men had cut off their queues, and women had unbound their feet.

As Eddy drove her home, Stella considered. She had never been around a real family—a family where everyone got together for dinner, where people squabbled good-naturedly, where people cared about each other. And that store, it had hypnotized her, seduced her, enveloped her in something—what?—forbidden, enchanted. Stella knew one thing for certain. She'd never been in such a beautiful, mysterious place, and she would do everything within her power to stay there forever and ever.

CHAPTER 9

THE KIDNAPPING

1925–28

Down in Chinatown, tongues wagged about Fong See's divorce from his white wife, but during these years there was plenty else—good and bad—to keep everyone occupied. Electricity was installed, streets were paved, and sidewalks laid. Opportunities blossomed. In 1922, Y. C. Hong, a hunchback who had worked as an interpreter for the Immigration Service, became the first Chinese to pass the California state bar and spent the rest of his years in Chinatown doing immigration work. In 1924, Anna May Wong, the daughter of a local laundryman, starred as a scantily clad slave girl in *The Thief of Bagdad,* simultaneously scandalizing the inhabitants of Chinatown and creating a stereotype of the China doll/vixen that would tap into the lustful fantasies of men around the world.

Chinatown was gradually becoming more westernized. In 1924, the Los Angeles Chinese Chamber of Congress met, hoping to correct the bad impression among whites about the enclave. By the end of the meeting, these honorable men had resolved that Chinatown was a good place for tourism and a safe place for women, accompanied or alone. The businessmen promised to suppress "rowdyism among the lower class of white people visiting Chinatown," and invited one and all to drop by during Chinese New Year's festivities.

Two years later, in 1926, a teacher at the Macy Street Elementary School in Chinatown approached the Southern Pacific Railroad, which now owned the land under the old part of Chinatown east of Alameda Street, to ask if the area that had once housed the stables for the vegetable peddlers could be converted to a playground. Young and old came out to remove debris, haul stones, and smooth the land. Once completed, the Apablasa Playground had a sandbox, bars, slides, swings, and a field.

The following year a group of boys from the Brethren Chinese Church formed an all-Chinese baseball team called the Low Wa, or Chinese Owls. Although Japanese businessmen had already sponsored close to twenty teams, and wineries and breweries had sponsored several Mexican teams, Chinese merchants refused to pay up. They couldn't understand the frivolity of the sport when there was so much real work to be done. As a result, no two Chinese Owl uniforms were alike: some were purchased secondhand from the Goodwill store, while other team members bought bits and pieces of new uniforms.

Perhaps these changes inspired Uncle. In 1923, he approached his powerful older brother, saying, "I would like to go out on my own, but I need your permission." Fong See remembered all of his brother's hard work and granted him his freedom. "I will always be loyal to you," Fong Yun promised. On May 1, 1923, he opened his own store at 807 West Seventh Street, across and down the block from Ticie's new enterprise. Like other Chinese, Fong Yun formed a paper partnership with four partners. His only true partner in the Fong Yun Company was his dead sister's husband, Jun Quak. Each of them invested two thousand dollars, enough to make them legitimate merchants in the eyes of the immigration officials. Sadly, Uncle wasn't the businessman his brother was.

Uncle had chosen an "exclusive white district" to set up shop, and, like Ticie, began to rent props and set pieces to the motion-picture studios. Goldwyn Studios, which sent a purchasing agent to see Fong Yun once or twice a week, was a particularly good customer, renting rugs, embroideries, screens, porcelain, and furniture. (Goldwyn Studios had once rented one of Fun Yun's screens, valued at seven thousand dollars, for $150 a week. This was just peanuts. The studio had recently paid Fong See ten thousand dollars for set pieces for a street scene.) But the rent for Fong Yun's location—a whopping $450 a month, while his brother paid a mere sixty-five dollars a month on Los Angeles Street—drained his resources. In 1924, during the greatest boom in the history of Los Angeles, Fong Yun carried thirty thousand dollars in stock, did seventeen thousand dollars in gross sales, and lost $1,070.

Just one year later, Fong Yun lost his store due to an unfortunate combination of his distracted thoughts for his family in China, his high rent, and his kindly disposition, which rendered him weak in bargaining sessions. Yun went to his older brother and asked for help. Fong See stepped in and took over the business. Fong Yun's emotional debt to his older brother grew even deeper.

Despite Fong Yun's failure, two of Fong See's other "partners" also decided to go out on their own. Ho Wing, who had managed the Long Beach store for so many years, bought out his benefactor's share. Now the Long Beach directory listed "Wing's Chinese Art—Bronzes, Brassware, Cloisonné, Jade, Silk," where "F. Suie One—Curios" had been before. The false Fong Lai, with a wife brought over from China to help him, opened the Chinese Art Company, at the arcade in the Jergins Trust Building in Long Beach. Immigration inspectors noted that the store was just forty by fifty feet, but that it was an up-to-date place with "an immense stock of goods consisting of vases, pottery, silk goods of all description, curios, ladies' ware, shoes, slippers, wooden ware, blankets, and practically everything carried by similar stores." Fong See's "partners" had learned well.

In addition to the loss of these partners, Fong See's business had suffered a blow from which it would never entirely recover. He had been trying to achieve success ever since he had first set foot on the Gold Mountain. His dream was very "American." He wanted to make money, have influence, be respected, have a wife and children who loved him. In 1919, when he traveled to China, he could look at his life and say he had achieved his dream. But once in China, he suddenly saw his life in a different context. In America, was he really rich? Could he live where he wanted? Did he make an impact on people? Did *Americans* care what he thought? Was he truly respected by his white customers, or simply enjoyed as "that funny Chinaman"? Had his wife and children ever shown him the deference he deserved? The answers played in his head—no, no, no.

In this emotional state, he was seduced by his home country. His American dream turned into a Chinese dream. All that he had desired—respect, wealth, power—was actually possible in China. But his impulsiveness in marrying Ngon Hung—either as a business deal or out of physical desire—cost him dearly. Much of his success had resulted from his marriage to a white woman who could make customers feel comfortable. As her longtime friend Richard White said in a 1921 interview, Ticie was "the brains of the establishment." She oversaw and directed everything, and she took that knowledge with her to Seventh Street. Fong See tried, ineptly, to replace his Caucasian wife by hiring another Caucasian woman, Helen Benjamin. He paid her a high wage—one hundred dollars a month—but somehow it just wasn't the same. In 1926, for the first time, Fong See reported to an immigration inspector that the art store had shown a loss—two thousand dollars—but he expected to make it up in future profits.

With this change in Fong See's fortunes, immigration harassment intensified. After returning from a brief visit to China to see Ngon Hung this same year, Fong See found himself hounded for the birth dates of his children. He listed them all by their Chinese names—from his eldest son, Ming, to his new daughter, Jong Oy—but he couldn't remember any of their birth dates. It took two months to sort it all out. Fong See anticipated that one day he would be able to bring over his new wife. He hoped she would rejuvenate him so that he wouldn't turn into an old man.

*

In Dimtao, Uncle's household included five children, an amah, and two servants, including Lui Ngan Fa, who helped with the younger children and did chores. They lived in Shue-ying's old house. Though hardly the mansion of Fong See where Ngon Hung lived, the house boasted a big room for living, with two bedrooms flanking it. The sitting room had a wide shelf near the ceiling, used for storage. Each bedroom held two large beds built on wooden platforms. A loft had been added in one of the bedrooms for extra sleeping space for the children.

The courtyard, which housed a well with cool, fresh water, was small and cozy enough for a few people to sit and chat. Off the courtyard stood a half-open kitchen where, in a small alcove carved into the outside wall, a figure of the kitchen god watched over the family's activities. At the beginning of the New Year's celebrations, the kitchen god would be carried outside with a flurry of firecrackers set about its feet to be sent on its annual trip to make its report to the Emperor of Heaven on the behavior of the family during the past twelve months.

With Fong Yun usually away in the Gold Mountain, the family developed its own routine. Servants woke up the children, washed them, fed them. The younger children stayed at home during the day. The older boys—Kuen, Ho, and Haw—went to school, where they studied the teachings of Confucius, classical poetry, and the new ideals and ideas of the Republic.

People in the village treated Fong Yun's family kindly, because he was the brother of Gold Mountain See. But although everyone in Dimtao was thankful for the charitable works of Fong See, not everyone was good. One of Fong See's cousins was known as a bad man in the village. While the populace didn't permit an opium house, this cousin always had an ample supply of opium that he bought from bandits and ruffians who lived in hidden camps in the distant hills. No one bothered to do anything about this crime, but then the bad cousin stepped beyond the boundaries of what was acceptable; he became an inside spy. Bandits offered to buy information from him about Gold Mountain See and his family. Since Fong See was away in America and the cousin couldn't gain direct access to his family, which was safely protected in the mansion, he did the next best thing. He befriended Fong Yun's wife. He did errands for Leong-shee, telling her how hard it must be to have her husband gone all the time. He played with the children, memorizing their names, faces, and ages: three older boys—Kuen, thirteen, Ho, twelve, and Haw, ten; a six-year-old girl, Choey Lau; and another baby boy, Duk, born on the third day of the second Chinese month of 1925, who was sick with pneumonia.

People in the village tried to warn Leong-shee, but she wouldn't listen. On a night in late January 1927, twenty men—too many for Dimtao's two guards to stop—clambered over the village's protective walls and made their way to the home of Fong Yun. They chose the weakest spot in the compound's brick exterior—the inset alcove where the wooden statue of the kitchen god held sway. Uncle's family awakened to hammering and the sound of the kitchen wall giving way. Inside the main bedroom, Leong-shee and a servant cowered in fear. The bandits pushed their way past the women, calling out, "We are here for the sons of Fong Yun!" They overturned baskets and pushed aside the few pieces of furniture. Some pocketed small treasures they found. In the third room, the children darted back and forth, trying to escape the grasp of the foul-smelling men. The bandits knew they were to take three boys. "Leave the girl behind," their leader ordered them in his crude dialect. "She is of no value to us."

Ngan Fa, the servant girl who slept with Choey Lau, whispered to her charge to feign sleep. Her eyes shut tight, Choey Lau felt the rough hand of a man pinch her earlobes. Feeling her earrings, he said, "Not this one. She's the girl." Easily they grabbed Ho and Haw, but where was the third boy?

Kuen, the eldest son, had hidden under his wooden pallet and pulled an earthenware storage jar in front of him. He was completely concealed from view. As villagers came out into the alleyways to see what all the commotion was about, the kidnappers snatched up baby Duk, then quickly retraced their steps.

At first, no one tried to stop the bandits, then one man called out, "Stop, there!" But his neighbors chastised him. "Let them take the Fong sons. This family lives too well. They have too much. It is not right." Even in his fright, Haw wondered, How can they be so jealous? My father, my uncle, they both took a chance. They went away. They had to work hard. Nobody gave anything to them.

Unhampered, the bandits swept through the dark alleys and out through the main entrance of the village. They traveled on foot for several hours. Ho and Haw scuttled along, afraid to complain, afraid to cry or plead for help if they fell. Ho, the elder of the two boys, whispered to his brother, "They don't care. It is just a business with them. We must be careful." On and on they went, running along the raised pathways between the rice paddies, stopping at an occasional village to demand hot tea, then slowly climbing the mountain of Sha Han. Finally they reached the bandits' home village.

Baby Duk died within two days from the illness that had already weakened him. When his body arrived at Uncle's doorstep, Leong-shee was overcome by grief. She could not let this happen to her other sons. A letter writer was sent for, and soon a missive was dispatched to make the long journey to Los Angeles, imploring Uncle to please come home and negotiate with the kidnappers. It was early February 1927.

Ho and Haw spent the next eight months with the kidnappers on the mountain of Sha Han. As far as they could tell, these men weren't the only bad men of this village; everyone who lived here was a bandit. Although devoted to the crime of kidnapping, ransom payments hadn't made this a town of wealthy men. The dwellings were little more than shacks, a far cry from the sturdy, tile-roofed brick buildings of the Pearl River delta. Behind several of the houses were pits. In other villages, these might have been used for refuse or the storage of vegetables and rice; here they held men kidnapped from their homes in the countryside. Older men were often held for months, their half-dead bodies returned to their families only after their ransoms had been paid.

Uncle's sons saw that they were lucky to be just small boys. Chun Kuen, the leader of the bandits, took them into his own home. Ho and Haw became part of his family, doing chores, even receiving occasional demonstrations of affection. Still, they were careful never to oppose Chun Kuen. They learned never to say anything that could be taken as a complaint or a threat. They were valuable only as long as they were alive, but Chun Kuen didn't like to be crossed. To risk that would mean to risk death. Sometimes the boys conspired to run away, but what could they do? They were small boys. They knew they were in the mountains, they knew they had crossed fields, but they could never have found their way home.

During the long months of their capture, the boys adapted to village live, even discarding their own Nam Hoi dialect to learn the dialect of the bandits. Some days were even fun, like the time they all camped out when the bandits traveled to their ancestors' graves during the spring festival. But the reality of their situation was never far from them. Late in their stay, after their father and uncle had come back to China, mounted troops would ride up onto the mountain looking for the boys. But a bandit could not remain a bandit by being careless. "Come with us or we'll kill you," Chun Kuen would tell the children. By the time the troops arrived, the village would be deserted.

In early March of 1927, Fong Yun received word that two of his sons were being held hostage, and that Duk had died at the hands of the kidnappers. Although Yun needed to get to China as quickly as possible, the Immigration Service moved slowly and precisely. Witnesses needed to be called, affidavits signed. On March 15, Inspector J. C. Nardini wrote a letter to the U.S. Department of Labor asking that Fong Yun's file be forwarded. A month later, on April 15, the interrogations began. At no time was the word *kidnapping* uttered. Fong Yun, whose sons had already spent ten weeks with the kidnappers, couldn't take a chance on the inspector's investigation bogging down with further complications.

Inspector Nardini had interviewed Fong See as recently as a year ago, and had asked at that time if there had been any changes in his family, only to receive the response that his mother had died. Now Nardini took the opportunity to delve into Chinatown's most persistent item of gossip: Fong See's new marriage. As a result, Fong See received just one standard question—"State your name"—before Nardini began: "What is the name of your wife in China? When did you marry her? Have you any children by her?"

Fong See answered these queries, then added, "Jong Oy is an adopted daughter. She is my wife's own child."

"Who is the father of this daughter?"

"I don't know," Fong See responded.

"Give us the particulars of how you happened to get her."

"She came with my wife."

"Where did your wife get that girl?" Nardini wanted to know.

"She was born to her."

"How old is your wife?"

"Twenty-three."

"How old was your wife when you married her?"

"Twenty-two," Fong See lied.

"And you claim then that she was the mother of a child by some other person?"

"Not my child," Fong See stated.

"You didn't answer my question," Nardini flared. He riffled through the pages of Fong See's last reentry transcript. "You said here that your youngest daughter was Jong Oy, five years old, and today you say she is your stepdaughter. How do you account for that? You said nothing about her being the daughter of your wife by a former marriage at all."

If Mr. Nardini had thought that Fong See would cave in, he was vastly mistaken.

Fong See shrugged and said, "According to Chinese custom, she is my daughter."

This answer momentarily stumped Nardini, who moved to the crux of the issue. "Were you in a position to marry this second woman as far as the law is concerned? Have you separated from your wife in such a way as would permit you to marry a second one?"

"We've been separated for years."

"How were you separated? Through the courts?"

"It is not necessary."

"You must answer my question!" Nardini snapped.

"There wasn't any court action taken."

The inspector sat back, nodded smugly to the stenographer, and said, "Then you are not legally divorced? How can you be married legally to another wife?"

"I wasn't married legally to the first wife," Fong See answered in his most superior tone.

"In what way were you married to the first wife?"

"We just lived together."

"Your first wife was a white woman?"

"Yes."

"Do you mean to tell me that a native of this country, a white woman, agreed to live with you without being married under state law?" the inspector asked, his voice dripping sarcasm.

"Yes."

"And now you go on record as saying that you married a Chinese widow in China?" Nardini asked in disbelief.

"Yes."

The inspector tried a new tack, questioning Fong See on the name change of his company. "My wife went away and I can't help it," said Fong See.

Finally, Nardini lost his temper. "What's that got to do with it?"

"I changed the name so that my first wife could no longer claim an interest in my store," the businessman responded.

Licked once again, Inspector Nardini wrote a favorable review to the district director of the U.S. Department of Labor Immigration Service. On May 31, 1927, Fong Yun received his return permit, and he set sail shortly thereafter. His sons had now been held captive for four months.

Fong Yun was a kind man who loved his family, but under the stress of the kidnapping, coupled with his failed business, he reverted to old Chinese ways, adopting the view that children were collateral against old age. Boys were born to take care of their parents. Yes, a first son was precious; fortunately the kidnappers had not taken Kuen. But the other boys—how much were they worth to Yun in dollars and cents? He knew he would have to confront his wife, who loved the children, but he couldn't allow himself to be swayed by her. Women were nothing to *care* about. As girls, they were bought and sold, or often left to die after birth. Yun, with his heart firmly in the wrong place, decided to take a tough stance with his wife.

When Fong Yun finally arrived in Dimtao, negotiations between the kidnappers and intermediaries were at an impasse. Before joining the negotiations, Fong Yun tried to reason with his wife. "This is a time of bad famine," he said. "If we lose Ho and Haw, we will still have Kuen and Choey Lau. We are still young, and you can have more children. Let the kidnappers have their way."

Another village woman might have seen the practical wisdom in her husband's words, but not Leong-shee. During her married life she had been alone much of the time. She had done all the disciplining of the children. She was independent and courageous, wise and compassionate.

"I want my children," Leong-shee insisted.

"I can't go to talk ransom," Fong Yun declared. "I am a man. It would be too dangerous for me."

"Then I will go."

While her husband stayed in Dimtao, Leong-shee traveled alone to meet with the kidnappers, knowing that they wouldn't hold her for ransom, for all females, even after the Republic, were useless and easily replaced. Sometimes she was gone for days. When she came home she pleaded with her husband to meet the bandits' demands, but he insisted, "We have other children. This is famine time." Then Fong Yun would try to assert his marital rights in the conjugal bed. At this, Leong-shee drew the line.

"I have no time for love. I have no time for sex. I don't have any time for that. My children are in the hands of kidnappers!"

Night after night, Fong Yun listened to this reproach. He had been away from the family for so long. When he returned to Dimtao, he had expected to find a compliant wife, not this harridan. So Fong Yun did what he believed any normal man would do.

The servant girl, Lui Ngan Fa, had been bought by the Fong family when she was eight, had worked diligently, and had never asked for anything that might imply a desire for a high standard at living. She was always happy as long as she had enough food to eat and clothes to wear. She made the beds. She helped with the babies. She never argued with others in the household. She showed her respect for the family by never sitting down in their presence or eating in front of them. At nineteen, Ngan Fa was old enough to marry. Fong Yun had been on the lookout for a good husband for her, but now, barred from his wife's attentions, he found himself attracted to this young woman. They lived in the same small house; they took care of each other when Leong-shee was away. Leong-shee felt she had no right to complain; she had done the same thing herself when her husband's Number One wife was dying from her coughing disease.

By November of 1927, Leong-shee had negotiated a ransom of two thousand American dollars to be paid by Fong See. The boys were returned—dirty, a bit tattered, their hair long and unkempt. It would take them many months before they would forget the language of the bandits and once again speak the pure—to Leong-shee's ears—sounds of the Nam Hoi dialect. Ultimately, the bandits came to a "no good end" and were captured and executed. The bad cousin stayed in Dimtao until he did another "bad trick" that finally turned the other villagers against him. For the next several years he languished in a Fatsan jail while the evidence was collected for his trial. Eventually he was found guilty and shot.

Fong Yun and Fong See decided that the risk of leaving the family in China was too great. Leong-shee and her family of four applied to the American Consulate General in Canton to accompany her husband to the United States. Fong Yun also asked that Ngan Fa, pregnant with her first child, also be allowed to enter the United States as a servant of Leong-shee. Ngon Hung, Fong See's wife, and her six-month-old son, Ming Chuen, also applied for entry. Ngon Hung and Leong-shee were issued non-immigrant visas to enter the United States as the wives of lawfully domiciled treaty merchants.

On February 6, 1928, a year after the kidnapping, they all landed in San Pedro, where immigration officials were familiar with the Fong See name. Despite the rigid enforcement of the National Origins Act, Fong See had enough power to bring in his new wife, his brother's wife, his brother's concubine, and all but one child. Applications for Jong Oy continued to be denied. The little girl was, for the time being, left behind in China to live with Ngon Hung's mother.

Once in Los Angeles, the two families moved into an American version of a traditional Chinese compound—carved out from the city's first Department of Water and Power building—on Marchessault Street, adjacent to the Plaza and a half-block away from the Fong See On Company. The triangular, two-story brick building had a courtyard large enough to drive trucks into and unload goods, and there were several outbuildings.

The older children were enrolled in school and encouraged to take American names. (Kuen was renamed Charlie, Ho was renamed Danny Ho, and so on. Perhaps because he was from a different mother, only Danny Ho embraced his name, using it consistently throughout his life). Too old to begin in first grade, the boys started in an "opportunity class," where they learned English and tried to catch up with classmates their own age.

Everyone who knew Milton wondered how he could stay married to Dorothy. She was a gorgeous woman, all right, with big, dark brown eyes. She was petite and had delicate features, but these surface manifestations hid a troubled interior life. It wasn't just that Dorothy's manners were crude, which they were, but everyone recognized her for the tramp she was. "He's too nice a person to be married to a woman like that," people said behind Milton's back. "But she has him under her thumb, and he's so madly in love with her."

Milton and Dorothy didn't care what anyone said; they were having a jolly time. They lived extravagantly. Milton rented a house out west, off Wilshire. Dorothy had affairs. Ming had affairs. They gave great parties.

"Come and have another drink," Dorothy would cajole her friends. "Be as crazy as we are."

"Dorothy won't be happy unless you all have a drink," Milton would add, topping up everyone's glass with the best bathtub gin money could buy.

At one party, Dorothy was so drunk that she stumbled and fell flat on her rear end on the heater grate in the living room. She sat there laughing, and everyone laughed along with her. When her friends finally got her standing again, they saw that the squares of the grate had burned straight through her clothes and into her flesh. She'd felt nothing.

Most of their friends suspected that it was this aspect of his wife that decided Milton never to have children. Only a few heard Milton's real reason. "I don't want them to go through what I've been through," he would say when his guard was down. "It's not easy to be Chinese in this country."

Ming's younger brother, Ray, focused on his ambition. Much as he would have hated the comparison, he was just like his father. Ray wanted to get ahead, to change his life. He thought for a while that Milton would go along with him. Buy real estate. Open a club. But Milton was so secure in the knowledge that the F. Suie One Company was his that he had, it seemed to Ray, become complacent. Milton liked life in the store, while Ray had spent years wanting to escape. Now that his father was out of the picture, Ray understood that it wasn't Asian art or his brothers that he disliked about the family business. He didn't care for the slow pace—the boredom of waiting for a customer to walk in, the weariness that overcame him as he followed the customer around the store, the monotony of price negotiations. He wanted to do something more exciting, where he could play a dynamic role. Now, with his brothers married or getting married, it was clear that one or two stores couldn't support all of the families. With so many opportunities in the world, Ray wondered, why stay locked in the store?

Ray listened to people when they came in the F. Suie One Company. Lucky Baldwin, one of the great real-estate tycoons in the city, had long been a customer. Lucky's daughter also frequented the store on Seventh Street. One day she came in to buy some silk pajamas for her chauffeur. Ray had vowed to himself that this wasn't the type of life he was going to lead, and here he was, doing just what he abhorred most—following some dame around the store selling bits of silk. But Lucky's daughter had a passion for ivory carvings, and on this day she batted her eyes at Ray and asked, "But where will I put them all?"

And Ray, like the son of his father that he was, responded, "We will build you a cabinet to put them in."

Then Ray went to Bennie, the one in the family who loved woodworking above all else, and said, "Do you want to go with me and open a factory, or stay with them and be a dutiful Chinese son?"

Bennie answered simply, "With you." Eddy also agreed to help out.

In 1928, armed with a ten-thousand-dollar loan from Baldwin's daughter, the boys opened See Manufacturing—"makers of fine furniture, mirrors, novelties, and objets d'art"—in one of the warehouses of the F. Suie One Company, down on Ceres Street in the industrial section of the city. The factory quickly caught on. With the boys' Hollywood contacts, See Manufacturing got orders to custom-make furniture for Mae West and other prominent celebrities. Ray did the designing, while Bennie and Eddy built the pieces.

Ticie insisted that everyone stick together. She didn't want the boys going on their own without the security of the steady income that the Pasadena and downtown stores brought in. None of them wanted to model their business on that of Fong See's. There would be no paper partnerships here. Instead they created a family pot. The profits from whatever new enterprise each child embarked upon would go into the pot, to be redistributed equally among the family members. Only Fong See wasn't entitled to a share. He had made a choice to separate himself from the family. With the family pot, Ticie's children widened the rift even further.

While his brothers jockeyed for position and wavered between trying something new and sticking to what was familiar, Bennie maintained his usual equilibrium. He'd always relished the feel of wood, and now he spent his days doing what he loved best. From the time he was twelve, Bennie had insisted he would marry Bertha Weheimer. Now, with his future secure, Bennie followed through on his promise, driving Bertha down to Mexico to get married.

In 1928, four years after her first date with Eddy, Stella still hadn't released her tenacious grip on him or his family. She had patience. It was the same patience, the same obsessive focus that enabled her to concentrate for hours on designing a rug. Stella intuited that if she just *stayed* with the family, something would happen.

Over the years, she had fallen into the Sees' rhythm of life. On Tuesdays, Mr. White came for dinner. Sometimes Ticie would make Chinese food. At other times she sent Stella and Sissee down the block to buy thick steaks. On Wednesdays, Mark Robbins, a character actor from the movies, dropped by. He was a great friend of Ray's, so on that night there'd be a lot of drinking and wild times. Mark liked Stella and gave her a parrot, which she then gave to her mother. On Fridays, Mrs. Morgan, who doted on Sissee, came for dinner. On Sundays, all the married couples came over: Milton and Dorothy, Ray and Leona, Bennie and Bertha.

Stella realized early on that her main ally was Ticie, who was more of a mother to her than Jessie Copeland had ever been. Ticie was good and kind to Stella. Stella saw her as a very gentle soul. Ticie, in turn, had taken to Stella right away, recognizing the blue-eyed, red-haired girl as another lost soul like herself. Ticie hadn't pried, hadn't asked questions. She didn't need to because Stella could have been Ticie herself: small-town girl, on her own, lonely, with no one to love her.

During the last couple of years that Stella and Eddy had been going around together, Ticie found that she herself got lonely for the girl. "Did you see Stella today?" Ticie would ask her son. "Wouldn't you like to ask her to supper?" To her daughter she would say, "Stella's a good companion for you." Ticie never noticed that Sissee had mixed feelings about Stella. On the one hand, it was wonderful to have a friend—Sissee's first true friend since Jennie Chan. On the other hand, Sissee felt transitory pangs of jealousy. I am your daughter, she longed to tell her mother, not Stella.

When Eddy came home with his pants ripped up the back after one of his evenings with Stella, Ticie decided it was better to keep them together under her roof, where she could make sure things didn't go too far. She knew what it was like to be young, to be in love, and how a lifetime's caution could be thrown to the winds. As the years passed, it had been easy for Stella to stay the night, or two nights, or three.

Stella and Eddy continued to see each other. Part of the time, Stella stayed with her cousins in Los Angeles. Part of the time she stayed with her parents, who had moved down to Redlands. The rest of the time she spent with the Sees—either downtown or in Pasadena. These long driving distances had made it difficult for Eddy to keep up with his premed studies at USC. Stella and Eddy were enough in love that neither of them felt bad when he dropped out. They just wanted to be together as much as possible. For Stella, that often meant using the excuse of helping Ticie or baby-sitting Ray and Leona's daughter, Pollyanne.

Now, in 1928, while Leona was out in the desert recovering from an illness, Stella stayed with Eddy's mother and had Pollyanne to herself. Stella had such feelings for the baby. What a hard life she'd already had! Leona had almost died giving birth to Pollyanne. The obstetrician had spoken privately to Ray, and had told him that Leona was going to have twins, and that they were so tangled up inside that one had to be cut out to save the other one. Ray had been forced to choose which one would live. One baby had died, while Leona and Pollyanne had lived.

"I love you, Pollyanne. I love you so much. I'll always be here to take care of you," Stella cooed, then nestled the infant's sweet-smelling neck. How she longed to have a baby, a girl baby, of her own.

Everything would have been perfect if Stella hadn't had this terrible sore throat. She didn't want to say anything to anyone, because she didn't want to go home to Redlands, but she knew she couldn't wait any longer, and finally told Ticie. "Ma, my throat is pretty bad. I'd better go home."

Ticie looked at her quizzically, but took the baby and said good-bye.

Stella took the train out to Redlands, where Jessie and Harvey were living in an old shack with no windows and a dirt floor. Harvey was drinking an awful lot. Ted, Stella's new baby brother, cried like nobody's business. And Jessie, who had tried many times to have another baby, only to miscarry all except this one, didn't have the energy to take care of the child.

Stella's throat worsened. Jessie made her daughter tea with sugar and lemon, but it didn't help. Then the fever came. Stella overheard her parents arguing.

"She needs a doctor," Jessie said.

"I won't spend my money on that. The girl's strong. She'll get better."

Back in Los Angeles, Ray fretted over reports of an outbreak of diphtheria. "What if Stella has it? What if she's given it to Pollyanne?"

The baby seemed fine, but Ticie worried about Stella—the way she'd barely been able to talk, the way she'd been so embarrassed about leaving, the way her freckles had stood out on her pale skin. "Did Stella say anything more to you about how she was feeling?" Ticie asked Sissee and Eddy.

"No," Eddy answered.

"She said her throat hurt like . . . well, it was hurting her a lot," Sissee said. "She let me look in there once, and the back of her throat was really red."

"Eddy, I want you to go out and get her," Ticie said. "We don't know much about her people, but I want to make sure a decent doctor sees her."

By the time Eddy got to Redlands, Stella was delirious. Still, he had no trouble talking her parents into letting him take her. The mother seemed relieved; the father was too drunk to care. Eddy packed Stella in the car and listened to her harsh breathing during the long, dusty drive back down to the store.

"Open your mouth, Stella. I need to see your throat," Ticie ordered the girl after she'd been tucked into bed.

Stella opened her eyes and looked up into that beautiful face. She would do anything Ticie asked. She opened her mouth and watched as Ticie involuntarily recoiled. That morning Stella had seen it herself in the bathroom mirror—great globs of green pus clinging to her inflamed throat like moss on a rock.

"Get Dr. Lovejoy," Ticie said calmly, recovering her composure. "Sissee, you take the baby over to Ray's. Stay there until I come for you. Hurry along, both of you."

Later, the doctor came, burned away the pus from Stella's tonsils, then said, "I'll have to put her in the pesthouse."

Stella began to weep, but she knew there was nothing anyone could do about it. She needed to be quarantined.

She never remembered much from the pesthouse, except for one time when she felt someone moving next to her in the bed. "Stop moving so much," she cried out. "Stop that. It hurts me when you move like that." Then she felt herself lifting up out of the bed and looking down to see not an empty bed, not just herself lying there, but two of her—one the wiggler, the other the complainer. She was twenty-three and had almost passed from this world again.

After she had recovered, Stella helped Ticie, Eddy, and Sissee move into a house out west, on Maplewood Drive. Stella acted enthusiastic about Ticie and Sissee moving into what they called "a real house"— one without a store attached to it. But Stella didn't really understand their excitement. What difference did it make if the family lived above the store? To Stella, the Sees had more, and lived better, than anyone she had ever met. But in keeping Ticie company and listening to her stories, Stella learned why the Maplewood house was so important. Fong See would never buy the family one, even when Ticie had begged and begged. When she talked, Stella could see that Ticie still carried a torch for Fong See.

In late 1928, Stella's persistence finally paid off. Eddy proposed. Stella couldn't remember how it happened, so maybe he hadn't proposed at all. Maybe it was just that they'd been on this track from the first moment he'd taken her down to the F. Suie One Company for dinner. All she knew was that one day she and Eddy were driving out to Redlands to talk to her mother and father and Grandma Huggins. No one seemed to mind that she was marrying a Chinese. Well, that wasn't exactly true. Grandma Huggins said a couple of things, but as soon as she met Eddy she decided he was a nice person. Besides, why would any of them object? They'd never really cared what happened to her. Ticie certainly didn't object, and no one asked Fong See anything about it, although he did send over an immense pair of carved doors of red lacquer and gold leaf for a wedding present.

On November 17, 1928, Stella, Eddy, Ticie, Sissee, and Mr. Preston (Eddy's friend, the principal from Polytechnic High, to stand up for the groom) piled in the car and drove south to Tijuana, where they found a justice of the peace. It was a good thing that Ticie always carried money with her, because it turned out that Stella and Eddy were supposed to have lived in Mexico for so long and have health certificates and other documents. After Ticie paid a bribe, the justice of the peace asked, "Do you want the ceremony in Spanish or English? In English it will cost more."

Sissee said, "I took Spanish in high school. I'll translate, if that's all right."

So Stella listened to the justice rattle off his words while Sissee did her best to translate. Then they were all back in the car and driving north again. That night in the house on Maplewood, Ticie pulled Stella aside. She thought her mother-in-law was going to tell her about the facts. Instead, Ticie looked at her with those sad, kind eyes and said, "I don't know, Stella. I love my son very much, but you should always keep a little money for yourself." With that, Ticie kissed Stella, who then went into Eddy's room for her long-awaited wedding night.

CHAPTER 10

DEPRESSION

1929–34

THE Chinese had known hard times for so long that the Crash, at first, didn't seem significant. Those who were poor—the laundrymen and vegetable peddlers—kept at their jobs, working fourteen-hour days the same as they had since they'd first come to the Gold Mountain. To the more prosperous Chinese—who never would have gambled in the stock market—the Depression was something *out there* in the Caucasian world that could have no effect on Chinatown or their prosperity. For that reason, in the early years of the Depression, many risked opening new enterprises in the Caucasian parts of town, believing that the time must surely be right.

Leong Jeung—the vegetable-peddling husband of Mrs. Leong, the Chinese-language teacher—had wearied of the hours required to keep a stall in the City Market. With money he'd saved, and a little borrowed from other local Leongs, he opened the Chinese Garden Café, two doors west of the intersection of Hollywood and Vine. Leong Jeung envisioned a dine-and-dance place. He hired a four-piece orchestra, a woman singer, and cooks who could turn out steaks and chops as easily as chop suey, chow mein, and egg foo yung. His elder son acted as the maitre d'. His younger son, Gilbert, who'd just entered USC, wore a tuxedo and waited on tables.

In the beginning, the Chinese Garden Café enjoyed fairly good patronage, but very quickly business fell off. At night, Leong Jeung watched as his wife counted out small change to make up Gilbert's $350 tuition. Finally business got so poor that Gilbert had to drop out of school, and Leong Jeung had to close the restaurant and move back to Chinatown. Stories like these began to cast a pall on the neighborhood.

The elder See boys also had minds and hearts filled with big dreams. Undaunted by their failure to push through the deal for the building at the corner of Bixel and Seventh, Milton and Ray found another building, on Wilshire at Berendo, almost directly across the street from the new Bullock's Wilshire department store—one of the first big businesses to set the trend for the city's westward migration. While Ticie continued to run the Pasadena store, the boys closed the Seventh Street venue and signed a climbing lease for the new space on Wilshire, which, at the beginning of 1929, seemed harmless enough. It was a beautiful building, with two stories and a sweeping staircase. Milton and Ray opened a store downstairs, then immediately got to work drawing up plans for a nightclub upstairs.

Following his mother's advice, Milton continued to improve the merchandise. He turned up his nose at the "backscratcher trade," preferring expensive and unusual antiques of better quality to the curios and souvenirs that still served Fong See well. "How do you set value on a piece of art?" Ming would ask rhetorically. "By how much you paid for it? By the trouble you went to find it? By how long it took to bargain for it? By how rare it is? Art is not like a can of peaches. You determine the market. You determine the scarcity. You look at the clumsiness, the delicacy. You consider how much straw it will take to cushion the piece in a packing case." In August 1930, to prove his expertise, Milton traveled to China for a four-month buying trip.

The See family appeared to be doing well. Stella and Eddy lived with Ticie and Sissee on Maplewood. On July 4, 1930, Stella gave birth to a boy, whom they named Richard. Ray and Leona bought a house in Nichols Canyon. Bennie and Bertha, and their daughter, Shirley, settled in Beverly Hills. Ming and Dorothy had also moved out west. Sissee went to UCLA to study business.

But just like Leong Jeung with his Chinese Garden Café, the Sees discovered the Wilshire store to be an elusive dream. The nightclub never came to pass, as the grip of the Depression took hold of the city. Instead, a wrought-iron business rented a portion of the deserted space. And as customers' discretionary income declined and was diverted to more pressing living expenses, the climbing lease jumped relentlessly from five hundred to seven hundred to one thousand dollars, then into the thousands.

After so many years of living without financial stress, the Sees had to tighten their belts. Each family member continued to put his or her earnings into the family pot to be redistributed. For many months, each household got as little as five dollars a week. Sissee, who dropped out of school to take a job at a weatherstripping company, brought in the largest share, at ten dollars a week. This meant that the See Manufacturing Company and the two branches of the F. Suie One Company were clearing as little as fifteen dollars a week combined. At the same time, the family was saddled with considerable expenses—four separate households, salaries for other employees, the leases on the two stores and the factory, and maintaining the quality of the stock.

In early 1933, Ticie called her children together. "The stores have been very profitable," she said. "We've had the market all to ourselves.

We've had a luxury business. But people don't want antiques when they need to eat. I think we're bust.''

"What can we do?" Ray asked. "We're locked into the lease on the new building."

"The lease must be unlawful," Milton said.

"We're not using all of the space," Ticie went on. "We're not even living upstairs. We don't even go up there to sleep. We simply have to get out."

Having reached a consensus, the brothers all drove into town, each with his own truck. They packed up the Wilshire store under cover of darkness, driving goods out to the ranch in La Habra, over to Ticie's on Maplewood, and to back bedrooms and garages at each of the boys' houses. Within days, Ticie returned to Chinatown and rented a store at 528 Los Angeles Street, at the corner of Marchessault, across the street from Fong See's compound in the old Water and Power building, and a few doors down from where Fong See still had his store at 510. Ray, Eddy, and Bennie worked in the factory, while Ming and Ticie set up shop. To evade bill collectors, the store was put in Sissee's name alone. Like the Leong family, the Sees had gone home to Chinatown.

This move nearly broke Ticie emotionally. She had kept everything and everyone together for so many years, reaching into herself and drawing upon reserves she hadn't known she possessed. The separation. Starting up a new store. Worrying about whether the factory was a good idea or not. She'd made it through all of those things, but now, at fifty-seven, she faced the defeat of the Wilshire store, the sense that she had nowhere to go, the humiliation before her old neighbors, and her desire to be with Suie. She felt completely drained, weak, unable to put a brave face on things and persist, *again*.

She thought wistfully that if she couldn't be married to Suie, if he couldn't protect her, if they couldn't be together, at least she could see him from afar. Every day she sat in a wicker chair at the back of her store on Los Angeles Street, looking out the window and wondering if Suie would stop by on his walk either to or from his compound. Probably not. Perhaps not ever in her lifetime. Nevertheless, not a day passed that she didn't hope she would hear the tinkle of the bells that hung on the door and look up to see him. It hadn't happened yet. Could it ever happen? It almost didn't matter. She was sustained by her slim faith that it might.

Her anger at him had long burned out, to be replaced by grief, then a final, horrible emptiness. She was a ghost of herself. She went through the motions of conducting business, but she pushed Ming to take on more responsibility. She did her duty as a mother, knowing that none of her children really needed her anymore. She acted the part of a good friend, but she could be in a roomful of people and feel the deepest loneliness.

She tried to accept the hollow sensation—the feeling that there was nothing but a black void under her skin. Only alcohol warmed the cold desolation.

On an early morning in January 1934, Fong See left his compound at the Water and Power building and looked across Marchessault Street to Ticie's store. Most mornings, and in the evenings when he returned, he could see his Number Two wife sitting in the back of the store near the window, waiting for him to walk by. It was a western concept— love—but he knew that she still loved him.

Little had changed on Los Angeles Street in the twelve years since his first family had left Chinatown, but now, on their return, he saw it as they might. Looking to his left as he crossed Marchessault, he glanced down to August Alley, behind his wife's store, where the block's small businesses had warehouses. Just across August Alley on the downhill side was the Sam Sing Butcher Shop, which had been in the business of supplying pork to Chinatown's residents and restaurants for as long as anyone could remember. No point in looking any farther down Marchessault. Too much destruction down there.

He paused to gauge the merchandise in his wife's windows. The large, narrow storefront had the same dimensions as his, but with plate-glass windows fronting both Los Angeles and Marchessault streets. Ticie and her sons would be competition, he thought. Their new place had a mezzanine and a basement—both unused, as far as he could tell. Upstairs, the Methodist Church rented several rooms where Fong See's young sons attended Mrs. Leong's Chinese-language class.

Next to Ticie's store was a curio shop, but most people knew that the real wealth in that establishment came from the gambling den in the basement. Then came the Lugo House, with the Canton Bazaar on the street level and the Hop Sing Tong upstairs. After the Lugo House there was another curio shop and an herb store. His store, the F. See On Company, stood in the middle of the block and to his mind was still the most prominent, with the name of the company painted in giant letters on the side of the upper story. The Chinese Professional Building, where a Chinese dentist, a lawyer, and others had set up practices, was upstairs.

Just beyond lay Tom Gubbins's Asiatic Costume Company, marked by two large paper lanterns that cast a pale glow on the street. Brightly colored kimonos shimmered and glittered in Gubbins's windows, attracting customers. Like Ticie and Fong See, Gubbins had become increasingly reliant on the film industry, renting out costumes and props, and acting as a middleman when studios required Chinese extras. He rented the upstairs to Leong Jeung, who had just opened a new restaurant, Soochow.

The Leongs claimed to have the number-seven restaurant in Chinatown. For their white customers, they also claimed to have invented the "family-style" dinner. Wealthy Chinese families also took advantage of the low prices, using Soochow for banquets for up to 150 guests. Finally, at the corner of Ferguson Alley was Jerry's Joynt, a bar that had once housed four gambling dens, but now catered to the City Hall crowd for lunch and Hollywood film people for dinner. All of these businesses faced the old Spanish Plaza.

Chinatown had always wakened slowly. Old men were the first to rise, emerging sleepily from dark doorways. Gradually, shopkeepers would take down the heavy boards that protected their store windows. Grocers would bring out crates of onions, rutabagas, and winter melon, stalks of sugar cane, and the freshest baby bok choy, to set about in attractive displays along the sidewalk. Next, their wives might bring out bean sprouts grown in the family bathtub. Down the street, another enterprising soul might set out a tub containing terrapins or snails. Soon runners from neighboring restaurants would be bustling back and forth, delivering tea and covered dishes of steaming food to busy citizens. By ten o'clock in the morning, doors would be propped open and business begun. But this activity belied the fact that business was slow for everyone.

Fong See did not hold with introspection, but sometimes he looked at his life and considered. Now, twelve years after his separation from Ticie, he knew he had ceased to be a driving force in his first family. He was only peripheral in importance to those children—Ming, Ray, Bennie, Eddy, and Sissee. They hadn't come to him when their business had turned sour. They hadn't sought his counsel when they'd decided to move back to Chinatown. Over time, they had become closer to their mother, adopting her values.

In many ways he had also ceased to be a driving force in Chinatown. At seventy-seven, he had evolved into a patriarch to whom people came for help and advice, for blessing and permission. Although his customers still called him a variety of names, in Chinatown he was now called See-bok, an honorific title for a man of his age and station.

But at home, See-bok was the important man he had always aspired to be. His marriage to Ngon Hung was far more traditional than the one to Ticie. He could communicate in Chinese with Ngon Hung, though never about business affairs. He could tell Ngon Hung what to do and she did it—she had to. It was her duty. She understood it was her role to be subservient. Ngon Hung waits on me hand and foot and doesn't complain, he thought. When I am sick and in my final years, she will still be young and strong. And he had his new children—Jong Oy, Ming Chuen, Ming Yun, and May Oy—all full Chinese.

He ran his household in an old-fashioned Chinese way. Ngon Hung stayed in the compound and took care of the children. She never walked about on the street where single men could stare at her. She sent servants or the children out to do shopping. (Sometimes even Fong See picked up fresh pork or chicken on his way home from work.) In 1932, he'd finally been able to bring Jong Oy over from China, and now Ngon Hung worked hard to train this daughter—as she would teach their new daughter, May Oy, once she was old enough—how to be a good wife and mother, how to run a household, how to embroider, how to obey.

Ticie had never obeyed him. She'd walked wherever she wanted to go. She'd said whatever she wanted to say. She'd done whatever she wanted. She'd tried—an American expression again—to crow like a rooster. Fong See could treat Ngon Hung the way he wanted, showing off his wealth and prestige through her. Since he'd married Ngon Hung, he'd seen how pleasant it was to have a young wife. So, in China in 1929, he'd married again. Si Ping, a girl about Ngon Hung's age, was a concubine in the normal tradition. He had no intention of bringing Si Ping to this country.

See-bok had the life of a respected father and gentleman that he felt he deserved, but, like so many others, the Depression was hitting him. In 1932, he received only five shipments from China. In 1933, only two shipments arrived. Like Ticie, he closed his shop on Seventh Street and consolidated back on Los Angeles Street. For the first time in thirty years, he had only one store. The value of the stock held steady at fifty thousand dollars, but the store didn't make a profit. In fact, in the last two years Fong See had lost approximately ten thousand dollars. As he told Inspector Nardini, "Of course, nobody knows that. It is between me and the government."

Everywhere in Chinatown, business slowed. Fees for washing and ironing shirts dropped from fifteen cents apiece to only five cents. Men were lucky to make twenty-five cents an hour. Most were happy if they could earn a dollar a day. They considered themselves fortunate if they also got room and board. Even work in Mexico dried up, leaving countless Chinese stranded there. See-bok had heard that as many as three hundred Chinese a month sent their pitiful earnings home, walked across the border to be deliberately caught by U.S. Immigration officials, then allowed themselves to be deported back to China, getting a free trip home and thus the nickname of "free trippers."

By 1933, what inroads had been made in terms of expanding opportunities were dashed. Wives and families were sent back to China, where living was cheaper. Uncle's family—his wife and all her children, as well as his concubine and her daughter—had already set sail, and See-bok knew it was just a matter of time before he would send Ngon Hung and the children back to China to wait out the Depression. (Which wasn't to say that Fong See didn't have money. He had plenty of cash secreted away that he could use for buying gifts, merchandise, or more property in China.)

Chinatown was once again becoming an enclave of single men, the only sounds their low, murmuring voices, the clackety-clack of freight and passenger trains, and the rattle of trucks along Alameda. There were no soup lines, no people on the dole, just a mental depression as men squatted on their haunches in doorways, staring listlessly into their folded hands, waiting. None of them would beg; they'd rather go hungry and weaken. The Chinese Benevolent Society, tongs, and district associations did the best they could. If a man was in trouble, he could go to his tong or association house, where at certain hours meals were laid out.

When it seemed things couldn't get any worse for Fong See's neighbors, they did. See-bok found it ironic that the railroad was the culprit again. Back in 1913 there had been talk about demolishing Chinatown to build a railroad terminal on the site of Juan Apablasa's old vineyards—the whole dilapidated area east of Alameda Street, which made up the majority of Chinatown. For the next twenty years the plan was entangled in one lawsuit after another. First the Apablasa family and the City of Los Angeles argued over who owned Chinatown's streets. Once that was settled, the Apablasas sold the land to an entrepreneur, L. F. Hanchett, who said he wanted to develop it for commercial purposes and at the same time build a "Chinese colony." When it was discovered that he'd planned a railroad terminal all along, his land demolition plan was thrown out of court. In 1928, the Southern Pacific Railroad bought the land, consolidated it with other purchases made over the years, and, with the Union Pacific, began planning a terminal that would be a monument to both train travel and the importance of the burgeoning city. On May 19, 1931, the California Supreme Court upheld a decision to condemn the land east of Alameda and begin construction for the station. Fong See hadn't been concerned, because his store was in a block just west of Alameda.

Two years later, eviction notices were distributed, giving tenants thirty days to vacate; this was extended to forty-five days. The city disconnected water, gas, and electricity. The few sidewalks that had been put in were pulled up. Some shopkeepers and families moved away, but many others stayed on—suspicious, ignorant, afraid. As one man told a newspaper reporter, "We no like to leave home where we have lived so long. We just wait." Another said, "Yes, we will move on. We don't know just where. Some say a new and better Chinatown will be built.

Yes, we will move there." Since many of the Chinese couldn't read English—some reports suggest that residents confused the eviction notices with deportation threats resulting from tong activity—the wrecking crews came as a surprise. See-bok wondered how many Chinese were dislocated. Twenty-five hundred? Five thousand? Who could tell, when the inhabitants had shunned census takers, avoided immigration officials, and hidden friends and relatives for so many years?

On December 22, 1933, the actual demolition began. By the end of the month the old Chinese School, the original produce market where for so many years vegetable wagons had parked in the square and hardworking men had eked out a living, the old joss house at the corner of Marchessault and Juan, the blacksmith shop, the Apablasa Playground, as well as noodle shops, meat markets, and tea shops, had been razed. In their haste to abandon their homes and businesses, longtime residents left behind both the detritus and the precious. Tractors buried jewelry, clothing, rice bowls, chopsticks, soup spoons, fan-tan buttons and other gambling chips, cleavers, portable stoves, oil, wine and soy sauce containers, glassware, medicine and cosmetic jars, toothbrushes, shoes. Children left behind marbles, dolls, and other toys.

Overnight, hundreds were left homeless. Most scattered to the Ninth Street area, by the City Market. Some moved in with relatives or business associates living in the remaining part of Chinatown west of Alameda, which included Fong See's block on Los Angeles Street. Anyone who had a brain—both Chinese and Caucasian—began to dream of what a new Chinatown or new Chinatowns could look like, and how they would make their fortunes building them. In this new year, See-bok decided he wouldn't worry about all that.

"Come on, stay," Tyrus Wong said one final time, as he walked over to the table to help with dinner.

"Okay," George Stanley answered, pulling up a chair and sitting down.

Eddy smiled. He should have been the one doing the inviting, not Tyrus, but what the hell. What mattered was they were down in the basement of the store, hanging out and putting together a cheap meal. Over the last few months, Eddy had become good friends with Tyrus Wong and Benji Okubo, two students from Otis Art School who'd originally come down to the store to look at art. Tonight they'd brought along George Stanley, an aspiring sculptor. He'd been standing around looking dignified and nervous. Tyrus had been cajoling him to stay, but George couldn't make up his mind.

Tyrus cracked a salted egg to separate the white from the hard yolk. He squeezed a little too hard, and the yolk flipped up into the air, landed, and rolled across the dirty cement floor. Tyrus picked up the yolk and carried it over to the sink to wash it off. George abruptly stood up again, and said, "Oh, I just thought of something. I have an engagement. I have to leave."

As soon as George left, they fell over laughing.

"The way the egg went *flit!*" Tyrus giggled. "It's like a gold ball rolling across the floor."

"I have an engagement," Eddy hooted.

The more they replayed the scene, the funnier it got.

Eddy loved being back in Chinatown. There was something about it that you just didn't get out in the other world. Of course, everyone interpreted Chinatown through their own eyes. Reporters got a kick out of it. They weren't just satisfied with tong wars, opium smuggling, prostitution, and gambling. One reporter in town for *The New York Times* had called Chinatown "a dark, crowded section, hot and thick, as full of mysterious ingredients as chili con carne, and as quick to burn." The old Plaza, which lay directly across the street from the store, was "a hotbed of vivid, violent life, as fertile as Hollywood is sterile."

This wasn't the world Eddy saw every day. He felt more like Louise Leung, the daughter of one of the city's most respected herbalists, who'd gone to USC and was the only Chinese working as a reporter at the *Los Angeles Times*. Recently she'd written an article titled "Please, What Am I? Chinese or American?" She described how she ate toast and eggs and coffee for breakfast, and rice, fried tofu, and spareribs for dinner; how she wore western clothes, but her friends at the paper thought she should wear Chinese clothes; how her parents had never tasted cheese or butter, considering these dairy products an abomination. Eddy thought that Louise had done a good job of illustrating the delicate balance between the two cultures. Like Louise, Eddy also wondered how a person could place himself.

So many of the old traditions and prejudices still held true. Sure, a guy could graduate from college, but no American company was going to hire a Chinese. A few were polite about it, but most weren't. It was like those restaurants that posted signs that read "No dogs, Orientals, or colored allowed," or the movie theaters where the cashiers hung up Sold Out signs when a Chinese walked up to the window.

Eddy knew he didn't belong *out there*. But did he belong here? He was happiest in Chinatown, hanging out with Benji and Tyrus, and yet . . .

Eddy also had friends like George Wong. He'd come down from San Francisco in 1929, opened a fish and poultry store east of Alameda, then moved up to Spring Street after the demolition. He had an attitude about Caucasians that was different from the prevailing view when Eddy was growing up. "Caucasians are always coming into Chinatown to steal and rob," George would say. "They come down here and take our pictures without asking us. I don't like that. Then the Caucausian says, 'Who in the hell do you think you are?' I say, 'I told you once. Don't do it. *Don't do it!* You do it one more time, you better get out of Chinatown—fast!' Then they send us their policemen. There's one who's too sassy. He's always looking down at us and calling us 'yellow.' "

Sometimes George would act out what he wanted to say to the policeman, brandishing an imaginary knife: "You want to start a fight? Come on. *I'll* change your mind." After some Chinese guys had gotten together and attacked the policeman, George scoffed, "The only difference between that policeman and us is that he wears a badge. If he were here today, I'd say, 'Don't call me "Chinaman." Don't say anything about my straight black hair. My hair is the same as your hair. Don't say anything bad about Chinese people, or don't come back to Chinatown.' That policeman was lucky that day he got beat up. When in America, you follow American law, but if you insult me, don't come to Chinatown!"

Even though George didn't like Caucasians, he got along with the See family. "You're half and half," he said. "You don't cause trouble." George was hot-tempered but a good guy.

To Eddy, coming back to Chinatown had also meant seeing more of his father. This year, 1934, Fong See had bought all of the children from the first family matching four-door Plymouths. These were hardly the low-slung beauties that Ming and Ray had grown up with, but Eddy had read the gifts as a kind of peace offering. Then Pa had invited Sissee and Eddy to drive him and his son, Chuen, first to the Chicago World's Fair then on to New York. It had been like the old days. Eddy and Chuen—so many years apart—had ogled a robot that spouted smoke, moved, and talked. In New York they'd gone to Macy's and bought matching Lindbergh jackets and goggles.

But Eddy was at loose ends. His job at the factory hadn't worked out. His mind drifted when he spent the day running wood through a table saw. It drifted so much, in fact, that he'd lost a few fingers. Now, at twenty-eight, Eddy was making jewelry, learning from the man who owned the Jin Hing Jewelry Store, and spending the rest of his time in the store with his mother and Ming.

Business at the F. Suie One Company had changed. Merchandise now settled into three categories: one-third for collectors, one-third for movie rentals, and one-third that the family planned to keep forever. Movie rentals were currently the most lucrative aspect of the business—if anything could be considered lucrative these days. Since the release of *Broken Blossoms* in 1919, the F. Suie One and F. See On companies had rented steadily to the studios. The films *Shanghai Express,* in 1932, and *The Bitter Tea of General Yen,* in 1933, had recently brought in particularly good revenue. Ma didn't like to deal with the set decorators, because they were, according to her, "a rough-and-tumble lot." So it fell to the boys to deal with the studios. But Eddy, as the youngest son, was consistently left out of these business dealings.

How could a man fill time? Drink. Women. Work. As for drink—he couldn't stand it. It made Eddy heartsick to see his mother drinking now. He felt powerless when his mother sent Pollyanne down to the corner store to pick up a bottle, or when she was too drunk to function. There'd been that night when Mary Louie, who worked in the store, had been invited over for Sunday dinner. Ma had started the day just fine, walking to the market, selecting a leg of lamb, bringing it home, and rubbing it with spices before putting it in the oven with peeled and sliced potatoes tucked around the edges. Ming and Ray were there that night, and kept filling Ma's glass. Soon the roast was completely forgotten. Mary asked aloud why the brothers were trying to get Ticie drunk. Stella answered that it was because Dorothy and Leona didn't like to be at the house. But Eddy thought that his mother just felt left out of things.

Then there were women. Eddy had been married to Stella for six years and had known her for ten. Some days he just couldn't stand the way she nagged him, the way she always complained about how hard things were, as if they weren't hard for *all* of them. He couldn't stand the way she followed him around, dreary and reproachful. So, with time on his hands, Eddy had discovered the pleasures of a dalliance. The woman he chose was a friend of Ming's. Helen Smith had been coming into the store, covering up her flirtation with inexpensive purchases: twelve nut cups for a dollar, a chop suey bowl for forty cents, a tablecloth and napkins for eighty-seven cents. Eddy thought the affair with Helen was harmless. Besides, Ray and Ming did it all the time and no one seemed to make a fuss.

As far as work was concerned, everyone talked about Ray's dreams, Ming's dreams, but no one ever thought about Eddy that way. He had dreams. He often fantasized about the life he could have had if he'd stayed in China in 1919. He'd be wealthy, powerful, always in touch with his father instead of just seeing him walk past the store every day and watching his mother pretend to be on the lookout for the mailman while everyone—and he meant *everyone* in Chinatown—knew that she was pining for him. Eddy had a vision of life that involved art and beauty, but Eddy wasn't an artist. Oh, he was handy, all right. Everyone in Chinatown knew they could come to him to fix a broken lamp or make a picture frame, but that wasn't the same as actually creating something.

Then he'd met up with Benji and this whole art group. Benji Okubo was a Japanese guy—strange, loony, bohemian. He'd grown up in Riverside, then studied art at Otis on scholarship, earning his keep as a busboy in the cafeteria, mopping the floors and taking home leftovers for dinner. He wore long sideburns that he twisted into spit curls. He liked to tuck his collar under, and wear his shirt open down to his navel. Sometimes he wore an ankle-length overcoat, and stood with his arms crossed, looking foreboding. Now he divided his time between the Art Students' League and a barn off Alvarado where he taught painting.

Tyrus was born in China but had been around Chinatown for a long time. He was a scrawny little guy and talked like a character in a movie. He was funny, and a great artist. Tyrus lived with his father—a lookout for a gambling den—in one of the boardinghouses for single men. Tyrus had started dropping by the store, and soon Ma had begun asking him, "Have you eaten yet?" Tyrus had stayed, and they'd become fast friends.

Then there was Eddy. He had a loose way about him. He liked his clothes on the baggy side to allow for expansive gestures and to have the freedom to perform whatever task someone asked of him. He was certainly huskier than Tyrus. Eddy's hair was unruly and long, but hardly the wild cut that Benji preferred. And while Benji had those spit curls, Eddy had grown a goatee.

If anything tied them together, it was their admiration for the artist Stanton MacDonald-Wright, who had founded the school of Synchromy in Paris with his friend Morgan Russell. MacDonald-Wright had eventually abandoned Synchromy, claiming it had become stultifying to him, and moved back to California to take over the Art Students' League. The artist—who was now using Chinese and Japanese motifs in his own work—encouraged his Asian students to look to their roots for inspiration. But when Eddy looked at the work, he wondered who was influencing whom—MacDonald-Wright his students, or the students their teacher.

So here were all of these Asian artists and artists inspired by Asian art, and no one paid attention to them. Sure, some of them, like Tyrus, worked for the WPA. But it wasn't the same as *acknowledging* them. This was where Eddy's idea of work came in. Eddy talked to his mother and Milton. "We have the mezzanine," he said. "Customers don't go up there. It's not a great place to show merchandise. We could open a gallery."

The first exhibit featured Tyrus's work—lithographs, prints, and paintings. Then Eddy mounted a combined show with Benji, Tyrus, Stanton MacDonald-Wright, and three other artists, Hideo Date, Jake Zeitlin, and Jimmy Redmond. The show had been so successful that the Community Arts Association, Public Library and Art Gallery of Palos Verdes Estates had sponsored another. The gang had all snickered over that show's brochure, which praised Tyrus as an "ardent admirer

of Michael Angelo [*sic*], El Greco and the Chinese masters of old."
Next April, Hideo, Benji, and Tyrus would have an exhibit at the Los
Angeles County Museum of Art.

But they were all still stone broke, which was why most nights—like
tonight—the gang came to the store and went downstairs to the basement to hang out and eat. Most evenings they only had enough money
to make *fan jiu,* crusty rice boiled in water, flavored with a little "bug
juice," Benji's name for soy sauce.

"Hey, Benji, you know that girl, that Caucasian girl, who went to
Otis for a while?" Tyrus asked. "She tells me she wants to be seduced
by Wright. Why not? All the girls want to go to bed with him. She goes
over to the Art Students' League. You know what happens?"

"We're going to hear about it whether we like it or not," Benji said.

"That guy's so smooth. He says to her, 'God created millions and
millions of little girls. Will this one little girl be a little bit naughty?' "

Everyone laughed, and Tyrus went on, "I say to her, 'What's the
highlight?' She says, 'He wore silk stockings.' "

"Silk stockings?" Eddy asked.

Tyrus moved on in his typical jumpy style, telling a story that they'd
heard before. "Everyone knows that it's the thing to make sketching
trips to Mexico. It's only two or three hours away, and then you're in
a foreign country. The scenery, the colors, everything is different. My
friend says, 'Let's go to Mexico for the day.' I think, he's got a big black
Packard, what the hell? So we're coming back across the border and I
don't have my papers. The immigration man says, 'You have to go to
Mexicali.' That's a hell of a long way, you know? My friend, his wife,
his daughter—they're all in the front seat. We're driving through the
desert and I'm as sick as a village dog. We get to Mexicali. They say,
'No, no, no. You have to go through Tijuana.' I go back there and wait
and wait. I'm there for about a month."

"You weren't incarcerated," Benji interrupted. "You were free to
roam around. Did you sketch?"

"I couldn't! I was too scared!"

"A Chinese family befriended you," Eddy said. "They took you
home."

"Yeah," said Benji, winking. "And they had a daughter."

A lot of this badinage was to keep Tyrus from brooding about a
Chinese girl who worked in the drugstore down the street. He'd told
them how he'd spotted her in a bookstore and been smitten. He'd asked
a friend if he knew her.

"That's Ruth," his friend had told him. "She won't be interested in
you. She went to UCLA, and you didn't even finish junior high."

"I'm going to ask her out anyway," Tyrus had responded. Later he'd
gone up to Ruth and said, "Can I buy you an ice cream cone?"

"No thank you," was all she'd said, and turned away. Tyrus's friend was smug: "I told you she wouldn't be interested in you. I told you, and you wouldn't listen."

Eddy and Benji tried to keep Tyrus off the subject of Ruth, because if she came up he would gloomily repeat over and over again, "Geez, I'm hit with a sledgehammer." As an artist, you didn't have to worry too much about fitting in and being American, Eddy thought, but you could still worry about getting the girl.

Drink? Women? Work? None of these things interested Eddy that much. He loved a dumb joke, preferably a dumb dirty joke. He loved hanging out with his pals and trading silly stories. He loved to have fun. Now all he had to do was figure out a way to have fun and do a job that he liked.

CHAPTER II

MEMORIES:
TYRUS TELLS HIS STORY

Sometimes people ask, "Do you miss China?" I don't know. I don't remember that much about it. I remember a stove used to be in one corner of the house. I remember we used to hang our food in a basket from a hook in the ceiling, so that rats wouldn't eat it. I remember a brick sticking out just so in front of our house. One time I fall down there. No, actually, I'm lying in my grandmother's lap and she drops me and it hit me here like that! Bam! I still have an itty-bitty scar right here, see? We had one family on one side, another family on the other. On one side is an opening and when it rains the water would come down inside. On the other side everyone keeps their pigs. Grunt! Grunt! And chickens too. It wasn't very sanitary, not like here.

In China we didn't have baseball or games like that. We play with flying bats. You take a pole and try to hit them. Oh, we have hundreds of them at night. You whack them and they squeak like this—*eek-eek*. They show their teeth like this. During the summer we had cicadas. They make a tremendous noise. You get a long pole and that Chinese rice tamale, *na maw,* you know that yellow one? And you pound it and pound it and put it on the end of a pole. You catch the cicada with that sticky rice, see? You put it in a cage and take it home. When it dies you give it a decent burial.

My father had a job in Sacramento helping out a grocery man. In those days finding a job wasn't too easy, but my father saved his money and he came to get me. I was nine years old. We went to America on a ship called the *China*. The *Nile* was the smallest one. The *Nanking* was a bigger one—a sister ship to the *China*—like the one you guys go on. Maybe we see each other at sea, because it was about the same time. That would be a funny thing. There were three of us in one room on the boat—my father, myself, and one other guy. It was the first time I used a toilet. You know how you lift up the lid and then there's this horseshoe-shaped seat? When I lift the lid up I think, What's this horse-shoe thing? I think, You can't possibly *sit* on this. So I swung my leg over it like this. A steward comes and yells at me, "You sit down like this!" He scared the heck out of me. You know how they say "a slow boat to China"? This was a slow boat *from* China. It took us about a month—not too bad.

When we get to Angel Island, I go one way and my father goes another. My father already has his papers. He can go ashore, but I have to stay on Angel Island. The women were in one place, the men in another. I was with the men. The guards give you three meals a day. They open the gate and blow a whistle, *wernk,* and you run down these long steps and eat as fast as you can. Otherwise the food would be gone. Lunch, the same thing. Dinner, the same thing. They have that *choy*— that Chinese green—and maybe some meat, and a great big pan of rice. Eat as fast as you can, run back up those long stairs, and they close the gates like a jail until the next day.

For a pastime I had chewing gum, American chewing gum that the guards gave me. You know how you chew, chew, chew. We had these steam-heat radiators. I'd stick the gum in there and let it run down. I'd sit there and watch it, then chew, chew, and let it run down there again. It was a way to pass the time. I didn't play cards or write poetry like the grownups.

I was a kid, so they made me take the top bunk. They had one, two, three, you know? All that steam heat up there? It was hotter than hell. You could almost touch the ceiling. From up there I could watch the men writing their poetry on the walls. Some people did beautiful calligraphy. They were real educated, but a lot of them died in there. Maybe they had problems with the questioning and answering. Sometimes if they stayed inside too long they would commit suicide. They would never get out and they couldn't go home. Too much disgrace. The officials asked the women embarrassing questions. How many times do you sleep with your husband? How many times in a night? Some of them just can't stand it. The Americans didn't do that to any other nationality, not even the Japanese, because they were a stronger nation in those days. My father sent me a note and a man slips it to me under the table. It says, "If they ask you such-and-such, you be sure to answer like this." They never did ask me that question. They knew that the answered questions were fake, but it was all for red tape. I was there for two weeks but it felt like two months. That's Angel Island.

Then we are in Sacramento. Right next door is a man who paints landscapes copied from postcards. My father would say, "You take lessons from him." At the time we thought he was pretty good, but now I look back and think, geez, he was just copying postcards. A couple of Caucasian ladies live on the other side of us. Old, old ladies. All night long they are hacking and coughing. One lady, her hair is all white like a ghost. She never goes into the sun at all. Her hair is long like a witch. She scared the hell out of me.

My father is a cobbler for a while. He is a partner with this Caucasian guy. My father, what did he know about fixing shoes? He would come home and his fingers would be all cut up. That Caucasian man cheated him out of the business. What could my father do? I felt sorry for him. He got a raw deal.

So he comes here to Los Angeles for more opportunity, and I'm alone in Sacramento, sharing a room with four men. I helped in a store during the day. At night they had a restaurant. I bring bean sprouts over there from the basement where they had these big cockroaches. It was pretty bad, but I learn how to cook there.

Did I say I went to McKinley Grammar School? Most of the kids were Caucasian. I remember one time we had this spelling bee, and the boy in front of me kept twitching around. If you did that, they'd take a credit off your line. I got so mad I said, "For Christ's sake, George, sit still." Only I don't say "for Christ's sake." I say "for crysake," because I think it is one word. I didn't know that "for crysake" was bad. I didn't think it was a dirty word, not a cussword like a four-letter word. Miss Lockhart makes me stay after school for three days. I didn't know about that. For Christ's sake! I knew a four-letter word that was a bad word. But "For Christ's sake, George, sit still" was bad too? The teacher says, "Don't you ever do that again, Ty." I'm crying, going *a-woo-a-woo*. But then she is shaking me and her wig is coming down lower and lower. I burst out laughing. That makes it worse, but it's not my fault.

When you look at this face it's kind of an angelical face, but I was a bad kid. To tell you the truth, it was the language barrier. I was cute when I was small, but I didn't speak much English. I still don't speak much English. I remember a song we used to sing, "Columbia, Gem of the Ocean." But I thought it was, "Columbus, Jump in the Ocean." If we had a fight, they'd send me to the principal and I'd point and say, "Him. Him." It was an action thing to prove that a boy hit me. If the teacher says, "Tomorrow I want you to bring in a current event and make a report to the class," I don't know what she means. What's a current event? I don't have a newspaper. In Sacramento, I'd buy the Sunday paper, read the comics, wrap it back up, and sell it again. That's what I'd do. Most immigrant kids are good in arithmetic because everywhere the numbers are the same. Everyone was good except for yours truly. I wasn't any good at all.

So pretty soon I take one day a week to be "sick." I go fishing in the park. I think that fishing's pretty good. Then I play hookey for two days, then four days in a row. Finally, what am I going to say for an excuse? That I had an ulcer? That I had a headache? Finally I was absent for about a month. Miss Hansen, my new teacher, says, "Ty, you are a very bright boy, but I can't teach you if you're going to be absent every day." She's crying about not promoting me. Father got her report in Los Angeles and had it translated. Right away a letter comes with money and instructions to come to Los Angeles. When I got off the train, my father hit me for doing so badly.

Then I am maybe eleven or twelve years old and we are living in Chinatown in a community house for single men on Ferguson Alley. The men come and go. When they find a good job, they leave. We are all sharing one bathroom and one sink, with cold water only. We have a tiny room and gas heat which is always hissing like this—*sssssssss*. We have one lightbulb. We have one wash pan. To get water you go down to the bathroom.

My father is working in a gambling house. He's a dealer—four, four, four. Fan-tan all day, all night. There are maybe two or three gambling houses in Chinatown at that time. Hardly any Caucasians in there—just Chinese people and some Filipinos. It's not like in the movies, with hatchetmen.

We're right next door to a house of ill repute with about three Chinese girls. There are even some Caucasian girls. Can you imagine that? When those girls get old, they're out of business. What do you think happens to them? Sometimes a customer would refuse to pay and the girls would chase them out in the street, cussing them.

We're sharing a room with a lot of other men. We all slept on these cots, only the bedbugs are so bad that they put the legs of our cots in little pans of kerosene to keep them from crawling up. When that doesn't work, you take the bugs and squish them between your fingers and thumbnail. All that blood? That's your blood, see? You pull back the sheets in the morning and see streaks of blood. That's your blood. They eat you alive.

My father sends me to Pasadena, to the Methodist school. We have a whole bunch of foreign students—from China, from Russia, from Mexico. I'm also working. My first job is working as a houseboy for a buyer at I. Magnin. She's a nice lady. Well, I only met her once. She left five pieces of chocolate and fifty cents on the mantel and says, "All you have to do is dust the furniture and sweep up." I think, This is a nice job. Fifty cents. Five pieces of chocolate. I start getting lazy. What happened? I sweep everything under the carpet and spend the rest of the time looking at a magazine. Then I take my fifty cents and go home. She says, "I'm sorry, but I don't think you can do the work. I have to let you go." I feel like a heel.

Then I read in the paper that a family is looking for a schoolboy to help on weekends. The lady lives on Belle Fontaine. I remember this clearly because I used to call it Belly Fontaine. "I want you to help me with the breakfast and so forth," the lady says. Then she asks, "Do you iron?" "Yeah, well, I know a certain amount of it," I say. She brings out a basket. I swear it was this big and it was full of sheets. I had to iron, iron, iron. I thought, this is awfully hard for fifty cents.

At night the son comes in and says, "I'll show you to your room." He takes me to this room and says, "This was my brother's room. My parents left everything the way it was." I say, "What happened to your brother?" "He died." "He died?" I ask. He says, "I want you to stay in this room and be comfortable." But Chinese people believe in ghosts. I pull the covers over my head. I won't put my hands on my chest because I'm afraid there'll be a ghost. In the backyard they have some pigeons, and they're cooing all night long. Boy! I sweat, sweat, sweat. This is a good thing, because if I didn't sweat I might have wet the bed. Anyway, the next morning the lady gives me toast and eggs and a glass of milk and I think, Now it's time to take it easy. Then she brings in another basket of clean laundry. Iron, iron, iron. I say, "This is Sunday. I have to meet my father. Can I go and meet him?" "Be sure and come back now," she says. "Yeah, yeah. I'll be back." I never went back. Not for fifty cents.

All this time, I'm going to school. But I told you I'm not good at school. I'm only good at one thing. Art. I like to draw cowboys and things like that. Even when I'm in China, they had a drawing class and the teacher would put a thing like a turnip on the blackboard. I wasn't in that level, but I would draw the turnip anyway. So I'm at Ben Franklin Junior High and drawing all the posters for the school. The principal noticed, and said he would try to get me a scholarship to art school. "What's a scholarship?" I ask. "They give you money," he says. So I get a scholarship to Otis for one summer. I'm the youngest one there. From the window I can see my father waiting for me across the street in Westlake Park. The other students are laughing all day. "Who's that man? Who's that funny Chinese man?" I don't say that's my father, but at lunch I go over there and he gives me a pork sandwich from See Yuen.

I love art. Sometimes after class, when I'm walking back to China-town, I stop at the library. I look at the Japanese sumi-e painters. I learn if you put down just what's necessary to make a point, you will have a great painting. If you can do a painting with five strokes instead of ten, you can make your painting sing. I look up the Chinese brush painters of the Sung Period. I learn that nature is always greater than man. It is the balance and harmony between man and nature that is important.

All this time my father is trying to help me. He had been well educated in China. He could recite poetry, stories, legends. My father is not an artist, but he appreciates fine calligraphy and makes me practice my calligraphy every day. We don't have enough money for ink. I use water on newsprint so I can use it again and again. Sometimes my father sees art on the street. I don't know, something like a sign for spaghetti. He says, "See how the steam is painted? See how it looks like it's real? That is good art. You make it look like that."

Sometimes I think I hate my father. He is so strict. You remember that playground down on Apablasa? My father's doing bootlegging down there in a little shack. For fifty cents or a quarter my father will sell you a jigger of his stuff. It's real rotgut. Anyway, I used to sneak down there and play baseball. If I saw him coming, I had to drop everything and run like hell. When he caught me, he would yell, "Look, you got two hands. Suppose you break one of your fingers. You'll ruin your whole life." Or sometimes he says, "You're very skinny. You have to do something that will fit you physically." When you're a kid you don't think about things like that. You just think about ditching school and fishing in Westlake Park.

One time he takes me to meet this man who does buckeye painting. You know buckeye painting? Well, it's a formula. The sky is a certain blue. The mountain has a little snow on it. Down here in this corner is the same old tree. There's a pond with a reflection. Maybe you get paid twenty-five cents and the man sells it for five dollars. It's not a work of art at all—just a quick thing you do. You do half a dozen, then go home. My father introduces me to this man, Ingerholt, who does buckeye painting. My father says to me, "He's good." My father says to Ingerholt, "Will you teach my boy to paint like that?" You know what that guy said? "You don't want to paint this shit. You go to art school and learn the real thing. You learn how to draw and paint real well."

When the scholarship was up, it was time to go back to regular school. I didn't want to go back. My father says, "Is this what you really want to do?" I say, "Yes." So he borrowed the money—ninety dollars. That was a lot of money! Later I got a five-year scholarship. I never finished regular school. That's why my English is so bad.

But I earn some money while I'm in school. There's this movie producer who likes to go to Africa and hunt animals. He asks me to come over to Reseda and do a painting job. He has these animal skins everywhere. The seats at the bar have zebra skin. There's a lion on the floor. He says, "I want you to paint some monkeys on this panel." So I paint some monkeys. They're hanging from their tails and look like a bunch of grapes. That man comes in and looks at it. "Very good. Nice job. But tell me, Wong, I've seen thousands of monkeys. What type is this?" I don't know what to say. I'm using my imagination. Finally, he says, "Well, I like it," and he pays me one hundred dollars.

Another time, the people at Otis say, "There's a company on Hollywood Boulevard that wants an artist to do a sign for them. You want to go?" I say, "Sure." I go over there and the man says, "You see that building way up there? I want a sign ten by twenty feet." I say, "Sure."

We go back inside and the man says "We manufacture women's bras-sieres." I don't know what a "woman's brassiere" is. Chinese people never talk about things like that. My father never tells me things like that. I say, "I don't know what that thing is. I've never seen one."

The man looks at me. "You've never seen a brassiere?" He says to his secretary, who's about fifty or sixty and quite chunky, "Why don't you show the boy what a brassiere is." She goes away and comes back with the brassiere *over* her dress. I went back to school and I think, is that to keep their chest warm or what? I look at the model in art class, draw a brassiere over her, and take it back to the man. He says, "Okay, I'll give you thirty-five bucks for it." They have someone else to go up and paint the thing. My father takes me down to see it. He stands there and says, "I'm proud of you."

CHAPTER 12

DRAGON'S DEN

1934–35

SOMETIMES—perhaps just once in a century, if a family is lucky enough—there comes a time that appears perfect. It lives on in dreams and memories. It's seductive to children and grandchildren who wish they could have been there. It's a time filled with exotic and interesting people dressed in exquisite clothes, who speak in the sultry voices of romance and intrigue. It's a place where people use ivory cigarette holders, drink, and act elegant, and nothing bad ever happens to them. It's a place that's mostly found in the movies, but for a few short years it became the domain of Eddy See and his cohorts.

It began on a night in late 1934, with dinner in the basement of the F. Suie One Company on Los Angeles Street, and a conversation that is as mysterious and elusive as Dragon's Den itself. Eddy, the youngest son of Ticie and Fong See, probably would have been stirring up some tomato beef on the hot plate. Stella, Eddy's wife, would have been keeping four-year-old Richard amused. Tyrus Wong and Benji Okubo would have pulled down the table that hung from the ceiling, and Sissee would have gotten out the chopsticks and bowls. Later, as they lingered over fragrant cups of tea, their talk would have turned inevitably to art, dreams, and fortunes not yet made.

"Eddy, you should have another show upstairs," Tyrus said.

"Yeah, it was good for *you*," Eddy answered in his teasing way. "I hung the damn thing. I did the work. You guys got the glory."

"*You* did the work?" Benji snorted.

"It was a great show," Eddy said. "It was good work. But listen, there's no money in it."

They pondered that for a while. Art was great, but could you make money at it? Benji certainly didn't have what anyone could call a livelihood. Tyrus had been a prodigy at Otis, but they'd all been entertained by his tales of trying to earn a living as an artist. Sissee was still working at the weather-stripping company for two dollars a day. Stella had given up her fledgling career as a commercial artist to become a full-time mother. And Eddy? The gallery up on the mezzanine wasn't going to put bread on the table. It was like the store in that way. People still loved art, loved beautiful things, but no one had money to spend on luxuries.

"We have to figure out what people need," Eddy said.

"Sex," offered Benji. "You take the wife and I'll take the sex." They had heard this line from him before.

"Food," suggested Tyrus. They all laughed because he'd always been skinny.

Then Sissee echoed, "Food."

There was something in the way she said the word—so soft, so considered—that Eddy said, "Hey, let's open a restaurant."

At first it seemed out of the realm of possibility, but as they talked it began to make sense.

"What's the competition?" Eddy asked. "There's Soochow, Man Gen Low, Tuey Far Low, Grand East and Grand View. Then there's Yee Yung Gooey—a total disaster as far as an American name for a restaurant." They all thought about that place. The kitchen was exposed, sawdust lay on the floor, and customers selected their chopsticks from a dirty glass set on the table. No amenities, just a place where single men could get the soup of the house, a single main dish, a bowl of rice, and tea for twenty-five cents.

"There's Jerry's Joynt for ribs, steak, and lobster—American stuff," Sissee said.

"I like Sam Yuen and See Yuen," Tyrus added. Both restaurants served American food to Chinese families. The meals at these establishments were also cheap—roast pork, roast beef, soup with oyster crackers, coffee, fresh pie, and homemade salt-rising bread, all for just twenty-five cents, or thirty-five cents for a T-bone steak.

Someone mentioned that the Paris Café, a Chinese-owned establishment in the Garnier Building, had gone out of business, while the Paris Inn, an Italian restaurant, was still popular.

"What about the chop suey joints?" Stella asked.

"We won't count those."

"Okay, maybe seven good places that serve family-style meals in Chinatown," Eddy said. "We would be number eight in the city, but we would be the best. We'll have the best food. And look, I'm half *lo fan*! We'll be the restaurant for Caucasians. We'll cater to them."

"I wonder if we could really pull it off," Stella said.

Eddy went on. "This isn't going to be just another place. It has to be *the* place. We'll get in the society columns. We'll bring in the Hollywood crowd." Looking at the disbelieving faces, he asked, "Well, why not?"

No one had an answer. Then Benji muttered one syllable: "Art."

Of course, that was it. Art would make this restaurant different.

"Benji can do murals," Eddy said. "Tyrus will help." And in those sentences the boss and his helper were established.

"I'll need more than Tyrus."

"Okay, so you'll have more," Eddy reassured him.

"So, Eddy, where's it going to be?" Tyrus asked.

"Right here, Tyrus. Right here." They looked around the basement at the bare brick walls dark with age, the exposed floor joists, the huge water pipes running along the ceiling, and the large gate valve in the center to turn the water on and off. Some might have been daunted, but this group was thrilled. Benji pushed away the remains of dinner, pulled out some paper, and began sketching. Ideas expanded and grew.

"We could knock down this wall," Eddy said, thinking aloud.

"Good job for Tyrus," Benji said.

"I'll draw new menus every night," Tyrus suggested.

"First you knock down the wall, then you do the menus."

"I could be the hostess," Sissee offered.

"We'll have ice cream," Eddy said. "Not the regular flavors, but lichee and ginger. We'll find someone to make those up. No one in the city has ever had those flavors. They'll be unique to us. We'll call the place Dragon's Den."

"Long Gam Low," Tyrus translated.

The gang worked on the plan until they felt it was ready to show to Eddy's eldest brother for approval. Ming thought it was a bad idea. "You don't know anything about the restaurant business," Ming pointed out. "That's a basement. No one wants to go to a basement to eat. No one wants to go downstairs. People like to go upstairs. They like nice places, not places filled with rats and dirt."

At that, Ticie intervened. "Ming will give you the money."

"Six hundred dollars, and not a penny more."

That six hundred dollars—a fortune miraculously saved by the family during those cash-lean years—went a long way. Eddy borrowed two large marble Foo dogs from the store for the entrance. See Manufacturing made up tables and chairs, a cabinet to hold hats and coats, a cashier's desk, and room dividers, all at cost. The furniture was done in pseudo-Chinese fashion: carved designs decorated the backs of the chairs, blue and white ceramic fish were used as pulls on the hat cabinet. The kitchen was outfitted with huge woks and a deep double sink. Dishes were purchased in bulk through the store. With Prohibition still on, the area that could have held a little bar—a freight elevator that led to the sidewalk—was converted to Eddy's ice cream bar. He hired two waiters and two waitresses at a dollar a day, plus tips. He found four men to work in the kitchen—a head cook, a second cook, a fry cook, and a prep man. He hired others as dishwashers. The kitchen help would receive between forty and sixty dollars a month.

When the tongs came calling, offering protection, Eddy said, "You can kill me or do whatever you want, but just remember I have three brothers. No matter what happens, they'll come and get you." Later, when his friend told him how stupid he'd been, Eddy shot back, "Fuck the tong. If you have enough people to back you up, you don't need them. Besides, they're not as strong as they used to be." Everyone hoped he was right.

Eddy let the artists conceive the overall design. Tyrus spent days knocking through the wall that divided the two dining rooms, leaving the edges jagged so that it looked like a dragon's den. Another friend from art school, Marian Blanchard, painted the rough edges. In the end, people would laughingly remember that the most money was spent on paint. Gallon after gallon of primer, followed by imperial yellow enamel, sank into the porous brick. Again and again, Eddy went out for more cans of Du Pont Deluxe.

Benji's perfectionism showed itself repeatedly as he supervised the crew made up of students from the Art Students' League and Otis, as well as a few who worked for the WPA. The murals merged Japanese and Chinese styles and owed much to the teachings of Stanton Mac-Donald-Wright, who had said the West had to stop thinking in linear patterns. Western rationalism would never be the answer. The idea was to juxtapose different colors without using traditional western techniques of perspective to create an illusion of depth.

Benji, MacDonald-Wright's most promising protégé, created his own mural on the raw brick walls of the basement. On one wall he painted the Eight Immortals, incorporating each of their symbols: the fan that Chung-li Chuan used to revive the souls of the dead; the sword that Lu Ting-pin, the scholar and recluse, used to rid the world of evil; the lotus of Ho Hsien-ku, who had eaten of the supernatural peach, become a fairy, and lived on powdered mother-of-pearl and moonbeams; the pilgrim's gourd of the beggar Immortal Li Tieh-kuai; the castanets of Ts'ao Kup-chiu; the flute of Han Hsiang-tsu; the flower basket of Lan Ts'ai-ho; the bamboo instrument of the magical and often invisible Chang Kuo-lao. On another wall, Benji drew a large Buddha. On a third wall, a warrior fought a dragon. The way the dragon moved in and out of the clouds, with each scale perfectly rendered, was reminiscent of MacDonald-Wright's WPA-sponsored mural in the Santa Monica Library.

Benji drew the outlines and his helpers filled them in. He was a fine colorist and the pigments glowed like jewels, but Benji was also finicky and stubborn. At the end of the day he would shout, "No, no. Not like that. Paint it out. Tomorrow we start over." The next day, Benji would once again carefully draw the outlines of the Immortals, and his helpers would try to satisfy him. No one except Tyrus had the nerve to cross Benji.

"Geez, I know the Immortals have long earlobes, but these are *very* long."

The next day the lobes would be drawn in even longer.

"Geez, I know the Eight Immortals have hair coming out of their nostrils and ears as a sign of longevity, but those are bushes."

In response, Benji directed his minions to paint each hair in separate, long, perfect curls.

Dragon's Den opened on February 1, 1935, to immediate acclaim. Los Angeles was still a relatively small city, and word of mouth traveled quickly. The arty crowd came to see the murals. Those who cared about food came to sample the "authentic" fare. Eddy served "family-style" meals, a concept still quite novel in America. Until the mid-1930s, Chinese restaurants were universally known as "chop suey joints," and all Chinese food was called chop suey. At Dragon's Den, a party could order an entire meal for fifty cents, seventy-five cents, or a dollar per person. The inexpensive dinner comprised soup, chow mein, Chinese peas with *char siu,* egg foo yung, fried shrimp, and rice. Prices for à la carte dishes were based on the size of the serving bowls of almond duck, sweet and sour pork, and soy-sauce chicken. These Americanized Chinese dishes—tame by today's standards—were exotic and adventurous in the thirties. (But, as did most other restaurants in Chinatown, Eddy provided a separate menu printed in Chinese that listed more-authentic dishes, at more-authentic prices.)

The restaurant was hot, and that brought in the Hollywood crowd. On any given night, Sidney Greenstreet and Peter Lorre could be found at a back table dining together. Already those names meant something—mystery, adventure, a walk on the seamy side of life. But it wasn't Casablanca. There was no search for a black bird. These celluloid images would come later. Walt Disney might be at another table with his entourage. Walt Disney—what an odd image *that* conjures up. But he was a man at the top of his form. So in our memories Disney must have had some other aspect to his character—not the all-American family-entertainment man, but a man who would go to Chinatown, step down into a dark basement, and treat a table of friends and colleagues to a fifty-cents-a-person family-style dinner of soup, almond duck, fried shrimp, and egg foo yung.

Between tables dotted with the well-known were others, aspiring artists who were mad about everything Chinese. To them, the See family seemed like a *force.* Dragon's Den *was* art in Los Angeles. Others—the men and women who created illusion in Hollywood—came as part of their work. There were directors, producers, cameramen, costume designers, set designers, and set decorators. Upstairs, Milton and Ticie spent the day with them as they searched for authentic pieces to use in films. At dusk, Ticie would say, "Ming, they've been here so long. Why don't you take them downstairs for a good Chinese meal?" And of course he would, because, skeptical as Ming had been, there was nothing like success, and the waiting line that wound up Marchessault and around the block onto Los Angeles Street bespoke success. This was good news to all of the Sees, for even now everything still went into the family pot—whether it was from the store, the factory, or the restaurant. As the Depression wore on, Dragon's Den supported a total of five separate households.

To a different world the "different" came. Dragon's Den became a haven for homosexual men and women. What other place in the city would accept them the way that Eddy and Sissee and Tyrus and Benji could? Who else would take them in, treat them with joshing respect, allow the individual preference?

No one ever took a photograph of the interior of Dragon's Den—or if any were taken, they haven't survived—and only in municipal archives do photographs of the exterior even exist. They show a brick building sloping down a hill, with the characters for "Dragon's Den"—in Chinese and English—painted by Tyrus Wong along the side. But the rest—the murals, the people, the food—live only in a handful of memories tinted by nostalgia. Beyond these images of the concrete are the more ephemeral feelings imprinted on patrons of golden evenings, of love and mystery, of the conviction that they were *in the world.* In one sense, these perceptions are absolutely valid. In another, they are pure fantasy, illusions created by the camera of the mind, for just under the surface of this romantic façade a marriage threatened to fall apart.

When Stella had married Eddy, she'd thought her life would change. Then the Depression reversed the family's fortunes. Instead of having a career or servants, traveling, dressing up, or going to nightclubs, Stella spent her days and nights on Maplewood. She worked hard to be a good mother, but it was a thankless job. She'd washed Richard's diapers by hand with Fels Naphtha soap the way Grandma Copeland had taught her. She'd knitted and crocheted sweaters, hats, and blankets for him. As he'd grown older, Stella had sacrificed her love of art to spend hours with her son cutting out pictures from magazines with pinking shears and gluing them onto paper.

Stella had done what they told you to do in magazines, things she saw other mothers do. She'd stayed with Richard all the time. She'd been there when he woke up, when he got dressed, when he ate. She'd walked him to kindergarten and suffered when he cried every single day. She'd checked to see if he'd gone to the bathroom. She'd made sure he took his medicines for his allergies and asthma. Wasn't that what mothers were supposed to do? Be with their children?

Still, she only had to look at others to see her own lack. Ticie adored the boy. The two of them would sit together in the kitchen, and Ticie would slather thick slabs of butter on crackers or toast, and Richard would dreamily eat them. Even Sissee, a spinster, was better at mothering than Stella was. She knew how to scold without hitting. She was stern without yelling. Once, when Richard said something naughty to his grandmother, Sissee took him aside and said, calmly but sternly, "Don't speak that way to Grandma ever again." He didn't.

Why did one child, one husband, and no job create such a crushing burden for Stella? Because she had already been crushed by her childhood, by parents who had neglected her, by the lack of a formal education when she was such a bright and gifted artist. Because her hopes, her expectations, her dreams had been crushed. Because she spent her days in a hot little bungalow, crushed by a never-ending series of chores—washing and ironing for five, cooking for five, cleaning for five—with only a sickly child for company while all the time she thought her husband and mother- and sister-in-law were out and about having fun.

Stella had found solace in food, especially white food. It soothed her to have tapioca pudding, mashed potatoes, or thick buttermilk slip down her throat. The weight she'd gained when she was pregnant with Richard had never melted off as the baby books said it should. Instead it had grown—from 112 to 130, to 140, until she hit 154 pounds. If she ate like this, she must have been terribly unhappy. She also must have known that she was driving her husband away. When the doctor told Stella that she was pregnant again, she was momentarily happy. Then life—not surprisingly—conspired against her in the form of the outright knowledge of Helen Smith.

On February 15, 1935, two weeks after Dragon's Den opened, Stella stood on the screened porch of the house at Maplewood Drive, sorting through the clothes to get them ready to wash. It was an unseasonably hot day in Los Angeles, and the muggy weather worsened Stella's morning sickness. As she separated the whites from the colors, she fought her nausea by letting her mind drift from her chore. She gazed out at the lawns and swaying palm trees that lined the street. Absentmindedly she reached her hand down into the toes of socks and pulled them right side out or plucked bits of string, rocks, and other forgotten doodads from her son's pants pockets.

She was calmly working this way, repeating her simple task with her husband's pants—a receipt in this pocket, some coins in that—when she pulled out a piece of stationery folded over and over again into tiny squares. A feeling of dread crept over her. Somehow she knew what it would be, as she unfolded the paper crease by crease.

"Hello Ol' Precious," the note began. "How's my valentine today? Thanks for the call. I answered quickly because my husband was home this a.m. Please let me hear from you later today. Hate to miss my call. Just in a happy mood since you made me so happy yesterday. Once a week means a heap to me. Perhaps you already know. Bye ol' sweet. Expect call about 5:30 or 6:00." The note was unsigned.

Stella started to scream. Her legs collapsed. Her heart broke. Her tears ran. Sissee and Ticie came running to the porch. "Are you all right? Is it the baby?" Stella tried to speak, but her voice was choked with sobs. She handed Sissee the note, and watched as her sister-in-law read the words. Sissee, who had long ago overcome her childish jealousy of Stella and had become her closest friend, set her mouth in a grim line. Her brother, Eddy, whom she loved the most of all of her brothers, had deceived them all. Ticie shook her head, her eyes filling with tears. That her son had hurt Stella—Ticie's soul-daughter—was almost more than she could bear.

Sissee tried to pull Stella together. "Who do you think this woman is? Do we know her?"

"Helen Smith," Stella said, and Sissee knew immediately that her sister-in-law was right.

How is it that a woman often knows exactly who her husband is fooling around with? Is it woman's intuition? Is it that she perceives some lack in herself and recognizes it in the other woman? Is it that she senses a subtle tone in her husband's voice when he talks about the woman in question, or is it the peculiar silence that falls over conversation when that woman's name comes up? For Stella, it was a little of all of these things, and in the months ahead she would berate herself over and over for not saying or doing something sooner.

Helen Smith, like so many of the better customers, liked to hang around the store. Only instead of spending time with Ticie, she seemed to prefer to linger at Eddy's jewelry table. She asked him to make her picture frames. People always asked Eddy to make things, so this hadn't seemed strange to Stella. Nor had she thought twice about it when Eddy went up to the Smith house to deliver the frames. That was what all the boys did.

This past Christmas, Stella had sent a doll to Helen's daughter in appreciation for her parents' patronage, and Ticie and Sissee had sent the Smiths a teapot. The thank-you note from Mrs. Smith was predictable: "The teapot is just precious and matches beautifully with our other pewter. We shall think of you both whenever we use it. Thanks just heaps and heaps." Stella's letter from the daughter was quite different in tone. "You stupid fool," it began. At that point Stella could have done a lot of things—spoken to Helen or shown the note to Eddy; instead she chose to dismiss the episode—the girl obviously had problems.

But when Stella saw that note in Eddy's pocket, all of the signs that she'd ignored suddenly coalesced. One memory in particular gnawed at her. Though Dragon's Den had only been open two weeks, the Smiths were already regular customers. One night when Stella was down at the restaurant, Helen had had too much to drink. Stella had taken her upstairs to the store and let her lie down on a cot in the back. As Stella slipped off Helen's high heels, the woman had made the strangest comment: "Why does your husband always have holes in his socks?"

Stella had passed it off as too much alcohol, and had gone back downstairs to get Mr. Smith. On the way back upstairs he had goosed Stella, which had completely startled her. Still, she'd stayed with Helen until she felt better. Now, sitting with her sister- and mother-in-law, Stella poured out all of this. "How could I have been so stupid? How could I have taken care of that woman while all the time she was fooling around with Eddy?"

"We're going over there right now," Sissee said. "We'll tell that Mrs. Smith what's what."

They drove to the Smith house, which perched on a hillside sheltered by eucalyptus and hedged by lantana. Helen Smith must have seen them drive up, for she stood at the top of the stairs and ordered them not to come any farther. "Mr. Smith is sick," she said. "Don't make any noise. Go away."

Stella screamed, "I don't care if he's sick, you bitch!" She wanted to run up the stairs and, in the phrase of the day, "scratch Helen's eyes out."

But with Helen standing above them like that—so in control—and cowed by the thought that there was a man in the house, Sissee held Stella back. "Come on," she said, "we'd better get out of here." Stella continued to yell and struggled against Sissee as Helen Smith disappeared back into the house. Finally, Sissee dragged Stella back to the car.

The house on Maplewood Drive must surely have seemed small that night. Ticie and Sissee in one room; Richard, not yet five, in another; and Stella and Eddy having it out in the living room. He promised he would never see Helen again if Stella forgave him. Soon after, Helen Smith—rather indiscreetly, it must be assumed—went to the store. Bennie chased her out, yelling, "And don't you ever come back!"

In those first few weeks after discovering the affair, Stella didn't know what to do, except she knew she didn't want to have her baby. She went to Ticie and Sissee, and told them, "I don't want Eddy to think I'm having the baby just so I can keep him." Her regular doctor wouldn't perform an abortion, but he told her where to go. It was a desperate move, but Stella made it.

For all of them—especially Tyrus—Dragon's Den combined art with money. After graduating from Otis, he'd worked for the WPA, doing paintings in public places, and got the odd commission, but that was it. At Dragon's Den, he'd been able to work on the murals and design the menus and matchbook covers. Though Eddy didn't pay him for that, Tyrus did earn money as a waiter. He always seemed to take a light-hearted view of things.

As customers came and went, Tyrus saw stories unfolding, most of them funny—like the time when, while bringing a pot of soup to a customer, he looked up to see a rat running across one of the ceiling pipes. Just as the thought passed through his mind—*If that rat falls in the soup, that will be really something!*—the creature disappeared. Tyrus began ladling the soup. The customer suddenly screamed, "A rat just ran across my foot!" Tyrus looked at her calmly and said, "No, we don't have any rats *here*. But we do have a nice little kitty. That's why we don't have rats." And even as he said it, he knew it would make a good story.

But Tyrus was lonely.

One day Eddy said to Tyrus, "We're running a little short of help. Didn't that Ruth work over at Soochow for a while? Do you think she'd be interested?"

Tyrus practically beamed. "I'll find out."

Tyrus went up the street, climbed the stairs to Soochow, and asked Mrs. Leong if he could speak with Gilbert. When his friend came out, Tyrus asked, "Do you have Ruth's phone number?"

He called her up and asked if she'd like a job. "Sure," Ruth said. "I'll come down." Then Ruth, too, became part of the gang. Tyrus could be with her every night without having to ask her out. He could joke with her about customers without trying to impress her with "intelligent" conversation. Between them, they got good tips, which they split.

One night after closing, Tyrus finally got up his nerve. "Would you like to see *David Copperfield*?"

"Sure," she said.

Afterwards they stopped for a bite to eat. He told her his best stories. Ruth laughed at all the right parts, then it was her turn. Back in China, her grandfather, a woodcarver for temples, couldn't make a living during the famine. "One day he walked my mother to the harbor," Ruth began. "He told her, 'You're going to the Gold Mountain with your auntie. She'll take care of you, and you'll have rice every day.' When she got on board, she didn't see her auntie anywhere, and when my mother arrived in San Francisco, she heard the broker say, 'She's too small. We can't use her.' "

Ruth recounted how her mother, instead of a life of prostitution, found shelter at the Cameron House, where she learned needlework and English. She stayed there until she married a preacher who interpreted for people hiring Chinese laborers. "She was seventeen and my father was thirty-four," Ruth continued. After the San Francisco earthquake, the family packed up a wagon and moved south to Santa Barbara, then to Bakersfield, where Ruth's father became a farmer.

"I was in the third grade when my best friend stopped talking to me because I was Chinese," Ruth told Tyrus. After college, and before working in the drugstore and at Dragon's Den, she'd been a secretary for Y. C. Hong, the lawyer. "He told me you can fight discrimination in a diplomatic way. When you do things in a soft way, you make the other people believe they've thought up something to do for you, when actually you're directing them."

Later, Ruth discussed the role of a wife. "I grew up in a family of women who worked," she said. "My mother was a midwife and took care of the children of people who worked in the fields, and my sisters have always helped their husbands at their jobs."

After this first official date, things moved quickly. Tyrus visited Ruth's family in Bakersfield, where he sometimes helped them pick vegetables. They seemed to like Tyrus even though he was penniless and appeared to be without a future. They gave him a tiny duckling for Easter, raised it for him, and slaughtered it to make a fine meal. But when Ruth's sister presented the dish, Tyrus grew glum. "I can't eat it, you know? It would be like eating my own baby." They may have thought him foolish and sentimental. But they liked him just the same.

Ruth decided their wedding should be a family affair. Eddy, Sissee, and all the rest of the Dragon's Den gang weren't invited. Instead of moping with hurt feelings (of which there were plenty), Benji and Eddy drove out to Bakersfield in the middle of the night and banged on the windows of the wedding chamber. Finally, Tyrus came out. "Of all the goddamn nerve!" he said in usual movie-dialogue way. "You could wait a day or two. Geez!" Benji and Eddy just laughed and kept up their raucous noise.

In June, 1935, Stella received an anonymous typed letter at the bungalow on Maplewood: "Do you know your husband and girlfriend have been and are still seeing each other? They will deny it and lie as they did before, but I know this for a fact. It may not make any difference to you, for you seem to put up with most anything."

Stella had not survived rheumatic fever, smallpox, and diphtheria to let her life be ruined by an unfaithful man. Stella was a survivor. She got on a streetcar and went to the home of Helen Smith's parents. "Please tell your daughter to leave my husband alone," Stella said. "I love my husband very much, and we have a son. We need Eddy, and Helen already has a husband." Helen's parents listened, and she went home feeling that she had done something positive. Of course Eddy went through the roof when he heard about it.

As summer wore on, Stella took comfort from Elsie Robinson's "Listen World" column in the paper, marking sentences that seemed pertinent. "We can spend our days in the midst of excitement—have countless things happen to us and all around us—and yet remain as ignorant as turnips," Elsie wrote. "Turnips also are born, live and die, yet remain total dumbbells; and many humans remain equally dumb, for the same reason as the turnip. . . . You can't learn about living unless you live. You can't live unless you take a chance; and your living is limited by the chances you take." On another day, Elsie seemed to be writing directly to Stella: "Love is always worthwhile, no matter what it costs. . . . Hate is never worthwhile, no matter what it costs. . . ."

Just as Stella cut out pictures for Richard, she snipped helpful advice from the newspaper for herself. "Your husband may be one of the men who simply isn't [*sic*] going to be faithful; that may be your slice of the trouble of life. Don't try to dodge it when it comes. Face it as you would sickness, poverty, war, with spirit and courage. Remember, in the matter of your husband's affection, no woman takes anything from you. You lost it before she found it." Stella pored over these words, trying to glean from them a way to win Eddy back.

She told anyone who would listen about Mrs. Smith. She told the family. She told customers when she was in the store. She told her friends. She felt that if she said it enough, Eddy might give Helen up. All the while, the anonymous letters kept coming. On August 13, 1935, Stella received the longest one yet.

Don't you think you're carrying this too far? From all indications you are the one that's stirring up trouble and not herself. . . .

I believe you show very poor taste in telling people how little you've always had and how you've sometimes not had enough to eat. Anyone knowing the family knows better than that. You should consider yourself lucky to have your husband's family treat you as kind as they do. It's been said that you have more since your marriage than you ever had before. . . .

I don't believe I would air my personal affairs to outsiders to the point of telling them you had to live sometimes on five dollars a week and about all the privations you've had to contend with. . . . You say you are capable enough to get a job. Why don't you do so instead of being so sore and envious of what others have. . . .

It's unfair of you to keep saying the friend ran after your husband for after all you know very little about the affair. If you had used good sense that Sunday instead of getting so wild perhaps you would have learned more. I can assure you it was a mutual affair and you on the outside looking in know so little. Do you think for one minute he will be so dumb as to tell you the truth when he has to live with you? I happen to know a lot about it all and he was as foolish over her as she was over him. . . .

You had best forget it all and continue slaving and depriving yourself or get out and make yourself useful. You should be able to make as much money as she (Helen) is making since you consider yourself such a helpmate. The trouble is you are lazy and you know if you gave him up no one else would have you. I've heard how you cry and carry on. If you're smart you wouldn't check on your husband so. The girlfriend said once your husband said you followed him around like a leech.

Stella had no idea who this anonymous letter-writer was—perhaps a friend of Helen's, perhaps Helen herself—but this note, like the ones that had come before it, only strengthened Stella's resolve. If she left Eddy, she had few options. It was the Depression, and jobs—especially in art, the only thing that Stella was really qualified to do—were practically impossible to find. She couldn't turn to her parents; she had little in common with them anymore. Her father, Harvey, had owned two barbershops, but the customers had drifted away as his drinking got worse. He'd always been verbally abusive; now he'd taken to beating Stella's mother. Finally he deserted Jessie once and for all. He was living on "the Nickel," Fifth Street, better known as Skid Row. Jessie and Ted, Stella's eight-year-old brother, had left Redlands with nothing more than a suitcase and their parrot, and had gone to stay in Grandma Huggins's new cottage in Glassell Park—up the street and around the corner from Stella's cousins Ida and Vernon.

Stella did what she had done since she'd first met the See family. She hung on tenaciously and waited, for she knew that if she left, she would not only be losing a husband, but also the only real family she had ever known.

PART IV

CHAPTER 13

SNAPSHOTS

1936–38

I N 1935, Fong See decided he would return home to China. He ordered Yun to come back to Los Angeles to take care of the business, leaving his wife, Leong-shee, their daughters, and the youngest boys in Dimtao. Kuen, Danny Ho, and Haw—Yun's older sons—returned to Los Angeles with their father so that they might earn money to bring their newly acquired wives to the Gold Mountain. By early 1936, Fong See and his young family had been living in the mansion in Dimtao for a year. See-bok was nearing his eightieth birthday; Ngon Hung had just passed her thirtieth.

In China, See-bok's wealth continued to grow. He owned the Fatsan Grand Hotel, the best hotel in the city. He bought two pawn shops— owning one of these was similar to owning a bank in the United States— where he gathered items similar to those he'd sold in his early days as a merchant—rattan furniture, baskets, and inexpensive clothes. He also expanded his philanthropic activities. Harboring a general concern for the villagers of Dimtao and seeing that the children had no opportunity for formal education, Gold Mountain See provided funds to set up and operate a free private school. Looking at the muddy roads that had long inconvenienced the villagers, See-bok denounced fears of evil spirits and anxiety over bandits. It was time to modernize, he told villagers. He then donated funds for a three-slab-wide road which extended from Dimtao to the outskirts of Fatsan. Their old fears forgotten, the villagers praised the roadway for its convenience.

See-bok never concerned himself with politics. Because he couldn't read, he only knew what he heard through gossip. Since conquering Manchuria in 1931, Japan had been mounting periodic raids into China. The Japanese will come and go, but China will stand, he thought. Since 1927, Mao Tse-tung had been promoting communism; beginning in 1932, Chiang Kai-shek had begun "extermination campaigns" against Communist troops. Chiang and Mao will come and go, See-bok thought, but China will stand. The way he saw it, these two men could fight all they wanted and it wouldn't affect him or his family.

Free from worries about politics or money, See-bok settled into the mansion and enjoyed watching the goings-on about him. The mansion, known in those days, as it is today, as the *gway* house—the house of white ghosts, in remembrance of the time that Ticie had spent in the village—had grown more exquisite with time. The mango tree that Fong See had planted years ago in the center of the garden cast a cooling shade. In the courtyard were two kitchens: one for the daily meals, the other for banquets for up to sixty people. During festive times, See-bok hung brightly colored lanterns, ordered good-luck dishes, and hired blind girls to sing for the guests. Outside the compound's walls, rickshaw boys waited for the guests to leave, and beggars lined up along the cobblestone pathways for leftovers. See-bok also brought in extra guards—who modeled their appearance rather dramatically on an amalgamation of Chiang Kai-shek's strongmen and Hollywood gangsters. When the inevitable attempt to kidnap Fong See's sons came, the guards hung on to the running boards of their powerful black cars, shooting their pistols with abandon. This time the kidnappers were shot dead.

From his favorite spot on the balcony, Fong See could observe Ngon Hung and Leong-shee, who spent each morning sitting by the large marble goldfish bowl that served as the centerpiece of the garden. In Los Angeles, life was lonely for Ngon Hung, but at least she didn't have to worry about protocol with relatives, narrow-minded gossips, or difficult servants. In China she was too young and inexperienced to exercise much authority. Her children—two sons and three daughters—were young enough that the other village women felt that Ngon Hung needed to hear all of their best (and usually unwanted) advice.

"If a pregnant woman dreams of red flowers, she will have a girl," an old auntie might say.

"If she dreams of white flowers, she will have a boy," offered another.

"Eat a lot of egg whites and your daughter will have fair skin," opined another.

Each mother, grandmother or auntie had a theory, but when it came to actual child-rearing, the women became autocratic. Only their way was the right way.

"Don't baby your sons or they won't grow up to be strong."

"Give your children sweets and they will have a sweet disposition."

"Don't listen to that auntie. Listen to me."

In this arguing, Ngon Hung found an ally in Uncle's wife. "In China, the aunties always give advice," Leong-shee said. "If you do something one way, then you'll satisfy one auntie. But what about the others?"

Ngon Hung and Leong-shee also spent many hours together commiserating about how their husbands had taken concubines. "I have a better life in America, where I don't have to see Si Ping," Ngon Hung might complain.

"Your husband is someone people can come to," Leong-shee answered. "You don't realize how powerful he is. It is true our lives are hard, but they could be harder."

"I am strong in many ways," said Ngon Hung, her belly swelling with yet another child. "Still, I am more than hurt that the old man"—as she called her husband—"has taken a Number Four wife."

"Si Ping is not going to America," said Leong-shee, who had suffered the humiliation of having her husband take a servant as a concubine, bring her to Los Angeles, sire three children with her, and return them all to China to live in the same house with Leong-shee and her children. "You are secure. I know how much it hurts. No matter how you are raised—whether you are educated or uneducated, rich or poor—it is still painful for your husband to need more than one wife."

Woman's talk—even if it included gossip about concubines—held no interest for See-bok's younger sons, all of them younger than ten. See-bok could see that they fidgeted at the restraints put upon them by village life. They had to wear peasant clothes. They had to go to school and learn their calligraphy. They had to sit quietly and attentively when the villagers came to pay their respects. The boys' only excitement came with holidays, festivities, and the scary stories of fox spirits and ghosts that old women told under the village's ancient banyan tree.

During these long, easy days, See-bok allowed himself the pleasure of enjoying village life. Lounging on his balcony, listening to Enrico Caruso on his Victrola, See-bok could survey his domain—the luscious grounds, the activities of the peasants who tilled the fields for his benefit, the domestic squabbles of his wives, the children underfoot. See-bok thought that he would remain here and live out his last days.

In early 1932, the film producer Irving Thalberg bought the motion-picture rights to Pearl Buck's Pulitzer Prize–winning novel, *The Good Earth*. "I would rather scrap every inch of film and every cent invested than to show a film which might give rise to ill-feeling between the two countries," he announced. "The whole object is to produce a film which shall establish a clearer and more sympathetic relationship between the peoples of two nations." Hearing these words and tired of the roles she'd been cast in over the years, Anna May Wong approached MGM Studios.

"I'll be happy to take the test," she said. "If you let me play O'Lan, I'll be very glad." But the studio only wanted her for the part of Lotus, the singsong girl who served as Wang's concubine and the villainess of the piece. "You're asking me—with my Chinese blood—to do the only unsympathetic role in the picture, featuring an all-American cast portraying Chinese characters." Indeed, for all of Thalberg's intentions, Caucasians got the plum parts: Paul Muni as Wang, and Luise Rainer as O'Lan. Shattered, Anna May left Hollywood and traveled to China.

In America, a call went out through Pacific Coast newspapers and radio stations to enlist players for the other sixty-eight speaking parts. Three hundred tests were made. Accents proved to be a problem. Given that Chinese can be found in any part of the world, many were excused owing to their Australian or Spanish accents. Some, born in America and eager for parts, were dismissed because their English was too good. Others, with appropriate accents, often wouldn't leave their businesses to take part in the film. Still, Ching Wah Lee, the editor of the *Chinese Digest,* became Wang's Friend; Keye Luke, a former art student from Chouinard, was given the role of Elder Son: Caroline Chew, the daughter of Dr. Ng Poon Chew, the famous editor and economist, played a teahouse dancer. Jennie Chan, Sissee's old friend, worked on the movie for six weeks as a nonspeaking extra. Ray See did a screen test, but was rejected because his voice was too "soft."

While casting decisions were being made, Thalberg sent director Sidney Franklin and a crew to China to collect a total of 390 packing cases of Chinese needles, cooking and farming utensils, doors and windows, water wheels, baskets, and clothes. Franklin also saw to the crucial mob scenes that would dominate the film. He recruited four thousand "refugees" from the countryside, each of whom was paid $1.50 a day. Another four thousand soldiers from China's Twenty-fifth Infantry and Artillery Division performed whatever other duties Franklin could conceive.

In 1936, production returned to California, where the studio had purchased five hundred acres in Northridge to create a working Chinese farm. Under the keen eye of a Santa Barbara grower, Yee On, a hillside was terraced, plowed, and planted with onions, leeks, bok choy, mustard, chard, red cabbage, water chestnuts, and China peas. On the floor of the valley an artificial river was constructed and decorated with stone bridges, water wheels, and other irrigation devices. A few weary water buffalos made the trans-Pacific trip to lend further authenticity. In the end, the farm was deemed so realistic that the Department of Agriculture sent a representative to study it for Chinese erosion-control techniques. In this setting, Wang and O'Lan fought desperately against the locusts. Between shots, Luise Rainer hunted rabbits with her dog, Johnny.

A walled "city" was built, with more than two hundred "shops" where roast duck hung in windows, barbers tended to queues, antique dealers plied their wares, and peddlers walked the streets with salted fish or sausages on poles. Extras spent days sitting on overturned straw baskets, waiting, gossiping. For some, it brought back memories of their youth— of the rich in silken robes, looking down from balconies glowing from the light of many lanterns, and of the poor in tattered clothes, sitting below with beggars' bowls. To others—many of whom had been born on the Gold Mountain—it was their first glimpse of the "real" China.

Practically everyone in Chinatown had a piece of the action. People were hired to make sure that extras were dressed in the right costumes: jackets that closed down the side for women, jackets that closed down the front for men. Women with short hair wore blunt-cut wigs; those with permanents wrapped their curls in black cloth. Even with those 390 packing cases of goods, MGM sent set decorators to Ming See at the F. Suie One Company for additional props. Ming checked the list of desired goods and found them either at his shop or at his father's store, the F. See On Company. In this way, Ming kept all of the business within the See and Fong families. The two stores rented out wheelbarrows, rickshaws, lanterns, and furniture for the peasant scenes being shot at the Wang farmhouse, as well as screens, embroideries, and carvings for the wealthy city sets.

Tom Gubbins of the Asiatic Costume Company hired extras and worked as a translator on the big location shoots. When MGM ordered three hundred or more extras, the studio got a discount. But most extras were paid a standard "five dollars a chink" for nonspeaking parts. As a proper "Chinese" comprador, Tom Gubbins made a fortune, skimming a fee from every extra who worked on *The Good Earth.* When the movie premiered, on January 29, 1937, it was hailed as the most authentic view of Chinese life ever filmed.

Five months later, on July 7, 1937, Japan suddenly mobilized its impressive war machine, attacking and seizing nearly all coastal cities and industrial areas, effectively closing off China from the sea. These events persuaded Mao Tse-tung and Chiang Kai-shek to put aside their own bitter disagreements temporarily and work together against their common foe. Fong See abandoned his idea of remaining in China, packed up his family—leaving his fourth wife, Si Ping, behind—and returned to Los Angeles. Yun's wife, Leong-shee, her children, and the wives of her three eldest sons also traveled with Fong See; Ngan Fa, Yun's concubine, and their three children stayed in China.

The Chinatown that Fong See came home to was in a state of flux. Ever since old Chinatown had been leveled, everyone knew there had to be a new Chinatown. But what form would it take, and where would it be? After several aborted plans, two viable projects emerged: China City and New Chinatown. China City was developed under the auspices of Christine Sterling, a socialite who had created Olvera Street, a touristy Mexican marketplace just off the old Spanish Plaza. With significant help from a handful of Caucasian businessmen, including Tom Gubbins and Harry Chandler, the scion of the *Los Angeles Times,* the money was raised for China City's site, which was bordered by Spring, Ord, Alameda, and High streets.

A few blocks to the northeast, New Chinatown was developing under the inspiration of Peter Soo Hoo, the first Chinese to be hired by the Department of Water and Power as an engineer. He thought that North Broadway—the area of the old French and Italian quarters, and currently the storage yards for the Santa Fe Railroad—was an ideal place for a Chinatown that would be owned and operated by the Chinese themselves. In many ways, New Chinatown would be as different from Old Chinatown as humanly possible: the buildings would be constructed strictly to code, with all earthquake, fire, and sanitation regulations adhered to. The streets would be wide, open, and airy, creating a safe ambiance. Prostitution, gambling, and opium would be forbidden. Only a few ideas would carry over from Old Chinatown: each building would have apartments upstairs for shopkeepers, and the buildings themselves would have Chinese motifs.

As these plans went ahead, the last section of Old Chinatown along Los Angeles Street remained the heart of the city's Chinese community. Ironically, Dragon's Den, which was owned by a half-Chinese family, attracted the most customers—for lunch, dinner, and midnight snacks. Now that Eddy finally had his liquor license, Dragon's Den closed at two in the morning. On Saturday and Sunday nights it stayed open until four in the morning—not as a place to drink, but as a place to hang out. After locking up for the night, Eddy, Sissee, and whoever else wanted to tag along went to the City Market to buy provisions for the next day.

Sissee knew that the responsibility of the restaurant was giving her brother Eddy ulcers, but she loved the unpredictability of the place: the way the chefs fought with their cleavers or got in foul tempers if they lost the lottery; the way her brother hustled to get water chestnuts as imports from China dwindled (recently the chef had begun substituting jicama for water chestnuts); the way Eddy had to fire Benji for going out to fill the wine kegs and not coming back because he was too busy drinking the merchandise (and all with no hard feelings).

Sissee loved the customers. James Wong Howe, the cinematographer, and his writer-girlfriend, Sanora Babb, were regulars at Dragon's Den. Since Jimmy's career was governed by the morals clause in his contract, he couldn't marry Sanora, a white woman; because he was a traditional Chinese man, they wouldn't live together. For several years, then, they took two apartments in the same building. Going out in public always posed problems. One woman, incensed by seeing a white woman with a Chinese man, banged Sanora's head on the ground. Another time, Jimmy and Sanora thought they'd try a restaurant in town; one wouldn't serve them, another turned them away at the door. As they drove downtown to Dragon's Den, a woman started shouting from her car at Sanora, "You must be a whore." The woman followed them clear to Marchessault Street, where she parked her car and got out. As Jimmy stood at the entrance to Dragon's Den, Sanora went back to the woman, took her hat, and threw it in the gutter. "Oh, my hat!" the woman cried. "My hundred-dollar hat!" Sanora just laughed, took Jimmy's arm, and walked down the stairs to their one sure refuge in the city.

But no single person held customers in thrall as much as did Anna May Wong. Seductive, sultry, beautiful. A curvaceous figure. A "wicked" past. A family that disapproved. On many nights—except for the ten months she was in China after the debacle surrounding *The Good Earth*—Anna May, dressed in silk cut on the bias, with a full-length ermine coat draped over her shoulders, could be found holding court at her own table. She would seductively extend her hand to those who came to pay respects—even those Chinese who scorned and ridiculed her behind her back.

Eddy got along famously with Anna May, for she liked a dumb joke as much as he did. Every time she came to the restaurant, Anna May would treat him to a tale or two. "One day a fisherman throws out his line," Anna May might have begun as Sissee's brother pulled up a chair to her table. "He catches this beautiful mermaid with long blond hair. He reels her in. She's a gorgeous-looking thing. The fisherman picks her up, examines her all over, then tosses her back into the sea. His friend, another fisherman, asks, 'Why?' The first fisherman responds, 'How?' "

Eddy might laugh and return a joke in kind. "An old guy loses his potency. He goes to a Chinese herbalist who says that the gland of the monkey will do the trick, but it's very expensive. The doctor says, 'But don't worry. I've heard that rye bread works just as well.' So the man goes to a Jewish delicatessen and asks for twelve loaves of rye bread. The woman behind the counter asks, 'Are you having a party?' 'No,' the man says. The woman says, 'Then it will get hard before you finish.' The man says, 'Why does everyone know about this bread but me?' "

Anna May might smile, then say, "You know, Eddy, the Japanese don't have jokes like that."

To Sissee, Dragon's Den was an oasis of culture, fun, and tolerance. Chinatown, conversely, was still a rough place. Toughs—and those who weren't so fierce, but knew a good opportunity when they saw one—loved to venture down to Chinatown on a Saturday night to get in trouble, knowing that there would be little if any recourse for their victims. These were known as "rambunctious Caucasians." "Sometimes they throw their plates on the floor. Sometimes they go in the bathroom and put linen in the goddamn toilet," the son of the proprietor of Man

Gen Low complained. And sometimes the waiters would take ice picks, go find cars on the street that looked unfamiliar, and "do the tires."

"We can't fight them any other way," the proprietor's son said. "Hell, they're six feet tall and we're only . . ."

If George Wong, who now supplied fish and poultry to most of the restaurants, was around, he'd add a thing or two: "If there's a problem in your restaurant, you have to run out and holler. We'll come and try to get that thing straight. If there's any trouble, fight. You know if the policeman comes, he'll just tell those people, 'Get out of here. Get out of here.' He won't arrest that guy. That Caucasian guy? He won't have to pay."

If Sissee and Eddy were there, someone would be sure to add, "There are a lot of nice Caucasians, too." But even that elicited smiles, because everyone in Chinatown remembered the time Sissee's second brother, Ray, had drunk too much, said some "snotty" things, and gotten into a fight with the waiters at the Grandview Gardens. "They beat the shit out of him," people said in recalling the incident.

Dragon's Den wasn't immune from these shenanigans. Eddy confronted a couple of troublemakers on the stairs as they were leaving without paying their bill. Words were exchanged. Suddenly the toughs were on top of Eddy, pressing their thumbs on his eyes. Sissee dashed out from behind the cash register, climbed on top of the pile, and squealed, "Let go of my brother! You can't do that to my brother!" Then Tyrus—who had recently taken a job filling in cartoon backgrounds at the Disney Studios for $2.50 a day—edged his way into the scuffle, yelling, "Don't kick them too hard. They're friends of George Stanley's. He just designed that statuette for the Academy Awards."

On another night, Sissee looked up from her desk into the muzzle of a nickel-plated revolver. The Mexican man holding it spoke in a low voice. "Empty the cash register," he ordered. When she refused, another man stepped behind the counter, put a gun to her back, pushed her aside, and took one hundred dollars. She didn't yell or scream. As the *Times* reported later, the robbery occurred as "a score of patrons remained oblivious."

Now when Eddy went to the restaurant, he looked like a gangster in a movie. He wore double-breasted pinstripe suits over which he sported a big black coat belted at the waist. He also carried a couple of guns—a .22 automatic and a .32 revolver—for protection against the "rowdy element" and for when he was carrying paper bags full of cash. The latter reminded Sissee of the old days, when Pa used to come home from the Pasadena store with his paper bag full of money.

So Sissee worked. She tootled around town in her Plymouth. She stayed out late with her friends, going down to the City Market at two o'clock in the morning after the restaurant had closed to buy produce and laugh. And at dawn she'd roll back to the house on Maplewood. This level of freedom made Sissee one of the most independent young women in all of Chinatown, and some would say in the larger city as well.

On the other hand, Sissee spent as much time as possible with her mother. In Chinatown it was said that Sissee and her mother were so close you couldn't put a piece of paper between them. Sissee banked for her mother. She lived with her mother. She drove her mother wherever she wanted to go. Everywhere Sissee went, her mother was usually with her. Sometimes, after the restaurant closed, Sissee would pick up her mother and go driving until three or four or five in the morning—anything to keep Ticie from focusing on her loneliness. "My mother's a real good scout," Sissee told boys who came to pick her up for dates. "Anything I want to do, she'll do." So, for all her gadding about, Sissee's life was, in many ways, a sheltered one.

Sissee, at twenty-eight, was still unmarried, though several men had their eye on her. Jack, a jeweler in the same block as the F. Suie One Company, taught Eddy how to make rings and set stones, in the false hope of making an impression on Sissee. Down at City Market, a grocer who operated his own stall had a bad case on her. Another guy, "Accordion Joe," who owned a restaurant in Hollywood, "sparked her up," but lost his chance when he took her to a boxing match. One of the waitresses at Dragon's Den had a brother who wanted to marry Sissee, but he also wanted to open a funeral parlor. "That's as bad as the squeeze box," Sissee confided to Stella.

Although Sissee was half-and-half, she was the daughter of Chinatown's most important merchant and was expected to marry somone from a good family. The only person who fit that bill was Gilbert Leong. His mother was a powerhouse, teaching the children of Chinatown their home language; his father, Leong Jeung, whose Soochow Restaurant was a success, served as president of the Chinese Benevolent Association. It wasn't love at first sight between Sissee and Gilbert. After all, they'd seen each other around for years, first as children aboard the *Nanking* in 1919, and later, when Gilbert, who lived over on Ninth Street in what was called the Market Chinatown, had gone to his mother's mission school, which was in the same block as Fong See's store.

In 1933, when Ticie moved back to Chinatown and before Dragon's Den opened, Sissee used to go over to Soochow for a bowl of noodles. Now that they were going around together, Gilbert kidded her about it. "You'd sit there absolutely straight-backed, staring into your book. You'd eat your noodles and pretend not to see me, but your book was upside down." Sissee always laughed at this, because she knew it was at least partly true. She had liked to stare at him when she thought he wasn't looking.

Gilbert was still the same skinny kid he'd been on the *Nanking,* but now he was a sculptor and an aspiring architect. Three years ago, for their first date, Gilbert had taken her to see the James Wong Howe film *Viva Villa.* Afterwards they'd talked about the lighting in that film, how real the clouds looked, how Jimmy had been able to get such a wonderful sense of atmosphere. Their second date had been a dance at USC. Now Gilbert was a regular visitor at Maplewood. It made Sissee mad, the way her brothers hovered about. When Ming came over, he'd have a couple of drinks, then start dancing and causing a ruckus. All the while, Gil would be trying to get his arm around Sissee and she'd be wanting him to.

One thing troubled Sissee. She'd been going with Gilbert for three years already. Why hadn't he proposed?

Every day since she'd gone to live with Grandma Huggins in Glassell Park, Jessie Copeland—Stella's mother—sat listlessly at the bedroom window, looking out onto the street. Sometimes she clicked her tongue at the parrot her daughter had given her. Jessie continued to sit and stare, until one day late in 1937 something snapped in her brain. She leaned over, opened the birdcage, and strangled the parrot. Grandma Huggins took Jessie to the County Hospital, where it was determined that she would have to be institutionalized indefinitely. Stella's brother, Ted, went to live with Stella and Eddy in a house they rented on Kingsley, a few blocks from Ticie.

Unfortunately for Ted, he was entering a home that was totally incapable of handling another crisis. Eddy—between his responsibilities at the restaurant and trying to rekindle his relationship with Stella—didn't welcome the child. As for Stella, she was still on a slow burn over Eddy's affair. In some of the darkest days for the See family, Stella—who had held her anger in check for so long—lashed out at her powerless ten-year-old brother.

Sometimes Ted would say something and, like her mother, Stella could feel something snap. She had no control over her rage. She beat Ted, hitting him over and over until she was depleted. Then guilt would set in. How could she have done it? He was helpless. It wasn't his fault. One time as she hit Ted, he looked up at her curiously and asked, "Why do you always hit me? Why don't you ever hit Richard?" And without even thinking, she turned and slapped Richard. It was only later, in the calmness of release, that she realized Richard had done nothing wrong.

Stella didn't like to visit her mother in the hospital, because she never knew what response she'd get on any given day. Sometimes Jessie recognized her daughter, but usually she just stared at the wall. No one ever explained Jessie's problem. Sometimes Stella heard the word *stroke.* Sometimes *manic depression.* Sometimes *schizophrenia.* Sometimes *nervous breakdown.*

It simply wasn't spoken about, just as no one ever mentioned Stella's father, because what could they say? "The man's a wino, a bum." Occasionally, Stella got a call from a police station where Harvey was being held. Sometimes he showed up at Stella's door, smelling of vomit, cheap alcohol, and sweat. "Do you have any money I could borrow? I'll pay you back." Eddy would pull out a few dollars, and Harvey would go back down to the Nickel.

The only person who benefited from Ted's arrival was Richard. Stella allowed him to walk with Ted to the movies, to the market, or over to see Ticie. She permitted the boys to put on capes, pretend they were Superman, climb on the roof, and jump off. Ted was such a *boy,* not like Richard, who wasn't good at sports and suffered from asthma, eczema, and allergies. Some days he swelled up until his eyes, cheeks, and lips puffed into an unrecognizable blob. Stella gave him pills to relax him so he could breathe. She rubbed his skin with green salve to relieve his itching. She took him to the doctor for shots. At night, she put a vaporizer medicated with tincture of benzoin in the room that Richard and Ted shared. What she didn't know was that when the vaporizer was spewing its foul-smelling steam, Ted would climb out the window and sit on the roof; often he was out there all night.

On February 1, 1938, just months after Ted came to live with her, Stella intercepted a final note from Helen Smith. This time it was a little store-bought card with a schoolgirl on the front. It read: "To my friend. Oh, I had a little dime and I had a little time. So I hunted very hard to find a little card to send to you to say I think of you each day." On the back, Helen had written, "Couldn't send you the flowers this year. Sincere wishes and congratulations on your third anniversary of Dragon's Den." Stella understood that the affair was really over.

Shortly after this, a friend asked Stella if she'd like to take a housesitting job in Pasadena. Realizing that she could finally loosen her grip on her marriage, Stella jumped at the chance to take Richard and get away for a while. (Ted stayed with Eddy.) Stella relished this time alone to temper her anger and try to forgive. At the same time, she earned a small income—her own money, the kind that Ticie so often told her to put aside for herself.

Richard visited his father on the weekends. One evening when Eddy had to work at Dragon's Den, he left Richard and Ticie at the house on Maplewood. Richard watched silently when his grandmother started to drink. When Eddy phoned to check in, Richard heard the slur in his grandmother's words. Twenty minutes later, Eddy pulled up to the house.

"How could you drink like that when you're taking care of Richard?" Eddy screamed. "How could you be so irresponsible? You're a drunk! You're a lush!" Then he pushed Ticie. Richard watched as his father's pushing turned to hitting. Ticie cried, but didn't say a word. Then she left the house and started walking down the street. Even Richard could see that her leaving wasn't fair. It was *her* house.

Eddy sat on the couch with his head in his hands and waited. Finally he stood up and they got in the Plymouth and drove up and down the streets until they found Ticie. She got in the car and they drove home. No one said a word.

Not long after this, the house-sitting job ended and Stella and Richard returned home permanently. Ticie seemed to stop drinking.

Since he'd first set foot on the Gold Mountain, Fong Yun had been at the mercy of his brother's every whim. If Fong See wanted Yun to go to China, he went. If Fong See wanted Yun to lie about a piece of furniture, he lied. But if Yun suffered, he was partly to blame. The family considered him a scholar, since he'd received a full education through the goodwill of his older brother. For this reason, the family thought Yun had his head in the clouds. He wasn't good at business, they reasoned, because he'd been spoiled by his older brother.

Yun had come to Los Angeles—young, optimistic, dedicated—only to see his dreams evaporate. In 1923, he'd opened the Fong Yun Company on Seventh Street, and failed. In the early thirties he'd opened another store, and gone bust again. After returning to Los Angeles in 1935, Yun had watched his oldest sons—Kuen, Danny Ho, and Haw— try to make a go of it with Fong Brothers, a five-and-dime at the corner of Seventh and Figueroa. But a curio shop in the heart of the business district in the depth of the Depression could not support three families. Danny Ho took over, leaving his brothers to go back to work for Fong See. They were young. They still had time to find their futures. Yun, on the other hand, felt trapped.

He had always planned to retire to China once his older sons were situated, but the world seemed to conspire against him. First, it was harder than expected for the boys to get established. Second, Yun had to bring Leong-shee, the younger children, and the older boys' three new wives back to Los Angeles. These women—who'd led privileged lives in China with servants to dress them, feed them, and clean for them—didn't easily adapt to life in Los Angeles. American-born wives, who'd seen plenty of hard times, took particular offense at the uppity Fong wives: "Those girls are spoiled. They've never worked. They thought they were going to come here and never lift a finger. . . ." The result of all this was that Fong Yun was burdened with more mouths to feed, at a higher rate.

Each evening Yun returned home to his rooms in his brother's compound. Over dinner, surrounded by his wife and younger children, he wept. "My brother is a tyrant," he'd say.

"Why don't you fight back?" Leong-shee inquired. "Why don't you stand up for yourself?"

"I owe my life to my brother," he answered. "When I was young, we were so poor that my brother would go and cut grass in the rain to earn money for food. I owe my education to him. I owe this life to him."

As low as he got, Fong Yun never forgot that his brother had brought him to the Gold Mountain. Despite years of menial chores, he remained faithful to See-bok. Yun honored his brother according to filial precepts. When his children asked to go camping or skiing, Yun said, "You must go ask your uncle. You must show the proper respect."

The children often speculated on their father's relationship with their powerful uncle. "Each person has his own personality," Kuen might offer. "Each person has his way of doing things. If See-bok's personality wasn't the way it is, he wouldn't be making the money he does." Still, Fong Yun had eight children and a wife here in the United States, and another three children and a concubine in Fatsan. He had the responsibility to care and provide for all of them. The construction of New Chinatown and China City gave Uncle the opportunity to escape what amounted to indentured servitude.

Fong Yun spoke to his brother: "I can't make ends meet. I would like to go out on my own again." Although Fong See didn't want his brother to leave, he wasn't angry. Uncle was too close to his heart.

"We can't afford new Chinatown," Fong Yun told Leong-shee. "You need two thousand dollars, maybe three thousand dollars to open there. We'll go to China City."

Fong Yun was among the first to rent space—the largest in the complex—and became the first president of the China City Association. Choey Lau, his eldest daughter, asked her father to buy insurance if the family was going to take on a such a big risk, but he refused. "I am an honest man," he told her. "I don't believe in gambling, and insurance is just a way of gambling. It's more important to spend your money on merchandise." Which is exactly what he did.

On June 8, 1938, China City officially opened. A reporter, observing the scene for the *Los Angeles Examiner* and caught up in the spirit of the day, wrote of exploding firecrackers and "Orientals sputtering the English equivalent of 'whoopee.'" He went on to describe the lotus pools, temple gongs, curio stands, dance pavilions, and "slim Oriental girls in silk jackets and trousers pattering back and forth." China City pandered unabashedly to Chinese stereotypes, evoking the "exotic" atmosphere of a Chinese village. The entire one-block complex was

enclosed within a miniature "Great Wall of China." Inside, small cob-
blestoned alleyways were filled with leftover sets from *The Good Earth*.
Ducks and chickens pecked the ground outside the Wang farmhouse;
tourists rode in rickshaws down the "Passage of 100 Surprises" and
nibbled on "Chinaburgers."

Just three weeks later, on June 25, 1938, the grand opening of New
Chinatown took place a few blocks away. Visitors entered through one
of two large gates—the first dedicated to "The Gathering of Best Tal-
ents"; the other built with donations from Y. C. Hong, the hunchbacked
lawyer, in honor of his mother and all "maternal virtues." Lanterns,
banners, and flags of the United States and the Republic of China
festooned the area.

Lovely maidens dressed in traditional costumes guided visitors
through the red-carpeted streets with such topical names as Mei-Ling
Way (from the given name of Madame Chiang Kai-shek) and Sun Mun
Way (for Dr. Sun Yat-sen's *Three Principles of the People*). Tyrus Wong,
Keye Luke, and Gilbert Leong contributed art for an exhibition. After
a parade, a lion dance, and musical interludes, the politicians and celebrities, including Anna May Wong, retired to the newly relocated Man
Jen Low Restaurant. Late into the night, crowds danced and swayed to
music under lantern light.

With the dual success of China City and New Chinatown, it felt as
though the Depression was finally over for the Chinese in Los Angeles.
And, for a short time, China City was a beautiful dream for Uncle and
a wonderland for his children.

Not long after China City opened, Choey Lon, Uncle's five-year-old
daughter, stood at her mother's side in the Sam Sing Butcher Shop,
watching and learning. Leong-shee surreptitiously pointed to a center
piece of pork. "I want that cut," she whispered to her daughter, "but
it's not time yet." Every day, Choey Lon and her mother followed this
same routine, walking over from China City several times until the
butcher had sliced to Leong-shee's chosen cut.

For Choey Lon, China City was a magical place where the fragrant
smell of incense wafted from a temple and gentle breezes passed through
wind chimes hanging before shops. At one gate were Chinese characters
reading, "As China's Lion Awakens, the City Grandly Opens"; at the
other were two larger-than-life door guards painted by her older brother
Kuen. The lovely curves of Gilbert Leong's sculpture of Kuan Yin graced
the Court of Confucius, where the cobblestones had been purposely laid
unevenly. The streets and plazas—the Court of Lotus Pools and the
Harbor of Whang Po—were great places to play tag or hide and seek.
Rickshaw boys pulled tourists through the bumpy alleyways for twenty-
five cents, yelling, "Coming through! Coming through!"

Magical characters lived in China City. An Italian fortune-teller. A Buddhist monk, tall and strange-looking. Choey Lon's mother explained, "He's from the North. They're tall like that." *Lo fan* women came and chanted with him. Another man acted like a door guard. He had his stall at the very entrance to China City. He was small, dark, and buggy-eyed. Everyone called him Peanut, not just because he sold peanuts but because he looked like one, too. Finally, Choey Lon liked to watch Tom Gubbins, who had moved his shop into China City, because he seemed so different with his English accent, piercing blue eyes, carefully trimmed beard, and cocked hat.

Queens and princesses came to visit China City: Eleanor Roosevelt, Gene Tierney, Anna May Wong, and Mae West, who was so moved at the Temple of Kuan Yin that she signed a photograph of herself with the words "You must come and see my temple sometime!" Choey Lon thought the actresses were especially exciting, even though her father didn't approve of Hollywood people. "Beware of easy jobs and easy money," he said. "Don't work for the movies. It is a bad business, full of bad types. I know Anna May Wong since she is a baby. But I'm telling you that entertainment is the lowest. You have to make an honest living."

Lon wasn't the only kid who loved China City. Children throughout Chinatown liked to come here. Sometimes Richard and Ted (her cousins? what they were exactly she didn't know, except they were relatives and white) would come down and act like kid tourists, with their cone-shaped lollipops and snow cones. Other children worked in China City. Lilly Mu Lee, who sold gardenias for fifteen cents and double corsages for thirty-five cents, sang "God Bless America" for a penny.

Lon believed she lived in a white fairy tale. China City was the huge castle, and she was Snow White. Like a princess, she didn't have to study, for nothing was expected of a princess but to be beautiful, reside in a beautiful palace, and be surrounded by delightful things. In her fantasies she conjured up a white prince.

Her mother and father tried to set her straight:

"White men drink a lot."

"White men beat their wives."

"White men are unfaithful."

Could these things be true? Lon wanted to find out.

If Lon thought of herself as Snow White, then she thought of her mother as Cinderella. Leong-shee worked in the back of the store, making food for everyone. Since there was no running water, she washed the dishes in a pan, then carried the bucket of greasy water outside to dump it. Nobody helped her—not Lon, not her father. He treated Leong-shee like a slave.

Choey Lon knew her father thought he was a high-class merchant.

He had aspirations, but even Lon could see they didn't gel. His shop was beautiful, well done. He had good antiques left over from his Seventh Street store, but mostly he carried cheap curios—backscratchers, little teapots, and ashtrays. And her mother was not a woman of leisure.

Lon adored her father and felt he loved her best of all. He gave her lots of attention—not the western kind, with hugging and kissing—but it was true and pure anyway. He called her teasing names—"sugar dumpling" and "turtle egg." When she asked him for something, he gave it to her. He didn't believe in discipline. "Children understand who you are," he said. "If you call it bad, then a child will gravitate toward it. They must learn by observation." As a result, all harsh words and punishments came from Leong-shee.

Today, as the late-afternoon shoppers made the last of their purchases, Leong-shee once again took her daughter to the Sam Sing Butcher Shop. Lon could see that the piece of meat her mother had picked was ready for slicing. Lon knew she was here to watch and learn, but she saw more than just her intended feminine lessons. She saw that her mother was the provider in the family. Leong-shee watched out for her children. She was an ideal Chinese mother who followed Buddhist philosophy, taught tradition and reverence, and obeyed the rules for being a good wife in her day-to-day living. At her mother's side in the meat market, Lon learned about perfection. She saw how well her mother did her job. She saw how women did things in the world that didn't show and weren't acknowledged.

Lon promised herself she wouldn't grow up to be like that. She didn't want to get married. She didn't want to have children. She was convinced her father wouldn't mind. "There's no use trying to beat children into something," he said, "because they will follow what they want to follow. Little dumpling, you will just have to be who you are." She believed him.

CHAPTER 14

ANNA MAY SPEAKS
(FROM THE GRAVE)

DURING my lifetime, nobody asked me what I thought. Nobody asked me if I liked it when one of my brothers used to brag to his classmates about me, hoping my fame would rub off on him. Nobody explained that even after I was dead, my family would try to keep me a secret. Nobody told me that practically the only thing people would remember about me was that I had created "bad stereotypes," and that only a few people would cherish me in their "fanzines" and their fantasies. Nobody ever asked me what *I* thought. But you go ahead. Ask me where I belong, who I am. I'm going to tell you, and you can believe it or not. I don't care. Because whatever *I* say, you will change anyway.

You ask me, *What is your home? Is it California?* I ask you back, How could it be the United States, where I cannot buy property? Where I cannot marry a white man? You ask me, *Is your home Los Angeles, where you were born? Is it Chinatown? Surely you must be comfortable there.* Of course I loved Dragon's Den. I was there almost every night. But the rest of Chinatown? The people didn't want me unless they could profit from me. So, when they wanted to raise money for China Relief, they held a Moon Festival. They said, "We need a grand marshal. We need a star." They knew in their filthy hearts there was only one person to ask. "We will ask Anna May." Naturally I went, knowing that the day after the Moon Festival they would go back to their old ways and I would go home alone.

What of Europe? You must have been happy there. That is where you had so much fame.

This is what I know. I couldn't get a decent job in America and I wanted to be a star. When I went to London, someone asked me, "Why did you leave America?" This is what I said: "I left America because I died so often. I was killed in virtually every picture in which I appeared. Pathetic dying seemed to be the thing I did best."

Another time a reporter asked me that same question and I answered, "When I left Hollywood I vowed that I would never act in films again. I was so tired of the part I had to play. Why is it that the screen Chinese is always a villain? And so crude a villain—murderous, treacherous, a snake in the grass! We are not like that. How could we be, with a civilization that is so many times older than that of the West? We have rigid codes of behavior, of honor. Why do they never show these? Why should we always scheme, rob, kill? I got so weary of it all—of the scenarists' conception of the Chinese character. You remember Fu Manchu? *Daughter of the Dragon?* So wicked!"

I'm telling you this because I *knew* I was creating bad stereotypes. That's why I wanted the part of O'Lan so badly. *The Good Earth* showed Chinese people in a good light, but Thalberg wanted *white* actors for the leading roles. Today, when they say *I* perpetrated those stereotypes, I wonder.

I couldn't take any more of America. So, in 1928, I sailed for Germany to make *Schmutzies Geld.* Someone told me that means *Dirty Money.* Then I went to Paris, then London, then back to Berlin. I learned to speak German and French. At least I *said* I learned those things. Perhaps I just learned how to pronounce the words before the camera. Perhaps I had no idea what I was saying. Perhaps I learned my lines by typing out my scripts. It doesn't matter, because I was a star. In 1929, I was in *A Circle of Chalk* with Laurence Olivier. At night, at the stage door, people waited for *me.* Did they wait for Olivier? Never. I would walk outside into the fog or rain, and they would be there—young men in their tuxedoes, young women with their bangs cut straight and blunt. Those young men lusted for me. Those young women tinted their faces ivory with ocher powder, hoping to duplicate my complexion.

In 1931, Sessue Hayakawa said, "Come back to America to star in *Daughter of the Dragon.*" I told reporters, "It is good to be home. I'm glad they want me back here to make a picture. I must confess I was discouraged when I left Hollywood. But I wasn't bitter. Everyone had been kind to me. And I'm grateful now; it wasn't easy at the start. It makes me appreciative of good fortune." The next year I was in *Shanghai Express.*

Is China your home country?

The Chinese have their own ways of being cruel. When I went to China after I lost the part in *The Good Earth,* I thought, Ah, perhaps this is my home. In Nanking, officials held a four-hour state dinner for me. I spoke Cantonese. They spoke Mandarin. Let me tell you something about these two languages. It's not like the difference between Spanish and Italian. Mandarin and Cantonese are as different from each other as German and English.

I told my interpreter, "Tell me everything they say. I want to know *everything.*" Through the dinner he whispered quietly in my ear what the others were actually saying as they stood to make their "toasts." "Does she know that her films are banned in our country? What of this courtesan in *Shanghai Express*? Is this how she wants the world to view Chinese women? Does she realize how she degrades our mothers and sisters and wives and daughters?" I sat there. I smiled. I listened. I told them in English, "When a person is trying to get established in a profession, he can't choose his parts. He has to take what is offered. I came to China to learn." When I was done, they gave me a standing ovation. And in America they wrote, "She was received like a princess."

I stayed in China for ten months. All my life I had been homesick for China, even though I had never been there before. The rhythm of life there harmonized with something in me that had been out of tune. I was no longer restless. It's hard to explain. Our Chinese expression "being in harmony with heaven and earth" is the essence of it. I went to Toishan to visit my home village. The women came out. They didn't believe I was real. They thought I was machine-made on the movie screen.

When I returned to America, I worked hard to raise money to help the people of China. I spoke everywhere. Paramount didn't mind. The studio was helpful. Publicists wrote press releases for me: "In view of current events in the Orient, anything Japanese annoys Anna May Wong, Chinese actress." I had an apartment overlooking a Japanese garden. When I looked at it I got angry. I wasn't soothed. I kept a bowl of goldfish. I always had fish, because it calmed me to watch them swim, and I could forget whatever bothered me. But I couldn't stop thinking about that garden. Paramount sent out another release: "Last night Miss Wong moved to a furnished home in another part of Hollywood, far from any landscaping suggesting Japan."

And you ask, *Was it enough not to look at a Japanese garden?* Of course not. I had one of the largest and most expensive wardrobes in Hollywood. I'd bought gowns in Paris, New York, Hollywood, and China. I auctioned off more than two hundred gowns, ensembles, wraps, accessories—including fans, jewelry, and headdresses. All the money went to relief funds.

This is what I know: When I kissed Jameson Thomas in *Piccadilly,* British censors cut it. When I was courted on screen by a Russian duke in *Haitang,* Hungarian officials banned the film. No film lover could ever marry me. If an American actress was made up with slanted eyes and eyebrows, and wore a stiff black wig and dressed in Chinese costumes, it was all right. But me? I was full Chinese. I always died in the movies, so that the white girl with the yellow hair could get the man.

My answer to all of your questions? I never *belonged* anywhere, because no place was home to me.

My father was a laundryman. You know what this is like—nonstop work, and people treating you badly and not paying the proper amount. My parents sent me to Chinese school after regular school, but I hated it. Instead, I went to the movie theater to see *The Perils of Pauline*. Do you remember, Stella, how we used to laugh about that, how you saw the same things in Waterville and wished you were *somewhere* else and I was in Los Angeles and wished I were *someone* else?

I was born Wong Liu Tsong. It means something like Frosted Yellow Willows or Frosted Willow Blossoms or Hoarfrost of the Willow Trees. All my life I wished for something different. I remember coming home from the serials and standing in front of the mirror and acting out all the parts. I remember walking to school and holding my eyes wide open so that I would look Caucasian.

When I was ten years old, I worked for a furrier. Sometimes I was a model. Once they dressed me in a mink coat and brocaded ankle-length pantaloons and took my picture for the rotogravure section of the newspaper. My father was so impressed by my elegance that he cut out the picture and sent it to my half-brother in China. My brother wrote back, "Tsong is indeed very beautiful, but please send me the dollar watch on the other side." You know what I say to that? A fur coat doesn't tick.

One day I heard about a movie they were making about the Boxer Rebellion—*The Red Lantern*. I went to a casting agent. Was it Tom Gubbins? No. It was Reverend Wang, the Baptist minister. He said, "Well, you got big eyes, big nose, big ears and mouth. I guess you'll do." He changed my name to Anna May Wong. I was twelve years old and I wanted to be in pictures. For two more years I went after school to work on different movies as an extra. My brothers, my sisters, they kept it a secret. They knew how mad my father would get. One day, one of my sisters said she had to tell Father, to soothe her own conscience.

My father was angry with me. He said people in Hollywood used harsh words. He said acting was not an honorable profession. He said things about white men: "They will take advantage of you. They will compromise you." My father got so angry he tried to arrange a marriage for me. He didn't ask me what I thought. But I'll tell you. I thought, I don't want a husband to boss me around. I don't want to live my life in Chinatown. I don't want to marry a cook or a laundryman. I don't want a husband who will take all my money, even if he lets me keep working. Besides, no Chinese man will marry me. I'd become too American to marry one of my own race.

My father gave up and I never got married. And when I was in *The Thief of Bagdad* my costume was so see-through that my family never forgave me. In their eyes, I was like a courtesan. Only my brother Richard remained faithful to me. Still, did my father complain that I brought home money? Did he complain when I supported the whole family? Did he complain when I bought one brother a typewriter and helped another to learn photography? Did he complain when I put all my brothers through private school? And here is the truth: I was beautiful as the slave girl.

After *The Thief of Bagdad,* the press began to call me "the celestial maiden." They called me "sloe-eyed." They called me "exotic." They called me "the Oriental Siren," "the China Doll," "the Lotus Girl," "the Chinese Flapper." They called me "the Queen of the B-films." They said I'd never cut my hair, never worn eyeglasses, never worn wool underwear, never curled my hair, never eaten lobster, never been on a bicycle, never owned a radio. They said I had the longest nails in Hollywood—which was true. They made it *news* when I cut my nails for *Daughter of Shanghai.* It was *news* again when I grew them back two inches and protected them with gold nail guards for *Dangerous to Know.*

Have you ever thought about what it would be like to be beautiful? In 1938, *Look* magazine called me "The Most Beautiful Chinese Girl in the World." I remember once in London I stopped a debate in Parliament when I walked into the visitors' gallery. They stopped everything just to watch me walk, watch me sit down. When I came back from my "Triumph Abroad," they said I was the "Toast of the Continent." They said my complexion was like "a rose blushing through old ivory," that my face shone on the screen like a Ming vase. But when Hollywood wanted a "Chinese," they hired Luise Rainer, Sylvia Sydney, Dorothy Lamour, Myrna Loy, and Sigrid Gurie.

Behind my back, people talked about how lonely I was. Even today, some say, "Didn't Anna May have tuberculosis?" "Didn't Anna May drink?" "Didn't she have sad love affairs?" "Didn't she become a virtual recluse?" "Didn't her brother have to take care of her?" Did any of them ever ask *me*?

This is what I want to ask you: What would you do if your family was ashamed of you? What would you do if you were their worst secret? This is what I did: It was the end of 1930 and I was on Broadway doing *On the Spot* with Wilbur Crane, when my mother crossed a street in Los Angeles and was hit by a car. My brothers called and told me. They left nothing out. Fracture of the skull. Broken leg. Internal injuries. They called later to say that our mother had died. Can you imagine how I felt to be so far away? Do you know how I felt when the police let the driver go free? But look, he was a white man. I filed a lawsuit. My father and my brothers and sisters joined me. What would they have done if I wasn't there?

So I say let people gossip all they want. Does it change my life? Does it make me disappear? When I returned from China, I found here a restless seeking for something that couldn't be found. The Chinese found it many years ago—a sort of serenity, an inner calm that comes from the understanding of life. This is such a short life. And mine was truly short. Only fifty-four years.

People say, Oh, she died of a broken heart. She died of disappointment. She died of too much bitterness. She died to pay for her sins against the Chinese people. But I say nothing matters one way or the other. I have learned not to struggle, but to flow along with the tide.

CHAPTER 15

SECOND CHANCES

1939–41

O N February 21, 1939, less than a year after it opened, a fire leveled China City. Officials blamed the fire on smoldering firecrackers used in celebration of Chinese New Year. Most of the shopkeepers, including Fong Yun, had no insurance. For a few unfortunates, it meant the loss of all their worldly possessions; beaten, they simply walked away. But many of the inhabitants dipped into savings or borrowed money from relatives to reopen; Fong Yun once again went to his brother for help and received it.

Three months later, on May 17, 1939, Union Station—built over the ruins of Apablasa Street—opened and was billed as "the most modern terminal in America." Angelenos were already producing more than half of the country's airplanes, and the most incredible traffic jams in the history of mankind. To combat the latter, a proposal for a four-hundred-mile network of freeways had been introduced.

On August 2, 1939, China City reopened amid great fanfare. A troupe of actors performed selections from famous Chinese operas. Lion and dragon dancers gyrated and shimmied through the alleyways. Magicians, musicians, and devil dancers worked their charms. Fireworks—carefully monitored this time—were set off. Café owners doled out souvenir chopsticks, while the proprietors of stalls and shops handed out lichees. But business would never be quite the same. China City would stumble along year after year, becoming more rickety and rundown as New Chinatown continued to prosper and grow.

Soon after China City burned, Stella discovered she was pregnant. Both Eddy and Stella regarded this as a chance to start their marriage afresh. But Stella sensed that there'd be problems with the pregnancy. Her doctor reinforced her foreboding by calling on weekends and at odd hours. At the end of December he began calling every day to ask when she was going to come in and have the baby. Stella always answered, "It's not time yet. I'll go to the hospital on January fifteenth."

On the day Stella finally went to the hospital, she stopped to see Ticie and Sissee at the house on Maplewood. "Take care of Richard if something happens to me," she said, so convinced was she that she was going to die. The last thing she remembered was her doctor talking softly, reassuringly, as the anesthesiologist put the mask over her face. When she woke, Sissee was sitting next to the bed.

"The baby?" Stella asked.

Her sister-in-law's eyes brimmed with tears. "He's alive, Stell, but he's not going to make it."

Strong as she was, Stella wasn't strong enough to see the infant, who'd been born hydrocephalic. The baby's head was huge and filled with water, the doctor explained. He'd be lucky to die quickly. A couple of days later the doctor came in again to say that the baby had died. Stella blamed herself. She believed that if she hadn't had the abortion when Eddy was fooling around with Helen Smith, the baby wouldn't have died.

Six months later, in June 1940, President Roosevelt signed into law the Alien Registration Act, which required the registration and finger-printing of aliens and made it unlawful for them to belong to "anti-American" organizations. In November, Roosevelt was reelected for an unprecedented third term.

This same month, Angel Island closed. Although as early as 1922 the immigration station had been deemed "too filthy and unfit for habitation," it wasn't until November 4, 1940, that the last 125 Chinese men and 19 women held on the island were moved to a temporary facility in San Francisco. Once war was declared, the U.S. Army conscripted the island for the detention of Japanese prisoners of war. After the war, the barracks would continue their slow decay.

As these world events and small personal stories unfolded, the people living in the four Chinese communities of Los Angeles—China City; New Chinatown; the last rundown blocks of Old Chinatown, west of Alameda; and the Market Chinatown, by the City Market—intensified the civic activities that had their inception during the Depression and now continued through the Sino-Japanese war. Horrified at reports of starvation and orphaned children, Chinese American women joined organizations to raise money to help China defend herself and to alleviate the suffering of her people. These women, who had for so long been silent, appealed to women of all races to wear cotton stockings instead of Japanese-made silk. They raised money for medical supplies and food. They organized bazaars, fashion shows, and theatrical and dance productions.

Beginning in 1938 and throughout the war, all the Los Angeles China-towns participated in a Moon Festival to raise money for United China Relief. Over several weeks, excitement escalated as a Moon Festival Queen was selected for her beauty and manners. David Soo Hoo, the brother of the founder of New Chinatown, suggested that other girls form a drum corps. In years to come, the Mei Wah girls would become a regular feature at parades and festivals throughout the southland.

During the coming years, Chinese Americans—who had traditionally avoided conflict or the appearance of being "troublemakers"—took to the streets in parades and demonstrations against American companies selling scrap iron and oil to Japan. Chinese picketed Japanese-owned factories and businesses. The Chinese boycotted Japanese goods, many of which had been mainstays in their small shops. (Sometimes the "boycott" meant simply sitting the whole family down for hours to peel off the little stickers that read "Made in Japan.")

No one lives on in the memories of Chinatown residents for her pro-China stance more than Mrs. Leong, the wife of the owner of the Soochow Restaurant and mother of Gilbert Leong. Mrs. Leong, who had female relatives who'd been raped, beaten, and murdered by Japanese soldiers, put the same obsessive energy into raising money for China Relief that she did into drilling her Chinese students on their calligraphy. When the Chinese Chamber of Commerce made up contribution cans printed in English and Chinese to put in stores and restaurants, Mrs. Leong boarded the bus and went all over the city to every place she'd heard there was a Chinese restaurant or laundry to drop off a can. She traveled out to Hollywood, the beach cities, and even to outlying areas that seemed to have no names. Each month, Mrs. Leong came out the leader in collected contributions.

With all this change, Chinatown's teenagers experienced a freedom that would have been regarded as unseemly as little as five years before. In a survey conducted in 1939, 210 Chinese boys and girls said they listened to the radio, and professed a deep admiration for Jack Benny and Eddie Cantor. The teenagers also enjoyed George Burns and Gracie Allen, Jack Oakie, Fred Allen, Al Jolsen, and Al Pearce. The girls adored Bing Crosby, while the boys preferred the Hit Parade Orchestra.

Where was Fong See during all this? He was being the maverick he'd always been. He had made his reputation and maintained his strength by avoiding the traditional roles of his fellow immigrants. Of course, he'd brought his family home from China before serious bombing started, but not before his children had participated in anti-Japanese rallies to protest the selling in China of Japanese-made toys and appliances. Naturally, he was disturbed when the Japanese captured Fatsan and decided that they would use his hotel for their headquarters.

But See-bok didn't concern himself with local anti-Japanese propaganda. He didn't go to rallies. He didn't care that shipping routes were closed and dangerous. In his Department of Water and Power compound he had great quantities of Japanese merchandise sitting in packing crates from numerous trips. His neighbors, who had lost relatives in the Rape of Nanking or in the numerous bombing raids of civilians, were incensed by See-bok's attitude. It wasn't just that Fong See wouldn't give to their causes, but that he flaunted his Japanese merchandise, displaying it prominently in the front windows of his store. "Fong See plays two ways," people grumbled. "He's on both sides. We ought to hit this guy."

For a brief moment See-bok gave the appearance of retiring. In 1939, J. J. Sugarman, an auctioneer and dealer who had been involved in the shooting of *The Good Earth,* approached him with an offer to buy the entire stock of merchandise of the F. See On Company, all cash. Fong See quickly agreed to the terms. Sugarman sold the merchandise at a "sale" from the store's longtime location at 510 Los Angeles Street. Once this was completed, Fong See resumed tenancy. He became famous for this transaction. Even forty years after his death, there would be those in Chinatown who would still shake their heads in a combination of awe, disbelief, and sheer happiness that a Chinese could best a Caucasian.

See-bok had held some of the best things back from Sugarman, and prepared to start over again. This time See-bok wouldn't have "partners." He would work solely on his own, without having to deal with the niggling harassment of the immigration officials. But he was eighty-two, an age when travel and negotiations were hard to do alone. Chuen, his eldest son by Ngon Hung, was only twelve, too young to be of any help on a buying trip. Instead, See-bok turned to his eldest son from his marriage to Ticie. "I wish to go to China on a buying trip," he told Milton. "You need to come. I am too old to do all of that bargaining by myself."

"Okay, I'll take this last trip with you," Ming answered. He packed his bag, said good-bye to Dorothy, and accompanied his father overseas.

The 1939 trip to China would serve them both well. Fong See had taught his sons that profit could always be made during unrest. Everyone in Chinatown sensed that war with Japan was coming in a big way. Fong See knew, and Ming agreed, that now was the time to go over and get out as much as they could. Together, Ming and his father would be able to buy in bulk, separating the goods once they got back to Los Angeles.

This trip would also expand the types of merchandise both stores carried. Collecting had changed in the years Fong See had been in business. Until China's 1911 revolution, Americans had followed long-standing European tastes when it came to Chinese antiques. Collectors filled their drawing rooms and parlors with either polychrome porcelains in rose, green, and blue and white, or monochromes—*sang de boeuf,* DuBarry pink, *blanc de chine, clair de lune,* flame rouge, and soufflé.

After 1911, royal artifacts—Ming scrolls, palace appointments, imperial robes, and Ming porcelains—had flooded the market. The following tumultuous years of the warlords had brought further hardship to China, with the result that many families were forced to sell heirlooms

Sissee, early 1920s.

Above left: Ming See as a handsome playboy, 1920s.
Above right: Ray See as a handsome playboy, 1920s.

Above left: Eddy's graduation photo, 1924.
Above right: Stella Copeland, 1924.

Bennie and
Bertha at the
beach, early
1920s.

Above left: Immigration photo of Ngon Hung and Chuen, 1927.
(*National Archives, Pacific Sierra Region*)
Above right: Immigration photo of Lui Ngan Fa, 1927.
(*National Archives, Pacific Sierra Region*)

Immigration photo of Leong-shee and her children.
Top row: Danny Ho and Kuen. *Bottom row*: Choey Lau and Haw.
(*National Archives, Pacific Sierra Region*)

The house in Dimtao, 1920s.

The old Department of Water and Power building on Alameda Street
where Fong See set up a compound for his family and that of his brother, Fong Yun.
(*El Pueblo de Los Angeles Historical Monument*)

Los Angeles Street. *Left to right*: Lugo House, F. See On Company
(after the separation), and Soochow Restaurant. Ticie's F. Suie One
Company was on the corner at the far left. (*Bison Archives*)

Tyrus Wong.

Painting of Sissee by Benji Okubo.

Sissee outside the
Dragon's Den,
late 1930s.

Exterior of Dragon's Den viewed from Marchessault Street.
The F. Suie One Company was upstairs.
(*El Pueblo de Los Angeles Historical Monument*)

Richard See, c. 1935.

Anna May Wong

Uncle Fong Yun's family, c. 1933. *Top row*: Haw's wife,
Haw, Kuen's wife, Choey Lau, Kuen, Ho's wife, Ho. *Seated*: Leong-shee
and Fong Yun. *Bottom row*: Gim, Chong, and Gai.

China City
(*El Pueblo de Los Angeles Historical Monument*)

New Chinatown

"Howard Yip goes to work daily with the sign above displayed on his back—notice to fellow workers he's Chinese and anxious to help smash the Japanese." Photo and caption from the *Herald Examiner*, January 1942. (*Hearst Collection, Department of Special Collections, University of Southern California*)

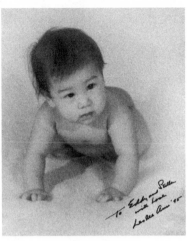

Ticie, late in life.

Leslee Leong, 1945.

Fong See's children from the second family, c. 1945.
Sumoy, Gary, Jong Oy, May Oy, and Chuen.

that many collectors and museum representatives considered superior to the royal ware. Most of these items dated back to the Sung Dynasty and included jades, early metals, paintings, jewels, and ceramics. New porcelains—snowy *tings,* Lung Chuans, Kuan crackles, splashed *chuns* or *ch'iens*—suddenly appeared on the market. During this same period, Chinese railroad crews were burrowing through mountains, breaking through city walls, and accidentally opening graves. As laborers unearthed works from the Han, Tsin, Wei, and Sui dynasties, a passion for primitive works took hold. Finally, as western collectors became increasingly sophisticated, they became more enamored of the great loves of the Chinese themselves—paintings, bronzes, and jades.

By the mid-thirties, no single genre was more popular and sought after by American collectors than archaic bronzes, some dating from as early as the eighteenth century B.C. (The Chinese themselves had harbored a passion for these vessels since the time of Christ, when copies first made their appearance. And as recently as World War I, the Chinese still cherished their bronzes, negotiating with Germany through the Versailles Treaty for the return of an antique bronze astronomical instrument taken from the Peking Imperial Observatory during the Boxer Rebellion.) Fong See hoped that he would be able to find bronzes at a decent price.

The trip through Korea, Japan, and China proved to be strenuous and difficult. The Koreans expected Fong See to kowtow to them, which he found unimaginable, unthinkable, intolerable. The Koreans insulted him and didn't show respect. He raged, while Ming tried to pacify him. That only made Fong See angrier and more belligerent. In China they traveled into areas already occupied by the Japanese. They went to Jingdezhen to what had once been a royal kiln, and loaded their purchases on barges and floated them down the Yangtze. Along the way, they advertised for people to come to the riverside to sell their belongings. Slowly Ming and See-bok floated from Nanking to Shanghai. The Japanese stopped them, boarded their boat, and attempted to confiscate everything. One legend has it that Ming and See-bok were afraid for their lives; another says that Ming acted like "an arrogant son of a bitch" and this time it was his father who tried to calm him down, instead of the other way around.

As See-bok predicted, business was good. In Yokohama, Ming bought six cases of mushrooms (for Dragon's Den), a rickshaw, and miscellaneous curios for $224.91 U.S. In Kobe he bought ten strings of pearls of varying quality. But most of the merchandise was purchased in China—Canton, Shanghai, and Peking. A random look at a packing slip from the P. H. Yui Company in Peking reveals the breadth and depth of type, quality, and quantity of merchandise father and son purchased.

Case number 1 (all brass): 12 pairs stirrups; 1 peach incense burner; 3 figures; 5 incense burners; 1 unicorn; 4 irons; 3 vases; 2 cows; 1 duck; 1 libation cup; 4 mirrors; 1 stove; 9 symbols; 43 ornaments. Case 67: 1 pottery horse; 2 lacquer trunks; 1 silk embroidery hanging; 2 silk embroidery bedcovers; 4 silk embroidery temple hangings; 2 silk embroidery door hangings; 230 yards of silk, satin, and velvet in white, blue, tan, yellow, and green.

All told, the goods amounted to 134 cases, weighing a total of 28,123 pounds. Cases were measured by overall weight, but also by the gross weight of particular items: plain lacquer, 1,015 pounds; lacquer inlaid with stone, 650 pounds; bone, 20 pounds; ivory, 34 pounds; horn lanterns, 20 pounds; silk embroideries, 120 pounds; porcelain, 607 pounds; Soochow jade, 58 pounds. The merchandise left Peking on November 25, 1939, traveled by train to Tientsin, then was placed on the SS *Norway Maru,* and arrived in Los Angeles on January 18, 1940.

Ming was caught smuggling on his return, although whether the charges resulted from this particular shipment is unclear. Two sets of packing slips had been drawn up—one set showing the real prices, and another listing much lower prices. But Ming, as arrogant as his father, carried both sets of papers on his person. After Ming paid an initial duty of $1,100.30, Customs performed a more thorough search. Four opium pipes were seized, as well as thirty rawhide cutout puppets, for a 100-percent undervaluation. Yet after close inspection of the merchandise, only another $73.77 in duties were required.

Neither Ming nor his father was a stranger to these antics; both had been caught for smuggling several times before. Although they were legitimately culpable, organizational problems within China made matching invoices and packing slips almost impossible. On the other hand, duty was steep, at fifty percent or more, so quite often the exporter would draw up a fake invoice listing goods at half the purchase price.

People on both sides of the Pacific were affected by Ming's error, as letters from the time attest. Mr. Shing of the Zing Hsiang Shing Company on Nanking Road in Shanghai wrote to acknowledge the trouble Ming was having clearing merchandise through customs at "a lower price." "We [were] sure you had cleared the trouble long ago," Mr. Shing wrote. "We are now having the same trouble over in San Francisco, the matter is unsettled pending investigation." He requested that "Mr. Milton" go to San Francisco and "get the trouble cleared."

Instead of being angry at Ming, See-bok was pleased. The way he saw it, smuggling was a bad word for an honorable undertaking. If you were smart, you did it. It was an integral part of business, and one of the skills—See-bok happily noted—that Ming had learned well.

Upon his return from China, Fong See decided to leave his Department of Water and Power compound, and rented the Methodist Mission's old space on Los Angeles Street. The basement of this building housed Dragon's Den. Ticie rented the street level and mezzanine for the F. Suie One Company. Up another flight of stairs, See-bok, Ngon Hung, and their many children took up residence.

Once his family was settled, See-bok began the arduous job of setting up a new business in his old storefront at 510 Los Angeles Street. His longtime Caucasian customers marveled at him. They took a kind of ownership of him, calling him "my Mr. See." "My Mr. See was rich," recalled one customer more than fifty years later. "He was a force, a builder who made things happen. The old boy had something. Well, look how I remember it. He had a bit of the pidgin thing, but I want to impress upon you the sense of dignity and quality. He left with me the memory not of a peasant in any way, though a Chinaman, of course."

By 1940, Gilbert Leong had been dating Sissee See for six years. When he looked at her, he saw a beautiful girl. She had a perfect oval face, not the harsh features of a girl of peasant stock. Her voice was melodious, not the high screech of some Chinese girls or the broad, rough tones of American girls. Her body was slim, without the flat front and back of Chinese girls or the unseemly bulges of American girls. She wore her hair in a chignon run through with elaborate Chinese ornaments. And she was kindness itself, as any person down on his luck knew. For all of these reasons Gilbert loved Sissee, but he still hadn't proposed. His parents were against the marriage, and Gilbert couldn't break away from their rigid religious beliefs or their old-fashioned Chinese traditions.

The Leong family had come from the South China village of Sun Wei, known throughout the region for its oranges. In 1896, Gilbert's father, Leong Jeung, traveled to the Gold Mountain as a laborer, entering the country as a "paper son." He worked first as a vegetable peddler, going door to door with a pushcart. Later, Gilbert's mother helped his father open a stall at the City Market. At the top of the market hierarchy were bonded, commissioned merchants who acted on behalf of the farmers to sell their produce. Next came second jobbers, who bought from people like the Leongs and sold to grocery stores. At the bottom were the *hang chieh mei*—the "walking behind the cart" men who took produce in their carts from neighborhood to neighborhood.

Everyone in the Leong family worked in the stall. Gilbert's father and older brother stacked the fruit and vegetable crates five or six high. Gilbert's mother helped sort the produce. Gilbert dressed the fruit, putting the best on top. As with the See family, all the money the children earned went into a family pot and was doled out as necessary by Gilbert's mother.

After so many years of eighteen-hour days, Leong Jeung had tired of produce, and opened his restaurant in Hollywood. Gilbert had worked as a waiter there, earning more tips when he spoke pidgin English than when he spoke his college English. After the failed Chinese Garden Café, the family had opened Soochow in Chinatown. Soochow had been the third restaurant in the city to serve *cha nau,* tea cakes. Gilbert's mother insisted on stocking a wide variety of teas—chrysanthemum, Sixth Happiness, oolong, jasmine, and poney with its strong musty flavor—which were always set on the table first. Then the waiters brought out steamers filled with *char siu bao* (steamed buns stuffed with roast pork) and other dumplings shaped like an ear or a pocketbook or an old man's scrotum. When the customers finished, the waiter figured the bill by counting up the empty plates. Any dumplings left on the table were taken back to the kitchen and steamed up again.

In 1936, with the success of Soochow, the Leongs moved away from the City Market area to the Italian neighborhood of Cypress Park, at the base of Mount Washington, just east of downtown. The house looked like a Southern plantation house, with two stories, big columns in the front, ten rooms, and plenty of land. Gilbert had heard all kinds of stories about the house—that it had once been a speakeasy, the home of a bootlegger, or the home of Jim Jeffries, the former heavyweight champ. Despite the house's rather unseemly past, the neighbors had balked at the possibility of a Chinese family moving in. But after the local minister spoke to the neighbors and introduced the Leongs, there hadn't been any trouble.

Gilbert was a proper Chinese son and an excellent student. He had grown up listening to his mother say, "Don't embarrass the Chinese people." His mother was strict in this sense: Gilbert and his brothers and sister knew their English and they knew their Chinese. They grew up speaking Chinese at home. "When I speak to you in Chinese," his mother had said when he was a boy, "I expect you to answer me in Chinese. Don't *ever* answer me in English. In the first place, I won't understand you. In the second place, we won't be able to develop a dialogue. Besides, how would it be for the sons and daughter of the Chinese teacher not to be proficient in Chinese?"

Gilbert started learning Chinese as a small boy, but not from his mother. His mother didn't have time to do the normal things—darn socks or cook—never mind give private lessons to her son. She was too busy—teaching her classes, traveling up to San Francisco to buy textbooks, brushes, and ink, and working in the produce stall—for things like that. Instead, they brought over Gilbert's grandmother. After her home chores, she sat with Gilbert at the kitchen table and taught him simple words and phrases.

When it came time for high school, Gilbert's parents decided that he should go across town to Lincoln, which meant that he'd be passing right through Chinatown after school and could go to his mother's class. He remembered walking up the dark stairwell and into the room, which faced out onto the corner of Marchessault and Los Angeles streets. He had known all twenty-five students—aged five to eighteen—who were divided into roughly five groups for their recitations. As for his primary lessons, they were indelibly etched in his brain.

"Each lesson will have thirty words," his mother instructed the new students. "You will pay attention and you will memorize." Gilbert learned quickly enough that those who didn't follow his mother's rules found their hands whacked with the punishing end of a bamboo feather duster.

"The Chinese language was invented by a ruler who watched how worms crawl," his mother explained. "The worms turn left. The worms turn right. Our language has gone through many centuries of change and evolution. Scholars revise it, throw it out, reinvent it."

Day. Sun. Earth. Moon. Those were his first characters. Combine *sun* and *moon,* and the meaning changed to *tomorrow.* The next characters in the primer were *Heaven* and *Earth.* Then *Father. Mother. Son. Daughter.* As he grew older he saw how the characters built upon each other. Add a stroke to the character for *door* and it became *home.* Add another and it became *marriage.* One stroke for *boy,* add another for *son,* double that to get *boy twins.* With every stroke the meaning evolved and became more complex.

"You must study so that you can fulfill your filial obligation and write letters to your grandparents in your home villages," his mother lectured. From their workbooks the students carefully copied out characters, then inserted the names of their grandparents. *How are you? We are fine. I am studying in school.* When they reached the third and fourth levels, they received new workbooks that taught the geography and history of China. *The shape of China is like a mulberry leaf.* Gilbert could still remember the indigo primers, which had been hand-sewn together in China. Somehow the smell of China had sunk into the wood-block prints and thin paper, so that Gilbert thought they were learning about China through their noses as well as their ears and mouths and fingers.

Gilbert needed to be the best student. It was expected not just by his mother, but by all the students in the mission school. Even so, of the thousands of Chinese ideograms, he learned perhaps a thousand requiring mostly four or five strokes, with a few of up to ten strokes. The characters with twenty-five or thirty strokes were rare words, with rich meaning for scholars of deep understanding.

Beyond his studies of Chinese, Gilbert's parents expected him to excel in the white world. Unlike Fong See, who was from the peasant class, Mrs. Leong had been educated. The family not only believed that the life of the scholar was one of the most pure, but they also believed that education was the only way to break out of Chinatown. Once the Leongs recognized Gilbert's drive and aptitude, they pulled his older brother, Ed, out of college so that Gilbert could go in his place. Gilbert went to USC and Chouinard to study art and architecture; his sculptures were exhibited in China City, and he was apprenticing with an architect, but his mother still wasn't satisfied with these accomplishments. He thought that she would only relax her hold on him once he was getting commissions to design his own buildings.

On an evening in late 1940, after the rest of the family had retired upstairs, Gilbert found himself sitting in the living room, listening to his mother lecture him. "There are other girls in this city," she said sternly. "Forget this girl, this Florence See. In time you will find someone who's one hundred percent Chinese. You tell me you like her, and I tell you it is like the sky falling down." The more Gilbert listened to these never-ending lectures, the more his resolve crumbled. "You're young," his mother continued.

"Mother," Gilbert interrupted, "I'm thirty."

She glared at him for a moment, then went on. "I'm not prejudiced. But I want my son to marry a Chinese girl. I'll tell you why. Interracial marriages don't work. You look at Fong See's family. You look at the Chew family. You will be stared at. You won't be accepted. And if you have children . . ."

Gilbert had never had time for outside activities. As a small boy he hadn't gone to the homes of other children. He hadn't had spending money for frivolous things. Instead, he'd been a member of the church's Epworth League for young people. They'd met once a week to listen to different elders tell of their experiences. Gilbert had never dated in high school. Then, in college, he'd met the Tom Leung family. The father was an herbalist. One daughter was a journalist. Another had married Peter Soo Hoo. After football games, the family had hosted parties with dancing. Gilbert had been to a few of those, had even danced with a couple of girls. That Elsie, for example. He shivered at the memory of her forwardness during a fox trot, when she had pressed her breasts against his chest and babbled about her trip to Shanghai, where she and Anna May Wong's brother, Jimmy, had, according to her, introduced the tango not just to the New Asia Hotel but to the whole mainland. "When I was in China, I had maids for everything," Elsie had whispered in his ear. "Food. Laundry. Cleaning. I didn't have to do housework, which would dull my hair and ruin my complexion." He could see that she wasn't the tanned tomboy who'd left a year ago. Now the pink chiffon of her dress molded across curves that most Chinese girls didn't have, and her skin was a creamy white. But nothing ever came of Elsie.

There was the other type of girl. The prostitutes and girls of bad reputation. Off Alameda in the crib section, Chinese girls still leaned over balcony railings and lured lonely bachelors upstairs. These women catered to Chinese men. Only rarely did he see Chinese men with Caucasian girls. They were not the high type of Caucasians. They were the lowest type of blondes; they were prostitutes painted up. Those men wouldn't walk down Wilshire or Broadway with those girls, but they would take them to Chinatown, where no one would voice their scorn. Even in Soochow there were men who brought in a certain type of girl, some of them quite famous. Like Johnny Weismuller with that Lupe Velez. She was a firecracker, hot, and with a body. But Gilbert agreed with his mother. Women of that sort were disgusting.

The fact was, Gilbert didn't know much about sex. He could joke with Tyrus and Eddy about the time he'd been delivering tea cakes to a winner at one of the gambling houses, and an ambulance had pulled up in front of one of the cribs and the attendants had brought out a man and a woman—both naked—stuck together like two dogs. "Too much Spanish fly," Gilbert had heard on the street.

When he told the story, Eddy had laughed: "He died with a smile on his face." But Tyrus had guessed Gilbert's confusion. "Didn't your father tell you about the birds and the bees?" Tyrus asked. "My father didn't tell me, either. I tell you what, if you go down to the herbalist you can find anything for below the belt. Believe me. Men's potency. Women's fertility. You say you've got a headache, they can't do anything for you!" Gilbert's friends thought it was all one big joke.

As much as he fought against his feelings, Gilbert only cared for one girl. How could he explain that to his mother? How could he explain who he was? *I am a sculptor. With my hands I take marble and form it into beauty. I make the stone yield to my desires. I am an architect. I want to take my visions and turn them into structures for life and for the living.* Gilbert longed to break free, but he knew he was the one chosen to get ahead, to be the scholar who would bring honor to his family.

Gilbert looked into his hands, bowed his head in submission, and said nothing. He knew—and he hated himself for it—that he would break off with Sissee as soon as possible.

One day in 1941, Ticie stepped out of the car, her shoes crunching on the gravel, and looked down the driveway of what had been her childhood home in Central Point, Oregon. The sky shone a rich, deep blue and the air was hotter than hell, just as she remembered. Otherwise, the whole place was different.

"What do you think, Ma?"

Ticie turned and looked at her daughter.

"There used to be a little pond over there." Ticie pointed. "And see the cook shed? A tobacco plant used to grow up onto the roof. It's dead now."

Sissee, sensing her mother's distress, said, "Come on, let's look around."

They spent the next hour walking around the property. Obviously no one had lived here for a long time. Weeds grew with abandon. The house was deserted. The barn still stood, and with a gentle shove the old door creaked open. The sun's rays filtered in through the cracks of the exterior planking. Dust motes floated through the streams of light. The barn was empty now, except for a few forgotten bales of hay banked along one wall. With the heat of the day and decades of use, the barn was redolent with the musty odors of farm animals, hay, and wood beams. Looking up, Ticie saw pigeons roosting along the crossbeams. It had been almost fifty years since Ticie had left Oregon, and the barn still seemed the same. She imagined that in another fifty years the barn would still be standing—perhaps a bit more rickety, perhaps even completely empty—but standing nevertheless, because what farmer in his right mind would tear down a perfectly good barn?

Ticie went back outside, sat against the bumper of the car, and watched as her daughter strode out across the fields. Ticie didn't know who currently owned the property, so she tried not to blame her brothers for letting the place get so rundown. Besides, who was she to complain, anyway? Ticie was pretty rundown herself, when she thought about it. She'd never been a vain person, but now when she looked in the mirror she couldn't deny her reflection. She was an old woman. Round. Gray-haired. She wore glasses. She was tired and old in her heart, too. These days she found it an effort to get up, get dressed, be driven downtown, and sit in the store all day.

As she looked back at her life, she could see that she had created what she had most longed for. A family. In 1919, when Fong See had wanted to leave Eddy in China, thoughts of keeping the family together had forced her to gather up her children and go home. When they'd moved out of Chinatown, she had pushed the children to form the family pot to make them financially secure *and* to keep them all together. These days they still got together for Sunday dinners, for every holiday, and for all of the grandchildren's birthdays.

Sitting there in the hot sun, she allowed herself the sheer pleasure of thinking about her children. Although she was still the titular head of the F. Suie One Company, Ming had taken over the day-to-day affairs. He had grown to be good at business. Ming was able to combine her eye for art with Suie's business sense. Her second son, Ray, had always been loyal to her and still harbored a grudge against his father for leaving her. She saw the irony in his ambivalence: Ray, of all her children, was the most like Suie—wily and ambitious. She admired her third son's straightforwardness; Bennie liked woodworking, Bertha, and his children.

Ticie was perhaps closest to Stella, Eddy, their son, Richard, and Sissee. Ticie saw them every day. Stella had been like a second daughter to her. Ticie was proud of Eddy, proud of his exuberance and his success with Dragon's Den. She admired the way he made an effort with Suie's second family. In this, Eddy was most like her: family came first. As for Richard, he was her favorite grandchild. She was delighted with his clever streak, his innate intelligence. She couldn't help but spoil him.

Finally, there was her daughter. Sissee was truly one of the most beautiful girls in Chinatown, and it wasn't just a mother saying that. Her thick, dark hair curled in the style of the day. She had high cheekbones and almond eyes. Her shy, welcoming smile stole people's hearts. She was a living, breathing, lovely girl with no one to hold her. Ticie acknowledged that she was partly at fault for this. She relied excessively on her daughter. She counted on Sissee to take her shopping, to Chinatown, to the store. Well, look! Sissee had brought her on this trip.

Now Ticie was dying. The doctor hadn't said it outright, but she knew it was true. And now that these last—what?—months, years, were upon her she focused on one final goal: to see her daughter married. Ticie needed to know that Sissee would be taken care of. On the trip coming north, Ticie had tried to talk to Sissee about this. "You should have someone in your life. You don't always have to be responsible for me." Sissee had laughed lightly and changed the subject. Ticie couldn't push too hard because she knew the reality as well as she knew her own daughter.

Sissee was thirty-two years old. She was a half-breed. No *lo fan* would ever marry her; no Chinese would ever marry her. Most Chinese families wouldn't even let their sons date an American girl. Ticie had overheard one mother in Chinatown say, "I would not want my son to marry a foreigner. It would be inconvenient to talk to a daughter-in-law like that, and my son would drift away."

After living in Chinatown as long as she had, Ticie should have been used to these old-fashioned ideas. This was, after all, the same community where marriages between people of different Chinese districts were discouraged. "Different dialect," mothers said. "Different customs. Too much worry for my son." Even now, marriages in Chinatown were often arranged formally, either through a matchmaker or just by two mothers getting together with photographs of their most perfect children. Many families—like Uncle's—still preferred to send their sons to China to marry a "proper" girl, one who had been raised with strict customs and didn't know the silliness of dancing, music, movies, or radio. Most girls were married by the time they were twenty-one. Sissee's friend Jennie had married and borne three children by that age. Only a few brave girls struggled against tradition and family to marry, as Ticie had, for love.

Being here at the Pruett homestead couldn't help but bring back memories of that girl who had carried such hopes for love. Now that Ticie's life was coming to an end, she looked back on her life with some detachment. She *had* married for love. She'd separated from her husband for love, too. Ticie had held her head up with pride, walked out the door, and opened her own store. How could she have known that the Depression would come? How could she have known how lonely she would be? Yes, she had held her family together, but at what cost to herself?

When she returned to Chinatown after the failure on Wilshire, she was no longer the wife of Chinatown's most prominent businessman. She became just the pathetic old *fan gway* woman renting space on the corner. But where else could she have gone? When she'd married Fong See, she'd given up many options. Chinatown was nothing if not a place for people with few options.

As a girl—churning butter, milking cows, baby-sitting all of those kids whose names she could no longer remember—she never could have imagined that her last vice in life would be the lottery. Many of the old men, who shuffled through the streets selling tickets on their circuit from Soochow to the butcher shop to her store, had been in Chinatown as long as she. She had helped some of them with their leases, their correspondence, and the immigration. They had all grown old together, and they had not forgotten her as so many of her neighbors had.

They waited patiently while she stared intently at the off-white paper with the green characters—eight across and ten down—for tree, cat, rat, cow. She would consider, then say, "I saw a cat today. Which is the character for *cat*? That's the one I'll mark." Or, "The moon was very beautiful last night, don't you think, Ah-soong? Show me the character for *moon*." Later in the day, the old men would come back to tell her if she had won.

As these thoughts drifted through her mind, Ticie watched Sissee pause at the far end of the field and turn her face to the sun. Since she was far away, Ticie visualized how her daughter looked. Sissee's cheeks would be tinged pink and shiny with a thin sheen of sweat from her excursions and the warmth of the day. As Sissee turned, waved, and began her slow walk back toward the car, Ticie thought, not for the first time, that her daughter was simply too beautiful to end up an old maid.

Ticie saw that her daughter was naive. Sissee didn't understand about Gilbert's family. She didn't realize how important it was to Gilbert that his mother served as the president of the China this and the China that.

Sissee, whom Ticie had raised to look at people for who they were, didn't understand that Gilbert's family saw only her "white" face. She didn't comprehend the pressure Mrs. Leong put on all of her children, especially Gilbert, her bright light. Ticie saw and understood all this, but over the last seven years she hadn't been able to think of a way to explain it to Sissee.

Like most couples, Sissee and Gilbert had their fights. Ticie loved to bake pies, and Sissee liked to invite Gilbert over for a piece. "Why don't you come over for pie tonight?" Sissee had asked Gilbert one day several months ago when she'd walked over to Soochow to borrow some bamboo shoots when Dragon's Den had run out. He'd said he'd be over about seven.

That night, Sissee had waited. Gilbert hadn't called. Stella had said reassuringly, "Well, it's Saturday night, maybe Soochow's busy." They'd all waited some more.

Finally, Gilbert had arrived. Ticie had brought out the pie and asked, "How big a piece would you like?"

"I don't want any," Gilbert had replied. "I already had some of Mrs. Coe's pie."

They'd sat there in shock. Later, Sissee had cried. And Gilbert had been locked out of the house for weeks. But eventually Gilbert and Sissee were once again an item.

Ticie remembered how puzzled the family had been when Gilbert told Sissee, "You're the one." Was this the proposal? Was this it? Then Gilbert had changed his mind again. "I'd like to marry you, but I have to do as my family says. You're not Chinese."

This time the relationship was off for good. Sissee was devastated. As in most families when one of their own is hurt, the anger had turned outward. "Who the hell do they think they are?" Stella had railed. "Who does he think he is? He's just the son of a restaurant owner. Big deal." But it had been a big deal to Sissee, and that was the real reason that Ticie had allowed her daughter to talk her into this trip.

Once Sissee got back to the car, they drove down the road a mile or so to the Central Point cemetery. Over the years, Ticie had grown accustomed to the Chinese tradition of caring for the graves of ancestors, so it shocked her to see the cemetery overgrown with weeds and poison oak. Ticie and Sissee wandered aimlessly, then became more systematic in their search as they picked their way among the headstones, looking for the graves of Luscinda and John Pruett. They'd gone on this way for nearly a half hour when Ticie paused and looked over and across a few rows to a pair of white marble headstones facing away from her. Ticie crossed straight to the two stones, walked around them, and saw her parents' graves. Moss grew at the base of each marker. Rain and snow had weathered the marble, sending dark stains over the words "He was a kind father and a friend to all," and "Jesus loves the pure and holy."

After they'd pulled the weeds, Sissee said, "Mom, let's see if any of your brothers still live around here."

Ticie walked back to the car, remaining silent through the drive to the filling station, where Sissee looked in a telephone directory. "There's a Pruett listed," Sissee called out.

"I don't care," Ticie said.

"We've come all this way. Don't you want to go over and meet this person?"

"No, I don't want to do anything like that. I just want to go home."

To see so much change in your lifetime wasn't such a wonderful thing, See-bok thought. What was it the *lo fan* said? No cloud without a silver lining? He thought there was no silver lining without a cloud. Here he was, a man in his eighties, an astute businessman, respected, feared. He had a beautiful young wife who had given him many children. He was sure she would bear him more, too. But he couldn't help feeling bitter.

He'd developed a different feeling about white people since marrying Ngon Hung. He'd had ideas. He'd had dreams. If just one *fan gway* had helped him . . . He didn't mean the friendship of Richard White or the simple business deal with Sugarman, but a real, true financial investment, then he could have been someone. He could have been someone *out there*. If he had been white, he would be famous and rich. He would live in Pasadena or Hancock Park. He would have a mansion filled with the most exquisite things the world had to offer. Now, as he looked back over his more than sixty years in this country, he could see the foolhardiness of his dreams.

So he'd become more Chinese. He'd abandoned his neatly tailored three-piece suits for mandarin robes. He'd relinquished his natty lizard-skin shoes for the comfortable cloth slippers he sold in his shop. He'd forgotten his English—or pretended to have done so. With a household of children babbling in Cantonese, he remembered the old sounds, phrases, and axioms of his youth. All those ideas of child-rearing that Ticie had laughed off, he now embraced unabashedly, knowing that Ngon Hung would never have the courage to speak up to him.

He had always been considered a far-ahead thinker. It became more difficult for him now. He thought about Ngon Hung. She was beautiful, but he was an old man. What if there were other men, younger men, who wanted her? He locked her up. He wouldn't let her out. Sometimes he wondered if she was unhappy, but his own jealousy made him dismiss those concerns. He never discussed business with Ngon Hung. She was neither his confidante nor a part of his business. The fact that she stayed home and had time to polish her fingernails gave him status in the community. She was young and attractive, even if she didn't have the latest hairdo or the newest clothes. He liked it that way.

He insisted that his second family act properly toward his first family. He made the children from his second family show respect for Ticie by visiting her regularly. (They reported that she was elegant but didn't speak much.) Each Saturday, See-bok arranged for Ngon Hung to send lunch over to Ticie and whoever was working in her store. Sometimes it would be a Chinese lunch, but mostly it came from See Yuen, on Alameda, which served American meals. The deliveryman walked up the small incline of Marchessault Street with a big tray heavy with silver-domed dishes of roast pork. These tribute meals paid off. The children of his first marriage—all grown now—called his wife *Ahpo*—giving her the respect of a "grandmother" though she was just a little older than Sissee—or *Ahji-ah*—"sister."

Try as he might, he never stopped thinking about Ticie. Sometimes he wondered, Do the others see I have a soft spot for her? He knew that Ticie still carried her love for him. Lately he wondered if she was ill or ailing in some way. Yet how could he go to her and not start gossip? Only when he went on his walks with his little Sumoy, his youngest daughter, did he stop at Ticie's store so he could talk to her.

Wives. It made him strong to have so many. It increased his esteem in the community. It was also good to have a warm young wife in his bed at night, but sometimes he thought it would also be nice to have some quiet time, too.

Children. When his children had come back from China in 1937, they were like low-class immigrants fresh off the boat; their English was terrible. Uncle's family, the same thing. See-bok didn't care. "One day we will all go back to China," he told his children. "We won't spend our money here. We'll save it for China." As for Chinese school, Fong See had come a long way from how he felt with the children from his first family. "Don't worry about your American education," he said these days. "You won't be living here forever. That's why you go to Chinese school. Pay attention and learn."

He ruled them with an iron fist. No bicycles. No roller-skating. No ice-skating. No movies. No radio. No sports. No football. No baseball. No dancing. No girlfriends. No boyfriends. No kissing. All of this went double—triple—for his daughters. When his children said that other fathers let their sons do or have these things, he answered, "Ah, but these things represent decay. These things are a bad influence." The difference between his second family and his first was that this time everyone obeyed him.

Grandchildren. At family banquets—weddings, births, deaths—all of his sons from the first marriage came with their families. He couldn't keep them straight. Ngon Hung did that for him. Oh, he knew Richard. That boy. But the rest? Some freckle-faced girl or long-boned, skinny girl would be presented to him. His wife would say, "This is Pollyanne, the daughter of Ray," or, "This is Marcia, the daughter of Bennie." He'd look them over, his attention already wandering, nod his head, say, "Yes, yes, yes, yes," then wave them away. Maybe a pat on the head depending on how he felt. These *lo fan* children were strangers to him.

Business. Mr. White was still a regular at both the F. Suie One and F. See On companies. He had dinner once a week with Ticie over on Maplewood, and dinner once a week with Fong See in his store, where the evening meal had always been provided for the employees. Mr. White came in, sat in a straight-backed chair or on a porcelain garden stool right next to the register, and calmly waited. But most of his old customers had died off, to be replaced by young decorators who knew nothing! See-bok had to teach them how to recognize a good piece of art. He worked even harder to cajole them into buying, to make them feel smart and clever.

He sized up these new customers just as he had the old government officials. Sometimes he put on a no-speakee-English routine. Sometimes he feigned to forget past negotiations, so that a young upstart would think he had bested See-bok and therefore came back to the store again and again. But just as in the old days, if a tourist walked in, See-bok yelled, "Get out! Get out! Don't bother me. If you can't afford to buy, then don't come in here. Go to another shop." He treated his few Chinese customers even worse: "I don't need your business. I don't want to bargain with you. Go away!" On the other hand, he still had his private den for those who had proved themselves worthy.

More business. He gave big parties in China, and he gave big parties here. He invited business associates home for tea cakes. He entertained them. When the delivery boy came, See-bok tipped him in front of all those business associates so they could see what an important man he was. Tipping wasn't a Chinese custom, but he had picked it up. Twenty-five cents, fifty cents, what was that to him? Was it for show? Of course, but it was always a big thing for the tea-cake man or the delivery boy from See Yuen. See? He was still a far-ahead thinker.

Business and family. He'd never wanted outsiders. "I'll bring someone from the family to help us," he'd always told his brother when they needed help. Why was this? His family had always helped when Caucasians wouldn't. Certain things were still important to him: money, property, and being a businessman, instead of a laundryman or grocery-man. He had never deviated from that course. Now people came to him for advice and guidance just as they did in the village. He had his favorites, and called in his markers when he had to. He didn't care what other people thought, as long as they agreed with him. He always had the last word.

"I need extra cash to bring someone over," someone might request.

"Who is this person?" See-bok would ask, then decide his or her fate depending on the answer.

"I need a job," a young man might say. "Can you help me?"

"What are your skills?" See-bok would inquire. "What do you know? What do you want to be?" When he had learned all he could, he would find a job for this or that young immigrant.

"Should I go into business with Lee Hom?"

"He has never been able to hold down a job," Fong See would opine. "You should look for someone else."

Someone might ask, "Arthur Chung has asked me for a ten-thousand-dollar loan. Should I lend it to him?"

Again, See-bok would consider. "No, two thousand is enough."

Even men with established businesses sought his advice.

"That boy from my home village, Jimmy, isn't working hard. Could you talk to him?"

And when Jimmy, a boy with the invincible attitude of youth, walked in, See-bok would question him: "Why aren't you doing your work in your uncle's laundry? Why are you not obeying him?"

If Jimmy was foolhardy enough to say, "I don't like to work hard," sure enough by the end of the day he would be without a job and learning what happened if you didn't follow orders.

The Japanese crisis. Some people in Chinatown still grumbled that See-bok kept Japanese goods in his store. That gossip had been started by no-accounts and people who talked too much. Why shouldn't he sell Japanese goods? It was his merchandise. He'd bought it before the war started. Who were they to tell him what to do? Why should he care what a bunch of no-accounts were yelling about? He remembered how his neighbors had come into his store to complain, then, later, had thrown paint on his windows. Did they think he would forget that?

When Mrs. Leong had come to call with her little tins for China Relief, he'd turned her away empty-handed. He knew how word of that had spread through Chinatown, but he didn't care. When his niece, who sometimes worked in the store, asked him about it, he explained, "I do my own charity. I give money to my village. I bring relatives over. You should give from the heart, and I do. Besides," he went on, "you don't know what they're going to do with the money. They're so greedy." To the son of the owner of Man Gen Low, he said, "I won't get involved with this anti-Japanese thing. Those people are corrupt. You give them money and they put half in their pockets. Why should I give my money to people like that? I don't need them. I don't rely on them. If I want to be patriotic, I'll do it the way I want."

Partners. He didn't have partners since he'd sold his business to Sugarman. Instead of simplifying his life, it seemed to make the most basic day-to-day affairs hard. Just a few years back, Fong Lum had been the family chef. He was a relative and a "partner." Each night he cooked a full Chinese feast in the back of the store. Everyone pulled up a chair to a round table like those in a restaurant. Fong See, who always liked fresh food, insisted on the freshest possible ingredients. He also liked chicken that weighed between three and four pounds. "They're the most tender," he told his sons.

One day Fong See had gotten the idea to buy a live chicken and slaughter it, thereby guaranteeing the freshest meal possible. Lum took the chicken out to the back alley, slit its throat, and threw it in a trashcan to thrash out its last moments. It jumped out, then scooted and dragged itself all around until there was blood everywhere and they'd all lost their appetites. Those days were gone, because Lum had deserted to work for Sugarman. That was that. Now Ngon Hung, who had never cooked before, had taken over.

Life story. When newspapermen interviewed him about Chinatown, he lied and told them he had been in Los Angeles since 1871. When customers called him Mr. See, Mr. On, or Mr. Suie, he never told them that his last name was actually Fong. When people asked how many wives he had, he answered one, two, three, or four, depending on his mood. When they asked him how he'd come to this country, he tried his best to make it into a good story, one that had never been heard before. Personally, he was sick of the whole thing. Why tell it again and again the same way? By now he had told so many stories to so many different people that he could no longer remember which was true or not.

On a Saturday morning in late 1941, Ngon Hung worked the woven frogs through their corresponding loops until each one had been fastened into place at her daughter's neck, armpit, and down her side. Then Ngon Hung pinched Sumoy's cheeks until they were a pleasant rosy color. "You're ready now," Ngon Hung said, gently pushing Sumoy through the room with the old organ and out into the main room of what had once been the Methodist Mission's main sanctuary. "He's waiting for you. Go on, walk with the old man."

Sumoy did as she was told. Born in 1935, Sumoy was the youngest girl in the family—the sweetest one, the most cherished. She was always good-tempered and never cried. Every day until she was old enough to go to school, she'd taken this walk with her father. Now she did it just on weekends and holidays.

Sumoy and her father left the apartment, walking down the two flights of dimly lit stairs. Pa took firm hold of her hand, reminding her, "Don't let go." Today they walked over to Soochow Restaurant, down to Dragon's Den, then to the Jin Hing Jewelry Store, the Eastern Grocery Store, and the Hop Sing Tong, where she sat on her father's lap and listened to him talk to the other old men.

On their way home, they stopped to visit "Mother" downstairs from where Sumoy and her family lived. Mother's store was a lot like Pa's. Mother was an old ghost woman. Even though she had many wrinkles, she was still very pretty. Sumoy knew Mother was part of the family; she just didn't know how or why. Sometimes Sumoy sat quietly while Pa and Mother chatted. But today Pa said, "You sit out here. Go over there and play." Mother handed her a toy butterfly on a stick. Then Mother and Pa disappeared behind a curtain that tinkled when they walked through it. Sumoy sat outside and waited.

Sumoy waved the butterfly back and forth, watching its paper wings flutter soundlessly. She had done something like this many times before, because Mother always gave Sumoy a book or crayons and paper to amuse herself. She never knew what Mother and Pa talked about. Even though Sumoy was only six, she knew she shouldn't ask.

Sumoy was in school and had learned that not everyone lived the way she did. She remembered her first day of kindergarten. Her mother had dressed her in Chinese cotton pants and a crossover frog jacket, just like today. When she'd gotten to school, all the other girls were wearing dresses. That night she'd begged her mother to let her wear a dress. But it had taken a long time for her parents to relent.

They didn't want her to do a lot of things. Pa didn't want her to join the Girl Scouts. "You're not the type of person to go on an overnight trip," he said. "Besides, I don't want my daughter to be viewed as sleeping on the ground." He didn't want her to go to the library: "If there's a book that's important for you to read, then you will get it at school. Otherwise you don't need it." He didn't like for her to go to church: "Don't spend active time there. No one should make up your mind for you. Don't give up your life for someone else."

Instead, her father wanted her to do her embroidery. He wanted her to learn how to knit. He wanted her to take piano lessons. She wasn't interested in those things. She watched her mother making shirts for her older brothers. She saw how her older sister, May Oy, was passive and shy, a good listener. May Oy was so quiet she was hardly there. Her oldest sister, Jong Oy, was lively. But everyone was always upset with her. They wanted Jong Oy to sit quietly and string macaroni necklaces to sell at Olvera Street.

Find joy in your family members only, Pa said. Sumoy thought that was okay for her older brothers and sisters; they had cousins their same age. Sumoy didn't. She was alone, so she spent her time with the adults. But she liked it when Pa took her over to China City to see Uncle and Auntie for lunch. Auntie was so nice to her! "Sit down," Auntie said when Sumoy visited. "Sit in this chair, because it is most comfortable." Auntie always asked Sumoy if she was happy. Auntie always retied the Shirley Temple bows in Sumoy's hair and whispered sweet words into her ear. Then Auntie would bring out sweets—sponge cakes, dumplings, coconut candies, or moon cakes made from winter melon and cut into thin slices. Sumoy would sit there feeling utterly content, because at home her father was so domineering and her mother always scolded, "Too many sweets. That's too sweet for the children. Why do you let them give those to her?"

The beaded curtain tinkled again, and Pa stepped out. Sumoy said good-bye to the ghost woman called Mother and followed her father. "Take my hand," he said when they got to the door. With one hand in her father's dry, papery palm and the other holding her butterfly on a stick, Sumoy went back out onto the street, blinking a few times as her eyes readjusted from the dimness of the store to the bright California sunshine.

Today she was too tired to remember her manners, and began asking questions. As they walked the few steps to the stairwell that would take them back upstairs to their apartment, she asked, "Pa, why don't you get a car so you can drive us around instead of walking all the time?"

"I'm too old to learn how to drive," he answered.

They began climbing the stairs. "Pa, why do we have to live here?"

"In fifty or one hundred years from now the city will still be growing," he said. "We are near the railroad. You want to be where people are coming and going. If we stay here, we will always be in the forefront of things."

Her father paused on the first-floor landing to catch his breath.

"Pa, don't you ever get tired of walking up and down these stairs?"

"We live *up*," he responded. "This building could be taller. If City Hall can be thirteen stories high, then other buildings can be higher than that."

"They'll be too heavy. They'll fall down," Sumoy said.

Pa turned the key in the lock and pushed her through the doorway into the comforting familiarity of their apartment in the old Methodist Church. "Sumoy, one day the whole city will be filled with buildings so tall that you and I can't even imagine them. We need to be ready for that."

*

From the day Fong Dun Shung left South China to become an herbalist on the railroad, the See and Fong family destinies had been deeply entwined in the political and economic conditions of the times. Some of these periods—Exclusion and the Driving Out—had been directed solely at the Chinese. Others—the Depression and World War II—had affected everyone across the country, including the Sees and Fongs.

December 7, 1941, marked several changes for the See and Fong families. The waterways remained virtually closed for the duration of the war, with the result that, through 1945, little new merchandise crossed the Pacific. No antiques. No water chestnuts. No silk. For many of the mom-and-pop shops in Chinatown, this meant buying cheap goods from Mexico. For stores like F. Suie One and F. See On, it meant a shift from high-grade merchandise imported from China to things that could be picked up at auction, items of lesser quality dredged up from the deepest and darkest depths of warehouses, even curios. At the end of 1941, neither Fong See nor Ticie could know how this would affect business. Nor could Ray and Bennie, for whom Pearl Harbor also marked a turning point. The See Manufacturing Company, which had flourished making bedroom suites for movie stars, was converted to the war effort, and this would change their lives.

CHAPTER 16

THE MISSION FAMILY GETS A DAUGHTER=IN=LAW

1942–45

Wʜᴇɴ the Japanese bombed Pearl Harbor, 42,000 native-born Japanese lived in California, as did 97,000 Germans and 114,000 Italians. The three groups were classified as "enemy aliens," and were forbidden to enter military installations or the Canal Zone—as if anyone were traveling down there. They weren't allowed to fly in airplanes or change residences within their own cities. They could no longer purchase or possess firearms, cameras, short-wave radios, codes, or invisible ink. Soon all enemy alien funds were frozen, and banks owned by enemy aliens were locked up—regardless of who the depositors were.

In addition to these governmental restrictions, the populace at large—petrified by the possibility of radio-directed air raids—began making life difficult for the most easily recognizable enemy, the Japanese. Landlords evicted Japanese families; wholesalers stopped supplying products to Japanese businesses. The Japanese couldn't get driver's licenses, credit from banks, or milk delivered.

On February 2, 1942, federal troops sealed the drawbridge and commandeered the ferry between Terminal Island and Long Beach. Of the four thousand people who lived on Terminal Island, more than half were Japanese farmers. The heads of all Japanese families were put under presidential arrest. On that same day, Attorney General Earl Warren recommended and received approval for a plan to have all Japanese aliens moved two hundred miles inland for the duration of the war. On February 19, a little over two weeks later, President Roosevelt issued Executive Order No. 9066, which authorized the Secretary of War to establish military zones within the United States from which any person might be excluded, subject to military regulation.

At the end of February, the worst fears of Angelenos seemed to be realized when an unidentified submarine sent a few shells into an oilfield near Santa Barbara. The next night an unidentified airplane was spotted farther south, sending the Los Angeles air-raid system into action. The night sky was pierced by sirens, while searchlights arced across the sky. Residents panicked, turned on their lights and ran out into the streets, totally invalidating the blackout. The army, meanwhile, fired 1,430 shells at the would-be attackers. No planes were hit, but five people died in the pandemonium—two from heart attacks, another three in car accidents. A few garages, patios, cars, and outbuildings were destroyed when the antiaircraft shells fell back to earth. The hysteria subsided only when it was determined that the "attack" had been a false alarm.

On March 18, Roosevelt created the War Relocation Authority, to be headed by Milton Eisenhower, the brother of General Dwight Eisenhower. "I feel most deeply that when this war is over and we consider calmly this unprecedented migration of 100,000 people," Eisenhower said, "we are as Americans going to regret the avoidable injustices that may have occurred." A few weeks later the evacuation began. On that occasion, General DeWitt, who was in charge of the evacuation, stated, "A Jap's a Jap. They are a dangerous element, whether loyal or not. There is no way to determine their loyalty. . . . It makes no difference whether he is an American; theoretically he is still a Japanese, and you can't change him."

The 42,000 native-born Japanese in California also had families—many with American-born children. This meant that 94,000 Japanese from California—and another 24,000 Japanese from Washington and Oregon—were viewed as "potential enemies" and subsequently interned. Amazingly, despite their internment, 33,000 Nisei—American-born Japanese—served in the U.S. armed forces.

Eddy's old friend Benji Okubo went—first to a place in Pomona, then farther inland to Heart Mountain in Wyoming. Another friend stored his paintings, promising him that she would return them when the war ended. Others weren't so lucky. Many Japanese had to sell their businesses or homes overnight. Others just walked away. Eddy, Stella, Richard, and Ted rented a house on the Micheltorena Hill from a Japanese family, the Okis, who were interned. They promised to take care of the house until the Okis were released.

While the Japanese suffered, many of the Chinese profited—in business, in status. The Woo family, for example, bought their produce company from an interned Japanese family, changed the name to the Chungking Produce Company, and went on to make a fortune. Another man bought a large quantity of rice at the beginning of the war. When imports from China ceased, he was able to sell his rice for greatly inflated prices.

The See Manufacturing Company, which had been in operation for a little more than twenty years, was converted to the war effort. In the past, Ray had designed furniture for Mae West, Anna May Wong, Edward G. Robinson, and Howard Hughes; Bennie had executed those designs with precision, speed, and cheap materials. Now, instead of making end tables, the factory turned out plywood map holders to fit snugly against an airplane's fuselage. Where once it had made intricately carved headboards, the factory now built airplane wings. Like the Woo family and the man with his warehouse filled with rice, Ray and Bennie were suddenly making a lot of money.

In a whole other category were the new opportunities for jobs that opened up as large numbers of white Americans shipped out. During the war, it was estimated that thirty percent of all Chinese American men in New York's Chinatown were working in defense plants. On the opposite coast, Haw, Uncle's third son, who now had a son and a daughter of his own, wanted a deferment. He got his nerve up, went to Fong See, his longtime employer and benefactor, and told him he was leaving the company. "I can't help it. They're going to start taking men with children." Haw took a job as a tool designer in a Culver City defense plant. His salary was doubled, then doubled again, so that he was earning one hundred dollars a week. "That's a lot of money," Haw boasted.

Odds were that after the war, Haw, like others who had gotten better jobs in the outside world, wouldn't come back to Chinatown. This would prove to be an accurate guess. Between 1940 and 1950—while the percentage of Chinese men working in restaurants and laundries would remain high compared to the rest of the population—Chinese men in craft occupations would increase from 1.4 percent to 3.5 percent, and in professional and technical occupations from 2.5 percent to 6.6 percent.

But, given their history in the country, the Chinese knew they had to be careful, too. The Chinese Consolidated Benevolent Association printed up insignias with flags of the United States and China flying side by side and the words "Your Allies" printed below. The association also distributed registration certificates stating that the holder was a member of the Chinese race. The people of Chinatown snapped up these items to paste in the windows of their homes, businesses, and automobiles. The Chinese wore pins with the Chinese flag and armbands that read "China" or "Chinese." About this, the *Los Angeles Examiner* wrote, "Make no mistake about it, a Chinese is a Chinese—and not a Jap." "Those *lo fan*," people in Chinatown said, mystified, bemused, and a little fearful, "they can't tell the difference between a Chinese and a Japanese."

The fact that the Exclusion Act remained on the books undermined the United States' stance as the protector of democracy. It didn't help that even though the Chinese population in the United States had sunk to between 75,000 and 78,000—of which men still outnumbered women three to one—nearly one-fourth of the men were engaged in the war effort at home and abroad. (It must be noted, however, that many Chinese armed-forces recruits were sent straight to cook school.) Many enlisted, not through any great sense of patriotism, but as a way of automatically gaining their citizenship, and thus opening the door ever so slightly to the possibility of going to China one day and bringing back a "wife of an American citizen."

Many joined the fight for repeal of the exclusion acts—from Ng Poon Chew, the Chinese journalist and lecturer, to Pearl Buck, who had become a celebrity after the success of the book and screen versions of *The Good Earth.* In San Francisco, the city board of supervisors—reflecting the attitude of the area's citizens—passed a special resolution encouraging repeal. But for every voice raised in support of repeal, numerous others opposed it, including the American Federation of Labor, the Daughters of the American Revolution, the Native Sons of the Golden West, and the Crusading Mothers of Pennsylvania.

In late June 1942, Mrs. Leong—language teacher, active fund raiser for China Relief, and mother of Gilbert Leong—sat in the main dining room of Soochow Restaurant, preparing for the banquet to celebrate the marriage between her son and Sissee See. She pulled out a bobby pin, scratched her scalp with it, then tucked a few loose strands of hair into the tightly woven bun which lay at the nape of her neck. Ignoring the high-pitched chatter in the kitchen, she tried to concentrate on the list of chores that would occupy her in the next few days. For fifty years now—ever since the missionaries had taught her how to harness her brain to shut out trouble—she had focused her energies on work during upsetting times. But today her heart was so broken that her mind wandered as if looking for that injured organ.

She knew what the people of Chinatown thought of her: that she was rich, that she would not mind her own business, that she put too much importance on old things, that she was too crazy liking that American football, that she kept her children—Ed, Gilbert, Elmer, and Margie—under her thumb. She knew the kinds of words they spoke behind her back. "Mrs. Leong wears the pants in the family." (Not true.) "She's a tough old dame who'll go clear to hell and gone to buy a leg of pork for the restaurant." (True.) "Mrs. Leong is controlling of her children. No wonder they've come out the way they have." (This made her mad!) Even her daughter Margie laughed off these stupid comments. "Ah, Mom, you don't run the family. You're just business-minded." But now Mrs. Leong's neighbors would see how she had failed. She knew they would laugh and jeer. She knew also that she would continue in her service to them, because, above all else, she was a good Christian woman.

For almost twenty years she had held classes at the Methodist Mission on the second floor of the building at the corner of Marchessault and Los Angeles streets, directly above the F. Suie One Company. Each day she had driven herself from her house on Ivadel down to this last remaining block of Old Chinatown, climbed the narrow stairs, and drilled her students on their memorization and written language skills. Every evening she had walked down the block past Fong See's store to her family's Soochow Restaurant, where she'd looked over the books, made sure the kitchen ran smoothly, and written up the order for the early-morning run to the wholesale stalls at City Market.

In all these years she had made it her business not to associate with the white woman who ran the F. Suie One Company with her half-Caucasian sons. When the mission had moved to New High Street, Mrs. Leong had thought she would never have to deal with Mrs. See. Now See-bok was renting the mission's old space and living there with his new wife—a clear lapse in decency, even if it was part of Chinese tradition.

If anyone had asked Mrs. Leong about her seemingly un-Christian stance on multiple wives, she would have answered hotly, "In China, we have multiple wives for many reasons. Sometimes a family cannot have sons. Sometimes a poor family has girls. Before you know it, there are concubines. That's been done for thousands of years! This is a Chinese tradition that does not conflict with my belief in Christianity." But no one had asked her, so she supposed people thought she was against the impending marriage between Gilbert and Sissee simply because See-bok had more than one wife.

There were so many things the people of Chinatown didn't understand about her. Her family celebrated Christmas and New Year's—with a combination of American and Chinese dishes—because they were Christians, but she insisted they also celebrate the Chinese New Year. "Why should we follow the Chinese New Year when we're here in the United States?" her daughter asked each spring. And each spring, Mrs. Leong answered, "We follow the Chinese calendar because we want to remember we are Chinese."

But Mrs. Leong always knew where to draw the line. No door guards stood vigilant outside their home to prevent evil spirits from entering. Her children lit no firecrackers to send the kitchen god to heaven to report on the household's behavior in the past year. She would not have the children worshipping idols. No red paper banners inscribed with pithy sentiments were festooned about the house. If her neighbors were afraid to use scissors or knives on New Year's Day because they might cut their luck for the coming year, this was not her concern. These things were all superstition. But the Chinese New Year was based on the lunar calendar. That was not pagan. It was a part of the Chinese culture and heritage. Her family could remember their ancestors, thank them for the gift of life, and ask for their blessings.

Similarly, she went to the herbalist for remedies and tonics for her family. She would go and sit in the carved teak chairs at the Gee Ning

Tong and wait for her prescription to be presented to her, folded in white paper. She would go home and brew the teas herself, or add them to a chicken dish for extra nourishment, knowing that most of the bachelor customers might still be waiting in the shop while the herbalist brewed their bitter tea, for they had no wives, mothers, or sisters to look after them. It could not be helped if her neighbors and her own children did not understand her thoughts on these traditions.

Now the wedding was just a few days away, and Mrs. Leong still had not met the mother of her future daughter-in-law. Even as the dowry negotiations continued and she and her husband considered how many bride's cakes—in addition to the whole roast pig—her own family should pay for the bride-price, Mrs. Leong meditated on this turn of events. How could Gilbert marry outside the race, after all she had taught him?

When her children were younger, she had told them, "You're more or less ambassadors. You represent all other Chinese kids. People are going to watch your conduct and the way you talk. Many of these Caucasians have never had contact with a Chinese person, so do your best."

"Do you want us to be American?" Gilbert or little Margie might ask.

"No," she would always respond. "You take the best of Chinese culture, you take the best of American culture, and blend the two. You are American citizens. You were born in this country, so you have to take on American culture too. Do not think everything has to be Chinese. You are Chinese American."

When they had lived on Ninth Street down by the City Market, and her husband still had the produce stall, she'd had certain rules for the children. Only speak English when you are outside the house. Speak English at school, on the street, even in the yard. The minute you walk inside the door, you must speak Chinese. These were easy rules to obey, and the children had done as she said. But later she had problems with Margie, who wanted to be a modern American girl. Mrs. Leong insisted—no lipstick, no cosmetics. Her daughter was from a good family and should dress properly—"to a T," Margie often complained reproachfully. This meant no dangling earrings, no silk stockings.

Now Mrs. Leong wondered what use all her rules had been. For eight years she had thought Gilbert would forget about Fong See's daughter and marry a Chinese girl. Mrs. Leong had kept her eye on Jennie Chan from the time she was five as a possible future wife for Gilbert. Jennie's family was poor, but she'd been a dedicated student at the mission. Mrs. Leong had often let Jennie teach the younger children their lessons. Jennie liked football, too, and in the old days, she was the only person Mrs. Leong had let come with her to watch the games at USC. All that was a long time ago. Jennie had married that Eddie Lee, had borne three daughters, and had been the first Chinese hired to work at Bullock's. Hat department, they said. Was that See girl any better? No! She was an old maid, thirty-three.

Mrs. Leong never encouraged an early marriage, hoping that Gilbert would take the time to meet a proper girl. Education should come first, she always said, thinking that he would find an educated girl—someone like Ruth Kimm. Mrs. Leong had often told Gilbert how much she liked Ruth. "Such a handsome girl, gracious, well-brought up, a good family, and her father owns a farm. Good fresh produce. She has a good job working in a pharmacy." But then Ruth married that artist boy, that friend of the See boys. This was not a good match, anyone could see that.

Still, Mrs. Leong kept wishing that the university held the answer. She told her son, "I do not care how old you are, you must go to school and study. If you do not have the money, I will pay for it." And she had. She'd paid for his tuition at USC, books, clothes, lunch money, music lessons and car expenses. Then her husband started the Chinese Garden Café in Hollywood. That had been a disaster, and Gilbert had to leave school!

What could they do? They went to Chinatown and opened Soochow right next door to Fong See's store. In 1933, Soochow was only the seventh restaurant in Chinatown to serve family-style dinners. Fifty cents a person bought chow mein, snow peas and *char siu,* egg foo yung, fried shrimp, and rice. No Chinese person would ever order this tourist meal! But Caucasians seemed to like it, and Soochow prospered, even during Prohibition. She would never allow her husband to serve liquor, ever, period. If white customers wanted that, they could go to Toey Far Low. That was a tough place! Let them go there! Finally they had earned enough money to send Gilbert back to school, and now even Margie had graduated from USC with a degree in social work. Mrs. Leong liked to tell people, "My son is an architect. He's working for Harold Harris, the architect. That Mr. Harris, he's a great admirer of Frank Lloyd Wright and designs avant-garde houses. You know what my Gilbert says? He says, 'That's not the usual run of the traffic.' And my Margie? Oh, she's a social worker." Her friends knew enough not to ask about Ed or Elmer.

All these things Gilbert did not understand, just as he did not understand her dedication to the mission. As a girl in China, she had been a "rice Christian"—sent to a Baptist mission school outside Canton to learn the ways of the Lord in exchange for a meal. Over time she forgot about her stomach to excel in her studies—both academic and religious. At seventeen, a go-between arranged for her to be betrothed, and she was married sight unseen to Leong Jeung, a vegetable peddler in the

Gold Mountain, who came over for the ceremony. He was much older than she was, but he was a good man, and by the time he went back to America, she had converted him. In 1910, when Ed was less than a year old, she boarded a ship for San Francisco. *Aiya!* Angel Island—so many months she spent there. All of them she still wanted to forget.

When she finally met her husband again in Los Angeles, she discovered he had become a Methodist. She was a Baptist, but she was Chinese first. Out of respect for Leong Jeung, she became a Methodist. She began to learn everything she could about the Methodists in Los Angeles. She learned how, along with the Presbyterians, Congregationalists, and Baptists, the Methodists set up missions after the riot and massacre of 1871; how a mission's success depended on the clergy speaking at least a smattering of Chinese; and how the missions offered spiritual comfort, lessons in acculturation, and language classes for young and old.

To honor her husband, she concentrated her efforts on the Methodist Mission, but she was hardly the first Chinese to do so. In 1889 several Chinese accepted baptism in the Methodist Mission and were listed in the parish's register. Among these were Chan Kiu Sing, a merchant on Spring Street, and his wife. He became the first Chinese in the United States to receive a license for preaching from the Methodists. From 1900 until his death in 1923, he was the pastor of the Los Angeles Chinese United Methodist Church.

Even today, Mrs. Leong couldn't think of his death without sadness. Reverend Chan had done so much for the community. When he hadn't been serving the church, he'd been working as the city's first Chinese court interpreter. He'd acted as social worker, minister, elder of the church, and governmental go-between. Many wives in Chinatown relied on Reverend Chan to accompany them to the Sam Sing Butcher Shop to select a piece of roast pork. Often he could be seen walking up Marchessault Street with paper cones filled with the fragrant meat to be personally delivered to the chosen few. (Naturally, Mrs. Leong was among them.)

In her early days on the Gold Mountain, Mrs. Leong had also learned about Caucasian women who left their families as often as three times a week to spend their evening hours teaching English to single men. She heard about and met Mrs. Emma Findlay, a Congregationalist, who never outwardly tried to convert, preferring to make herself indispensable to the women of Chinatown and their friends and relatives in the area around the City Market. Mrs. Findlay taught Chinese women English, bought them embroidery supplies, and took them to American stores to shop for western-style shoes, hats with ostrich feathers, and shirtwaist dresses with lace collars. She taught them how to put up their

hair in the pompadour style. She introduced them to the German midwife, supplied baby clothes, and, when the children were old enough,
arranged for them to go to American school.

All this Mrs. Leong observed. All this she learned. And one thing
she knew for certain. She could do better than any American woman!
In time, Mrs. Leong traveled north to San Francisco to take an exam-
ination, pledge her allegiance to the United States, and become the first
Chinese-language teacher certified by the State of California. She found
no "rice Christians" here in America. Most people, even if they were
very poor, had enough to eat, not like China. She'd had to figure out
another way to save the souls of the children. She could have called
them "tongue Christians," for all parents in Chinatown wanted their
children to know the language of their homeland.

Her work did not end with the children. A few years ago, Mrs. Leong
and Mrs. Chan, the Reverend's widow, started the Win One Circle—
the first Chinese women's religious organization in Los Angeles. They
quarreled a long time over that name—Win One. They decided it meant
to win somebody over or bring somebody in and then teach them about
the Bible. Many of the members were Buddhists and knew nothing
about Jesus, but they learned quickly enough. Those women were so
lonely. After years of separation, some had finally come to America
alone, with small children, staying on Angel Island sometimes for
months—as she had done—unable to fathom their interrogators' questions. Others had come as mail-order brides, meeting their husbands
for the first time when they left Angel Island. Some had even been sent
here as contraband, crossing the Pacific in sealed wooden crates down
in the holds of big ships, living quietly so as not to attract attention,
rationing their food, surviving their own horrible human smells. Any
way they came, the women arrived in Chinatown knowing no English,
having no faith.

The Win One Circle evolved into a personal triumph. Mrs. Leong
went herself to meet many of the wives and get permission from their
husbands for them to come to her house once a week. In the beginning
she had perhaps twelve ladies, but after a few years the group grew to
twenty. After a lunch of noodles and tea, they did a Bible reading
followed by songs, then lessons on American customs, everyday English
sentences, and what to do if you came in contact with an American.
During holiday time—and as the women converted, more and more of
them celebrated Christmas—Mrs. Leong instructed them on where to
find Christmas ornaments, how to select stockings for their children,
what a candy cane was, and how to make gingerbread.

She told them which stores were good, always recommending the
National Dollar Store on Broadway—"owned by Joe Shoong, who came
to San Francisco at age twenty-three and now owns forty department

stores." She told the ladies on which floor to find certain gifts. Men's socks and ties on the mezzanine, reindeer sweaters on the second floor. They should stop on the ground floor to see the Santa Claus, who would give their children rock candy and a little Christmas book. She taught them how to say "Can you help me, please?" "How much is this?" "I want one [or two, three, or four]," and "Thank you very much." She told them what to expect. "Look for a woman behind a counter to help you. Keep your money in a purse and count it out carefully. Take your time. The American may get angry, but it is your money."

Besides the Win One Circle, Mrs. Leong held a monthly tea meeting at the church by the Plaza for the mothers of her Chinese language students. The tea was "attendance required" if the women wanted their children to continue with their lessons, just as it was "attendance required" at Sunday school and church service on Sundays for all the students. The women came—even if they worshiped Kuan Yin or followed the teachings of Confucius—because they wanted their children to learn.

Like so many baby birds, the women begged nonstop: "I want my children to know about the culture and civilization of their homeland," they chirped. "I'd like my son to study Chinese so that he can read letters from his grandparents," they peeped. "I will give my child anything as long as he asks me in Chinese." Mrs. Leong did her best to feed their dreams.

She knew the children often complained to their parents that they had no free time. She held class every weekday from 3:30 to 5:00 P.M. and on Saturdays from 10:00 A.M. to 12:30 P.M. On Sundays, the service went from eight in the morning to eleven, Sunday school from eleven to three. No time was left to play, the children griped. They went to American school, then Chinese school, then to work in laundries, restaurants, or curio shops, and they still had their homework and home chores. She never listened to this nonsense—her Gilbert had to live this way, and had done well—but Reverend Chan did. He changed the whole Sunday schedule to give families free time. "This way," the Reverend had said, "people can spend the afternoon at the park or the beach." She hadn't understood his thinking, or that of Reverend Wong, who had taken over the ministry, but she had to live with it.

Mrs. Leong always found something more to do. Once a month the Congregationalists, Presbyterians, and Methodists got together for a Union meeting. Each group met at its own church for an early-morning service, then they all spent the afternoon together at a picnic—usually at Lincoln or Brookside Park. On the Fourth of July, children of all denominations piled into the back of the Methodist Mission's stakebody truck and bumped across town to the ocean, throwing firecrackers at pedestrians and cars along the way. They flew the American flag on one side of the truck and the Chinese flag on the other. Her memories of those noisy days were always of warm potato salad and sandwiches and fried chicken gritty with beach sand.

When she got tired, her husband often grumbled, "You are too tied down to the school. You should give it up. Why are you wasting your time? It's too much on you." There was no money in this work, she knew. Twenty-five dollars a month stipend for twenty years, paid by the Methodist Home Office in San Francisco. She was not teaching because she needed the money, she always reminded Leong Jeung. She was doing God's work. Wasn't it true that during the years she'd been teaching, the membership at the Methodist Church had grown to three hundred, surpassing the Congregationalists and the Presbyterians? "Oh, yes, then, that's all right," her husband always said, then dropped the subject.

So now this wedding. For eight years she'd told Gilbert no. She saw nothing wrong in this. "I am giving it to you straight," she had told him. "All Chinese parents—no, not just Chinese parents, but parents of any nationality—Japanese or Italian, I don't care—they want their children to marry someone of their own race. Florence See is half Chinese, yes. Of course she is Chinese. But she has too much *fan yin*— too much Caucasian thinking in her."

In these past years, she and her son had many arguments. He would say, "You only know the old school. You always say you have to be one hundred percent Chinese and know everything Chinese—customs, thinking, everything."

And she had always answered, "Even if you have only a little bit of a foreign element in you, you are going to sway over to that side. This Florence See—too much *fan yin,* I tell you." But in the end, Gilbert did not listen to her. It was because of the war, he said. If he was going to be a soldier, he was going to live his own life.

"Mom," Gilbert said, "I have to take the bull by the horns."

And he did! Just like that! So then he went to Fong See. What did she expect, that the old man would say no? Fong See said, "I am not unaware of gossip on the block. You and my daughter have been going together a long time. I have known your family a long time. Send your mother and I will speak to her." That visit—between Mrs. Leong and old See-bok—had set in motion the formal engagement and the protracted negotiation for the bride-price.

She let her eyes run down the list of characters she had written. If there was to be a wedding, all traditions would be properly carried out. Eastern Bakery, on Grant Street up in San Francisco, made the best bride cakes in this country, some filled with meat, some with lotus seeds or black bean paste. She ordered an extra two dozen of the lotus-seed dessert, since their name, *lin ji,* sounded like "continuously having children." The man who had taken her order had promised that some of the cakes would be baked in a carved mold with the character for "long life" on some and "double happiness" on others. Perhaps ten basket trays of those altogether, along with the roast pig and the money gift to Fong See, would be enough for the bride-price.

She went into the kitchen and checked with one of the chefs as he prepared the *bat ho lin ji,* the traditional dessert made from lily petals whose characters meant "everything will be united with these two people." The high-altitude tortoises would be here soon. The order for shark's fin had also been placed. In a corner of the kitchen, a large tub held dozens of black eels that slithered and slipped, setting the water in constant turmoil. Mrs. Leong nodded her head in resignation. These would make many good-luck dishes for the wedding banquet.

The wedding between Florence Luscinda See and Gilbert Lester Leong took place at two o'clock on the afternoon of July 2, 1942, in the side chapel of the Methodist Church on Colorado Boulevard in Pasadena. Since the bride and groom were both Chinese in the eyes of the state, they could be married in California, making Sissee the only member of her family to be married in the United States. The ceremony owed much to Mrs. Findlay, who had introduced western-style weddings—what the Chinese called *men ming* or "enlightened" weddings—to Chinatown. Yet the idea that a bride's family would have total control over a wedding was contrary to Chinese thinking. Sissee and Gilbert's wedding fell somewhere between a four-to-seven-day Chinese wedding—replete with sedan chairs, phoenix crowns, and banquets—and a western-style wedding with a white-gowned bride, church service, reception, and honeymoon.

According to Chinese tradition, the bride cakes, the whole roast pig, and a whole roast chicken for good measure—all wrapped in gold and red paper—were sent to Fong See. He, in turn, had the pig carved, wrapped in more red paper, and delivered to friends and relatives around Chinatown. Instead of the wedding with four or five hundred people that some in Chinatown expected, only forty guests—almost all of them family, with the exception of Anna May Wong—were invited to the church. It was wartime, after all. Sissee wore a white satin gown—stiff and flared—for the ceremony.

Afterwards, the wedding party drove to the Leong mansion on Ivadel, and swept in through the vast and airy entry for a luncheon reception for over one hundred. Sissee changed into a traditional red brocaded Chinese wedding robe and began circulating among the guests. On the bride's side were fourteen Sees and eight Fongs. Yun's family made up another twenty-four guests. The rest of Sissee's guests were friends: Ticie's cohorts—Mrs. Morgan, Mr. White, and six from Wing's family down in Long Beach; waiters and waitresses from Dragon's Den—Esther, Loy, and Juanita; and pals Tyrus and Ruth, Wally, Helen, Kay, and Pink. The Leong family accounted for just four guests since Elmer was already overseas, but they invited twenty-five Wongs, twenty-five Laus, the widow Chan and her daughters, and other friends.

The luncheon, the banquet at Soochow for the friends and relatives of the groom's family, and the banquet the following night for the friends (mostly Caucasian) and relatives of the bride's family gave each person time to reflect. As could be expected, the meeting between Mrs. Leong and Ticie was strained. The two women had little in common. Mrs. Leong tended to gravitate toward her own guests, while Ticie preferred to keep to herself.

Ticie wandered alone through this house that would now—according to Chinese custom—be her daughter's home. Years ago, the opulence and size of the Leongs' house would have appealed to her. She hesitated at the grand staircase, then passed through the living room with its huge fireplace and wood paneling to the dining room, where the gifts—jewelry, coins, silk, and embroidered fabrics—were laid out. Finding a quiet corner in the library, she sat alone to let the excitement of the day drain away. She was happy, relieved, tired. Ticie knew that, if nothing else, her daughter would be taken care of. Stella observed all of this with a keen eye. In the car, driving over, Stella had been overwhelmed by the sense that now that Sissee was married, Ticie wouldn't live much longer.

The children—of which there were many, between Uncle's numerous children and grandchildren, and Fong See's ever-expanding family—ran through the house, were chastised, giggled and ran some more. They *oohed* and *aahed* over the gifts—admiring some and groaning over others. Settling for a moment, Uncle's children—both young and old—traded stories about Mrs. Leong. The older ones remembered her as kind and patient. "She was a precious thing to our family," recalled one. But the younger children couldn't find a nice thing to say, for in twenty years of teaching, Mrs. Leong's patience and energy had worn thin. Where she had once used the bamboo end of a Chinese feather duster to rap on the table to get the children's attention, she now sometimes tied two or three together to make an impression on a young wrist or open palm.

"If we missed a word of our lesson, she made us hold out our hand and she whacked us."

"And Mom and Dad didn't believe us."

"I *was* bad," said Gim, one of Yun's younger sons. "I didn't memorize my lessons. When Mrs. Leong fell asleep, I made fun and played games."

"Then she hit you on the arm so hard that it swelled for several days."

"And Mom finally decided we wouldn't have to go back!"

The bride flitted from person to person, bashfully accepting compliments, blushing at the sometimes bawdy comments about the coming wedding night. On this day Sissee appeared as she had been and would be throughout her life—subservient. She was beautiful, kind, knowledgeable about Asian art and the restaurant business. But more than anything else, Sissee was a good Chinese daughter who followed the Confucian ideals of womanhood: As a small girl, she followed the rules of her father; as an adult, she obeyed her brothers and served as her mother's companion; as a married woman, she was prepared to bend to her husband's will and adhere to the customs of his family.

As Sissee talked to her guests, she consciously ignored the gift display, because when she glanced that way she saw only her father's dowry presents. She had grown up surrounded by beautiful things, and while she may not have known an authentic Ming from a fake at first glance, she did have an eye for quality. When she looked at the pair of carved wooden chairs her father had sent over, she noticed that they were late nineteenth century—respectable pieces, but not great. When she looked at the full service of Canton ware—with its bread baskets and demitasse cups—she saw only "export curio." When the china had arrived, she'd examined it carefully, comparing one piece to another in the store. Regarding two plates side by side, she saw the primitive quality of the painting, the brash color of the paste, and the thickness of her china.

The Canton ware brought bitterness to her heart. Her father had given her a "nice" dinnerware set, but she saw only the negatives. All she could think was that he'd gone into his store and selected a few meaningless things. But she was a realist. She knew she was lucky to have gotten anything at all. After this party, the china would be packed up in its original eight crates and never used.

After the gift-showing party, everyone got back into their cars to drive to Soochow for the first banquet given by the groom's family. Many of the guests drove the short distance along L.A.'s recently completed first freeway. In Fong Yun's car, pandemonium reigned. The small children played in the back. Gary, Uncle's youngest son, opened the door and fell out. The family pulled over, picked up the boy, and drove to the French Hospital—almost the last remnant of Frenchtown—in Chinatown. Doctors refused to see the boy.

"We don't have an emergency room," the woman in admitting said. Yun suspected that the hospital staff didn't want to treat a Chinese. In retrospect, it may have been that the family didn't have insurance. Either way, the family got back into the car—with sisters weeping, a mother wailing, and Gary feeling increasingly the worse for wear—and drove to County General, where Stella had been taken years before for her diphtheria. When Sissee and Gilbert heard what had happened, their hearts sank. This was the worst possible omen. The boy turned out to be fine, however, and—as is the prerogative of newlyweds—Sissee and Gilbert's spirits once again soared.

On this first night, Ed Leong supervised Soochow's kitchen with facility and dispatch. As soon as the guests were seated, a crew of waiters brought out steaming bowls of shark's-fin soup. Murmurs of approval swept through the room as the guests realized the lavishness of the feast about to be set before them. Like many brides, Sissee didn't have time to enjoy the banquet prepared in her honor. She circulated from table to table, pouring tea into little cups set on a tray. As she passed it around, each guest took a cup and replaced it with *lai see*—the traditional good-luck paper money.

"May every corner of the universe extend its blessing," said a well-wisher.

"Red eggs for next year!" another called out.

"Nine months and two minutes!" quipped another, to good-natured laughs.

The next morning, Sissee woke up in Gilbert's bedroom in the house on Ivadel. She dressed in a flowered dress and brushed out her hair. She was no longer an old maid, but as she looked in the mirror, she saw that she wasn't a young bride either. A few strands of gray already streaked her hair.

Downstairs, the Leongs waited. Sissee wouldn't be able to make the traditional visit to the ancestral temple where a new daughter-in-law customarily pays respects to her husband's ancestors. Sissee couldn't stand before the wall of the temple in the village of Sun Wei, where the names of every Leong going back as far as memory were recorded, and recite, "I, Florence Leong, have come to join your family." Instead, Sissee, like other young wives in other Chinatowns across the country, would perform the simpler and more easily accomplished tea-pouring ceremony.

Mrs. Leong stared sternly at Sissee, causing her to blush. Still, she didn't falter in her actions. She boiled water, poured a little into a teapot, and swished it around to warm the ceramic. She measured the tea leaves out into the palm of her hand the way her mother, who had learned so many years ago from the single men who worked in the back of the shop in Sacramento, had taught her. After placing the leaves in the pot, Sissee poured the water over them and waited silently for them to steep. Keeping her eyes downcast, she poured the tea into each of her new family members' cups—her father- and mother-in-law first, then her brother-in-law, and finally into Gilbert's sister's glass. Sissee felt a sudden rush of anxiety; she so wanted to do this right. As each cup was poured and presented, her in-laws, in turn, gave her a gift of *lai see* or a piece of jewelry.

Leong Jeung, Gilbert's father, observed the proceedings with openness in his eyes and heart. He was a simple, pleasant, thrifty man. Although people enjoyed his personal warmth and kindness, most were unaware of the good things he had quietly done. During the Depression he had written checks to the Kong Chow Association and the church so that many would be helped. He never sought recognition for his good deeds. In the Leong family, he was regarded as weak, for he didn't seem to strive for the high ideals of his wife. But he knew this for what it was: he was a country man who spoke with a country dialect; his wife was a city girl with a city dialect. Anyone could see that she had come from a good family with class. For that reason he had chosen to stay in the background.

As he watched his daughter-in-law pour his tea, he allowed himself the thought that perhaps this alliance would work. He looked across the table at his wife. He knew he would hear plenty about the girl's shortcomings in the months ahead, but for now his wife seemed satisfied. If this Sissee could perform the rest of her duties as well as the tea-pouring, then perhaps his son hadn't made such a bad choice after all.

Soon after their marriage, Sissee accompanied Gilbert first to Arizona, then to Tennessee, where he was stationed. Within weeks of Sissee's departure, Ticie took to her bed. She sent for an herbalist and drank healing teas. Nothing helped. She asked everyone in the family not to let Sissee know. "Let her be happy," Ticie said. "I want Sissee to enjoy her honeymoon and get to know Gilbert." When Ticie got sicker, she moved in with Ray and Leona.

This time gave Ticie a chance to see how much Ray had separated himself from the rest of the family in the way he lived. His elegant house nestled in Nichols Canyon, and was shaded by eucalyptus trees. She stayed in the Japanese-style teahouse by the pool. In the evenings, when he came home from the factory, he would come and visit her. With his highball in hand, he would sit in a chair, gazing out at the twinkling lights of the canyon, and talk. Frequently his thoughts drifted to his father. "I can't forgive Pa," Ray would say.

Ticie would think back to when Ray was a boy and chafed at having to sell jade rings door to door, make sewing baskets, or put furniture together. He'd eventually grown out of that dissatisfaction to enjoy his father's money during the late teens and early twenties. But the discovery that Suie had married Ngon Hung had rekindled Ray's ambivalence toward his father. In all these years it hadn't dissipated.

"If I can forgive him, why can't you?" Ticie asked.

"After what he put us through? After what he did to *you*? Ma, I just can't. I never will."

"Maybe when I'm gone you'll be able to make amends. You never know. One day you may need his help."

But Ray shook his head. "I'll never take anything from him."

And even as Ticie recognized that Ray, of all the children, was the most like his father, she also knew there was nothing she could say to change his feelings.

At the beginning of December 1942, six months after the wedding between Sissee and Gilbert, Ticie went home to Maplewood. In mid-December, Eddy and Stella took Ticie to Mount Sano Hospital. Over the next two weeks, Ticie refused to see any of her grandchildren, not even Richard. On January 4, 1943, Ticie died of a cerebral hemorrhage owing to advanced arteriosclerosis and hypertension. She was sixty-six years old.

When Sissee came back from Memphis for the funeral, she was beside herself with grief. "How could I have not known?" Sissee wept. "Why couldn't we have had more time together? I wanted to be able to take care of her." She would not be mollified or consoled.

It is a measure of how devastated by Ticie's death were all of her children and grandchildren that none of them remember much about the funeral except that it was held in the Little Church of the Flowers at Forest Lawn in Glendale. Stella doesn't remember going to the funeral at all, though other people say that she was definitely there. Pollyanne, Ray's daughter, remembers spending most of the service in the bathroom with Stella, trying to comfort Sissee. Chuen, Fong See's eldest son from the marriage to Ngon Hung, knows that his father and older sister, Jong Oy, went to the funeral, but when they came home the service wasn't discussed, perhaps out of deference to Ngon Hung.

Soon after the funeral, Sissee went through her mother's address book and wrote notes to those who hadn't attended the funeral. By return mail, the family received a letter of condolence from an Aunt May Pruett of Eureka, California. Was she Ticie's aunt? Was she the children's aunt? Was she the wife of one of Ticie's mean-spirited brothers? Now that Ticie was gone, the children would never know the answer, but just reading the letter gave them insight into what she had fled from all those years ago. "You can all be comforted by the thought that she is not dead but sleepeth as Jesus says in the Bible," Aunt May wrote. "You will see her and know her again. There is no Death, for God is our life." They puzzled over this missive and decided not to write back.

The general vagueness about Ticie's death crosses over into a vagueness about the rest of 1943. What is certain is that Milton was finally completely in charge of the F. Suie One Company. He had also met a young woman, Irene "Sunny" Rockwell, a white woman who had rented a little studio behind the F. Suie One Company. Ming said that the two of them were making T'ang horses to sell until he could get authentic pieces from China. Gossips in Chinatown had another idea: Ming and Sunny were making something all right, and it wasn't T'ang horses!

Ray and Bennie were entrenched in the See Manufacturing Company. Sissee, newly married and living with Gilbert in the south, was no longer active in Dragon's Den. Which left Eddy—who now had his December-seventh beard, a goatee that he began growing the day the Japanese bombed Pearl Harbor and maintained until his death—to deal with Dragon's Den alone. Stella has said that Dragon's Den closed because Sissee was "gone" and "somebody died." Eddy liked to say that he decided to close Dragon's Den when he asked a cook to mop the floor and the man refused outright, knowing full well that with the war on, the Chinese were finally getting decent jobs "out there." Whatever the reason, Dragon's Den closed in 1943, and Eddy went to work at See Manufacturing as an employee to get a deferment. Although Eddy and Dragon's Den had carried the entire See family through the Depression, he was no longer contributing to the family pot, a fact that was not lost on his brothers.

In their grief, the family ignored the visit of Generalissimo Chiang Kai-shek's wife, Soong Mei-ling, to the United States, where she campaigned for both war funds and the repeal of the exclusion laws. In Washington, D.C., she addressed Congress and met with President Roosevelt. On her way back to China, she stopped in Los Angeles. This visit highlighted years of work against the Japanese aggressor—the fund-raising of the New Life Movement, the Rice Bowl Campaign, the Seven-Seven Campaign (named for the 7/7/37 bombing of the Marco Polo Bridge in Peking), the outstanding sales in war bonds, and the $250,000 raised by the 1941 Moon Festival. All in all, the Chinese in Los Angeles had raised more money than had the larger Chinatowns of either New York or San Francisco. Madame Chiang Kai-shek did her best to honor those efforts.

On March 31, 1943, she appeared at the Hollywood Bowl, where, author Garding Liu noted, humanity hung to the hillsides like bees swarming in a tree. Madame Chiang was a Wellesley graduate and the most sophisticated woman the four thousand Chinese who attended could ever remember seeing. She appeared hatless before the throng, and her black hair glistened in the sun. Her ears were pierced with silver buttons. She wore a long black satin *cheongsam* lined in pale blue. (Though hardly as important as fund-raising or the campaign for repeal, Madame Chiang's visit started a fad among the young Chinese women of the community; for the first time, on special occasions they proudly donned Chinese dresses modernized to show the arm and accentuate the figure.)

Like the Chinese in the audience, Madame Chiang also wore pins on her lapel: one was the silver wings of the Chinese air force; the other was a ribbon showing the national colors of red, white, and blue. After the speech, Mayor Fletcher Bowron escorted her to a parade in her honor that passed along Macy Street in Chinatown. Later the Chinese Benevolent Association received her. These activities—along with her beauty, her elegance, her grace, her education—were dutifully followed in the press and, perhaps, swayed the readership of the country into believing that, indeed, the Chinese race was not so bad after all.

In a message to Congress, President Roosevelt called exclusion a "historic mistake." On December 17, 1943, Roosevelt signed the Magnuson Act, repealing the old exclusion laws and allowing Chinese to be naturalized. Actor Keye Luke, who had earned a reputation as Charlie Chan's Number One Son, announced that he wanted to be the first Chinese to be naturalized. However, on the day Luke had to appear in court, he was doing a picture with Wallace Beery, and a Chinese doctor became the first to be naturalized. Amused by this, newspaper columnist Walter Winchell carried the following item: "Keye Luke, Charlie Chan's Number One Son, just missed being Number One Naturalized U.S. Citizen."

In the heady days following repeal, no one paid much attention to the fine print, which continued the annual quota established in 1924. As a result, even while China and the United States fought side by side, Immigration and Naturalization officials still found it difficult to find "acceptable" and "qualified" Chinese to fill the annual quota of 105. In actuality, during the first ten years of repeal, the U.S. government found an annual average of only fifty-nine Chinese acceptable for admittance to the country. In addition, between 1944 and 1952, only 1,428 Chinese Americans—after presenting documentation stating that they were here legally, and passing tests on English competency, American history, and the Constitution—were naturalized.

The anti-miscegenation laws carried on, as did the laws barring Chinese from buying property. More immediately troubling were the cases of Caucasians mistaking Chinese for Japanese. Bennie, whose home in Beverly Hills had been bought in his wife's name, worried about what would happen to families of Chinese ancestry. He cautioned his daughters, "Don't tell the neighbors about your ancestry. Don't tell the people at school you have Oriental blood in you. Don't tell anyone anything." His daughter Marcia remembers those days: "I grew up thinking, It's a secret. Don't tell anyone. It's a no-no. Not because I was ashamed of being a quarter Chinese, because I'm not. We just didn't know what would happen."

And the war pressed on. Angelenos grew accustomed to blackouts. Radio spots such as "Viva Victory" reminded citizens to behave, be careful with their rations, and buy bonds. Jeeps zipped in and out of traffic. GIs streamed through Union Station, rode the Red Car out to the beach, and went to the Hollywood Canteen, hoping for a dance with Betty Grable. Sometimes they simply crossed Alameda and ventured into Chinatown.

Since many of the GIs were "seeing the world" for the first time, they got up their courage to sample Chinese food. Some restaurant owners did something they never would have thought possible back during the Depression: they closed and locked their doors to keep the crowds out. The restaurants were simply stretched beyond their capabilities; supplies were impossible to get, and most of the help had either gone to war or into defense work. The Leong family, which had opened a second Soochow in New Chinatown, closed it for lack of dishwashers, busboys, and waiters; Gilbert and Elmer were in the service and Ed was working at See Manufacturing for his deferment. The Leong family gave the New Chinatown space to the USO for the duration, and focused their energies on the original Soochow.

On April, 30, 1945, Hitler committed suicide. The very next day, Sissee gave birth to a baby girl, Leslee Ann Leong, in Memphis. One week later, German resistance ceased. On August 6, 1945, America dropped the bomb on Hiroshima, followed three days later by a second bomb on Nagasaki. On August 14, Japan unconditionally surrendered. The war was finally over, and the boys started coming home. Soon Sissee, Gilbert, and Leslee would be reunited with their families back in Los Angeles.

PART V

CHAPTER 17

HOLLOW BAMBOO

1946–47

$\mathbb{B}$ ETWEEN 1940 and 1950, the population of Los Angeles doubled, with nearly eighty percent of the people migrating from the Midwest. Los Angeles was now home to more Iowans than lived in Des Moines, more Indianans than in Terre Haute, and more Nebraskans than in Lincoln. Where once fields of lima beans or asparagus had grown, now hospitals, parking lots, and row after row of tract houses appeared to spring up overnight. The numbers of automobiles also mushroomed. Angelenos owned more cars than the number registered in Alabama, Arizona, Arkansas, and Colorado combined, with the result that Los Angeles now ranked as the country's number-one smog city.

During the war, Los Angeles had established itself as "the arsenal of democracy." Its aircraft industry, the largest in the nation, was the city's number-one moneymaker and employer. But the city also ranked first in other industries. Los Angeles produced more movies than any other city in the world. As *Time* magazine reported, Los Angeles "lands more fish than Boston or Gloucester, makes more furniture than Grand Rapids, assembles more automobiles than any other city but Detroit, makes more tires than any other city but Akron. It is a garment center (bathing suits, slacks, sports togs) second only to New York. It makes steel in its backyard. Its port handles more tonnage than San Francisco." What most people didn't know was that the county was still the richest and most profitable agricultural and dairy area in the nation.

Not since the railroad pricing wars of the 1880s had Los Angeles experienced such prosperity and change. That first Christmas after the war, downtown was gaudy with lights and decorations and families together again. Department stores filled their windows with fantasy displays of everything from electric trains to washing machines. Santas, puffy with padding and fake beards, handed out strings of rock candy and lollipops to rosy-faced children. GIs still in uniform prowled the sidewalks in groups or honked their way down congested streets in their jeeps. Women, basking in the radiance of early pregnancy, window-shopped past the Broadway, Silverwoods, and Barker Brothers. At night, the women linked arms with men they'd thought they'd never see again, and stood in line to take in a movie at the Orpheum, Lowe's State, Pantages, Paramount or the Million Dollar.

During these postwar years, Chinatown mirrored the growth of the rest of the city when, from 1940 to 1950, the population increased from 5,300 to 8,000. For the Chinese this boom was fueled by the War Brides Act of 1945, the Act of August 9, 1946 that put Chinese wives of U.S. citizens on a nonquota basis, and the Displaced Persons Act of 1948. So, while the official quota for Chinese immigrants still stood at a mere 105 a year (by contrast, Poland had an annual quota of 6,524), over 7,000 Chinese women entered the U.S. between 1946 and 1953 as war brides and another 3,465 Chinese students, visitors, and seamen were granted permanent resident status as "displaced persons."

Many Chinese—both young and old—became citizens: Chuen Fong, Fong See's eldest son from his second family, who had been inducted into the army one month before the end of the war, was naturalized after he was released in 1947. Fong Yun was naturalized a year later. Like other American GIs, the Chinese veterans took advantage of new opportunities for education and housing. By the spring of 1949, 3,610 Chinese Americans across the country had enrolled in American colleges and universities, more than ever before. With these successes, education became recognized and accepted as a way out of Chinatown.

Although the Supreme Court had declared restrictive covenants unconstitutional as far back as 1917, California had continued to enforce them. In May 1948, a ruling passed the state legislature that effectively banned restrictive covenants barring Chinese and other minorities from buying property; such covenants would no longer be enforceable in state court. This—combined with the influx of immigrant women—changed the structure of Chinese communities. American-style nuclear families developed and settled in traditionally white suburbs to find superior housing and schools.

The miscegenation laws had also hung on with tenacity. As a quarter-Chinese, Pollyanne, Ray's daughter, still fell under the state's racial code. Like her parents before her, she and her Caucasian fiancé made the trip to Tijuana. Two weeks later, on October 1, 1948, the California Supreme Court finally declared the miscegenation laws unconstitutional. The following year, the L.A. County Marriage License Bureau issued eighty licenses for interracial marriages, of which eleven were for marriages between whites and Chinese. Bennie's daughter, Shirley, who, along with her sister, had been sworn to secrecy about her Chinese background during the war, was the first in the See family to be married to a Caucasian in the United States.

But attitudes were stubborn. "After World War II, we were considered either dumb or stupid, because whatever we earned we gave back to our parents," recalled David Lee. "Once we got out of our territory, we were shell-shocked. They didn't want us. I remember Sammy Lee, the Olympic diving champion. He came back a captain or a major and he couldn't buy a house in Orange County. If you died, you couldn't be buried, because the cemeteries were segregated." Those who moved into new neighborhoods scouted things out ahead of time. Tyrus and Ruth Wong, for example, asked the existing owners to inquire if anyone would object to having a Chinese family in the neighborhood.

Wilbur Woo, who had lived as a child behind the Leong residence in the City Market Chinatown, was one of fifteen Chinese students at UCLA: "After the war, some of us became professionals—doctors, lawyers, maybe a few owned supermarkets in black areas. But things hadn't really improved. I remember driving to Sacramento in the late forties and being stopped by a policeman. The first thing he asked was 'What restaurant do you work at?' " Choey Lau, Fong Yun's eldest daughter, married an Army Air Force pilot who couldn't get a civilian job because he was Chinese. In 1951 they would move to Hawaii, where he would be hired by Aloha Airlines, which had been founded by a Chinese.

It didn't matter if you were important, either. In New York, when the chief Chinese delegate to the United Nations knocked on the door of the wrong hotel room, the woman who answered wordlessly handed him her laundry. Closer to home, James Wong Howe, the cinematographer, took a portion of his Hollywood money to open a Chinese restaurant. When a photographer came to take publicity shots of the exterior, Howe walked over and asked, "Can you move over just a little bit so it will make a better composition?" The photographer sneered. "What the hell do you know about photography? Why don't you go back in the kitchen and do some cooking?"

The residents of the last block of Old Chinatown remained resolute in the face of any change. The old businesses—the F. See On Company, the F. Suie One Company, Soochow Restaurant, the Chew family's curio shop, and the herbal emporium—still held sway. Along the small alleyways bisecting the block, wives still bought their pork at the Sam Sing Butcher Shop, city pols stopped in for drinks at the three-thousand-year-old carved bar in Jerry's Joynt, the religious sought advice and good luck at the Kong Chow Temple, and bachelors bought entire meals at See Yuen for a quarter. The Lugo House continued as a refuge for single men. But the once-grand Pico House had become a flophouse, and in the Plaza on Sundays, evangelists hurled hellfire and brimstone at a sorry collection of derelicts, drunks, and hobos.

In a city that prided itself on the new, it seemed that everyone had a plan to make Los Angeles bigger, better, cleaner. In the last years of the decade, many of the city's landmarks would come down. Old Chinatown, an eyesore to some, also came under fire. On November 6, 1946, City Attorney Ray Chesebro filed condemnation proceedings in Superior Court against the twenty-two property owners in the last surviving block of the city's original Chinatown. His plan was to raze the block and create a park to "beautify" the approach to Union Station. In coming months this idea would change once again, as much of the area was allotted to the widening and opening of roadways in connection with the building of the Hollywood Freeway.

The residents of Old Chinatown greeted the news with a calmness that reporters found disquieting. But many, like Fong See, were old-timers who had lived through the Driving Out and had been shuffled from place to place at the whim of the larger Caucasian populace since they'd first set foot on the Gold Mountain. A reporter from the *Daily News* spoke with Fong See, who, it was noted, was "patiently philosophical." (The rival paper, the *Los Angeles Times,* supported this observation with photographs capturing the "venerable old man" appearing "unexcited" and "imperturbed" about the condemnation proceedings.) "Man requires but little space—less space than this cubicle in which I stand," Fong See told the *Daily News.* "And when my time comes, they will crowd me into less space than this. I have lived well, I am ready for what tomorrow holds." Yet another reporter asked Fong See if he had made much money in his fifty-eight years on Los Angeles Street. "There are three carloads of it piled up in the back," the old man laughed, "but I don't know what to do with it." The reporter commented that this was an example of "subtle Oriental humor."

Yet another interviewer seemed to speak with a very different man. "Allee time change," Fong See mused. "Allee time city glow and change. Move many time. Allee time people think change sad. Not sad. Change must come."

Photographers roamed the streets of Old Chinatown. One caught Fong See in his long, embroidered mandarin robe, posing with a feather duster before a statue of Buddha in meditation. Another captured a child climbing on one of the stone dogs that stood before the entrance to the F. Suie One Company. The camera lens froze the incongruities throughout the enclave—a carved figure representing the transcendence of man from the Lower World to a Higher Civilization next to a sign for "Rum and Coke—40 cents." Along this last remaining block, people wondered what they would do if they really did have to move.

In 1946, after the Oki family returned from the relocation camp, Stella, Eddy, and Richard moved into the basement of the F. Suie One Company, where Dragon's Den had once been. (Ted had joined the merchant marine.) Junk, which in the family could mean anything from antiques to piles of used lumber, occupied half the space. The other half was partitioned off for living quarters. Benji and Tyrus's murals of the Eight Immortals and the dragon still clung to the walls. Beautiful pieces of Chinese art enlivened dark corners. In the kitchen, the family took their baths in the prep sinks; rats still made their nests in the exposed rafters and scuttled along water pipes.

Some people might have seen this paradox—living in a rat-infested basement surrounded by expensive things—as inappropriate. But what constituted inappropriateness? Fong See had grown up in the close quarters of village life. His children had been raised in the close quarters of immigrant life. Now Eddy carried on that tradition. His family had always lived in small places—out of habit, thrift, or necessity. Eddy, Stella, and now their son learned to shut themselves off and establish their own space. They learned how to be in the same room and not talk to each other.

The job at See Manufacturing hadn't worked out for Eddy. His brothers had put him in charge of the assembly line, but he had realized they were never going to let him do anything really important. After working day after day behind a table saw, he was also overcome by the drudgery of the work. So he'd quit and now simply walked upstairs to help Ming in the store. Eddy set up a table for making jewelry just inside the front entrance. It was a much calmer life, one that helped relieve his ulcers, which still hadn't healed from the Dragon's Den days.

Stella also renewed her interest in the F. Suie One Company. As a teenager she had kept Ticie company in the store on Kip Street. When Stella was first married, she had walked over to the location on Wilshire every day to visit her mother-in-law. Stella had done odd jobs—a little polishing, dusting, sweeping. Now that Richard was in high school, Stella once again spent much of her time in the store, where her art background served her well. For years she worked on the restoration of a coromandel screen, pressing filler into the cracks, recarving it, replacing the broken slivers of mother-of-pearl, and laying on fine coats of black lacquer.

Richard celebrated his sixteenth birthday in the basement of Dragon's Den. He was one-quarter Chinese, and his looks showed elements from both his Asian and Caucasian blood. He was a sweetly handsome boy, slightly taller than his cousins and uncles and just a touch huskier. His hair was a soft and silky shade of black. He had an endearingly shy smile. But perhaps his most striking feature was his green eyes, of which he was immensely proud.

Richard began to live a triple life: partly with Benji Okubo, partly in the white world, partly in Chinatown. During the summer and on vacation, Richard worked with Benji—still gruff and wild under the domesticating influence of his wife, Chabo, whom he had married in the internment camp—on landscaping jobs. Benji and Richard would drive out to Ava Gardner's or Elizabeth Taylor's house, then trim, cut, shape.

When they were done, they'd buy a six-pack of beer, and sit and talk.

For nine months of the year, Richard was in school. Rather than go to Belmont or Poly with the other kids from Chinatown, Richard enrolled at John Marshall High, near Silverlake, where his friends were the only Jews in a predominately Gentile school. He hung around with a guy who wanted to become a doctor. Their affiliation had less to do with being ethnically different from the others—which they certainly were—than it did with simply being different. They weren't part of the in-crowd. They weren't *popular*. They certainly didn't date or hang out with girls. Instead they competed against each other for grades and talked about where they wanted to go to college.

After school, Richard went back down to Chinatown. He worked in the store, doing many of the jobs that his father and uncles had done as teenagers. He drilled holes in the bottoms of porcelain vases and wired them for lamps. He put together furniture when it arrived from Asia. He spent time—as did everyone in the family at one time or another—on the coromandel screen. He became convinced that he didn't want to spend his life working in the store like his uncle and father.

For the first time, Richard began hanging out with his cousins (Fong Yun's children) and his half-aunts and -uncles (the sons and daughters of Fong See), as well as a few of the young men along the block— Albert Wong, the kid from the Sam Sing Butcher Shop, and Allen Mock, the son of a gambler. Although they saw him as definitely Caucasian, they accepted him because he was a relative.

The boys, Richard included, were like so much hollow bamboo, Chinese on the outside, hollow on the inside. They didn't fit into the world of their parents. They certainly didn't fit into the world of their white peers. They didn't even fit in with girls in Chinatown. The basic philosophies didn't mesh. The American work ethic—success, occupational prestige, educational attainment, the expenditure of wealth to compete with the Joneses—just didn't jibe with how these boys had been raised: to save for buying trips and banquets, to work for the family and not for yourself, to think of returning home to China, and not to disgrace yourself in front of Americans or bring harm to the family through your actions.

Like their fathers and grandfathers before them who had suffered from having their culture belittled, so too did these young men. The larger world spoke loudly and clearly: You are different. What you feel has no value. You are bad. You are dirty. You are unpleasant to live near. Consciously and unconsciously, they had heard, felt, and seen these things since the day they were born. Be careful. Watch out what you say. Don't make a mistake. Their bodies, which should have been filled with all the hopes and dreams and spunk of young men around the world, were filled instead with a withering combination of insecurity and a what's-the-use attitude.

But Richard didn't think about these things when he climbed the stairs from Dragon's Den to his grandfather's apartment and a world that seemed purely Chinese. Straight-backed chairs lined the four walls of the main room. The old organ of the Methodist Mission still stood on its raised platform, and sometimes the younger kids pumped the pedals, creating horrible wheezing moans. Even without the organ, the noise level was always high. Nine people lived in this apartment: Richard's grandfather, his wife, and their seven children, ranging in age from infancy to their early twenties. They were often joined by what seemed like half the population of Chinatown, who came over unannounced to sit and gape before the new television set—the first in the neighborhood. Over the cacophony of voices—babies crying, teenagers giggling and roughhousing, old folks calling out to each other in high-pitched tones—the set blared out wrestling or newscasts.

Richard didn't pay much attention to his grandfather or Ngon Hung. His grandfather seemed fossilized. His step-grandmother—though just a couple of years older than his aunt Sissee—appeared ancient, with her crooked back and her shuffling steps. Carrying, birthing, and caring for seven babies had taken a toll. Following ghetto tradition, all of her children had been born at home—some easily, as when she went to the bathroom and the baby simply slipped out, and some—according to family story—with difficulty, as when she was home alone, in pain, and pushing for hours.

Richard grew familiar with the routine in this bustling household. Each month his grandfather called his children together to dole out ten dollars or fifteen dollars—their portion of Fong See's family pot, now called an allowance in keeping with contemporary times. To May Oy, who was quiet and home-loving like her mother, Fong See might say, "Go out and buy something for yourself." To his eldest son, Chuen, he would say, "You did a good job this week in the store." He might compliment Yun on his efforts in putting together a piece of furniture. To Sumoy he would say, "I understand you did a good job in school." Other times he subtracted dollars, saying, "I heard you were mean to your sister," or "You didn't help your mother make *joang*." To Jong Oy he might rail, "You think I don't know when you sneak out at night to be with that military man? This is not the right type of person for my daughter. You will get nothing this month." He was always sterner with the girls, hoping to control their modern ways with less money and harsh words.

Once they were older, Richard and the other guys went out. Chuen and Yun had a car—a World War II Jeep bought from army surplus—and they'd all pile in and roam about town for *siu yeh,* "midnight snack."

They drove to Van de Kamp's on San Fernando Road for hamburgers, fries, and malts, or out west to Ocean Park for a pastrami-and-cole-slaw sandwich at Zucky's, or to Micelli's in Hollywood, where the Italian waiters treated Richard like a movie star, or simply down to Ninth Street by the City Market for noodles, dumplings, or a bowl of *jook* (rice gruel) seasoned with salted fish.

They visited Anna May Wong in her Chinese-style house with its moon gate, courtyard, and tall, narrow doors. These social calls—often with Sissee, Gilbert, Stella, and Eddy—brought out the very best in them all, as they remembered good times at Dragon's Den. Sometimes others showed up—Tyrus and Ruth; Dorothy Jeakins (an old friend from art-school days and now an Academy Award winner for her costume designs); Norman Foster (the film director); James Wong Howe and Sanora Babb; and Katherine DeMille (the niece of Cecil B. DeMille). Anna May's younger brother, Richard, would also be there, watching over his sister as he had done for so many years.

When it was just Anna May and the boys, they'd play poker, drink, and tell dumb stories. Sometime during the evening, Anna May—dressed in black slacks and black sweater, her bangs just as black as when she'd danced as the slave girl in *The Thief of Bagdad*—would look over and mutter, "You know, fifty million Chinamen can't be Wong," and they'd all laugh as though it were the funniest joke on earth.

In the summer, the boys ventured even farther afield—camping in Yosemite, Mammoth, and Yellowstone parks. Sometimes they went to San Diego to hunt and fish. Over time, Richard understood how unusual he was, compared to others. Sure, Chong and Gai, Uncle's sons, were on the tennis team. Sure, Chuen had been in the service and Yun, Chuen's younger brother, was doing auto shop. These were things Richard could relate to. But in other ways they'd been raised very differently. Uncle had never allowed his sons to join the Boy Scouts, because he didn't trust uniforms. He hadn't let them try out for team sports, because he'd grown up with rickshaw races and thought running was low-class. But the biggest discrepancy was that Chuen and Yun *had* to work, because they were being prepared to take over their father's business. Uncle's sons *had* to work, because they wanted to open their own shop in New Chinatown. Albert Wong worked hardest of all, delivering, bookkeeping, managing property, cutting meat, and shining shoes at the City Market on Saturdays and Sundays. No one really *expected* Richard to work. He was the family scholar; his parents simply wanted him to go to school, get good grades, putter around the store, and help Benji during the summers.

During their sojourns, the boys drove all night, all day, never thinking about discrimination or racism, knowing how easy it was to avoid if they chose not to notice it. They encountered trouble only a few times. Upon arriving at the Canadian border, they weren't allowed to cross, because they had "too much junk in the car." Driving from Los Angeles to New York City to visit Jong Oy, who'd run off with her military man, they couldn't get a room because of "who we were." When they stopped at a public swimming pool to go swimming, they were stumped by a sign that said WHITES ONLY. Unsure about what they counted as, they just left.

When they weren't on the road, they hung out, usually in an area next to Uncle's store in China City, where the boys built model airplanes, amateur radios, and electric gadgets, and repaired furniture. They tinkered with cars in the alley. They'd put away a few beers or maybe some wine—Richard more than the others—and talk. Just as Fong See had reinvented himself over and over again, they too reinvented his story—elaborating, changing, guessing, simply making it up.

"How do you think my father met your grandmother?" Chuen might ask Richard.

"He had that underwear factory . . ."

"Do you really think that's how it happened?"

"You mean that she just walked in and he gave her the job?" Richard asked.

The guys looked at each other, considering.

"It doesn't make a lot of sense."

"Maybe he met her when he was out selling door-to-door," Richard suggested. "Maybe she was a customer. You know what I mean? Maybe he was getting a little on the side."

"Knowing my dad, I wouldn't doubt it," Chuen said.

"What about your mom?" Richard asked. "Did he really *buy* her?"

"I think my father needed a new wife because he wanted more children," Chuen speculated. "My mother was scared, but he was kind and gentle. When she was five years old, my mother was on her own. She had to scavenge in the garbage for food, because people wouldn't feed her."

"Our mother always wanted to learn how to speak and write English," Yun might add. "She wanted a teacher to come in, but my father chased him off."

The boys thought they were hot stuff with their hair slicked back and their leather jackets, but they never went out with girls. Not ever. In earlier days, Fong See would have found brides for his sons, but now he was too old. Ngon Hung could have met with other mothers to make a match, but she was too loving of her sons to notice that they needed anyone besides her. The boys were so well cared for that they didn't have a deep desire to look elsewhere. They would have liked to go on dates, but none of them thought they knew how.

Their sisters and girl cousins seemed to adapt more easily. While the boys roamed the streets, the girls gathered together, climbed up on a bed, and perused magazines for the latest fashions and hair styles. They permed their hair or curled it into flips. They gave each other American names: Jong Oy became Joan. Sumoy wanted to be called Carol, "without an E."

The girls seemed better equipped to handle the conflicts between the imperatives of the American world and the strong traditional styles of their home lives, where it was taboo to show any part of their bodies, have ambition, aspire to more than embroidery and motherhood, or show any disrespect for male family members. Perhaps the American school system exposed them to more opportunities than it did their brothers, who were expected to work in the family business after school. Perhaps, because the girls weren't "working," they could do their homework. (A father would have scoffed at a son doing homework: "This is just a devious means of wasting time!") Perhaps, because the girls weren't uncrating goods in the back alley, they had more exposure to the western customers who came through the store. Choey Lau found a *kai ma,* or fairy godmother, in a white customer who took her to the opera, the ballet, and the philharmonic. In turn, Leong-shee scolded her daughter, "You should never have been Chinese." Choey Lau listened to this with equanimity, and later was to claim, "Because of Mrs. Morrison, I got westernized."

Her younger sister, Choey Lon, veered away from traditional Anglo cultural manifestations, preferring to sit at her window and listen to the mariachi music that wafted up from nearby bars. When she went shopping, her older sister might select a sedate pink dress. But Choey Lon would opt for, say, white with red stripes; what she really wanted was the one with the glitter and sequins and ruffles like what she saw the Mexican girls wearing on Olvera Street. She also liked to dance. When her family said, "Gee, Lonny, you've got rhythm," she would answer, "Yes, I do, and I'm not afraid to show it." She experimented with different kinds of food, begging her mother to make tacos and her father to eat them. To all this, Leong-shee just shook her head and said, "I can't believe you're from my stomach."

For young men, finding a suitable Chinese girl to marry was still difficult. Mothers who had been sold in villages told their sons, "High cheekbones are unlucky." Fathers, who still longed to return home, spoke frankly to their sons: "Small ears mean a lack of blessing." Even the old bachelors that every family had around their table, come dinnertime, were requested to advise lovestruck young men: "The world knows that a short underlip means a short life."

Interracial relationships were problematic at best. In his book on Los Angeles Chinatown, author Garding Lui tried to explain the perils from the Chinese point of view: "Colored" women were okay, because they were good workers; Mexican girls were bad, because they would bring their families and require too many bedrooms; Japanese girls believed themselves superior. Lui then described an affair between a Chinese man and a white woman. The couple was driving to a picnic in the country, making "dove-eyes" at one another, when a white man stepped up to the car and accused the Chinese man of being a white slaver. The woman interjected, "I have divorced three untrue husbands; I've had enough of such guys as you, and now I have a Chinese husband who is kind, and good, and true." To this, Lui noted, "If that woman had three, or possibly five, husbands who were absolutely worthless and unfaithful 'guys,' and then finally met a golden yellow husband who was everything that could be desired; then, boys, give the Chinaman a big hand and don't be jealous in the matter."

This story aside, dating a white girl seemed ludicrous. The younger generation of Chinese men couldn't muster the unbridled nerve of someone like Fong See. Paradoxically, Chinese girls didn't seem afraid to date white boys, as long as they could keep the news a secret from their conservative elders. Perhaps this was because Chinese girls were in the enviable (at that time) position of being treated like "China dolls." White men wanted to go out with Chinese girls; white girls wouldn't give Chinese men the time of day.

In this atmosphere of all the things that could be wrong or unlucky, Richard developed a crush on someone who would have been taboo for him in any culture—his half-aunt Sumoy.

Much of the change that was happening in Los Angeles, and indeed across the country, was the result of the sudden exposure of so many GIs to different countries, especially those in Asia, which until the war had remained relatively unknown. For every horror story told of long, treacherous days in the Pacific, there were countless other tales of the beauty of Hawaii, the simplicity of Japan, the richness of China. It all seemed to come together in California, where the influences of Chinese and Japanese immigrants had melded with the state's climate and landscape. It should come as no surprise, then, that after the war, the so-called California style of living suddenly took hold, capturing the imagination of the entire country. Everyone desired a palm tree, sunshine, a barbecue. They wanted moon gates, upturned eaves, stonework. Ray See saw these trends and recognized that his time had come.

He had been griping for years about putting his earnings into the family pot. The way Ray saw it, he alone—with a little help from Bennie—had built the See Manufacturing Company. (Ray totally dismissed Eddy's participation, because his brother had quit so early into the enterprise.) Ray had started in a little hole-in-the-wall down on Ceres Street where he'd done custom work for Hollywood celebrities and socially prominent families in the west. Later he'd done Monterrey- and Mission-style furniture—heavy stuff with thick arms and simple lines, but easy to sell in Los Angeles. Then he'd expanded again, doing lamp groups and Chinese-modern furniture for Stickley and Prevue right through the war. By that time the factory had moved to Eighteenth Street south of downtown, and covered an entire city block.

With the combined success of the furniture lines and the war contracts, Ray knew he was at a key juncture in his life. He could step forward and reap the rewards due him, or hold back and stay with the See family. When Morris Markoff, the president of the West Coast Lamp and Shade Manufacturers' Association and owner of the Marbro Lamp Company, approached Ray with the offer of a partnership, a large capital invest- ment, marketing expertise, and national expansion, Ray made his move. If he broke up the family partnership, then he and Bennie would be free to make their own fortunes. With Ticie gone, Ray felt he could do this with a clear conscience.

Over several weeks in early 1946, the See siblings met on the mez- zanine of the store on Los Angeles Street. The various life choices each of them had made seemed obvious. Ray had decided to live in the white world, where he'd pursued the life of a playboy, with his affairs and high living. He was solidly built, and his face had the fleshy quality of someone accustomed to the good life. His height, at just over six feet, helped to create a presence that the other brothers couldn't muster. Ironically, of all the sons, Ray was the most faithful to his father's vision of life in America. He was an entrepreneur through and through.

Ray's partner and sidekick, Bennie, was a family man. He dressed simply, in baggy clothes more appropriate for the mess of the factory than for a businessman's lunch. He didn't put on airs. Although he had affiliated with Ray, the two families rarely got together. Ming had re- mained the essence of the eldest Chinese son. He kept one foot firmly planted in the family business, not for any love of Chinese art, but because it was his role. All of his friends were Americans. Eddy's life, on the other hand, was anchored in Chinatown. Everything about him seemed Chinese, except his wife and son. And Sissee, by marrying Gilbert, had made the most complete decision to live as a Chinese.

At stake were two businesses: the F. Suie One Company and See Manufacturing. Ming ran the store, but it had been in Sissee's name since the family had bailed out of the lease on the Wilshire store during the Depression. Eddy, Ray, and Bennie had started the factory, but Eddy hadn't liked the work. He'd opened Dragon's Den, but it was closed now, leaving him in the position of being the only one in the family who didn't have clear ownership of a business. Unfortunately, Eddy didn't have anything to bargain with.

Sides were drawn and redrawn. Affiliations were tested; some held, others collapsed. During the loud arguing—which Ray's daughter, Pollyanne, and Eddy's son, Richard, remember not for its content but for its vituperativeness—years of angst, resentments, and petty peeves poured out. Old rivalries showed themselves. Instead of bickering over who had the fastest car, the most expensive car, the biggest car, they argued over whether or not the family partnership should be dissolved, and, if so, who should get which business.

Ray was a formidable force. Eddy, Ray claimed, no longer pulled his weight.

"But I supported the family through the Depression," Eddy retorted. "I carried you and your families for five or six years."

"That was the Depression," Ray said. "Those days are gone and we owe you nothing. Bennie and I have an opportunity now, and what happened in the past doesn't matter." He sat perched on a stool, one hand tucked into a trouser pocket, a silk handkerchief peeking out of the breast pocket of his well-tailored herringbone jacket.

"I helped start the factory," Eddy said. "Doesn't anyone remember that?"

"Bennie and I are the ones who worked it, who built it up," Ray said. He took a drag on his cigarette, then continued, "It's always been ours."

"But I had ulcers. I had to take it easy for a while! Now, as soon as I'm sick and not productive, you drop me?"

"I'm not dropping you. You're the one who closed Dragon's Den," Ray reminded him. "And remember, there's the store. Why can't you be partners with Ming?"

Ming, who had remained silent through most of the discussion, turned to Ray. "Well, I've been doing the work in the store for years, while Eddy was showing off with the restaurant. After Dragon's Den closed, he went back to the factory."

"But as an employee!" Eddy snapped. "Why should I have been an employee?"

But Ming went on, "And Eddy quit. So then he came to work at the store, doing jewelry." Addressing Eddy directly, Ming said, "I have to say that I don't see why you think you have the expertise to run the store. You haven't gone on any buying trips. You haven't worked with the decorators. You've never spent much time with the Hollywood people except to give them dinner. I don't see why you should be my partner."

"You know I could do those things as well as you," Eddy said, but Ming only shrugged. The store was his by virtue of the fact that he was the eldest son.

But this exchange gave Eddy something to work with. He *did* feel that he knew enough to run the store, and in fact he had often chafed at Ming's arrogance. As the meetings wore on, Eddy went to his sister and said, "I'm the one who should have the store. Ming thinks he's the big boss, but I could run it better." When Sissee didn't respond, he tried a different approach: "I could do what Ray's doing. I can design. I can get contracts." She listened to these entreaties, but revealed nothing of her thoughts.

In another meeting, Eddy, desperately trying to keep his dignity and not get cheated by his brothers, attempted the one argument that he thought they would listen to: "Ma never would have wanted you all to do this. She wanted us to have the family pot so that we would stick together."

"Ma's gone," Ray said. "And I don't see any reason why I should be supporting your family."

"And I'm asking you again, is this what Ma would have wanted? She always said family's family and that we had to stay together."

Soon after this, Eddy was admitted to the hospital with a severe flare-up of his ulcers. With Eddy out of the way, his siblings decided to make their decision. They gathered once again on the mezzanine of the store. The brothers and Sissee agreed that *if* Eddy were there, he would choose to keep the family together. Bennie and Ray agreed to separate. Ming, having listened to Eddy's argument about what their mother would have wanted, voted to keep the partnership together. That made the vote two for breaking up the partnership against two for staying together. Suddenly the pressure was on Sissee. Here was the surprise that none of them expected. Although Eddy was her favorite brother, Sissee sided with Ray and Bennie. Her vote was less for breaking up the partnership than against what Eddy had told her in their private conversation. In asking for her support in trying to take the store away from Ming, Eddy had alienated Sissee.

While Eddy recovered in the hospital, the partnership was officially dissolved. Ray and Bennie got the factory; Ming and Sissee kept the store. Eddy got nothing, except a promise that he would always have a place working in the F. Suie One Company. He could keep his table at the front of the store, make jewelry, and repair lamps.

If it comes as a surprise that Sissee voted against Eddy, what is really astounding is that none of this was *ever* spoken about. The children only heard rumors, for none of their parents wanted to fully explain their individual roles in the breakup. Nevertheless, Eddy and Stella made certain assumptions. It was obvious that Ray and Bennie were together. Eddy never truly forgave them, but the truth was that he didn't have to see them every day. It never even crossed Eddy's and Stella's minds that *Sissee* had voted to separate.

So it was that Ming received the most blame. What possessed Ming to accept it? Affection for Eddy? Love for Sissee? Respect for the relationship between Eddy and Sissee, which, except for this one disagreement, remained extraordinarily close throughout their lives? Or was it the sense that, as the eldest brother, Ming had to try to maintain some semblance of family harmony? For the next fifteen years Ming and Eddy would work side by side. Eddy harbored his resentment and Ming took it, while Sissee continued in her role as the cherished younger sister.

In some families this scenario would be unbelievable, but not for the Sees. Eddy, even at his most disheartened, would often say, "Family's family. We still have to stick together." Or, if he'd had a disagreement with Ming, he might say, "He's my brother. And you really only have your family." Though he certainly never absolved Ming, Ray, or Bennie—and though none of them ever socialized again the way they had when Ticie was alive—it was inconceivable that Eddy would start a long-term feud with his older brothers, just as it had been inconceivable for Ticie to leave him behind in China. The others may have divided Ticie's physical estate, but Eddy had received her one true legacy—her love for the family and her belief that her children were stronger together than apart. Family—and this included his full brothers and sister as well as his half-brothers and half-sisters—meant everything to Eddy. Family always came first, no matter what the personal cost.

CHAPTER 18

FIRE

1947–50

I n 1947, Fong See turned ninety and went into the hospital to have his gallbladder removed. Before the surgery, the doctor said, "I don't think you're going to make it. As a precaution, you should take care of your personal affairs." See-bok didn't like this advice one bit! He decided he would show that doctor by living through the operation. Then, after the surgery, while Fong See was still recuperating in the hospital, the doctor came in and said, "You're not going to live much longer." Now, for the first time in his life, See-bok tried to think about what would happen if he died, but he found it nearly impossible. Instead, he considered how very much alive he was.

Despite his brush with death, he looked much younger than his age. He had always been a slim man. With each passing year, whatever excess fat had been on his frame melted away until he appeared to be just bones with skin stretched tightly over them, giving him the appearance of someone fifteen or twenty years younger. He walked with a shuffle, keeping his feet firmly planted on the ground, but his carriage was still proud and upright.

He was far from being disengaged from the world about him. He was vigilant about business. He had sources who reported to him on the goings-on about Chinatown, Los Angeles, and the world. He was the master of his home, keeping a tight hold on the activities of his children and Ngon Hung. He also kept tabs on the children of his first family— all of them in middle age, all of them married, all of whom he saw in relation to himself. Ming was learning how to be a patriarch; he fulfilled his familial obligations even when they made him unpopular with his brothers and sister. (See-bok remembered how he, too, had learned to accept responsibility and make sometimes unpopular choices for the family.) His second son, Ray, was doing what See-bok had hoped to do himself: make a reputation in the white world. (It troubled See-bok that he had no relationship with this son, but what could he do? The boy would not visit or call, as was his responsibility.) Fong See didn't know much about Bennie, except that he was a good boy who obeyed his older brother.

Eddy. Now here was someone Fong See liked. Eddy came to visit almost every day. He had relationships with his younger half-brothers. He taught them how to repair things, how to put furniture together, how to fix their cars. He talked with those boys, kidded them, teased them. And Sissee was a good daughter. He could see this in the way she was raising his granddaughter Leslee to be a good Chinese daughter with proper manners. His second family? Those seven children were still too immature to have opinions that mattered. They were too young to be doing anything interesting. His youngest son, Gary, was only two; his eldest daughter, Jong Oy, had married and moved away.

Finally, there was Ngon Hung. As Fong See lay in his hospital bed, he thought about his Number Three wife. He realized that he had come to care about her in his own way. It was not the western idea of love, by any means, because in truth Chinese women were nothing to *care* about. Throughout his entire lifetime, girl babies in China had been abandoned at birth, sold as servants, prostitutes, and concubines, or matched into marriage with men they had never seen before. Women— Chinese women—lived to care for their husbands and have sons. Ngon Hung had fulfilled both of these duties. She was passive, submissive, and obedient; she had given him four boys and three girls. He concluded she had been a good wife all these years.

He thought, What will happen to Ngon Hung when I am gone? Who will look after her? My boys are still young, and she is inexperienced. Fong See reached for the phone and called Mr. Ogden, the attorney who had handled the separation from Ticie. The next day Mr. Ogden came to the hospital to consult. "You should marry Mrs. Fong in this country to make sure there is no confusion about your estate when the time comes," Mr. Ogden said.

A justice of the peace was found and brought to the hospital. Fong See was propped up in bed. Ngon Hung—forty-two and old beyond her years—stood at her husband's side. Within minutes, Fong See and Ngon Hung were married according to the laws of the State of California.

For now, Fong See kept the rest of the details of his will a secret. Besides, he had no plans to die yet. He still had to get through his honeymoon.

On October 10, 1947, Anna May Wong, the aging screen goddess, slipped her arm through Ray's, tilted her head to his ear, and whispered. She wanted to leave. She was tired of talking to people, tired of shaking hands, tired of standing in high heels for the last two days. She wanted to go up to her room, and she wanted him to come with her. Ray shook her off. "I didn't bring you two thousand miles to give you free drinks," he said. "Go get some coffee. Come back in a half hour and do your job." Anna May stared at him for a minute, turned, and wobbled away.

Why had he brought her to Chicago? The dancing girls would have been enough. Edith and the rest of them looked cute and demure—if a bit clumsy—as they glided across the platform around his furniture pieces. They didn't have big tits like the girls in the other booths, but the buyers thought they were cute, and ordered like never before. He'd brought Anna May along as a novelty, but after the last couple of days he wished he'd left her back in Los Angeles for her brother to look after. Last night, she had even proposed to Ray. "Divorce Leona. Marry me. It will better both of our fortunes," she'd said. Ray had to admit that Anna May had a head on her shoulders as far as money was concerned, but that didn't mean he wanted to divorce his wife and marry an actress!

He put these thoughts aside and focused on the business at hand. After the family partnership had split up, Ray and Bennie had formed See-Mar of California with Morris Markoff, the lamp manufacturer. Now Ray and Markoff were at the Drake Hotel in Chicago to introduce their line to the Furniture Mart. The booth was crowded, as it had been since the doors to the hall opened two days ago. The samples for next January were selling well. Better yet, the local media had made several appointments for interviews.

How could Ray have guessed that he would be making this kind of money? Hand over fist, was how he liked to think of it. He tried never to brood about Ming, Sissee, and Eddy. Why should he? They were so stuck in the past. Ming hung around the store, turning into an old man. Sissee and her husband did good deeds all over Chinatown. And Eddy? What had happened to Eddy was too bad, but business was business. If Ray's father had been right about anything, it was that you couldn't let family stand in the way of your achieving the American Dream.

Business, Ray loved it. He got a kick out of posing for photographers, doing interviews, meeting people. He delighted in watching the look on the face of some skirt from the *Times* when he told her about designing furniture for Bob Hope and Walter Brennan. He loved it when he could take the wood left over from his war contracts and turn it into table/lamp combinations. He enthused in his descriptions of See-Mar of California, which manufactured lamps and occasional pieces.

It seemed as if the entire See family had been in the lamp business in one way or another, practically from the beginning. Years ago, Ray's mother had gotten his father out of the underwear business by making lampshades out of China silk. Decades later, Ming still sold lamps by drilling through the bottoms of Chinese vases and wiring them. Even Eddy did his bit as the one man in Chinatown who could fix anyone's broken lamp. Now Ray was designing lamps in truly unique designs: Mongolian horsemen, T'ang horses, chess pieces, and heads of Greek gods; a column lamp with hand-carved acacia leaf; a modernized "candlestick" in green, black, or red; a Chinese woman in flowing robes and sashes carved from a "tablet" of alder. His lamps had interesting shades in China silk, rayon, or tropical cotton prints of the kind he had designed for D. N. & E. Walter in the past.

The idea of function in domestic furniture intrigued Ray. As a result, many of his tables held recesses for cigarettes, hors d'oeuvres, record albums, and magazines. Others had built-in spaces for glasses, ashtrays, even radios. He'd designed a blond wood coffee table in the shape of a Chinese ideogram. Each corner sported a rectangular box for growing plants—"always an attractive note in a room," noted one reviewer. The base of one of the most popular lamps held a pot for a live philodendron or a more durable plastic one.

Ray was a long way from the Chinese antique business. While what he made wasn't junk, you couldn't call it art either. "Nothing wrong in no-good product so long you make money," his father used to say, ordering the boys to bury brand-new ginger jars in manure to "age" them quickly. His father had been a genius when it came to fooling customers, Ray had to give that to him. He remembered how his mother and sister had spent afternoons "antiquing" baskets fresh off the boat with that smelly mixture of asphalt and turpentine. Those "antiques" had made a tidy profit, just as the lamps were easy money. When his salesgirls talked about teak and ginger finishes, Ray knew that a finish was all they were. Using cheap wood, he had incorporated marble, latticework, and walnut-burl overlays to create what many interior decorators were calling "unique surprises." Make a handsome product from inexpensive materials, and it will always sell. And his did—to Barker Brothers, Widdicomb, Stickley Brothers, and Lord & Taylor.

Anna May came back holding a newspaper. She looked sober, too sober. He hoped she'd done nothing embarrassing. When she reached him, she flipped open the paper to a headline that read, FIRE RAZES L.A. FURNITURE PLANT, WATCHMAN KILLED. Her pale skin and trembling hands told him who owned that factory.

Ray didn't read the full story until he was on the plane heading back for Los Angeles. Eleven fire companies, with twenty-one pieces of equipment, had battled the blaze for hours. After the flames had been extinguished, firefighters had found the body of the night watchman. Ray looked at the photograph of the ruined building and shuddered. The article estimated a $25,000 loss on the structure alone. Ray knew the real value lay inside. From what he could see, all the machinery, as well as the plant-lamps, chess-lamps, table/lamp combos, and all their matching shades, had been reduced to ashes, as had all of the occasional pieces. He pulled out a pad of paper, made some quick calculations, and tallied the figures. The loss looked to be in the neighborhood of a quarter of a million dollars.

Ray began making plans. Today was October 10, 1947. If they could lease space quickly, they might be able to get in new equipment by the end of the week. If they got to work right away, he might be able to ship in sixty days. If the new line could be out the door by December 10, he could still take advantage of the Christmas rush. No one ever bought furniture in December, but shoppers—fatigued and loaded down with packages—often sought refuge in the furniture sections of department stores to rest on sofas, chairs, and ottomans. They would come back after the holidays to buy for themselves. All he had to do was get the merchandise made and shipped. If everything went well, See-Mar would end up bigger and better than ever. These were, Ray acknowledged, a lot of ifs.

From Los Angeles airport he took a cab down to the industrial section of town. From the outside, the building didn't look badly damaged. The brick walls still stood, although they were smoke-stained and the windows had blown out. Ray heard someone approach and stop next to him. He turned to see an old Chinese man as frail as a dried leaf, wearing a gown down to the pavement. His hands were tucked up into voluminous sleeves. It took Ray a few moments to recognize the wizened stranger as his father. They hadn't seen or spoken to each other in years.

"What are you doing here?" Ray asked.

"Now you borrow money from me," Fong See said.

Ray appraised the old man who'd deserted his mother so long ago. Ray felt himself begin to shake with years of pent-up anger. His voice, when it came, was low and hoarse. "Not from you, not ever." Ray crossed the street and stepped into the gutted ruins of what had been the first material realization of his freedom. He never spoke to his father again.

On January 21, 1948, just three months after the fire that gutted Ray and Bennie's factory, another tragedy struck the family. While Ming was off spending the night with Sunny Rockwell, the woman who sculpted in the alley behind the store, his wife, Dorothy, probably drunk, fell asleep in bed with a cigarette. The house caught fire and burned to the ground, killing Dorothy. Unable to find Ming, the police called Eddy, who went straight over to the house and identified Dorothy's charred remains. When Ming arrived in the early-morning hours, he "went to pieces." In shock, he stared blindly, numbly, at the fireplace that still stood in what was otherwise a few inches of ashes. Ming was too upset to answer the questions posed by the firemen and the policemen.

Ming had to stay somewhere. There wasn't enough room at Dragon's

Den for another person, and he wasn't close enough to Bennie or Ray to be taken in by them. Sissee was the best choice, the only choice, Eddy reasoned, because Ming was going to need a woman's compassion to get him through his mourning. So Eddy drove his older brother to the Leong house on Ivadel, where Sissee and Gilbert had taken up residence since returning from Memphis. Ming—silent in his grief and guilt—was put to bed in the upstairs sewing room.

All through that day and night, the family came and went. They tried to talk to Ming, but he wouldn't speak. They rehashed the history of the See brothers. All but Bennie had strayed from their wives. Ray and Leona had a marriage in name only. Stella and Eddy had patched things up. Ming and Dorothy had been another story. The family knew he was having an affair with Sunny. But he had fooled around for so long that no one had reproached him for it until now. "If Ming had been with her, it never would have happened," Stella said angrily. "He had a responsibility." Through all of this, Sissee was a rock—providing coffee, tea, and snacks to her brothers and their wives, shutting off comments such as Stella's with an abrupt "We're going to forget about that. We're going to forget about that for Ming."

During the following weeks, Sissee was moved to action in a way she never could have been for herself, insisting that they all work to help Ming erase the fire from his memory, for he truly had fallen apart. His hair seemed to go white overnight. He had the shakes. When he spoke, his normally even voice was broken by a stutter. Close friends tried to comfort him: "No one can blame you. Dorothy treated you like a rat." Through all this, Mama Leong never questioned the fact that Sissee had moved Ming into the house. Mama Leong never lectured or complained. She simply allowed Sissee to care for her brother.

On a morning in May—four months after Dorothy's fiery death— Ming was still living with the Leongs. Sissee and Ming—quiet, as he had been since that night in January—sat together in the kitchen sipping coffee and listening to Bernice, Sissee's sister-in-law, tell a story from work.

"My boss said, 'We have coffee cake and coffee for breakfast. What do you eat?' I said, 'Coffee cake and coffee.' 'Gee,' he says, 'I thought you Chinese *just ate rice.*'" Bernice, who'd been the first Asian hired by Western Auto, laughed and Sissee giggled along with her. "They're all Midwesterners," Bernice went on. "They've never seen someone like me before."

"I'll bet they haven't," Sissee said.

"Then they say, 'Your English is quite good.' I say 'Well, it ought to be. I was born here.'" Again they laughed, knowing that they could look at this stuff either as discrimination or just as a joke. Bernice glanced at her watch. "I've got to go. I don't want to be late."

Sissee walked her sister-in-law to the door. She paused to watch Bernice drive away, then walked down the hall to the kitchen. Ming, without a word, went back upstairs where he would remain until Sissee called him for lunch. She straightened up the kitchen and the butler's pantry, then poured herself another cup of coffee, went back into the dining room, and picked up the newspaper to peruse the classifieds. Sissee relished these quiet mornings after the other Leongs had left and before she began her daily chores.

The house on Ivadel was perfect for the extended Leong family. The upstairs had five bedrooms separated by a central hallway. Three of the bedrooms held family units: Mr. and Mrs. Leong in one; Sissee, Gilbert, and Leslee in another; and Elmer and Bernice in yet another. The other two bedrooms were occupied by Gilbert's single siblings, Margie and Ed. There was also the sewing room, where Ming was staying, which frequently doubled as an additional bedroom for Leong houseguests.

Sissee and Gilbert, who was apprenticed to an architecture firm, had little privacy. They shared a common bathroom with the rest of the family; they shared their bedroom with Leslee. Their communication was circumspect. In China, custom would have dictated that all of their conversation be conducted through servants. But in the United States, Sissee and Gilbert had no servants to act as go-betweens. Instead they followed the next level of proper marital etiquette: "Ascend the bed, act like a husband. Descend the bed, act like a gentleman." During the day and at any time in front of the family, no kissing, no touching of any kind, no sweet words of affection were permitted. It was a careful, impersonal way to live, one that was insisted upon by the ever-righteous Mrs. Leong.

When Gilbert, Sissee, and Leslee had first returned from Memphis and moved into the house on Ivadel, Mrs. Leong hadn't softened just like that. She'd observed Sissee and made careful calculations of her character. Sissee, who had grown up working in the store and at Dragon's Den, had had to prove to her mother-in-law what a hard worker she was. When Mrs. Leong bought some rundown apartments on Bunker Hill, Sissee kept them up. Each time a tenant left, Sissee scrubbed down the apartments with ammonia and Clorox until her hands were raw. She never complained, never said a word. The housekeeping chores also fell to Sissee. She did the shopping and cleaning. (Except on Thursdays, when her father-in-law made dinner at home for all of them, Sissee made dinner nightly for her own family unit. And, except on Thursdays, Sissee and Gilbert were already in bed when the rest of the family got home from Soochow.) When she wasn't cooking, cleaning, or shopping, Sissee went to the F. Suie One Company to do the books. In her spare time she volunteered at the Chinese Women's Club and visited her mother's old friend Mrs. Morgan, which showed she honored older people. Sissee always told Mrs. Leong the truth and showed respect. But more than anything else, Sissee gave the appearance of being willing to listen to and adopt her mother-in-law's advice.

"If anyone comes to the house, welcome them with a cup of tea," Mama Leong might suggest, and Sissee would do it.

"Be careful what you say," Mama Leong chastised. "In Chinese, a wrong inflection will give a very different meaning."

Mama Leong instructed, "At home, we always use serving spoons for the communal dishes. At other houses, or sometimes at banquets at low-class restaurants, people will put their chopsticks into the common bowls. This is not how we do it. But if you are at a place that does it this way, then certainly do the same. To be polite, only pick up what is directly in front of you."

Another daughter-in-law might have said, "I know that. I wasn't born in a barn, you know." But Sissee kept her mouth shut, allowing her mother-in-law to think that she was docile and obedient.

The hardest part was having a small child in a house full of adults. Even though Sissee had been raised in Chinatown, there were certain things she could see about the way she'd grown up that were completely different from the Leong style. Sissee had been close to her mother. There had always been hugs and kisses and deeply felt expressions of love. In the Leong family, emotional demonstrations were held in disdain. As a result, Leslee never received hugs and kisses from her grandparents. Presents were not to be played with. Christmases came and went, birthdays came and went. Gifts—dolls and miniature ovens—were to be looked at, admired, then stored in the attic.

The Leongs loved Leslee, of course. She didn't make noise, run around, or bang into things in the house. "Best of all," Sissee had heard Mama Leong say, "Leslee looks like a typical Chinese baby." Although by all rights Leong Jeung should have given Leslee her Chinese name, Mama Leong had done it herself, giving her beautiful, quiet granddaughter the name of Man Gai En, for the famous musician.

Now, as Leslee got older, Mrs. Leong sometimes scolded, "Don't let Leslee forget she's a girl. She must act like a young lady—in how she walks, how she sits, how she talks." Another daughter-in-law might have said, "Oh, Mom, you're so *chong hai,* so long-winded," but Sissee simply nodded, and reminded Leslee to be quiet and remember that the house was filled with grownups.

Where other families might have resisted, argued, or harbored resentments, the nine Leongs—Sissee included—had settled into a comfortable routine shored up by tradition. Ed, Gilbert's older brother, accepted the responsibility of the family business and obeyed his mother. Margie was a social worker, but her schedule brought her back each night to Soochow, where she was still the hostess.

Elmer? Poor Elmer. Sissee could remember how handsome her brother-in-law had been before the war. He had been in military intelligence and had flown over Germany almost every day. Eventually he'd gotten ulcers, and one month before the war ended, the military had brought him home and he'd spent the next year and a half in a hospital. While he was away, he'd also gotten a bad case of acne. Once out of the hospital, he'd gone to a Chinese doctor, who sanded his skin off. Now Elmer was a wastrel. With his skin brutally scarred, he'd moved outward to the next layer, dressing in expensive clothes and shoes. But Bernice provided Elmer's real armor. She was a strong woman.

Bernice had been born up north, near Fresno, and had a life that was in many ways typically Chinese American—persistent in the face of hard times combined with the rare stroke of good fortune. Her family was practically the only Chinese family in the area, so Bernice was very westernized, with a modern haircut and makeup. She spoke English at home, and followed American traditions. Her father had owned a restaurant at the country's first miniature golf course. When the Depression hit, Bernice's father had moved his wife and five children into Fresno, where he was hired as a cook in a place that had gambling and prostitution. Bernice said he'd hated it because he was straitlaced and religious. He'd taken a chance and opened a little grocery store, then a restaurant in Fresno Chinatown, where he'd gained a reputation for his coconut cream and lemon pies. "People came from miles around to get them," Bernice told Sissee. "American people, not just Chinese." Then her father had contracted double pneumonia; soon after, he'd died of a heart attack. Bernice had been eighteen at the time.

She'd taken a job at Wu's Café, and it was there that she'd met Elmer, passing through Fresno on his way to a football game in San Francisco. In 1940, Bernice had moved to Los Angeles and gone to work for an herbalist. When she'd gotten tired of that, she'd taken a job as a secretary for an actress, Ona Munson, the woman who'd played Belle in *Gone With the Wind*. Bernice had a cousin, Pearl Luck, who had a gift shop in China City. Pearl, a Methodist, had gotten Bernice to go to the mission, where she'd renewed her acquaintance with Elmer. Then the war had come. Elmer had been sent overseas and Bernice had gone back to Fresno. After Elmer had gotten out of the hospital, he'd asked her to come back down to Los Angeles. Mrs. Leong had tried to discourage this, but the big difference between Gilbert and Elmer was that Elmer did what he wanted.

Elmer had listened to all of his mother's talk about Bernice's inferior family background and immediately taken Bernice and eloped to Las Vegas. Mrs. Leong had pitched a fit, but there was nothing to be done about it except have another marriage ceremony in a church. Afterwards, Mrs. Leong had wanted Bernice to perform the tea-pouring ceremony, but Bernice had refused. "I'm not going to kowtow to them," she had said. She hadn't given in then, and she didn't give in to Mrs. Leong now. But this wasn't Sissee's way.

Since Ming's arrival in the house, Sissee had enjoyed the truce with her mother-in-law, but she realized there was more to marriage than a good relationship between a wife and a mother-in-law. Sissee wanted desperately to move out of the house, but Gilbert repeatedly forestalled her attempts. For this reason, Sissee had spent much of her early marriage redefining her image of her husband. She had seen Gilbert as a sculptor. She had thought he was creative, romantic, bohemian. She had placed him in the same category as Benji and Tyrus. It had come as the biggest shock of her life when Gilbert had turned out to be a rigid Chinese man.

The more Sissee talked about finding their own house, the more she realized her husband wanted to stay with his mother. Still, every day Sissee looked through the classifieds, hoping to find a solution. This morning her eyes caught an advertisement, and she began to envision what might be. That night, when Gilbert came home, she showed him the ad.

"Army surplus is selling entire barracks," she said. "We could go in with Stella and Eddy and buy one. They'd like to get out of the basement and have their own place too."

"What? You want us to live all together in a barracks?"

"No, we'll take it apart and use the materials to build our own home. You'll be able to express yourself and build exactly what you want."

Gilbert laughed. "It sounds ridiculous. It sounds like something Eddy would do. You're a dreamer, just like him."

And without considering the implications, she said, "I want to get out of here. There are just too many people." Then, echoing her own mother, she added, "I want to have a house of my own. Either we move out of here, or I'll move out myself."

In a way that Sissee would never fully understand, Gilbert had made his choice when he married her. "Go ahead and check about these barracks," he said. "Perhaps they're a good idea after all."

In 1948, Sumoy, Fong See's youngest daughter and Richard's half-aunt, turned thirteen. She was petite and pretty in an innocent way. All who knew her loved her. "She is so sweet, she was born sweet," they said. Sumoy was the good daughter, the one who accompanied her father on his Christmas shopping trip to Sears, where she helped him pick out gifts—reindeer sweaters for the boys, Dan River gingham blouses for the girls, a hat and scarf set for Ngon Hung. Sumoy's father and all her older brothers guarded her for the precious jewel she was. Just as her father wouldn't let her go on camping trips with the Girl Scouts when she was younger, he now forbade her to go on overnight trips with the church or to the homes of her friends. When she wanted to spend the night at Betty Soo Hoo's house, Fong See said, "No, she has brothers." When Betty came over and said she had her own room, Fong See still wasn't satisfied. "Do you have a lock on the door?" Without a lock, Sumoy wasn't sleeping anywhere other than her own room. Yet, for all this protection, Fong See didn't seem to notice that Richard was ga-ga over Sumoy.

Richard provided excitement to everyone in the extended Fong family. The girls thought he was fascinating. How could he not be fascinating? He was eighteen. He was white, with black hair and skin paler than theirs. Yet he was connected; he was family. When he moved to Chinatown, everyone accepted him as though he'd just returned from a long journey. Richard wasn't simply another cousin; he was the son of everyone's absolute favorite uncle/cousin/half-brother. Eddy had never broken the tie. He had given the kids their first radio when Pa had said no. He had taken the boys out to Angeles Forest and cut down Christmas trees to bring back and set up throughout the Fong apartment. (Stella had shown the girls how to make ornaments out of toilet paper.) He was the ideal older brother, so it was only natural that in a family where blood truly was thicker than water, they embraced Richard completely.

Richard and Sumoy were like Romeo and Juliet—impossible, doomed, the stuff of stories. The other teenagers were bewitched by the pair's shy looks, their sudden blushes, their eyes locking onto each other, then just as quickly glancing away. "It was so beautiful," one cousin recalled. "It was love. I could cry when I think about how beautiful it was."

Part of the suspense was watching the energy flow between these two—the girl just out of puberty, the boy just graduating from high school. The other part was not knowing if it was real or imagined, because surely, if it was true, wouldn't one of the adults have done something? But not once did Fong See, Ngon Hung, Eddy, or Stella say anything directly. Rather, Fong See told his wife, "Keep an eye on Sumoy. Don't let her get out of hand. Don't let her do anything that will embarrass the family." Ngon Hung, who, when most girls are experiencing their first crush, was already married and a mother, counseled her daughter, "Men always have time to run around town. Society doesn't put a brand on them."

What none of them appreciated was that Sumoy had a brain. Even though she was a good Chinese daughter who might be expected to follow an inevitable course through a life of childbirth, chores, and early old age like her mother's, Sumoy wanted desperately to break the pattern, which seemed as immutable as granite. After a day at junior high school she went to the store, sat at a table in the back, and did her homework. Her father ignored her when she complained that it was too dark. Sumoy knew her requests were pointless. It was dark because they didn't want anyone to see the dust. Having finished her homework, she picked up a feather duster and worked her way from one end of the store to the other.

"What do you need school for?" her father asked. "If you have to work, be something like a secretary or an office assistant."

Her mother shook her head in confusion. "You know about the past, but you care more about the future."

Only Richard understood.

"I can't go on like this," Sumoy confided to him with an air of sophistication that belied her years. "I don't want to spend my life in the store. I want something different. Besides, they'll never let me in the store. Chuen and Yun are being groomed to take over, not me, not a girl. They're the ones out delivering furniture, driving the car, helping Father."

"You don't want that anyway," Richard said. "You can do other things. You could go to college."

Sumoy, who was close to her mother and still tied to home, knew she would never overstep any boundaries. She shut her eyes to the lovesick boy before her, preferring to see an understanding brother.

By late 1948, Gilbert, Sissee, Eddy, and Stella (who had bought a lot on Landa, a street that curved up the back side of Elysian Park and offered a view across the Los Angeles River toward Mount Washington) had made considerable progress in taking apart the barracks. Each weekend they drove out Alameda in a loose convoy: the adults in cars, the boys—Richard and Ted (who was between stints with the merchant marine and the army)—in a pickup truck. Along the way, the group stopped at a farm to buy fresh-picked corn. When they reached Long Beach, they crossed over the drawbridge to Terminal Island, where they drove the short distance to the barracks. There were about twenty barracks in all, and each had been sold to a family motivated by the same sort of wishful thinking as inspired the Sees and the Leongs. Tyrus and Ruth usually came along for the picnic and the jokes.

The barracks stood two stories high. Each floor had a latrine with several toilets, all hooked up to a single flush, a point that Tyrus couldn't let alone. "What are you going to do with these?" he jibed Gil and Eddy. "They have one flush, for Christ's sake." The toilets were also connected to the same water source—a huge tank, totally impractical for domestic use. The communal urinals took even more ribbing. Other things—like the two-story water heater and all its accessories—seemed to defy comprehension. But plenty of other stuff—wood, wiring, nails, electrical circuitry, faucets, and spigots—was usable.

The process was like constructing a building in reverse. The men—since much of it was designated "men's work"—started on the roof and slowly worked their way down. First they pulled off the roofing material and scraped off the tar. Then, very slowly, they extracted the nails and lifted out the wood planks, passing them down from person to person to be stacked in the back of the truck. As the roof and the walls came off the second floor, the men worked like spiders across the webbing of remaining joists and beams. On the ground, the women sat together and talked as they straightened nails and packed them in wooden barrels, wound up balls of electrical wire, wrapped windows in blankets, and stored fixtures in boxes.

They enjoyed being out here—the camaraderie with the other groups, the time spent with their families. They were middle-aged now. Ruth was still extraordinarily beautiful, with her jet black hair. Her eyes sparkled with an inside humor. Although Sissee was the youngest—if only by a few months—she looked the oldest, with her hair threaded by gray. Stella had undergone an amazing transformation in the last year. On Eddy's birthday in 1947 she had begun going to a diet clinic on North Broadway. After years of being overweight, she now weighed 112 pounds. The weight had settled into voluptuous curves on top and bottom, tapering in to a twenty-two-inch waist. Her hair was still fiery red, with tendrils that frizzed in the sea air.

Time had treated each of the men differently. With each passing year, Gilbert would become skinnier and ever more ramrod-straight. Tyrus would never change. He was thin, energetic, and funny, the most successful of them all. He'd left Disney and gone to Warner Brothers, where he worked on storyboards for John Wayne, George Raft, and Frank Sinatra movies. "I have a lot of freedom," he told his friends. "I don't have to punch a time clock, and when it's slow I can take time off and do my own work."

Since being cut out of the family partnership, Eddy had drifted—making jewelry, doing minor repairs on appliances for friends, visiting his father. Eddy still had his "December seventh beard" and was a bit wider through the middle, but these were just physical characteristics. He was an incorrigible goofball. Holding up a length of salami, he might widen his eyes and say, "How would you like to have *this* between your legs?" And every time he said something along those lines, Tyrus would laugh: "That's the trouble with you. Everything is always below the belt."

After the work was done, the three couples sat in a ragged circle around the fire. Richard and Ted sat slightly apart, talking in low voices. The four little girls—Leslee, and Tyrus and Ruth's three daughters—pedaled their tricycles in wide, noisy circles. This was the time they all enjoyed the most, when the work was finished and they could cook a pot of corn over a fire, drink coffee, and nibble on sandwiches and cold noodles.

A year later, in 1949, although the barracks was completely dismantled and all of the wood, electrical wiring, faucets, and spigots were stored in family warehouses and backyards, no dream houses were under construction. Gilbert said he was "too busy" with his own work to design a house. Instead of building the house on Landa, Stella, Eddy, and Richard moved into Stella's grandmother Huggins's house on Lantana Street in Glassell Park—close to downtown, and around the corner from Stella's cousins Ida and Vernon. (Stella had inherited the house on her grandmother's death.) From here, Richard enrolled at City College and began taking classes. The lot on Landa grew wild with patches of sumac, poison oak, and rye grass.

Eddy began several home-improvement projects that he never completed. He tore out the ceiling, exposing the rafters. He chiseled plaster off walls. He built a foundation for an addition, but lost interest. He took out windows to make a lanai, lost interest again, and replaced the glass with "temporary" sheets of plastic.

The garden, on the other hand, flourished under such neglect. Stella and Eddy—with help from Benji—planted bodhi trees, giant bamboo, tamarind, pittosporum, walnuts, apricots, and avocados. Abandoned projects proliferated into a thick jungle highlighted here and there with things scavenged from a Los Angeles that was being systematically "improved." Eddy tipped over a Chinese street vendor's cart and spread out leftover rice to attract birds. Against a wall he propped bamboo rakes, and leaf gatherers made from sheared-off five-gallon soy-sauce cans. The overall effect was wild, untamed, yet aesthetically pleasing.

A year after moving into the house on Lantana, Eddy became galvanized with the idea of preserving and honoring the history of the Chinese and other pioneers in Los Angeles. Part of what motivated him was that yet another fire had destroyed another portion of China City. Fong Yun's store hadn't been damaged, but many others had. Several shopkeepers simply gave up, and as they left, business dwindled. By 1950, China City was nearly a ghost town. At this same time, the city fathers decided to tear down the last block of Old Chinatown—the 500 block of Los Angeles Street that Fong See and Ticie had used as their home base since 1906.

Eddy proposed that the residents of Los Angeles Street create an "International Settlement," a $500,000 development that would include shops and restaurants. The International Settlement would represent all the different cultures that had come to Los Angeles and, simultaneously, save the last block of Old Chinatown from destruction. "You attract people through their stomachs," Eddy said. "Then they'll stay to buy souvenirs. All we have to do is get our neighbors to invest and improve upon what we already have." The Lugo House—built by a Spanish land-grant family of the same name, and then the first home of Loyola University, and for years after that a boardinghouse for Chinese bachelors—would be converted to a museum. Tyrus drew up renderings of the Lugo House fixed up as the International Settlement. The *Los Angeles Mirror* sent out a reporter and a photographer.

At first the City Council seemed receptive to the idea, then Mrs. Sterling, who'd been instrumental in the founding of Olvera Street and China City, decided she didn't want anything to conflict with her enterprises. She had the ear of the *Los Angeles Times,* which, in turn, owned the souls of several councilmen, or at least that's how Eddy saw it.

On September 28, 1950, all factions appeared before the City Council. Proposals ranged from turning Los Angeles Street into a parking lot to a German beer garden. Several argued that the International Settlement posed the threat of tong wars with café owners from China City. But all debates came to a halt when Mrs. Sterling arrived with a delegation from Olvera Street. Wearing flowers in her hair, pearls, and a dress with flowers appliquéd on the shoulders, Mrs. Sterling urged that the entire Plaza be renovated. "The Plaza should be cleaned up and commercialism eliminated or else everything should be torn down and the property used for a parking lot." She emphasized that the International Settlement was a purely "commercial" enterprise. (Amazingly, no one pointed out that both Olvera Street and China City had operated as commercial enterprises for years.)

She asked the council members to consider the important role that the Mexican and Spanish civilizations had played in the city's cultural heritage. Then, with great enthusiasm, she told the assembled crowd that she had brought with her a little surprise. The doors to the council chamber were flung open and in poured a group of Mexican folk dancers dressed in fancy costumes of ribbon and lace, who performed to the accompaniment of a mariachi band.

The councilmen were enchanted by this sudden, but colorful, display. Then Sissee stood to speak. "We didn't come in our costumes," she told the council. "We didn't bring music. We don't have to show off. We may be proposing an *International* Settlement, but we're *Americans* first." Eddy added that, in addition to the Mexicans and Spanish, the city owed much to the Chinese, the French, the Italians, and even—a daring suggestion so soon after the war—the Japanese.

But it seemed that the council members had already decided in favor of Mrs. Sterling. Still, there was one consideration: the Lugo House—which stood in the center of the 500 block of Los Angeles Street. "To me the idea of this historic building being destroyed is absolutely appalling," Councilman Ed J. Davenport opined. "This Council has been stymied at many points and not told the complete truth. We were told that it [the block] was needed for freeway purposes and then found out only a small portion was needed." He proposed saving the Lugo House, the Kong Chow Temple, and a few other buildings in the area.

Orville Caldwell, the deputy mayor and chairman of the Civic Center Authority, suggested that the Lugo House be moved the short distance to Olvera Street. But in the end, the State Parks Commission decided to turn the Plaza west of Los Angeles Street into a state park. Included in this plan were the Pico House, the Masonic Temple, the Garnier Building, and an old fire station. The Lugo House, the F. Suie One Company, the F. See On Company, Soochow Restaurant, and the other buildings that made up the last block of Old Chinatown would be torn down to make way for freeway ramps. Whatever was left over would be planted with grass. Eddy and Sissee left the meeting knowing that condemnation notices would be arriving soon.

On a day in October 1950, three years after the fire that had leveled his factory, Ray See strode across his new showroom to give a revision of a design detail to Bennie. As Ray crossed the floor, he overheard one of his salesgirls describing a table/lamp combination to a buyer from one of the big department stores. "While the piece is solid and substantially modern," she said, her hand arcing around its silhouette, "you will find a feeling of lightness and delicacy reminiscent of eighteenth-century styling. For this reason, Calinese fits perfectly into American Colonial and the more formal eighteenth-century English styles, as well as into most modern room settings."

Ray dropped off the drawing, came back through the showroom, eavesdropped again on the salesgirl, and reflected that a man does not become a millionaire by sitting on his haunches like some fool. He was on a roll, and clever enough to take advantage of it. With hard work and determination he had rebuilt his company. Within nine days of the fire, he'd rented space in another factory, while Bennie set about cleaning up the salvageable equipment. Samples for January had been made, production started, and orders shipped out within sixty days.

On July 26, 1948, just nine months after the fire, Ray, Bennie, and Markoff had sent out invitations for the opening of the new factory. The plant took up 26,000 square feet and had been built with a sawtooth roof that brought in natural light, allowing the factory to function as a "total daylight" operation. The showrooms—each paneled in gum wood with a natural stain—were triple the size of the old ones. An immense picture window divided the plant from the showrooms and offices, so that visitors could observe the manufacture of their wares. Through it all, Markoff had gotten on Ray's nerves—always hogging the attention, always giving interviews, always questioning production schedules. Finally, Ray had asked that the partnership be dissolved. Markoff readily agreed. Ray and Bennie had kept the See-Mar name, and business had started to take off.

In 1948, Los Angeles had produced $200 million worth of furniture at wholesale prices. Each year, that amount continued to grow. Some said it was because styles by West Coast designers were "fresh and daring." Others thought the trend reflected the growth of the television industry. In Los Angeles County alone, 456 sets were sold each day. With those sets came a new interest in seating arrangements, TV trays, and TV consoles.

Ray used these theories to create a new furniture line—Calinese. Actually, his wife, Leona, had come up with the name. "It will be a little bit of California and a little bit of China," she said. "Use something cheap, like myrtle wood. People will think it's exotic and innovative." Taking her advice, he'd incorporated myrtle and lauan, a mahogany from Luzon in the Pacific. He designed small cigarette tables in light and dark finishes, which could be placed around a room separately or together to make one large coffee table. He combined a chest and a bookcase to make a modern version of an old-fashioned hutch or china cabinet. And he still designed lamps—especially the table/lamp combinations. All of his ideas were turned into reality by Bennie and the other men and women who worked on the assembly lines.

Ray loved the pace: getting out new designs each season; setting up showrooms in Los Angeles, San Francisco, and Grand Rapids; wining and dining the buyers. He hadn't met a furniture man or a carpet man yet who didn't like to drink. Martinis and steaks and parties and women willing to spread their legs. People behaving outrageously at night and coming in the next morning to buy. Simply paradise, as far as Ray could see.

He especially loved the way it paid off. Baker, Knapp & Tubbs had been the first to take the Calinese line, filling their front windows with it. By 1950, Calinese could be found across the country. Frederick & Nelson in Seattle stocked it, calling Calinese "modern but not severe." James A. Cullimore & Company in Oklahoma noted the "richness of detail and softly rounded corners of the Orient." Stower's Furniture in Houston celebrated its golden anniversary by highlighting Calinese as perfect for "those just-married budgets." W. & J. Sloane in San Francisco promoted Calinese as "high modern at low prices." Even *The New York Times* had carried the news of Calinese.

Ray was at the height of his career and everyone knew it. The year before, in 1949, not satisfied with just Calinese, Ray had started designing fabrics again for D. N. & E. Walter, which had been in business in San Francisco since the building of the railroad. Ray had recently been feted by the company as the country's "eminent textile and furniture designer." His affiliation with Walter had also resulted in a documentary called "The Art of Handscreen Painting," in which Ray had the opportunity to show off his designs. His outsized, brightly dyed prints had names evoking the natural beauty of the state and the Orient: Giant Cactus ("as beautiful as a western sunset"), Flower Window ("from a latticework window in San Francisco's Chinatown"), Oahu ("a popular pattern for people who enjoy a Polynesian atmosphere"), Chungking ("distinctive as China herself and as modern as the moment"). All of them, as the narrator explained, utilized a "subtle new color combination and a trace of Chinese influence to create new designs lovely as a Ming vase and refreshing as the outdoors."

The people at D. N. & E. Walter talked about these new prints as a method of boasting about California to the entire country. "We're proud of our state and the way we live out here," the narrator said. "We try to get that across. With Walter handprints, everybody can have California sunshine right in their home." Ray's job, as the narrator explained, was to "combine Oriental mysticism, philosophy and charm with the vigorous beauty of the outdoors."

The new decade had begun auspiciously for Ray. Fifteen thousand Angelenos had passed through the doors of a "Calinese Touch-Plate" home in Santa Monica. The two-bedroom house had been furnished by Barker Brothers. Cocoa wall-to-wall carpeting flowed from room to room. Cocoa, turquoise, and tangerine had been used in the draperies and upholstery, with lemon yellow and lime green accents. The "Touch-Plate," an innovative remote-control lighting system, ran throughout the house and was served by four panels. Billed as the "House of Tomorrow," the home boasted the latest in modern inventions: exterior Venetian blinds; ceiling-mounted glass panels that emitted infrared rays (a new method to heat a bedroom and "do away with cold sheets"); an automatic garage-door opener; an indoor incinerator ("smog-proof and odorless"); and retractable hose reels and clotheslines.

Lamps, fabrics, furniture—Ray was doing them all. Sitting behind his desk, Ray glanced across the showroom floor to where the salesgirl was giving her pitch, echoing the words of a recent press release. "Mr. See has developed these occasional pieces in forms that have roots in the ancient past, yet every one of them reads 'today' in its effect. To achieve an Oriental feeling, Mr. See has used finishes in ginger, amber, and teak. Genuine coral and jade are used as color accents. The cloud design is taken from an ancient mandarin coat in Mr. See's collection."

Ray grinned. So much had been made of his "collection" of Oriental antiques. If only they knew how much he hated that stuff—the smell, the look, all the bad associations. After a lifetime of trying to get away from all that, here he was being reminded of it at every turn. It amazed him that the fantastic coverage on the Calinese line had come in large part from the "Chinese pioneer family" crap.

It was ironic, really. Most of his friends didn't even know he was Chinese. He never talked about it. His daughter, Pollyanne, knew enough not to ask. He was fairly proud of being Chinese, but he just couldn't forgive his father for leaving his mother and the rest of the family. He remembered a picture that Pollyanne had painted of a Chinese man. Ray had taken one look at it and wordlessly walked away. The drawing had looked so much like his father that it had made him physically ill.

As Ray See marveled at how far he had come and how he had built a life for himself, his father, now in his nineties, stood on frail legs outside his store at 510 Los Angeles Street. After all these years, See-bok was moving once again. This time he was going just a few blocks, to New Chinatown, where his son-in-law Gilbert Leong had designed a new showroom for the F. See On Company, as well as a warehouse, and living quarters above the store for See-bok's family. See-bok supposed he should look at this move as a new start, but he had had so many new starts in his life.

He watched as his eldest sons from the second family, Chuen and Yun, backed and sidled their way out through the doorway, carrying one end of an altar table. At the other end was Peter, the son of Fong Lai. See-bok barked out a few words—"Don't bump it! Be careful!"— and thought back to how his own true-life brother had been replaced by a new Fong Lai. When the second Fong Lai had wanted to bring over his son, Fong See had made the arrangements. Peter had originally come over from China to teach Fong See's children Chinese, but now he worked in the store.

See-bok looked around. Across the street, the old Spanish Plaza. To his far right, Olvera Street. To his far left, the Pico House and the other buildings that would be saved. But everything in his block was in disarray. Some of the buildings were already deserted: the Sam Sing Butcher Shop had moved over to Spring Street; the Leongs had consolidated Soochow with the branch in New Chinatown. But a few old-timers like him were sadly packing up a lifetime's worth of possessions and merchandise. Everyone was out or getting out before the bulldozers came.

See-bok watched his sons and Peter load the table into the moving truck. Inside the store, others—his younger sons and nephews—were up on ladders, prying loose carvings, rolling up scrolls, and carefully bringing down wall hangings. His daughters were packing ceramics and small bronzes.

He was too old to make this move!

Over the last few months, Fong See had watched while others tried to fight City Hall, but he knew that the only way to win was through money. It pleased him to know that rumors circulated around Chinatown that he had offered the city $250,000 if they would let him stay in his Los Angeles Street location. He liked it that people said, "He puts his money where his mouth is." See-bok wouldn't say what he'd offered, but when the city hadn't taken the bait, he'd gone to the Union Bank with his Caucasian accountant to see about a loan to move to New Chinatown. When he'd heard he'd have to pay points or cash under the table—he couldn't remember which—he'd simply refused and ponied up the cash for his new building. These stories kept his reputation alive.

Chuen and the others came out with more merchandise and loaded it on the truck. "Come on, Pa," Chuen said. "We're taking this over to the new place. You'd better come along with us."

Fong See's new store was on Chungking Court in a recently built block of New Chinatown, west of Hill Street. After his son had parked the truck, See-bok shuffled into the dark storefront.

"Pa, why don't you rest for a bit?" Chuen said. "We'll take care of things."

See-bok nodded, and wandered back past the packing crates and larger pieces of furniture left helter-skelter on the floor, to a back room where a cot had been set up. He sat down slowly, sighed, then lay down. He stared at the ceiling. He didn't worry about business. My customers will follow me, he thought. He would let his sons wait on clients from Beverly Hills and Pasadena, as well as the movie stars from Hollywood— Yvonne De Carlo, Anne Baxter, and Walter Pidgeon. It would be good practice for the boys, but Fong See himself would still wait on important customers like Charles Eames and Frank Lloyd Wright. (That old man! That Frank Lloyd Wright! He drove Fong See crazy! The way he came into the shop and tap-tapped at the merchandise with his cane! Fong See had shown him! "Get out! Get out!" he'd shouted until Wright fled. For years that story alone had made people wonder and come in to see if it was true. They would come to his new store to hear that tale again.)

Fong See was old, but he'd never lost his vision of life in America. He always thought ahead. He knew people wondered why he didn't take this opportunity to leave Chinatown altogether, but when the new City Hall had been built, he had seen the future. That building was so tall and sound that he became convinced that Los Angeles would always be a place where Caucasians would come first. So he stayed in Chinatown. Now, after sixty-three years in Los Angeles, he had finally bought a store. (It was still in someone else's name as a precaution.) It was as though Fong See was announcing, "I'm putting my roots down here. I came to America. I did well. Remember me."

It was hard for See-bok to think about these things as he lay on the cot in the back room of his new store. It was 1950, and Fong See, at ninety-three, was becoming increasingly disengaged from the world around him. His son Ming had recently married Sunny Rockwell, but Fong See hadn't gone to the wedding. (He wasn't invited because he was too old and unpredictable.) Fong See just barely observed the relationship between his sons and his grandson Richard. (That boy had troubles, drinking too much. But he told Chuen, "It's better to have bad friends than no friends.") His daughter Jong Oy had moved away, first back East, then to Taiwan, after marrying one of Chiang Kai-shek's officers. She had met the boy when he'd come over as a trainee. See-bok had already picked out the son of a businessman for her to marry, but she'd insisted on marrying this military man. Fong See had been too old, too weak, to prevent this. Now he supposed he'd never see her again.

Remember me, he thought.

He had always kept control over his family in China, but now he was an old man, powerless and ineffectual, totally isolated from his home village. Since he'd married Ngon Hung, all of his work had been geared toward leaving Los Angeles and going back to China, but just when he would have gone home to retire, his home country had thwarted him. He tried to look back and see what he could have done differently.

He thought back to the Japanese invasion. The Fatsan Grand Hotel had been conscripted by the Japanese to use as their headquarters. In the home village of Dimtao, his fourth wife, Si Ping, whom he had married in the 1920s, had done all right. They had never had children, and she had one hundred *mou* of land to sustain her. But Uncle's concubine, Lui Ngan Fa, and her three children had suffered greatly. With only six *mou* among them, they had been reduced to simple meals of *jook* or cabbage rice. Yet people said that no one left empty-handed when they went to her for money or food. No one realized then that Lui Ngan Fa's acts of generosity when others had nothing to eat but boiled bark would serve her well in the coming dark years.

When the world war ended, Fong See had gone back to China and seen with his own eyes how furniture had been destroyed, how his house had been torn asunder, how his land had languished. The manager of the hotel claimed that only three hundred U.S. dollars was left in the account. It was reported that Fong See had said, "This is evidence of the cruel act of Imperialist invaders. With this three hundred dollars, I might as well invite all my relatives and friends to a meal." Maybe he'd said that, maybe not. He couldn't remember exactly.

For a few brief years, Ngon Hung's mother, the business-minded Fong Guai King, had once again taken over the hotel. But this, too, was temporary. As soon as the Japanese were vanquished, the Generalissimo and Mao went right back to their civil war. In 1949, using the same guerrilla tactics they had used against the Japanese, Mao's troops drove Chiang Kai-shek off the mainland to the island of Taiwan. Soon after, the Communist high command claimed victory and rode into Peking to take up residence at the Forbidden Palace. In South China, lesser troops took over the Fatsan Grand Hotel to use as that city's Communist Commission Office. Fong See's town house behind the hotel was razed, with no apology or money paid for the insult. But this was not all! He sent six thousand U.S. dollars to Fong Guai King—not for her, she was too old, nor for Si Ping, his wife here would not allow it—but to help his young cousins and nephews leave China.

Fong See wasn't the only one to do this; all through Chinatown, people scrambled to send money back, hoping to get mothers and brothers and cousins and wives out before the Bamboo Curtain came down. When China first closed, families sent "tea money" back to relatives left behind in home villages. But now the risk was too great. In villages and cities across China, retributions were carried out against citizens reputed to have Imperialist relatives in the West. In American Chinatowns, since the outbreak of the Korean War in 1950, the politically powerful Six Companies—the federation of benevolent societies representing districts and counties in China—had mounted virulent anti-Communist campaigns. Spies were allegedly everywhere, and willing to report citizens sympathetic to the Communist regime. In addition to the fear of retribution that Chinese Americans faced from within their own communities, there was the apprehension about Caucasians that had continued unabated since the days of the railroad.

With the Korean War, Americans were also in the grip of anti-Chinese, anti-Communist propaganda. Chinese students and scholars from the People's Republic of China attending schools in the United States were barred from returning home. With the detention of Japanese American citizens still fresh in everyone's mind, there was widespread fear that now Chinese American citizens might face the same fate. (The passage of the McCarran Internal Security Act of 1950, which provided for the internment of Communists during a national emergency, certainly didn't help to quell these anxieties.) All these factors combined to produce a decline in the remittances sent to relatives in China from $7 million in 1948 to just $600,000 a year later. Now, in 1950, very little "tea money" left the United States for China.

Fong Guai King received the money, but gossips informed on her. She did her best to hide it, even giving some to Lui Ngan Fa to spirit away from inquisitive eyes. But while the Fong family had been able to slip through all the changes that had happened in China in the past, this time they were destined to be victims. Fong Guai King—her feet still bound, her hands still smooth and soft—was dragged to the village square, where she was forced to kneel in broken glass while new village Communists came forward to denounce her.

"She treated us badly."

"She was a bad woman, always selfish."

"She was rich, always taking fifty percent of the profits from the Fatsan Grand Hotel."

"She never thought of the villagers."

"She never worked hard. Look at her hands and you will see."

"She is one of the worst of the bad class."

On and on they went until Fong Guai King confessed, and no nephews or cousins were able to escape.

Though a terrible loss of face, this was just a preface to what would come. Because Fong See owned over one hundred *mou* of land, he was classified as an evil landlord. Still, the old-timers of Dimtao remembered Gold Mountain See's good deeds and therefore treated Si Ping well when she was detained. They remembered how she had financed the Arts and Handicrafts Fair every year on the seventh day of the seventh month. They remembered how women and young people from the ninety-six villages of Nam Hoi county had always come to enjoy the popular event. Only the farmers from rival villages were cruel to Fong See's fourth wife, occasionally beating and cursing her. Not too badly, it was reported. For a time, Uncle's wife escaped these torments. "She was always kind and humble," the villagers recalled. But eventually she was hit on the head and made to confess that she had hidden the money for Guai King.

The Communists were evil, or at least that's what most people were saying. But it was hard to tell. Many in Chinatown had forgotten what China was like: starvation, drought, pestilence, no opportunities. When Mao said, "Everybody works so everybody eats," Fong See, who may have been considered a landlord but had grown up as a peasant, recognized the irrefutable logic to those words. When relatives wrote that daughters of not very well-to-do families were being recruited to become orthodontists, doctors, and engineers, it was another sign—a woman could be something more than just a servant. But no one wanted to say these things aloud.

Americans were confused by all this. After so many years of "Free China" campaigns, the Communist takeover of China, followed by the outbreak of the Korean War, came as a surprise and a blow. Just as party loyalists wanted someone to take the blame in China, so too did Americans want someone to take the blame for the loss of China. Harking back to the last century, when the railroad was completed and the specter of yellow hordes petrified the Caucasian populace, once again politicians—with Senator Joseph McCarthy just beginning his anti-Communist campaign—dredged up familiar fears.

But while red-baiting demagogues and their minions ruined reputations, careers, and lives, some senators were passing special bills to bring in individual Chinese people who'd been caught in China when the Bamboo Curtain came down. This had happened to Woo Nguey, the wife of the owner of the Chungking Produce Company in Los Angeles, who got stuck in China during a visit. Senator Richard Nixon came to the family's aid, passing a special bill so that she could immigrate. To celebrate Mrs. Woo's return, the family sent the senator a crate of china, which he returned to them with a note saying that it was "wrong to accept a gift for doing right." In this way, the Woo family became convinced that Senator Nixon was an honest man.

Fong See had witnessed many changes in his home country during his lifetime—the fall of the Manchus, the Boxer Rebellion, the reign of the warlords, the rise and fall of Chiang Kai-shek. Through all of these struggles, he'd never wavered in his belief that he would one day return to China to live out his final days. This time, however, he knew he was too old to outlast the new regime. For Fong See, who had sent money back to China for seventy years, investing and buying property, this turn of events meant that not only had his family lost most of its land wealth to the Communists, but that he would never be able to follow the old proverb that said, "The fallen leaves return to the root." Lying on the cot in the back room of his new store, Fong See knew he would never be able to return to the home village, recline in his rooftop pavilion, and listen to Enrico Caruso on the Victrola. Fong See would never be buried in his homeland.

CHAPTER 19

ANOTHER MARRIAGE

1951–57

O N February 7, 1951, bulldozers, cranes, and steam shovels rolled down Los Angeles Street and began demolishing the nineteen buildings that made up the last block of Old Chinatown, including Jerry's Joynt, Soochow, the Kong Chow Temple, the Sam Sing Butcher Shop, the F. See On Company, and the F. Suie One Company. Debris and discarded furniture lay beneath piles of brick and shattered siding. The Lugo House, built in the days of hand-wrought square nails, was ripped apart. In structures not quite leveled, pipes and loose wires dangled. Below ground, passages and basements that had once offered a means of escape from police raids were crushed.

C. G. Byson, who was contracted to wreck the block for a cost of $16,794, personally inspected each broken wall, hoping to find hidden treasure. Instead he found lottery markers, piles of rags and waste paper, and forgotten camphor chests—the Gold Mountain chests of old, packed with quilted jackets, soap, and papers. Richard and Eddy also sifted through the ruins, collecting those hand-wrought nails and picking up shards of Chinese porcelain, ginger jars, and medicinal bottles. Richard found pieces of clothing—shirts with detachable collars—that he added to his wardrobe. Eddy appropriated granite cobblestones and curbstones for the garden on Lantana.

This demolition meant major changes for the family. The Sees moved the F. Suie One Company over to Ord Street, into one of the last remaining buildings of China City. The Foo dogs that had flanked the entrance to the old store and, before that, the entrance to Dragon's Den, now guarded China City's old moon gate, which led into the courtyard of the F. Suie One Company. Inside, the family converted each kiosk and cubbyhole into specialized rooms for merchandise. The central aisle, which had once seen rickshaws loaded with gawking tourists, now became the display area for furniture and knickknacks.

Just to the left, inside the entrance, was the bronze room. Next came the art room, which held the priceless pieces. In this room, Ming invited special customers to sit around a rosewood barrel table on little pie-shaped stools. "I have such a treasure to show you," he'd say, then slowly bring out his collection of rose quartz. Just past the art room was the porcelain room, followed by a small alcove with an eight-foot carved Shiva. At the back were glassed-in offices for Sissee and Ming, and a large shop area for restorations and custom work. On the right, coming back along the aisle toward the front, was the scroll room, followed by the embroidery room. Next came a vestibule leading to another warehouse area, and an elevator shaft that went to an upstairs workshop.

Finally, behind Eddy's jewelry table at the right of the entrance was the true "back," that area where the family hung out. It was in the back that Stella worked on that confounded coromandel screen and did other restorations. Here the family heated up noodles, nibbled on *char siu* sandwiches on sourdough bread, brought in tea cakes, or picked up french dip sandwiches from Philippe's, across the street. In the late afternoons the family entertained their friends, and had a glass of "something stronger" before heading home.

The family would stay in this store on Ord Street for the next thirty years. Business would change. Rentals to movie companies would gradually be superseded by rentals to television productions, and back again. With China closed, the Sees looked to other sources for merchandise. Old customers—some of them major collectors—would come in, wishing to sell. Grace Nicholson, who had learned about Asian art from Fong See when they were neighbors out in Pasadena in the teens and twenties, sold her Chinese antiques to the F. See On and F. Suie One companies when the trend seemed to ebb. When the Bernheimers—famous in Los Angeles for their Japanese gardens—decided to hold an auction to liquidate their estate, Ming, Eddy, and Richard attended to buy large bronzes and big stone pieces. The most spectacular purchase was a nineteenth-century freestanding Chinese conjugal bed designed for a house where all the relatives—aunts, uncles, in-laws, and children—lived together. In China the bed had served as private quarters—with an anteroom, then the bed itself—encased in panels of boxwood, fruitwood, and rosewood. In Los Angeles the bed became a playroom for the See grandchildren and great-grandchildren who came to visit the store.

Fong See, now in his late nineties, found all this change strange indeed. In his new shop in New Chinatown, he felt removed from everything and everyone he knew. Old Chinatown had been conservative and stuck in the old ways. New Chinatown was just the opposite—new, modern, all junk. It shocked him. His new neighbors seemed like strangers, and he felt too old to start new friendships. His children sensed his withdrawal. They seemed liberated somehow, and were always off skiing or some other foolish thing.

Just as Sissee took her mother up to Oregon for one last visit, Chuen now took his father to Sacramento. That Chinatown was completely gone now. They looked for the brewery where Fong See had worked as a teenager. He remembered the way, telling Chuen how he had walked five or ten miles a day just to get there. The brewery was long gone, too. The people—his landlord, the rancher, his neighbors, the man who had helped him import his first curios—were all dead.

Fong See slowly gave up. All the timeworn sayings honoring old age— "Your good fortune is like the eastern sea," "your longevity is as great as the south mountain," "may you have this same day every year"— didn't mean much to him now. He would spend his last days in the F. See On Company, performing for customers, telling far-fetched stories in his put-on pidgin English as he always had. He would spend his nights in the downstairs room behind the store—too sick, too tired, to walk up the flight of stairs to the family apartment.

As Fong See was coming to the end of his life, his grandson Richard was taking a few tentative steps into adulthood. To his Chinese pals, Richard seemed outspoken. He appeared strong. He drank boilermakers and made fun of his cousins and half-uncles when they couldn't hold down a beer. He would walk in with a stolen street sign or a light from the railroad yards, and blithely say, "Look what I got." If a guy was worrying about whether or not he should ask out a white girl or a Mexican girl, Richard would say, "Go after her." Since he'd spent two years at City College, he was meeting people who'd been to war, people who went out of their way to be different instead of conforming. He had conscientiously developed an "exotic persona"—a little bit beatnik, a touch of Chinese, and a tad swashbuckling in his attitudes, dress, and speech. To his friends and relatives in Chinatown, Richard seemed very *Caucasian*. He seemed as if he knew what was up, what was cool in the world outside Chinatown.

But Richard knew little more than his cousins and half-uncles. This boy who talked with so much bravado about taking out white girls had only been on two real "dates" in his life, both of them in junior high school. (He still had a crush on Sumoy, but that certainly wasn't going to go anywhere.) Now, like countless Chinese bachelors before him, he wanted to find out about "normal" American life; he wanted to find out about girls. But to Richard, dating seemed artificial: dressing up, going to the movies or a dance, trying to talk to someone you didn't know. It wasn't natural, but he'd turned twenty and knew he had to try.

Richard heard about a writer who had said that the only reason he wrote was to meet girls, not for marriage or sex, but just to learn how to *deal* with girls. In 1951, taking this advice to heart, Richard wrote a play and decided he would try to get it produced at John Marshall High, his old school. He knew that drama kids were a little off the wall. He also knew that the girls wouldn't be total dogs. Once he got to the drama department, he saw that all the girls looked basically alike in their angora sweaters, detachable Peter Pan collars, and straight skirts. He found that he physically loved the smell of greasepaint, so he was attracted to Carolyn Laws, who wore pancake makeup to cover a birthmark on her right cheek. She had light brown hair that curled delicately around her face, deep brown eyes, and an engaging smile, and she liked to laugh.

Carolyn had a wildly "American" family. In 1853, Carolyn's great-grandfather, George Washington Laws, had left Tennessee and become a pioneer farmer near Dallas. Her paternal grandmother was a Bowlin, descended from Sir John Bowlin, who was one of the earliest settlers in Virginia and who had supposedly married the daughter of John Rolfe and Pocahontas. (Carolyn said she didn't believe it.) The Bowlins, having lost almost everything in the Civil War, had made their way southwest to the Grapevine Prairie between Dallas and Fort Worth. Carolyn's father, George Laws, had grown up in Texas, then moved to Los Angeles to become a newspaperman. It was there that George met Kate Sullivan, who could trace her family back to New York State before the Revolutionary War. They fell in love and got married. Then the Depression hit and Carolyn was born.

When Carolyn was eleven years old, her father left, joined Alcoholics Anonymous, and remarried. Carolyn's mother, as Richard heard it, was an alcoholic bitch who hated her daughter. From the time George walked out until Carolyn was sixteen, her mother would say, ten or twenty times a week, "If you don't like it the way it is around here, then you can go and live with your father." Kate seemed to spend the rest of her time drinking Hill & Hill Blend or crying in her room.

Through it all, George came around every week, no matter what hell Kate had in store for him. Even when he didn't have a job, he'd get his girlfriends to help pay child support. So, as Carolyn saw it, her father kicked in money, kicked in attention, and braved Kate's tantrums when many dads would have disappeared entirely.

In 1949, Carolyn's mother married a drunk named Jim Daly, got pregnant, and had a baby girl. When Kate came home from the hospital, she kicked Carolyn out of the house, although she was only sixteen at the time. Carolyn went to live with her father and her new stepmother in a one-bedroom apartment. Carolyn slept on the couch while her father and stepmother took the Murphy bed.

All of this material was absolutely new to Richard. At the very least, he'd never met anyone whose parents were divorced; this was as "exotic" in the fifties as a Eurasian family. And despite, or maybe because of, her childhood, Carolyn Laws really did seem to know what was what. She was very popular and had never missed a dance or failed to go out on a Saturday night throughout high school. She had the lead role in the senior play. She got straight A's, because she wanted to go to college and become a writer or a teacher or possibly both. She had tremendous ambition and focus. In other words, strange as she was for that time and place, to Richard's eyes she was "making it" in the regular world.

Carolyn and her friend Jackie Joseph liked Richard, but he was completely different from anyone they'd ever seen in their lives. He wasn't like those boys with the stuffed argyle socks hanging from their rearview mirrors, or like those Valley boys in their leather jackets—smoking reefers and crashing parties. Richard wore collarless shirts that his mother made for him or that he'd found in Chinatown. He was unbelievably cute: black hair, a darling smile, high cheekbones. Though he was only one-quarter Chinese, his eyelids had epicanthic folds, which Carolyn found extremely attractive. The Caucasian part of his background came out in the color of his eyes—green. What this meant was that Richard looked just enough Chinese to be positively beautiful but not too foreign. Richard was shy, but in another way he wasn't. Some days he was goofy and silly, and would say anything to anybody. On other days he'd say nothing. The girls decided he was just "struggling with his shyness."

He drove a beat-up car—his dad's old 1936 Plymouth—that was filled with junk and listed to one side. Carolyn and Jackie always needed a ride somewhere, and Richard was always happy to oblige. "I'm always driving you hither and thither," he bemoaned jokingly. "I'm like Saint Joseph, the eternal chauffeur."

One day Richard invited Carolyn, Jackie, and a guy named Jack Hensey over to his house on Lantana Street. The kids lined up on two couches that faced each other in the musty darkness. They saw all this stuff—strange and beautiful things—but couldn't make any sense of it, because it was in a house that hadn't been "finished." Foundations snaked about the perimeter of the house, seeming to wait for the next century for construction to continue. The kitchen had no finished walls, just dried plaster oozing out between lath strips. The tiny bathroom was only half hung with plywood, and the door didn't close all the way. The living-room wall had been knocked down but never completed, so that the guts of the house hung out. Right where they'd taken down the wall was Richard's parents' bed for all the world to see.

As they sat there, Richard told them about how his parents celebrated Christmas. "We go out on Christmas Eve and buy five or six trees," he said. "We bring them home, stick them in old soy-sauce cans, and put them all over the house. Some we even hang from the ceiling."

The high school students—as conventional as the times dictated—couldn't look at each other for fear of laughing, or blurting out, "Jesus, will you *look* at this place? Will you *listen* to this guy?" They were impressed, horrified, appalled. Richard See was either the coolest boy who had ever lived, or the spookiest creature who had ever come down the pike.

After that, they went over to Jack's house, where his mother set out lemonade and cookies. It wasn't just that Richard's house seemed poor and Jack's seemed rich, but that the kids were more comfortable in the familiarity of a beautiful, old, Spanish-style house that hung on a palm-covered hill beneath the Hollywood sign, where everything was immaculate, clean, spacious, and run by some screechingly correct mother. Wordlessly they promised themselves they'd never go back to Richard's.

Finally, after months of hanging around together, there came a time when Carolyn asked Richard to drive her alone out to her mother's house in the Valley. As they sped along the back road of Griffith Park, Richard said, "I'm a quarter Chinese." Then he told her he loved his half-aunt Sumoy. "But there's nothing I can do about it," he said. "My heart is taken, isn't it a shame?" Embedded in all this information—all of which was an entirely different sort of conversation from what Carolyn was accustomed to listening to in the front seat of a boy's car—was what Richard had told her on the first day they'd met: that he'd played poker with Anna May Wong.

"She's my favorite actress ever," Carolyn had said. To herself she thought, My favorite actress *by far*. Carolyn had loved Chinese things forever. When she was little, her parents had given her *Tales of a Chinese Grandmother* and little Chinese teacups. At a deeper level she hoped that Richard might be an agent of change who could bring her dream life and her real life together.

When they pulled over, Carolyn knew what to expect. He kissed her, pulled away, and asked, "Have you ever listened to 'Two Sleepy People'? That's a very cogent song."

She was impressed that he could use the word *cogent* in a sentence. Richard wasn't some dumb high school student; he was a smart clever college man. And as these thoughts whirled through her brain, she realized that he was her soul mate, because he did her the honor of *talking* to her like a human being and not as if she were some stupid fifties girl. He listened to her. He cared what she had to say.

They began going out a little more seriously. Richard took Carolyn to see foreign films, and to see *An American Tragedy,* with Montgomery Clift and Elizabeth Taylor. He took her down to Chinatown, where he walked her through Union Station to show her the murals and the stenciling on the ceiling. They strolled along Olvera Street, stopping for burritos and taquitos. These weren't like the usual dates Carolyn had had with nameless, interchangeable high school boys. Dipping her taquito into a mound of guacamole, Carolyn couldn't help but remember one boy who'd also brought her down here, taken a bite out of a burrito, and spit it out into a trash can. Richard would never do anything gross like that. Instead he would drive her up to his parents' lot on the backside of Elysian Park, and they'd sit together and talk, talk, talk.

Richard had something Carolyn craved—not marriage, not a house or even a family, but culture. Richard had culture in spades, because what other boy would take a girl to Union Station instead of a Joan Crawford movie? What other boy would laugh and be goofy? What other boy would *listen* to her when she talked about wanting to have a career? Who else would meet her halfway in these daydreams by saying that one day they would build a house on the Landa lot and live together forever, even if it was just a fantasy?

When Carolyn graduated from high school in June of 1951, Richard wrote in her yearbook, "If you have to have this to rember [sic] me by then there is no use of me writing this. I will see you after you graduate. If I do not see you, then you should not want this to remember." He also sent her a two-page letter. At the top of the first page, its edges ragged where they'd been torn out of a binder, he wrote, "Twenty Years from Now, or Who in the Hell was He?" The letter began, "I am a fool perhaps, but I think there is a possibility that we will marry (each other that is), depending upon yourself, myself, and the millions of other people that influence our lives." Further down he wrote, "All these things above and below were written by Richard See, God's gift to the children of broken homes who are seeking, who are seeking perhaps, a father more than a husband, to give them security. Or perhaps they are seeking a child to give security to. I am both, and neither, father and child." In the event she might get her hopes up, he added, "I don't know if I'm in love now, but I do know that I've never been in love before. I'm not even sure I think I'm in love, but I'm sure that I am almost to the point of making myself believe that I am." Carolyn guessed that he was still crazy about Sumoy.

Richard's letter wasn't the only ambiguous thing to happen to Carolyn after graduation. Within days, all that had been so tenuous slipped away. Carolyn's dad didn't exactly kick her out, but he didn't invite her to stay, either. In this limbo state, Carolyn was taken to Barney's Beanery by her friend Jackie Joseph. "I don't want you to be sad," Jackie said, "because we're going to have a good time. We're going to be okay." By the end of the day, Carolyn had moved out of her dad's apartment— with George promising to pay ten dollars a week for her upkeep—and into a one-room apartment in Atwater, near the Los Angeles River, with Jackie and her mother, Belle. Jackie and Carolyn shared one twin bed; Belle got the other.

Belle was hardly a typical fifties mom. She was gone most of the time, at the liquor store she owned down on Skid Row. She never cooked or cleaned. Jackie could only remember two things that her mother had ever cooked. Once, Belle had put a rabbit in the oven to bake. Months later, motivated by idle curiosity, someone had opened the oven and discovered the rabbit still in there, covered with so much mold that Belle had remarked, "Well, look at that. The bunny's grown back his fur." The other time, Jackie had come home to find her mother—dressed in black net hose, black patent-leather high heels, and a black bat-wing sweater—rolling out bread dough, twisting it into interesting bow ties and question marks. But again, Belle's interest flagged and the bread was never baked. Meals were always of the open-the-can-and-eat-the-contents-cold-right-out-of-the-container variety. When it came time to clean up, Belle, who'd seen *A Streetcar Named Desire* one too many times, cleared dinner off the table by sweeping it off onto the floor like Marlon Brando. This lack of traditional domesticity translated as well into a vague detachment about who her daughter and her friend were seeing. Never once did Belle ask the girls of the many boys who came to pick them up for dates, "What are his intentions?" or even "Who is this bozo, anyway?"

All through that summer, Richard hung around. Carolyn and Richard even set up Jackie and Chuen for what would be a disastrous double date. Both Richard and Chuen were slight, small-boned, and shy. But where Richard was funny, Chuen was deadly serious. Where Richard knew a little something about Chinese furniture, Chuen was already fluent—trained as he was to take over his father's store. Chuen had nothing to talk about with Jackie, and she had nothing to say to him.

But mostly Richard came over to Belle's. The girls would heat him up a can of soup, and he'd say, "Do you have any Chinese soup spoons? I can't possibly eat soup with these tin things."

And Jackie would say, "This is an *American* house. Take it or leave it."

He would shrug, then suck up his soup from the brim of the bowl. "This is how the Chinese do it," he'd say. The girls would look at each other and think, How weird, how exotic.

Or he would come in with a pile of books—by H. Allen Smith or Max Shulman—and sit on the couch and read. Occasionally he'd slap his thigh and laugh, but never—not once—did he look up and say, "Hey, you guys should hear this." Again, the girls would look at him, then at each other, and think, What a lunatic, too cool.

It was part of the American courtship ritual to drive a car, loaded down with your friends for moral support, over to some girl's house and stand around on her lawn. Just like the white boys, Richard drove his car up onto Belle's lawn. His Chinese buddies—the sleeves of their white T-shirts rolled up—piled out and stood around. This was the one time Belle drew the line. The woman who would permit nearly anything, who slept in her dress, who had bunnies "growing" in her oven and hundreds of chinchillas dying from neglect in her garage, said, "I can't have this!" and "There goes the neighborhood!" and finally, "They've got to go!" Even Carolyn had to agree, because *who* were all those guys, anyway? They all had names like Haw and Maw and things she simply couldn't understand.

Not long after this incident, Richard wrote the first of what would become many twelve-page letters, saying that Carolyn was a wonderful person, but that she would never understand the nature of love because she was too frivolous. He's just thinking about Sumoy, Carolyn thought. If he doesn't appreciate me, then I'll find someone who does.

City College, 1952. Everything that had seemed strange and bizarre in high school now seemed absolutely normal. Carolyn, as had all her girlfriends, sheared off her curls to just a few cropped inches for a more "vogue-y" look. She eschewed her Peter Pan collars for black turtlenecks—important for making a statement about alienation and conformity, and practical because they didn't require ironing. Men? Carolyn found plenty of new and different men to go around with, but she still liked Richard, who'd transferred to UCLA, where he was studying anthropology. Although Richard wasn't around, Carolyn was reminded of him every time she saw Sumoy, who had also enrolled at City College.

Carolyn looked up Sumoy's schedule in the admissions office and— as sedately as possible—stalked her rival from English to History to Psych. On nights when Carolyn had nothing better to do—few and far between as these might be, what with dates, studying, and night shifts at Van de Kamp's—she went to New Chinatown, where she stared at the yellow lights of the upstairs apartment above the F. See On Company and wondered, What does Sumoy have that I haven't got? Listening to the melodious tinkling of wind chimes hanging from balconies, she thought, Well, Sumoy's Chinese, and I'll never figure that one out.

Carolyn tried to forget about Richard, but Los Angeles was still basically a small town. While out on a double date with Jackie, one of the boys squealed, "Oh my God, will you look at that!" And there was Richard in his wacky car, alone, singing in full voice, "Be My Little Bumblebee." Three people in the car became hysterical, laughing, crying, hooting. Then Jackie said, "Carolyn's *gone out* with that guy!"

"Yeah, I know him. So?" Carolyn said. Years later she would reflect, "But who knows who those guys were and what ever happened to them, while Richard went on to live in memory."

Soon afterward, Carolyn got up her nerve, called the F. Suie One Company, and asked for Richard. A Chinese person answered in words she couldn't quite understand. It sounded like, "Lichald almy foo-day." Richard had been drafted, and he hadn't even told her. That's that,

Carolyn thought. So she took up with a fellow named Stan Guild, which wouldn't have meant much in the great scheme of things, except that Belle Joseph had her eye on him too. Carolyn was no longer welcomed by Belle. The way Carolyn reckoned it, she was batting 0 for 3. She'd been kicked out of her mother's house, uninvited to stay with her father after graduation, and now pushed out of Belle's. From here, Carolyn began living in a series of furnished rooms.

In 1952, four of Fong Yun's children—Chong, Gai, Gim, and Choey Lon—decided they would open a little shop, Fong's, in New Chinatown, just down the promenade from the F. See On Company. A few months later their father finally gave up on China City and moved his store next door to that of his children. This same year, Sissee and Gilbert bought an original Craftsman-style building—formerly a library—atop Mount Washington. They began turning the house into a showplace, with gold-leafed ceilings and exquisite pieces of Asian art. In December they would host their first Christmas party. (Over time this gathering would become known for its fabulous food, wonderful decorations, and joke gifts.) Ming and Sunny would miss this first Christmas party, because they were living in a small village outside Tokyo. This trip would convince the couple that they should alternate between spending a year abroad and a year at home.

A million light-years away from year-long trips to Asia, buying a house, or even opening a little shop in New Chinatown, Carolyn Laws continued to struggle and try to build a life for herself. She hooked up with Dick Jones—a Van de Kamp's customer—and together they took a set of furnished rooms in Hollywood. Since it was 1952 and you were supposed to get married, buy a dishwasher, and have three kids, Carolyn didn't tell her parents how or where she was living, and they never asked. She never mentioned Dick Jones—who said he was in the process of getting a divorce—and they never asked. Her parents didn't call her, because that meant the landlady would buzz Carolyn's room and she'd have to buzz back, then scurry downstairs to use the phone; and she didn't call them, because, again, that meant going down to the front desk. For fourteen months, Carolyn waited on tables at Van de Kamp's, played housewife with Dick, took English classes, and studied hard.

Things went along pretty smoothly—she ate breakfast at a little café on the corner, rode the streetcar to school, and went off in the middle of the night to watch Dick solder aquariums—until she developed a crush on a guy who worked the soda fountain at the restaurant. As a lark, a friend wrote in one of Carolyn's notebooks, "You love Bill. Use your will." When Dick saw that, he said, "You're not getting out of this crummy apartment alive." With his fingers around her throat, Carolyn had the presence of mind to lean on the telephone buzzer until the landlady came up, wanting to know what was going on and demanding that they stop making that infernal noise!

Carolyn went downstairs and called her dad, who came straight over. Instead of punching Dick in the nose, as some fathers might have done, George shook his hand and said, "I'm sorry we have to meet like this, pardner." George helped Carolyn pack. He took her to lunch, told her to "stay out of trouble," and dropped her off at another rooming house. Noticing that the place was inhabited by hookers, he suggested that she might not want to stay there too long. Then he drove off. Kate was equally unhelpful. Hearing the news that her daughter had been living with someone, Kate didn't wash her hair for three weeks. "You're just like your father," she wailed.

Now batting 0 for 4, Carolyn moved into another furnished apartment, this one just two blocks from City College, which had a fake window with a curtain draped in front of it. From her new place, she began to write Richard, who was stationed in Newfoundland, and he wrote back.

[undated]

Dear Carolyn,

I am now a prisoner of the United States of America, in other words, I am still in the U.S. Army. I am now living on a sort of Arctic Devil's Island. I'm stationed at McAndrews Air Base, in Newfoundland. The country is rather beautiful around here, but it is extremely difficult to see beauty when you are living under certain conditions. My main diversion has been drinking, with frequent intellectual discussions with numerous eccentric people added to spice up life, and perhaps the occasional pillow fight to get rid of pent-up aggressions. Otherwise life is quite dull. . . .

BY ORDER OF PRIVATE SEE

December 11, 1953

Dear Child,

I must see you on my leave. Among other things I can make indecent proposals to you (or should I say propositions) and also insult you in all kinds of devious and subtle ways. . . .

Sumoy, as an item of oblique interest, intends to get married within the next few weeks or months. This of course makes me extremely happy. . . . She is not marrying me by the way. Oh well.

December 23, 1953

You asked about Chiang and Mao, I prefer neither. The Chinamen I like are Chuen, Grandpappy, Tyrus Wong, Albert Wong, Sumoy, Buddha (who was an Indian—sorry), and a few others too obscure to mention. Mao and Chiang are just crazy mixed-up old gentlemen that I never met and therefore can form no definite opinion as far as my liking or disliking them.

Dicky Boy
Lover First Class See

January 1, 1954

I don't know when in the hell I'll get the goddamn leave now—I don't know if I'll get a leave at all. . . . The leave, it seems to me, wouldn't accomplish exactly what I had planned—I had thought we might shack-up for approximately two weeks—but apparently I misjudged you—so to hell with it—Yes—you're a person, a very wonderful fine person, you're crazy, mixed-up, cool, you go to my head. You're all kinds of nice-nice and goodie-goodie—but I don't think I'm in love with you—and I'm pretty sure I'll never marry you—and even more sure that if we did marry it would be a mess, but I think I'd like to sleep with you—or any other fairly good-looking girl between the ages of 13 and 52 (if well-preserved). By the way, how old is Marlene Dietrich? Did I tell you I was going to marry Pier Angeli, Eartha Kitt & Gigi (Audrey Hepburn), with sex and kisses. . . .

January 25, 1954

I'm so happy to get out of this stinking hole. . . .
P.S. My next play will be entitled, "How Wide Thy Pelvis!" or "How Wide They Pelvis?"

By the time Richard arrived in Los Angeles at the end of January and knocked at the door of Carolyn's room, it was, as they say, a done deal. A mild feeling of doom surrounded the whole encounter. Richard driving up, climbing the stairs, expecting—what? Carolyn, sitting in her room, waiting, answering the door, and saying, "We have rules here. I can't close the door if you're in here. I can't even have men in my room." Then climbing in the car, driving desultorily through the city, stopping for dinner at a forgotten restaurant, going back to Richard's parents' house on Lantana, walking through the house to the screen porch behind the kitchen, and finally "doing it." (Of this "it," so long anticipated and hinted at, Richard has said, "That was the first time I'd ever done that sort of thing. I liked it a lot.")

Carolyn and Richard spent the rest of the furlough together. They went to the beach. Richard, who had heard Charlie Parker, Les Powell, Lester Young, and Lionel Hampton in New York on his way to New-foundland, took Carolyn to the Haig, on Wilshire Boulevard, to hear Gerry Mulligan and Chet Baker. Carolyn dressed in black, listened attentively, didn't move a muscle, and got "very drunk." They made themselves part of the arty crowd, knowing that if they weren't, then who was? They went with Chuen and Allen Mock (a neighbor in China-town, who was studying to be an architect) to the Beverly Cavern. They went to see _One Summer of Happiness_, a Swedish film about young love, then spent the rest of the evening discussing adolescent awaken-ings. They went to see _Ninotchka_ and ate pizza. Almost every other day of the first week, they drove up to the lot on Landa that Stella and Eddy had bought years before, sat on the rim of the ravine, and talked.

"My dad owns this land, and when we get married we'll have Allen draw up plans," Richard said.

And Carolyn, who hadn't lived in a house with more than one bed-room since she was eleven, asked, "How many bedrooms shall we have?"

"We don't want bedrooms. We'll just have one great room and live all together in it."

"What about kids?"

"Eight, at least. Sixteen is better."

"Isn't that a lot?"

But Richard's position was that he was a lonely child, practically an only child.

Carolyn, ever practical, asked, "How will we raise them? What will we do for money?"

"Should I work?" he mused. "I don't think so. In the Chinese tra-dition, the son of a wealthy man is expected _not_ to work as a sign that the father is rich."

"We're not in China. And your father isn't rich."

"All right, then. I'll be a gardener in a convent."

"No, you won't. You need to make a living and support your wife and children."

"Maybe we shouldn't get married after all," he said. "You're too conventional."

It was a thirty-day leave, and by the middle of the second week, Carolyn's period was seven days late. It was ten weeks too early for a rabbit test, which was the only sure way to determine whether she was really pregnant. She was too scared, too poor, and it was too early to go and get an abortion. All Carolyn could do was try various folk remedies; all Richard could do was try to figure out what to do when he had just two weeks left of his leave. Now instead of romantic tête-à-têtes on a ragged hillside, Carolyn—her ears ringing from high doses of quinine and sick to her stomach from taking castor oil—sat in a steaming bath, trying to boil away the theoretical baby, while Richard sat on the edge of the tub, trying to wish it away.

"If you're pregnant," he said, "I want you to go ahead and have the baby."

"If I'm pregnant and you just go back to the army . . . well, you can just forget that."

Richard fell back on the same lines he'd used in high school. "Do I really love you? I'm not sure. I'm so sensitive."

"I'm seeing how sensitive you are."

"I'm only twenty-four," he insisted. "And you're my first girl."

Carolyn considered, thinking, That's true, but I don't exactly see anyone else falling all over themselves to be with you.

He said, "I haven't seen the wider world. I'm too young to get married."

"Well, I'm only twenty, and if I'm pregnant . . ."

"But I didn't come back with the intention of marrying you."

"What about your letters? What about all your proposals?"

The only true answer to these questions would have been "Hey, I was only trying to get laid." Richard was just wise enough not to let those words fall from his lips.

Always the discussion drifted back to the problem at hand. "If you're really pregnant, I'll be happy to marry you when I get back. But I don't want to marry you now."

"That's fine," Carolyn answered stiffly. "If I'm not pregnant, that's fine. Just fine! But I'm telling you, Richard, if I am, you can just *forget it.*"

In this atmosphere of mutual trust and love, they decided to get married, because Carolyn's period was now almost two weeks late, and Richard had to go back to Newfoundland. It was the fifties, and they felt they had no other choice. Yet none of what followed was done in a sad atmosphere. They liked each other a lot. "There was something jaunty about the whole thing," Carolyn remembered.

On February 18, Carolyn and Richard drove to the store on Ord Street. Richard had told his parents about his engagement the night before, and they were waiting to see this Carolyn Laws. Stella gave Carolyn a hug and said, "So this is the little girl Richard is marrying." Then they walked back along the main aisle of the store—past the bronze room, the art room, the ceramic room—and into the back office, where Eddy waited for them.

He was beside himself. "This is a terrible idea!" Eddy yelled, whacking his hand through the air like a karate master trying to split a pile of bricks. Half of Carolyn's mind absorbed what he said; the other half seemed mesmerized by Eddy's gyrations.

Richard, bound by silence concerning their real reasons, said, "*We* think it's a good idea."

"It's the worst idea I've ever heard! It's indiscreet!" Eddy shouted.

Carolyn, who'd survived her mother's fits, stared at him and thought, Oh, have a tantrum. Just go ahead. It won't change a thing.

But when Eddy went on about how special the family was and asking who she was to be marrying into it, Carolyn began to burn.

"You're not just marrying Richard," Eddy said. "You'd be marrying into our whole family . . ." The way he let that hang, she knew he was saying she wasn't classy enough or good enough for their son.

Stella sat nearby, wringing her hands and saying, "I don't get it. I just don't understand."

On the face of it, Eddy's reaction seemed strange. After all, though the particulars were different, Carolyn was as much an "orphan" as Ticie and Stella. But Eddy didn't see it that way. Perhaps he recognized that Carolyn was—despite her naiveté about birth control, which he didn't even know about—a modern woman. She had ambition. She wanted a career. Ticie and Stella had worked, but it was always in the family business. Carolyn, on the other hand, looked outward. Perhaps Eddy recognized that she was never going to put the See family first.

"Well, you certainly can't get married without asking Pa," Eddy spat out. Carolyn took that to mean that Fong See would say no and the whole thing would be called off. Richard and Carolyn drove over to New Chinatown. Rather than invite the couple in, Fong See stood with them in the courtyard outside his store. To Carolyn, he seemed older than God. He wore long Chinese robes, and she watched, bewildered, as he gibbered and twitched and—to her mind—gave an imitation of a crazy old Chinaman. He pinched her behind. He pinched her arm. He said, "Good stock." Then he turned to Richard and asked, "You got five dollars?"

"I'm thinking of getting married, and I wanted to ask you if it's okay," Richard said.

Fong See didn't say no.

The next day, Carolyn went to see her mother. At no time did the words "I might be pregnant" enter into the discussion. Again, the announcement of her upcoming marriage was done in the same jaunty fashion as going to a jazz club or out for a pizza. Carolyn remained upbeat, cheerful, a little ditsy.

"Richard's a nice man," she explained. "He wants to grow a beard,

Above: Eddy (with his December 7th beard), Stella, Sissee, and Gilbert at the Earl Carroll Theatre Restaurant in Hollywood, late 1940s.

Above: Ray See as a successful businessman, late 1940s.

Right: Chuen, Yun, an unidentified friend, and Richard, with their fishing gear, early 1950s.

Left: Ray with friends at New Chinatown.

Right: Stella and Eddy in late 1940s or early 1950s.

Below: See-Mar showroom

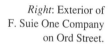

Left: Fong See outside the Los Angeles Street store just before it was torn down, c. 1949.

Right: Exterior of F. Suie One Company on Ord Street.

Left: Interior of F. Suie One Company, showing old China City kiosks.

Richard as
a cute high
school student.

The wedding of Richard See and Carolyn Laws, 1954.

Fong See as
a very old man.

Gilbert Leong,
successful architect,
with Miss Chinatown.

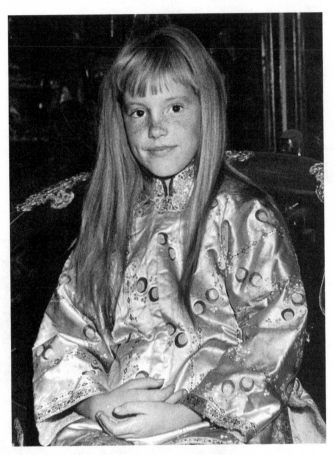

Lisa in the F. Suie One Company, 1963.

Ming and Bennie (*seated*) in the "shop" at the F. Suie One Company on Ord Street in 1960s.

Eddy and Peanut at work.

Right: Stella and Sissee, November 5, 1988. On this night the F. Suie One Company received Centennial Honors from the Chinese Historical Society of Southern California for "a century of excellence in pioneering achievements as a member of the Chinese American community in Southern California."

Left: Ngon Hung celebrates her eightieth birthday in 1987, with Sumoy and Frank Quon.

Sissee's seventy-fifth birthday, 1984. *Top row*: Si (Gilbert's brother-in-law), Margie (Gilbert's sister), Gilbert, Nick Nichols, Bernice (Gilbert's sister-in-law), and Yun Fong. *Bottom row*: Stella, Ngon Hung, Leslee, Sian (Leslee's daughter) Elizabeth (Leslee's cousin), and Sissee.

Leslee Leong with her daughters,
Sian and Mara (*seated*), 1989. (*Adam Avila*)

Alexander See
Kendall and
Christopher
Copeland
Kendall, 1994.
(*Patricia
Williams*)

Right: Lisa and relatives have lunch in Foshan (formerly Fatsan), China, 1991.

Above left: Lui Ngan Fa, Fong Yun's concubine, in Foshan, 1991.
Right: Fong See's house in Dimtao, China, 1991.

Left: The F. Suie One Company in Pasadena, 1995.

but it's not a pose, because his father has one. He has black hair and green eyes, and he skis . . ."

"Is he in school?"

"He's in the army, but he wants to be an anthropologist."

"And his family?"

"They're very close," Carolyn went on. "That's the way they do things, at least that's what Richard says. Family is everything to them, and even though they've lost a lot of traditions in this country, there's still a big effort to keep it all going." Carolyn hated it that she was taking the very words that had so upset her when they had come out of Eddy's mouth and using them to sell her mother on Richard. But this way of keeping the conversation going also kept her mother from saying anything mean. "Richard says it's their identity crisis, so that they can subdue the stresses that impinge upon any marginal subculture in this society . . ."

"What *is* Richard?"

"What do you mean, 'What *is* Richard?' "

"You know what I mean."

"Didn't I tell you? He's a quarter Chinese, didn't I mention that?" Then, not caring after all, she added the phrase that Richard had learned from Anna May Wong: "Oh, Mother, fifty million Chinamen can't be Wong." No laughs, but no objection either.

Visiting George and Wynn turned out to be far more of a trial. George sat Richard down for three hours of homespun Southern wisdom on marriage, family, and the responsibilities of a man and wife.

"Happiness is the absence of aggravation," George proclaimed. "A clean conscience is a comfortable companion. What's good for you is bad for you."

"I'm sure we'll be happy," Richard ventured.

"I don't give a damn what you say, kid. In your youth and loyalty you may feel required to say you love Pee Wee so much you'd trust her drunk, undressed, and in bed with Errol Flynn."

"Daddy . . ."

"Pee Wee, forget yourself for the next few months and think instead of Richard, or Richard-and-Carolyn, as a married unit. Put some personal sacrifice in the bank for the long months ahead. I want you to invest in a little insurance for the years to come—insurance of a life free from the flippant crack and the lifted eyebrow."

As Wynn came in with iced tea for everyone, George went on, "I happen to like Richard and think he's a good dish for any girl, you included. Now you must think I'm for sure a cornball."

"Oh, George," Wynn said.

"All I'm saying is, don't ever get daunted."

As they got in the car, Richard sighed, "My God, that man *needs* to drink."

Looking at this round of visits, Carolyn saw only that her family was extremely relieved. Everyone was supposed to get married, settle down, have kids. The fact that the Sees were Chinese and that the state's miscegenation laws had been overturned not quite six years before? No one cared. Kate was lost in anger about her own life, Wynn thought the marriage was cool, and George was relieved of his guilt.

Still, Eddy fought the idea of his son marrying Carolyn. Eddy took George out for tea cakes, and tried the same arguments that he'd used on Carolyn and Richard: they were both too young; they weren't up to the responsibility of a family. Finally, desperately, he said, "Carolyn doesn't know how to make *bao*. Richard should really marry a Chinese girl."

"You didn't," George pointed out.

"Yes, but Stella had our whole family to help her. Your daughter won't have a Chinese mother-in-law." Then Eddy laughed as though it was an intolerably funny joke. Except that it wasn't a joke at all. This was the crux of it. Although his father had married a white girl and he himself had married a white girl, it was heartbreaking to think that his son would marry one. Just like his friends and neighbors, Eddy, the most "Chinese" of all the brothers, had hoped for a Chinese daughter-in-law—American-born would have been fine.

For the next week, Richard and Carolyn were caught up in a round of activities. They went to La Golondrina on Olvera Street for dinner. They saw *One Summer of Happiness* again. Carolyn threw up at work—another sign that she might be pregnant—then went to the movies with a friend. The day after that, Carolyn and Richard got their blood tests and went to another movie. The following day they got their license, and Eddy made Carolyn a ring out of twenty-four-carat gold. That night they had dinner with Kate. The next day Carolyn bought a wedding dress—a pale blue linen dress with a little matching hat—and an outfit to wear to the wedding banquet—a tangerine silk blouse and a navy blue skirt. These purchases left her stone broke. That evening, the night before the wedding, they had dinner with Stella and Eddy in Chinatown.

The following day, February 27, 1954, Carolyn and Richard were married. For reasons of time, the wedding party was small—just thirteen people. Notably absent were Carolyn's stepfather, Jim Daly, and Fong See. (The former wasn't invited. The latter, at ninety seven, was simply too old to attend.) Both families met for the first time in the upstairs office at the Unitarian Church. Carolyn's stepmother, Wynn, wore a cream brocade suit with a very deep plunging neckline that left the men agog. Kate, mother of the bride and deserted ex-wife, took one look at Wynn—another first encounter—and began to weep. Stella wore a dark blue silk suit edged in velvet ribbon. Chuen stood up as best man, while Joan Wilheim, one of Carolyn's friends from junior high, served as maid of honor. (Jackie Joseph was working in Las Vegas as a showgirl. When she heard about the marriage, she commented, "Getting married? To Richard See? It's like marrying some chum you hang out with. It's not like he's rank or ugly or stupid. He's just on a different level than what you would think of as your romance.") The flower girl—Kate's daughter, Carolyn's half-sister—stood sullenly with her arms crossed over her chest. Sissee, Gilbert, and Richard's friend Allen Mock made up the rest of the witnesses. The minister read from *The Prophet,* and asked Carolyn and Richard please not to cross any picket lines during their married life.

Afterwards, Sissee took everyone to lunch at an Italian restaurant across from the Ambassador Hotel. Carolyn's father, usually blasé about not drinking, made a show of his abstinence by turning over his glass, motioning to his daughter, and pointing wildly at his glass to show how well he was behaving himself. Between George's conduct, Wynn's low-cut dress, and Kate's ratty fur coat and ridiculous sobs, Carolyn felt waves of embarrassment and shame wash over her. The plain fact was that the Sees *did* seem to know something about family, and they *did* seem to stay married.

After lunch, Richard and Carolyn drove down to Laguna Beach for a two-night honeymoon. When they returned to Los Angeles, Stella and Eddy hosted a no-expense-spared banquet at Soochow, where two hundred Fong and See relatives, as well as old friends and customers, turned out. A few days later, Richard went back to Newfoundland.

Following Chinese tradition, Stella and Eddy expected Carolyn to give up her apartment and come and live with them. She flatly refused. She said she'd keep her own place and continue on at City College. Still, the family tried to make her a part of the family. But Carolyn— unlike Ticie and Stella—was stubborn and independent. When, after countless excursions to orchid shows and countless teas at Sissee's house, where all the women wore hats and gloves, Carolyn's in-laws asked her for dinner, she begged off, saying she was sick. This incident wouldn't have mattered, except that Stella and Sissee took Carolyn a pot of soup and discovered that she wasn't at her apartment at all. She had lied to them, and they had found out. It appeared to Stella and Sissee that Carolyn didn't want to be a part of the See family after all.

Over the next few weeks, Richard sent a flurry of telegrams and letters:

3/9/54

The army will not let me bring you up here. Stay in school. If possible will write more later. Sorry. Love, Richard.

3/23/54

BUT FOR CHRIST SAKE. ARE YOU PREG-NANT??????? If you don't know by now, you are awful dumb.

3/25/54

I suppose you will not like this, but I am glad there will be no baby immediately. . . .

3/26/54

You asked what I want in a wife. Right now I want *me* in a wife. Ha Ha chuckle slurp drool quiver blurp giggle. . . . Mostly I like manic insanity and a sense of humor in a broad. But why should you worry about what I like in a wife, I am an extremely intelligent type of person and have the ability to choose what I like, and I did get married you know. To you, as a matter of fact, if memory serves me correctly, that is.

Many of Richard's letters to Carolyn illustrated what he referred to as a "joking relationship." She laughed when he signed his letters—"Richard E. See, boy loving husband. P.S. I lahve you (I think)"; or "Traumatic See Boy Husbang"; or "Slanteye de Sade." She, in turn, signed her letters, "Trained Professional Wife."

In May, Carolyn—not pregnant, and immensely relieved after her false alarm—finally joined Richard in Argentia, Newfoundland. Even now their jaunty attitude prevailed. They painted their rooms dark brown, hung bright orange curtains, put up Rouault and Tomayo prints. They went to the Airman's Club and Newfie square dances. Carolyn wrote her in-laws, asking them to send up "Chinamen-type spices" so that they might make something besides salted cod for a change. And since they'd gotten married because they thought Carolyn was pregnant, they went ahead and decided to have a baby. Carolyn was pregnant by the end of her first month in Newfoundland. In November 1954, Richard was discharged and they traveled to Paris to hang out with friends.

On February 18, 1955, Carolyn was admitted to the American Hospital in Paris, where she gave birth to a daughter, Lisa Lénine See. Congratulatory transatlantic telegrams and gifts were sent from giddy grandparents. A few months later, after traveling through France, Italy, and Yugoslavia, Richard, Carolyn, and their baby returned to Los Angeles and moved into a little house opposite the Micheltorena Hill. Carolyn and Richard enrolled at UCLA and began taking classes. For a time it seemed the marriage might make it.

During the time that Richard and Carolyn were away, there had been two deaths in the family. On July 15, 1954, after fifteen years in the Norwalk State Hospital, Jessie Copeland, Stella's mother, died. Her death certificate shows that her last days and hours offered no relief from the years of physical and mental trauma that had kept her institutionalized. Four weeks before her death, she had a "cerebral vascular accident." Twelve hours before her death, the hospital staff found Jessie in a state of hyperthermia. Eight hours later she was diagnosed with pneumonia. She died within four hours.

In March 1955, Ray's wife, Leona, succumbed to cancer. She had spent her last weeks at home in Nichols Canyon. She had asked her son-in-law to bring her a pair of binoculars and from her sickbed she focused the glasses across the canyon on the little house of her husband's mistress, Mary Marshall. Days before her death, Leona phoned both Sissee and Stella and said that she was leaving a letter for them in her bathrobe. When Stella and Sissee went up to the house after the funeral and searched through Leona's robe, they found nothing. Leona had died as she had lived—quietly and with no lasting trace.

At the end of February 1957, Fong See was admitted to Monte Sano Hospital, where Ticie had died many years before. As is often the case with divorced families, the situation had to be handled delicately. Some argued that Ming, as the eldest son from the first marriage, should have been in charge. Others thought Chuen, as the eldest son from the second and current marriage, should have taken the more active role. But Ming, for reasons of his own, chose to step aside, while Chuen was totally unavailable. He was in Tokyo, celebrating his marriage to the daughter of a Japanese innkeeper.

It fell to Eddy, the son who had tried the hardest to remain in contact with his father, to do the right thing. He went to the hospital every day. He consulted with the doctors. He translated the medical words as best he could to Ngon Hung. He soothed the broken hearts of his younger half-brothers and half-sisters.

Two weeks later, on March 9, Fong See died. His death certificate listed cerebral arteriosclerosis as the antecedent cause of death, with encephalomalacia as the direct cause, and auricular fibrillation as the "final manifestation." (A layman might as easily have said that he died of old age.) The rest of the death certificate was filled in with misleading information; the names of his mother and father were "unknown," but the line for date of birth was filled in with a precise "October 26, 1857."

This was just the beginning of what looked to be a final revision of the biography of Fong See. The newspapers carried the news as the "Death of Chinatown's Oldest Resident." With help from Eddy, obituary writers filled in blanks with whatever seemed plausible. "He was between ninety-six and one hundred," Eddy told the *Los Angeles Times.* The *Examiner,* on the other hand, simply gave Fong See's age as ninety-nine. It sounded all right for a man who on occasion had claimed to be well over one hundred, and would only tell his children that he was born in the such-and-such year of the reign of such-and-such emperor. Fong See's date of arrival in Los Angeles was adjusted to 1881. He was remembered as a "smooth-cheeked patriarch known to generations of Angelenos." The reporters recalled his favorite saying: "Don't worry and you live a long time." They also dutifully announced that funeral services would be held at Forest Lawn, pending the arrival from China of Chuen Fong and his new wife.

As Chuen traveled back to Los Angeles, Eddy negotiated with the mortuary. Fong See had said he wanted to be buried at Forest Lawn because Ticie was there. The man at Forest Lawn assured Eddy there would be no problem. It was only when Eddy and Yun went to look at the plots in person that the people at Forest Lawn realized they were dealing with a *Chinese* corpse.

"You can have any of those plots down there in the corner," the man said. "That's for people like you—"

"My father was an important man," Eddy interrupted. "We want him to be buried near my mother in the Gardens of Memory."

"He can't be buried there at all," the man answered.

For two weeks everything was put on hold as Fong See's fate was decided. The folks at Forest Lawn were all heart. They offered to sell Eddy a coffin with a diamond embedded in the top, an offer that Eddy rejected for reasons of taste. Then they offered to have Ticie disinterred and moved to the "minority" section in the flats. This was absolutely out of the question.

Eddy was beside himself. He wrote letters everywhere—to his insurance man, who was on the board at Forest Lawn, to people in city government—all to no avail. "All the bitterness," Eddy remarked to a friend. "I just thought that if we could somehow take my father back into our family for the funeral, that would make amends." Instead of being upset at Eddy's mucking about in their affairs, the second family welcomed his help. As Chuen would say many years later, "I was twenty-nine and I felt like I was fifteen. I didn't know a damn thing. I was glad Eddy took over. We were all grateful."

When Chuen arrived back in America, the will was read. Since China was closed, it was impossible to make official arrangements for Si Ping, Fong See's fourth wife. Nevertheless, Si Ping was assured that she would always have a roof over her head; since she was the only wife living in China, she had her choice of staying in the hotel, in her husband's town house in Fatsan, or in the mansion in the village. Over the coming years she would stay in all of these places. (When China loosened up, Ngon Hung was able to send a stipend to Si Ping.) Each of Fong See's children from the marriage to Ticie was left a crisp one-dollar bill—"to make it legal, so the will won't be contested," Mr. Ogden, the lawyer, explained. Everything else was left to Ngon Hung and her family.

It could be argued that the See family wasn't entitled to anything from their father. After all, when Fong See and Ticie had separated, she had taken half of his estate, which, upon her death, was divided between the five siblings. It could also be argued that the See children were not "children" at all, but adults with jobs and homes and families of their own. They didn't actually *need* anything, while many of the children in Fong See's second family were still quite young. (Ronny was fifteen. Gary was only twelve.) These were the logical arguments, but love and grief aren't logical. The See children felt extremely sad that in death their father had abandoned and rejected them once again.

While Eddy fumed over the problems at Forest Lawn, Bennie was enraged at this final injustice. "Mother worked—we *all* worked—unpacking those crates and the rest of it," he said.

"Who didn't work hard in those days?" Sissee asked.

"We should contest," Bennie insisted.

"It's a slap in the face," Ray snorted. "It's the crowning blow. It's just like the way he treated Ma."

Sissee agreed, but added, "What does it matter, anyway? These last few years, our paths didn't cross much. It's not worth it."

Eventually the family calmed Bennie down. "We can manage ourselves," Ming said. "We don't need anything from Pa." In the end, they took their one-dollar-bills and squirreled them away as final bitter reminders.

Only after mortuary officials had perused the list of invited guests, which included many prominent *white* citizens—old customers, a few politicians, as well as the minister who would conduct the service—were funeral services held in Forest Lawn's Hollywood Hills Chapel. (A hearse stood by to take Fong See to Rosedale Cemetery, where he would be buried in the section allotted to the city's most important pioneer families.) No professional mourners were hired; there was no parade through the streets of Chinatown, no firecrackers, no "road money," no gongs or cymbals. No artisans were hired to brush with red ink on wide white ribbons or banners the characters for "Your longevity is like age-old mountains," or "Your family will honor you for generations to come." Instead, the See family insisted on a Caucasian affair.

Although the family was not permitted to use the main sanctuary at the top of the hill, they could use the "integrated" church in the flats, which was big—and utterly tasteless. The walls of the nave were inset with little cages, and throughout the eulogies, live birds chirped and trilled. The Reverend Henry V. Lacy of the First Methodist Church reminisced about his sixty years in China as a missionary's son and a missionary himself. A friend of Sissee's sang "Sweet Mystery of Life." The only nod to Chinese tradition was that each mourner was handed a piece of candy "to sweeten sorrow" and *lai see* to bring good luck.

The church was packed. For many, it was the first time they'd seen so many Chinese women in one place. Although by this time women made up forty percent of the population of Chinatown, they were still hoarded like gold. Many of the wives—being of the old merchant class— had rarely set foot outside their homes, but were allowed this one day to sally forth to pay their respects to See-bok, to thank him for bringing them over and for giving advice to their husbands during times of adversity. The women clustered together in a little group—appearing to Carolyn's Caucasian eyes not so much foreign or fresh off the boat, but more as though they'd just arrived from another planet. (Many looked at Carolyn as an oddity as well. Noticing the makeup covering her birthmark, they wondered if she was following the Chinese custom of powdering her face white in mourning.)

Businessmen wept openly. During the days of Fong See's slumber, as his final resting place was being argued over, men had come to visit him, hold his hand, and talk. Now they passed before the silver-lined coffin and bowed three times before their mentor. Those who hadn't had the chance to pay back See-bok for past debts threw themselves on the casket in distress for having lost so much face.

Fong See's extended family sat in a special bereavement section. Ngon Hung, who had worked in the service of the old man since she was sixteen, sat dry-eyed. Her husband was ninety-nine, so his death had not come as a surprise. Immediately following his death, she had wept discreetly; now she didn't want anyone to see her lose control. Chuen sat with his new wife, Teruko, only just beginning to realize the responsibilities he would be taking on as the eldest son on his side of the family. His sister, Sumoy, didn't see much of the service. Instead she acted the part of the dutiful daughter, working the foyer, serving as liaison between the Chinese-speaking guests and the Forest Lawn officials, helping old family friends write their names in the guest book.

Despite their hurt feelings, the See family was in attendance: Ming and Sunny; Eddy and Stella; Sissee, Gilbert, and their daughter, Leslee; Ray with his daughter, Pollyanne, and her husband and children; Richard, Carolyn, and their daughter; Bennie and Bertha, who turned up with their daughter Shirley, but without Marcia, who'd asked her parents if she should try to get off work and they'd told her not to bother.

After the funeral, the mourners—relatives, customers, and business associates—lingered outside the chapel, talking in low tones, sharing anecdotes about Fong See. Some bemoaned the fact that he couldn't be buried at Forest Lawn; others marveled that there had been a possibility that he *might* be buried there. Everyone agreed that much had changed in the world, Los Angeles, and Chinatown during Fong See's lifetime.

The rowdy little town of Los Angeles had matured, and Chinatown with it. In the old days, Chinese food had been something strange, something to make fun of. By the mid-1950s, "Let's have Chinese" had become a common phrase, as over 150 enterprising Chinese restaurateurs spread across the city in the wake of new housing developments and shopping centers. Prepackaged chop suey wrapped in cellophane had appeared on supermarket shelves, and school cafeterias had "chop suey days." Chinese families still ran scores of laundries across the great desert city, although mechanization and profitability now brought Caucasian entrepreneurs into the field. Far from the environs of Chinatown, herbalists treated Caucasian patients. Many Chinese had triumphed as doctors, dentists, lawyers, optometrists, architects, and engineers.

New immigration laws continued to be passed. Some reversed decades of discrimination; others continued to limit the entry of Chinese into the United States. In 1952 the McCarran-Walter Act provided for immigration for purposes of family reunification and gave special consideration to those with special skills. But the McCarran-Walter Act also set national-origin quotas based on political affiliation. Democratic countries had virtually unlimited immigration possibilities, while those from Communist countries, including the People's Republic of China, were denied entry. This meant that great numbers of potential Chinese immigrants were, once again, excluded. Nevertheless, Chinese wives continued to come to U.S. shores in unprecedented numbers, thanks to the Refugee Relief Acts of 1953, 1957, and 1959.

Seven months after Fong See's death, Congress would pass the act of September 11, 1957, which stemmed from the U.S. government's persecution of accused Communists. Chinese who were living in the United States illegally—mostly paper sons—were encouraged to step forward, identify themselves to the INS, and, in the process, name other paper sons and those suspected of being Communists. Thousands of Chinese participated; in San Francisco alone, ten thousand Chinese came forward. In exchange, the government granted them legal status, as long as the Chinese proved they weren't involved in any subversive activities; ninety-nine percent of those who confessed were allowed to remain in the United States.

What Fong See's mourners realized as they stood outside the chapel in the crisp spring sunshine was that his death marked the end of an era. The world was vastly different from the days when Fong Dun Shung had left China to work on the railroad, and his wife had supported her children by carrying people on her back, changed from the nightmare of the Driving Out and Exclusion, altered by the overturning of restrictive property covenants and miscegenation laws. With Fong See's death, his family began to envision a new set of hopes and dreams. It was a tribute to Fong See not only how far they had already come, but how far his children, grandchildren, and great-grandchildren would go.

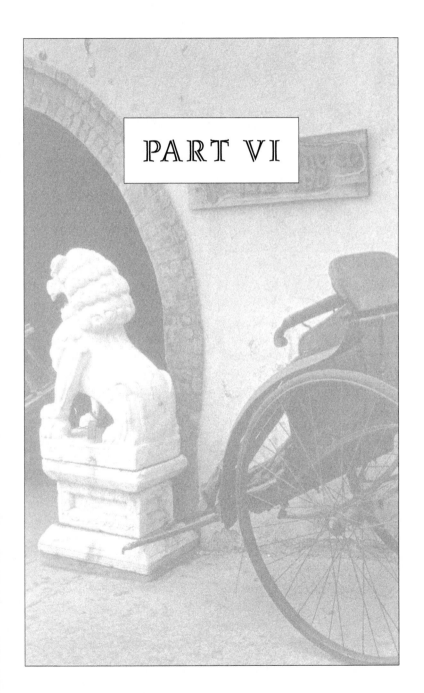

PART VI

CHAPTER 20

FAMILY MEANS EVERYTHING

1957–95

THERE were numerous reasons why the marriage between Carolyn and Richard didn't work out, but for a few years they both scrupulously chose to suppress them. When Carolyn—the daughter of two alcoholics and the stepdaughter of another alcoholic—married Richard, she ignored the fact that he'd written from Newfoundland that he was the company sot, that an oft-told family story recounted how he'd thrown up on Elizabeth Taylor's rug, and that he'd already been arrested twice for public drunkenness. Carolyn looked the other way when, at the family banquet at Soochow on their third day of marital bliss, Richard got so drunk that he vomited through his nose and had to be carried out by his buddies. In Newfoundland and Europe, she didn't worry about his drinking, because he drank "only red wine." When they returned from Europe and went back to school, Richard continued to drink. Finally she noticed.

Adding to their stress was Eddy, who, following old traditions, played the role of Chinese father-in-law. He meddled, intruded, bossed. Unlike a complacent Chinese daughter-in-law, Carolyn rebelled. She didn't think it was funny when Eddy suggested she walk ten feet behind her husband. She didn't laugh when Eddy said it was a joke. She refused to eat the mushy green center of the crab, even when her father-in-law said it was a delicacy. She complained when Eddy took her wedding ring, promising to size it, and never returned it. She got mad at Richard when his father came to the apartment every day, stood over the baby's crib, and said, "You haven't changed Lisa's diaper," or "Lisa's sick—*again,*" or "I'd like to declare Richard as a dependent again this year." She ignored Eddy when he repeatedly asked her to take Lisa down to Chinatown so that Fong See could give her a Chinese name. And all the while, Carolyn nagged Richard, "Why don't you grow up? Why don't you get a job? Why don't you stop drinking?"

If Richard hadn't been so cowed by his resentful wife and his interfering father, he might have shot back, "Why can't you obey? Why can't you curb your stubbornness? Why can't you show respect? Why can't you take a joke? On the other hand, why do you have to always see our differences as a *Chinese* thing? Why can't you *lighten up*?" Instead he just drank. Things were not going well.

Through all of this Carolyn and Richard were in school and managing a tenement apartment downtown. Richard was working toward his Ph.D. in anthropology—the culmination of one sort of American Dream and a legitimate measure of success in the Chinese culture. Carolyn was also in graduate school at UCLA, writing her first novel, and trying to raise a kid.

At the end of 1958, Carolyn found out she was pregnant again. They both knew that they couldn't possibly have another child, and scrambled to get money together for an abortion. Unfortunately, the abortionist turned out to be a con man who absconded with their borrowed money; fortunately, she miscarried at the end of January.

But none of this was what ultimately made Carolyn leave. What bothered her most about Richard was that he never once told her he loved her. The sad fact was he didn't. He also wasn't accustomed to communicating freely. Growing up, he had learned how *not* to acknowledge people when they were in a room, how to be in a crowded place and create your own space through silence, how to avoid confrontation.

In the spring of 1959, Carolyn met Tom Sturak, a fellow graduate student, and fell immediately and passionately in love. On March 6, 1959, she won second place in the Samuel Goldwyn Awards for her novel; it included a cash prize of five hundred dollars. In June, after five years of marriage, Carolyn told Richard she was leaving. (It might be noted that the night she walked out, Richard uttered the words "I love you," then went right back to grading papers.) Carolyn took Lisa and ran away to Reno for a quickie divorce.

The family partnership dissolved, China closed, Fong See's death, a divorce. Where are the happy endings? Where is the See and Fong families' achievement of the American Dream? Despite everything, just about everyone *did* have a happy ending, and strangely, for many, those happy endings can be traced back to the death of Fong See. Just as today China can't relinquish its ancient leaders, it was unthinkable that the See and Fong children could rebel against their father and his old ways during his lifetime. Now they had their chance.

In 1958, finally free of having to prove anything to his father, Ray decided to retire. As always, Bennie went along with his older brother. They sold See-Mar, and each went his separate way. Bennie, after thirty years away, returned to the F. Suie One Company; Ray did some designing for Widdicomb, the furniture manufacturer. In 1960, Ray married Mary Marshall, who proved to be extremely loyal and completely equal to the task of dealing with her husband's sometimes tempestuous moods. This same year, Ray and Mary traveled through Asia. In Taiwan they looked up Ray's half-sister Jong Oy. Ray and Mary went to the military compound where Jong Oy lived, but were told she was "not at home." Ray believed that she was ashamed to let relatives see her in such poor circumstances.

In 1961, after Mary and Ray returned from their trip, the See siblings decided to sell their half of the property in La Habra that Fong See had received in trade for rugs so many years ago. With their portion of the proceeds, Bennie and Bertha bought a ranch in La Habra and began fixing it up. Sissee—who had begun running her own shop on Los Feliz, next to Gilbert's architecture firm—bought a Thunderbird, and saved the rest. Ming and Sunny bought a house just down the street from Sissee and Gilbert and began transforming it into a Japanese retreat, with koi ponds and shoji screens. Stella and Eddy put all of their money in the bank and began to plan what they might do. Their opportunity came sooner than expected. In late 1961, Ming, Eddy, Bennie, and Sissee formed a new family partnership and bought an existing Asian art store, the Jade Tree, on Robertson Boulevard in the heart of Los Angeles's design district. Eddy, happily, was once again an equal partner.

With China closed, the family expanded its world. Ming and Sunny continued to alternate a year at home with a year abroad. They traveled to Thailand, Burma, Korea, Persia, and Japan; the types of merchandise available at the F. Suie One Company grew and evolved with each successive journey. In 1963, Stella and Eddy took some of their money from the La Habra property and traveled for a year to Vietnam, India, Penang, and other Asian countries. This trip renewed the wanderlust of their youth.

Eddy and Stella would never be rich, but they would make up for it with style and panache. Over the years—first living in the basement of Dragon's Den, then working in the store—Stella gradually gave up her cotton dresses for black pants, tunics, and pieces of Chinese folk jewelry. Eddy remained a friend to all. He helped Kuen, Uncle's son, open a restaurant. He helped the old chef and a waiter from Dragon's Den open their restaurant. And if Stella and Eddy chose to live in a "bohemian" way, well, what the hell? The house on Lantana was the most enjoyable place to visit, with the best jokes and the best food in town.

Sissee and Gilbert had to wait awhile before they could go on their big trip. Through the late fifties and the whole of the sixties, they were an active couple. Sissee became the president of the Chinese Women's Club—and one must imagine what a personal triumph this must have been. She was also instrumental in the running of three stores—her own on Los Feliz, the Jade Tree, and, of course, the F. Suie One Company. Gilbert lived up to his mother's high expectations, becoming the architect of choice in Chinatown. He designed the Sing Lee Theater, numerous bank buildings, and gorgeous homes, and became so respected that he was asked to serve on the board of directors of the East West Bank.

In 1969, Gilbert and Sissee finally got their chance to travel. They toured Asia for six months on what amounted to a second honeymoon. They would forever treasure the romance of Singapore, of listening to "Lara's Theme" and "Claire de Lune" waft up to their room as they watched junks sailing past on the glistening sea and coolies pushing wheelbarrows on the strand. Later, in 1972, Sissee and Gilbert traveled to the Far East again, with the first Chinese American tour group to go back to the People's Republic of China.

No matter where the See family went, they always returned to the F. Suie One Company. After decades in business, the family had developed the odd but profitable business of *not* selling. This practice encouraged stories, and brought in more customers. (Even today, a Procter heir of the Procter & Gamble company likes to recount how he bargained for ten years for a pair of carved Thai dogs.) Wise customers learned to approach Sissee to appeal to Ming or Eddy on their behalf. When complimented on her success, Sissee would just laugh and say, "It's nothing. I've been doing it all of my life." For the next thirty years, as the siblings died off one by one, life was reduced to simple conversations.

"A lady's in the store," Stella might announce. "She likes those two vases, but she doesn't know where to put them."

"How about on her mantel?" Sissee would say, pulling herself up slowly from her chair. "What price did you give her?"

"How much have we asked for them?"

"I don't know. I can't remember."

"How about four hundred seventy-five?"

"Want to try six-fifty? Seven-fifty?"

"Five-seventy-five?"

"Whatever comes to your mind."

"Five-seventy-five!" Stella might conclude, and at least one phase of the negotiation would be complete.

It sounds quiet, and it was. "I don't have anything interesting to say," Sissee said, not long before her death. "What am I going to say? Someone came in and looked at a piece of pottery today? My life is very shallow." Then she added, "It's hard to talk about how I feel about the store." I think I understand what she meant. The daily routine of business was mundane; what was important was the art, and the interactions with the family.

When I thought things were getting serious with my future husband,

Richard Kendall, I took him down to the F. Suie One Company. He met the relatives and passed their inspection with courtesy, respect, a hole in his corduroys, his sweet smile, and his proficiency with chopsticks. But he also needed to pass another "test": to step into those dark, murky, dusty rooms, to look and touch and *feel*—as Stella had done when she first stepped into the store—and, finally, to fall in love in his own way with this *stuff*. A few weeks later, Dick proposed. Very soon after that, his father asked my mother something along the lines of "Is Lisa stable? Does she understand about family?" And my mother could answer, without a hint of irony or falsehood, "Family means everything to Lisa."

In 1967, Eddy, the youngest See brother, died when an aneurysm burst next to his heart. He was only sixty-one. Stella went into a deep depression for close to seven years. When she came out of it, she asked a cousin and a girlfriend to travel around the world with her. When they returned, Stella went back to the store, where she worked full-time until she was eighty-three—long enough after Sissee's death to help Leslee complete an exhaustive inventory.

Ray died in 1974, at the age of seventy-four. Toward the end, he showed a sentimental streak. When he complained that he couldn't get a decent Chinese meal, Mary learned how to cook elaborate, multicourse Chinese meals from Madame Wu, the famous restaurateur. Just weeks before his death, Mary and Ray attended an auction at the Mission Inn in Riverside, where he instructed her to buy the ceramic water buffalo that he had rested against as a child. (Recently, Mary sold the Nichols Canyon house and moved into a West Hollywood condominium. She has remained faithful to his memory for twenty years.)

Ming died on June 17, 1978, at the age of eighty. For most of his life he had played the role of the aloof Chinese patriarch, but he remained conflicted about his heritage. If a friend happened to say that he wished he were Chinese, Milton would answer, "Are you crazy? The best thing that ever happened to us was that the immigration officials fouled up our last name." He never had children; he always told friends he didn't want them to suffer the way he had.

Two years after Ming's death, Sunny asked for her husband's half of the F. Suie One Company, so that she could move to New Mexico. An agreement was struck, and Sunny did indeed take a considerable amount of merchandise with her, leaving the rest of the family thankful that they had so many other things stored away in sheds, warehouses, attics, and back bedrooms from all those numerous trips abroad. At last report, Sunny was in her late nineties. No one knows what became of the merchandise.

Ming's death left just Bennie and Sissee. Bertha often accompanied

Bennie as he drove in from La Habra to Chinatown. In 1979, Bertha passed away. Bennie never got over losing his childhood sweetheart, but he promised to keep busy on his ranch and in the store.

In 1981, the F. Suie One Company moved from its longtime location on Ord Street to 1335 East Colorado Boulevard, in Pasadena. (Sissee was especially thrilled by this change, which brought back memories of the days when her parents had been so successful on Raymond Street.) Three years later, on March 5, 1984, Bennie died. He was eighty-one.

Sissee's sudden death from a heart attack, during the Christmas holidays of 1989, came as a shock to the whole family. Her funeral was hardly the sort of happy occasion that had been common in the past few years—festive rituals such as the huge banquet to celebrate the one-hundredth anniversaries of the F. Suie One and F. See On companies as two of a handful of continuously owned and operated family businesses in Los Angeles (Chinese or otherwise), and the small family banquet of three tables that we had had just months before for Sissee's eightieth birthday. (It was the latter event that prompted her to ask me to write this story.) But the funeral did have moments of joy, celebration, and triumph. The service was held at Forest Lawn—not in one of the chapels down in the flats, as her father's had been—but in the Church of the Recessional, at the very top of the hill. Everyone was there, except Stella and Ngon Hung, who were too broken up to attend.

During the eulogy, Gilbert tearfully reminded the assembly that Sissee's Chinese name was Jun Oy, which meant "true love," and that for forty-seven years—which included their long courtship—his had been a true love. Actress Beulah Quo recalled that Sissee's stuffed mushrooms and stuffed bitter melon were her best dishes. Munson Kwok spoke on behalf of the Chinese Historical Society, noting that Sissee's love of Asian art was in her roots; it was her avocation and her profession. Sitting there, I remembered when Sissee had made me a pot of Chinese "baby soup" of whiskey, ginger, and peanuts to "help bring in the milk" when my first son was born.

At the end of the service, Richard and Yun stood at the exit, handing out money and candy. Then everyone drove downtown to the Empress Pavilion, arguably the best restaurant in Chinatown, for a glorious banquet. Sumoy hugged my mother. Chuen, Fong See's eldest living child, came up to me and said, "Well, if Sissee said she wanted you to write this book, then I guess you'd better come over to my store and we'll talk."

Sissee See Leong, the last surviving child of the marriage between Fong See and Ticie Pruett, was interred in Forest Lawn's private Gardens of Memory. In death, Sissee is once again near her mother.

Since Sissee's passing, Gilbert has turned into a cranky old man who refuses to turn up his hearing aid. In a pattern found in families around the world, he has adopted many of the prejudices and controlling characteristics of his own mother. He has spent years torturing his daughter in the same way his mother tortured him for marrying into the See family. (When Leslee married a Caucasian man, Gilbert wouldn't let him in the gate for eight years, and wouldn't talk to him for twelve.) Yet Gilbert's love for Sissee has never dimmed.

"I kick myself today," he says. "Every day for the last ten years we drove past the Methodist Church where we were married, but I was always too busy to stop. Why didn't I stop and go in the chapel just once? I didn't do it. It haunts me. Everything else was too important. I wouldn't take the time to do things for the closest person, the one who was dearest to me, and all of a sudden I found out it was too late."

He's turned his attention to the store. For over a hundred years the F. Suie One Company has been a solace, a refuge, a world apart. Now it has also become a bit of a battleground between father and daughter over who owns it, who wants it, and whether it should survive. "When it breaks down to a discussion over every one of ten thousand items, it gets to be real hard," says Leslee, who graduated from USC, went on to UC Berkeley, traveled the world, worked as the assistant curator in the Far Eastern Art Department of the Los Angeles County Museum of Art, and came back to work in the store in the early 1980s so that she could be close to her mother and her aunt Stella.

"What my father doesn't understand is that turning any of these things over for a profit can be a real plus," says Leslee, who, after a long hiatus, has resumed the business of renting props to movie and television companies, for such films as *The Joy Luck Club* and *The Shadow*, and TV series including "Murder She Wrote" and "The Young and the Restless." "The family has just been so afraid to let it go, but I don't know where they thought they were going to take it." My advice, though perhaps unwanted, is that she should go back to the old ways and hang a sign in the window: "Ten Thousand Customers Coming Through the Gate!"

The happiest endings are new beginnings. Fong See—a peasant boy from a tiny village in the south of China—created a family that flourished in America. In the See family, Ray's daughter, Pollyanne, had three children. The two girls—an interior designer and a bookkeeper—have yet to marry; their brother is the CFO of a company, and father of a girl and a boy. Bennie's daughters, Marcia and Shirley, each married and had children. Marcia, a teacher, has taught her daughters that they too can combine work and motherhood: Heather, an engineer, has two young children; her sister, Gale, is a microbiologist with three children. Shirley had three children: Donna, who is a doctor's assistant, and Robert and Kenneth, who work in the family-owned printing business.

Among them, they have given Shirley and her husband seven grand-children. Sissee and Gilbert's daughter, Leslee, has two beautiful girls, Sian and Mara. Stella and Eddy had Richard, the only son in the third generation of the See family. He, in turn, produced daughters: my half-sister, Ariana, who just graduated from college with a business degree, and me. My sons, Alexander and Christopher, are thirteen and ten.

In my great-grandfather's second family, all three of the girls married, but only the eldest of the four sons married. In Taiwan, Jong Oy died of cancer in the early 1980s. One of her sons lives in Georgia, where he is a veterinarian. He and his wife gave Ngon Hung her first great-granddaughter. Jong Oy's other son has a doctorate in aeronautical engineering and has worked for NASA. He and his wife recently gave up their jobs to go back to Taiwan as missionaries.

The second Fong sister, May Oy, is a researcher. One of her daughters works in a library; the other works in the media. The youngest Fong sister, Sumoy, is still beautiful and adored. She is the principal of a multiethnic, multicultural school in Los Angeles where upwards of thirty languages are spoken. Her son, Robert, is a CPA and is married to a Japanese American woman. They have a three-year-old son, Austin, and a set of newborn twin boys, Brady and Tanner. Robert's brother, Tyler, is an insurance consultant, and he and his wife have a little girl, Stephanie.

Three of the Fong brothers—Chuen, Yun, and Gary—work at the F. See On Company on Chungking Court in New Chinatown. When their brother Ronny died two years ago, just days short of reaching his fiftieth birthday, Yun, in his early sixties, moved out of his mother's house and into Ronny's place. Yun is living on his own for the first time in his life, and loving it. Gary still resides with his mother, and has taken over Ronny's stamp collection.

Chuen and Teruko had four children, two daughters and two sons. Mari is a representative for a pharmaceutical company. She has two little girls, Jade and Shannon. Mari's sister, Sumi, sells computer soft-ware; her son, Ian, just turned two. One of Chuen and Teruko's sons died, leaving only Sean to carry on the Fong line. Sean has just entered college, where he is studying graphic art.

Finally there is Ngon Hung, now in her eighties and still living in Chinatown. It took her years after Fong See's death before she felt comfortable venturing out, making friends and joining the Chinese Women's Club. But with each step she took, her back straightened until, by now, she looks younger than when she was a shuffling, hunched woman locked in servitude. She divides her time between watching Chinese vieotapes on her big-screen television set and going on junkets with many of Chinatown's other senior citizens to Las Vegas. Her family reports that she is an inveterate gambler who always wins.

*

In a culture where only the eldest son has value, it is by default the role of the younger brother to stumble his way through life. This role was certainly assumed by Fong Yun, whose attempts at business were usually marked by failure. But with Fong See's death, Fong Yun, the oldest living "younger" brother, suddenly catapulted into the position of elder statesman of the family and of Chinatown.

In 1970, *Los Angeles Times* columnist Jack Smith interviewed Fong Yun in his shop in New Chinatown. Smith found Uncle painting a carved wooden figure in the back room of the store. To Smith, Fong Yun looked ancient, as indeed he was. Yun recalled his life in the City of Angels with good humor. When asked about the devastating first fire in China City, he said, "Oh, I lose everything," and laughed heartily. Later Smith asked Fong Yun his age. "How old?" Yun repeated, considering. "Not very old. Ninety-seven?" Then he laughed again. "Okay. Ninety-eight. Not old."

Surrounded by his large family, Fong Yun lived to paint a few more screens, repair a few more figurines, entertain a few more customers, and travel to Hong Kong to see his eldest daughter from his concubine. He died a wealthy man in spirit and family, and a *very* wealthy man by the standards of Dimtao. He made sure that his concubine and children in China were provided for, leaving them two houses in Fatsan, a home in Dimtao, and a modest yearly stipend that continues to this day.

Fong Yun also left a family of eight children in Los Angeles, each of whom has only kind words to say about him, for if Fong See was the brains of the family, in many ways Fong Yun was the loving heart. After Kuen, Yun's eldest son, closed his restaurant, he opened an antique store in Hollywood. Kuen is retired now and living in the Silverlake area of the city. He has six sons—including a lawyer, an architect, an accountant, an engineer, and an artist. They, in turn, have married and given Kuen and his wife eight grandchildren at the time of this writing.

Fong Yun's second son, Danny Ho, became the first multimillionaire in his family, with his huge rattan manufacturing company. He died in 1992, leaving behind two sons—who have taken over the business— and a daughter. Haw, Fong Yun's third son, became a tool designer; his sons are a lawyer and an engineer. Uncle's fourth son, Chong, became an engineer; his three children are either in or about to enter college.

Uncle's youngest son, Gim, is the only one in his family still in the antique business. He runs Fong's, the store in New Chinatown that he started with his siblings in the 1950s, and does cloisonné work in his spare time. He married the daughter of the pastor of the Methodist Church, and their two daughters are a bank executive and a CPA. One of the girls just gave Gim his first grandson.

Gim's sister, Choey Lau, has spent her married life in Hawaii. Her three sons have grown up to be a lawyer, doctor, and businessman. Lau's sister, Choey Lon, became a fashion designer. Several years ago, Lon, who used to pretend she was Snow White, living in the castle of China City, materialized her fantasy in a penthouse apartment that replicated the fairy-tale princess's mausoleum in the forest, right down to a pair of bronze deer. The execution of this vision was so complete that it appeared on the cover of *Architectural Digest*. Lon never married, and today lives just blocks away from Chinatown, in a high-rise condominium complex.

Concerning others who have peopled these pages:

After his wife's death, Harvey Copeland, Stella's father, stopped drinking, got off Skid Row, and began living a quiet life in a boarding-house. He adopted a cat to keep him company. After so many years of shirking responsibility, he took his pet-owning duties very seriously. In late 1957 he was hit by a car while crossing the street to the butcher shop to pick up fresh meat to give his cat.

Sadly, just as Harvey had begun cleaning up his life, his son, Ted, who was a barber like his father, began to sink into a life of alcoholism and barroom brawls. In the early seventies, Ted died from cirrhosis of the liver. His twin daughters, Lynn and Gwynn, have six children between them.

Peter, the son of the mysterious Fong Lai, still works for Chuen and Yun in the F. See On Company. Peter is considered a family member, and as such is always seated at an important table at banquets. Mary Louie, who started working in the F. Suie One Company during the influenza epidemic of 1918, and her sister, Dill, are in their nineties, in perfect health, and share an apartment in Hollywood.

In the late fifties, Tyrus Wong began designing Asian-themed Christmas cards for Hallmark in his free time. When he retired from Warner Brothers, his wife Ruth got so sick of having him around the house that one day she said, "Why don't you go fly a kite?" Today Tyrus, now in his eighties, uses his meticulous craftmanship to build and paint centipede kites up to two hundred feet long, which he flies on Venice Beach. He is very spry, and still loves to tell stories.

Fong See was an unquestionably unique man who rose above, ignored, and finagled his way around discriminatory laws. The majority of Chinese immigrants were not so lucky. Still, these faceless men and women were hardworking, resilient, and persistent. These characteristics helped to fuel their ambition, their hope for the future, and their desire to better their lives and those of their children—all those things that have inspired would-be Americans since the Pilgrims landed at Plymouth Rock.

Statistics on the numbers of Chinese immigrants to this country, as well as the number of Chinese Americans already living here, are, as ever, malleable and unreliable. The People's Republic of China estimates that the diaspora of Chinese totals about fifty million. This figure includes the twenty million Chinese living in Taiwan, who are Chinese but not Communist. It also embraces those Chinese living in Macao and Hong Kong. Although the figure is not precise, it can be said that the diaspora was so immense that it brings to mind certain clichés: that the Chinese can be found in any corner of the globe, that there isn't a country in the world where you can't get a decent Chinese meal.

This book has concentrated on those Chinese who came to America. Between 1950 and 1960, through immigration and births, the Chinese American population in the United States increased from 117,629 to 237,292. Already this was a tremendous increase from the mere 78,000 at the beginning of World War II. But the passage of the Immigration and Nationality Act Amendments of 1965, which repealed the old national-origins quota system, irrevocably changed the pattern of immigration. Although the new law still favored immigrants from the West, it did allow the entry of twenty thousand Chinese each year. Following the trend established with the War Brides Act, the emphasis was on family reunification, followed by a preference for highly educated, highly skilled professionals.

In 1976, the immigration laws were amended again to remove the inequities between the eastern- and western-hemisphere limitations; limits were now maintained at twenty thousand per country. (Those seeking family reunification and those with special skills were still preferred, however, and were treated on a first-come, first-served basis.) With these new laws, the Chinese American population exploded, doubling each decade. Between 1965 and 1984 the number of Chinese immigrants jumped to 419,373—a number that almost matches the 426,000 Chinese who came to the United States between 1849 and 1930.

In 1990, according to the U.S. Census Bureau and the LEAP Asian Pacific American Public Policy Institute, Asian Pacific Americans—comprising immigrants from thirty different ethnic groups, including those from Vietnam, Korea, Sri Lanka, Japan, Fiji, and the Philippines—are just 2.9 percent of the U. S. population. Chinese Americans total 1,656,472; sixty-three percent of that number are foreign-born. Like the numbers put forth by the PRC, these, too, must be looked at with care. How did people classify themselves? How much Chinese blood defined them as Chinese rather than Caucasian or "Other"? One-half? One-quarter? One-sixteenth? Did people call themselves Chinese only if they were full-blooded?

Amazingly, not even during the years of the worst persecution have Chinese Americans ever exceeded one percent of the total U.S. population; in 1985 they stood at only .42 percent. Despite this small number, contributions of Chinese sojourners and Chinese Americans can be found across the country and in every field of endeavor. Going back to the earliest days of the Chinese in California are the tough men who hacked and burrowed their way across and through the Sierras to construct the transcontinental railway. Many of those laborers went on to reclaim the land of the Sacramento Delta—even today some of the richest agricultural land in the entire country.

These, as well as other contributions, are taken for granted. Almost anywhere a person goes in the western United States, he will find not only those ubiquitous Chinese restaurants but also forgotten places—China Wall, China Gulch, China Creek, China Camp. Some of these names recall backbreaking work—a wall built to hold back a raging river, or a shelf carved out of the side of a mountain to support a railroad right-of-way. Others represent the abandoned sites of enclaves on the outskirts of towns, in scrub canyons, and along small creeks where the Chinese found safety and respite from the larger white population.

In 1994, as this book is being written, the diaspora continues. Based on recent trends, the combined Asian Pacific population in the United States will grow from today's 7.3 million to 20 to 23 million by the year 2020. In California this group will increase from 2.85 million in 1990 to as high as 8.5 million in 2020. Many of those people are having experiences strikingly similar to those of Fong Dun Shung and other early immigrants. Today thousands of Chinese pay up to thirty thousand dollars per person to smugglers who pack them aboard barely seaworthy vessels—without toilets and with little sustenance—and hope for the best. Often these ships drift for weeks without power, or languish two hundred miles offshore, beyond U.S. coastal waters, under the constant, wary eyes of the Coast Guard.

If the immigrants are fortunate enough to land unobserved, they, like their great-grandparents before them, must work hard—in laundries and restaurants, in garment factories and electronics assembly plants, as prostitutes and drug runners—to pay back their debt to the smuggling ring. If they are caught trying to land, the immigrants can apply for refuge on the basis of participation in the Tiananmen Square uprising or objection to China's one-child-per-couple policy. But these new immigrants (*all* immigrants, actually) aren't welcome. In Sacramento alone, twenty-one anti-immigration bills—most of them unconstitutional if enacted—are currently under consideration. The purpose of these bills, like those of the nineteenth century, is to stigmatize immigrants as "detriments, parasites, even criminals." And, just as in the old days, elections are won and lost on the issue of immigration. In 1994, California's governor, Pete Wilson, campaigned on this platform. Through Proposition 187, illegal immigrants would be barred from receiving *any* state funds; this meant no education, no welfare, and no medical care, except in dire emergencies. Wilson and the proposition won by large margins. The day after the election, several groups went to federal court seeking to block the new law as being unconstitutional, while in Washington, D.C., Congressman Newt Gingrich suggested that Proposition 187 be adopted nationally. The early court challenges were successful; the cases are now proceeding through the courts of appeals.

Even without Governor Wilson's proposed "reforms," conditions for new immigrants are almost as bad as they were in the 1880s. In New York Chinatown—the largest Chinese enclave in the country, in which sixty-five percent of the inhabitants reportedly have limited or no English—the median income is nine thousand dollars a year. In San Francisco Chinatown, the country's second largest Chinese community, annual earnings are slightly higher, at eleven thousand dollars a year. In addition to poor wages, these immigrants lack affordable health care and housing. Nationwide, one-fifth of all Chinese American housing is overcrowded. In San Francisco Chinatown, the population density is 228 per acre, the second highest in the nation after some parts of Manhattan. Over half of the housing is considered "old, deteriorated, and substandard."

Today, single men can still be found sharing eight-by-eight-foot rooms and sleeping in bunk beds stacked from floor to ceiling. Bathrooms and kitchens are shared by several families. Immigrants—children and adults—can expect to hear racial epithets, have food thrown at them, get beaten up, and be made fun of. And, just as in the old days, these immigrants are usually too afraid or too bewildered to complain.

But what about the "model minority"? What about all those Chinese American doctors, lawyers, engineers, and mathematicians? They're certainly out there. For every Chinese American who makes less than ten thousand dollars a year, there's another who earns more than seventy-five thousand dollars. According to the 1990 Census, Asian Pacific Americans are highly educated relative to the general population, with thirty-seven percent of those twenty-five years of age and older having a bachelor's degree, and fourteen percent having a graduate or professional degree. Nearly a quarter of all doctors, nurses, and medical technicians in New York, Los Angeles, San Francisco, and Chicago are Asian Pacific Americans. Over ten percent of all doctors across the United States are of Asian Pacific backgrounds, while in business, entrepreneurs have increased tenfold in the last decade.

But remember, Asian Pacific Americans constitute only 0.4 percent of the seats on the boards of directors among the Fortune 1000 companies. In California, where Asians make up ten percent of the electorate, there hasn't been an Asian in the state legislature for eleven years. Asians are 3 percent of the national population, but they make up less than one percent in the House of Representatives. In the newsrooms of daily newspapers across the country, Asian Pacific Americans comprise only 1.5 percent of the work force.

Los Angeles has the third-largest Chinese population in the country, but statistics are complicated by the fact that there are two Chinatowns: New Chinatown and Monterey Park. Many old-timers won't even go to the Chinatown along Spring, Broadway, and Hill streets anymore. "All the Cantonese people have passed away," says one family friend. "I won't go to Chinatown because of the parking and the new dialects." Just as in years past, this city-within-a-city still serves as port of entry to new immigrants. Vietnamese noodle shops stand beside traditional Chinese herbal emporiums. Cambodian record stores compete with T-shirt stands run by a new wave of immigrants from Kowloon and Hong Kong. Pajama-clad Laotian grandmothers clutching umbrellas stroll with children laden down with backpacks and Walkmans.

Farther to the east is Monterey Park, where the *feng shui*—the confluence of wind and water—is known to be auspicious, and a visitor can get the best Chinese meal on this side of the Pacific Rim. In the past thirty years, Monterey Park's Chinese population has jumped from just three percent to over fifty percent. Many of the families have come from Hong Kong and Taiwan, bringing with them, as Gilbert Leong reports from his position at the bank, grocery bags full of cash. Gilbert's stories are substantiated by a 1985 article in *Forbes,* which estimated that $1.5 billion was deposited in Monterey Park banks during that year alone— nearly $25,000 for every man, woman, and child. So, while Los Angeles may have the third-largest community of Chinese, it is the only one that can boast of having the "Chinese Beverly Hills."

Reminders of the old days can still be found. A portion of China City's Shanghai Street still stands in the parking lot of Philippe's Restaurant, one of the last remnants of the city's old Frenchtown. In Pasadena, the home of Grace Nicholson, the woman who got interested in Chinese antiques because of Fong See, has been turned into the Pacific Asia Museum; the garden, thought by many to be the finest example of a Chinese garden in the United States, was designed by Gilbert Leong. To the north, in San Francisco Bay, Angel Island, the notorious detention center for Asian immigrants, has become a weekend picnic spot. In Sacramento, the Chinatown along I Street has been reduced to a single modern edifice—with a mall, restaurants, and a Buddhist temple—evoking more of the modern China than the old. All that's left of the 500 block of Los Angeles Street is a grassy embankment—a temporary resting place for homeless men and women.

Then there's the "stuff." In these remaining years, my grandmother Stella agonizes over the material world. Who's going to deal with the unused stacks of wood and barrels of nails from the World War II barracks that are still just sitting around? Who's going to sort through the sheds on her property, and the back rooms of her house, which are jammed with merchandise? These are problems that the others have already faced in one way or another. Gilbert has solved it by hoarding—piling things up in his dining room, attic, and shed, and in the house on Ivadel where his sister-in-law Bernice still lives. (Of the rest of the Leongs, only Gilbert's sister is still living.) Even Ray was not immune. After his death, Mary cleaned out the garage, where she found utility bills dating back to the early 1930s. Why was Ray saving them?

The family learned early on that one man's piece of junk was another's objet d'art, that yesterday's curio could become tomorrow's priceless antique. The Satsuma ware that Fong See bought in Japan in 1919 has evolved from "import curio" to prized antique. The Canton ware that Sissee so disdained as a dowry gift from her father is considered valuable, if merely for the completeness of the set. Over the years there were countless customers who found special items. Bernard Gelbort, who bought a coromandel screen with weeping willows and egrets on layaway for $135 in the late 1940s, sold it recently at Christie's for $175,000.

Fong See understood that even everyday goods could have "value." The wife of a famous designer wowed Europe with the simplicity and elegance of Fong See's everyday clothes, purchased after his death, while Pietro Sandolar made a mini-fortune after casting the stone dogs in front of the store and mass-producing them in plaster. Today they can be spotted guarding banks, restaurants, and mansions. Even those little sewing baskets with the tassels and beads that the See children slaved over as kids, or chairs, chopsticks, and pottery from Dragon's Den, can be found in homes and antique shops around the city.

It wasn't always easy when I was growing up. My mother, Carolyn See, remarried, had another daughter, Clara, and got divorced again. We moved around a lot; I had gone to seven schools by the time I reached the third grade. During those early days we were broke a lot of the time, but then my mother's writing career began to take off. Today she is the author of seven books, a book critic for the *Washington Post*, a professor at UCLA, and a wonderful mother and grandmother.

My father, Richard See, was out of the picture for many years; he was simply too drunk. He finally got his Ph.D. in comparative anthropology and, in 1965, took a job teaching in Mississippi, where he met and married his second wife, Pat Williams. They moved to Orange

County, had my half-sister, Ariana, and got divorced. Soon after, my father, who now teaches at Cal State Fullerton, met the woman of his dreams—Anne Jennings, a fellow anthropologist. One of the best things about Anne is that she got my father to stop drinking. Another is that she has a sense of adventure—what some might call the See wanderlust. My father and Anne have traveled throughout Africa, Southeast Asia, and the Middle East. In 1992, after being together (and often apart, owing to Anne's fieldwork) for eighteen years, they finally got married. Which should in no way imply that my dad is just your average guy with a job, a house, and a wife.

He has always kept his unique style. At the baby shower for my second son, held at a *dim sum* restaurant in Chinatown, my friends thought he was the waiter—with his mandarin beard, his baggy pants, his collarless shirt, and his—sorry, Dad—*attitude*. He is probably the only person in the country who was devastated when Russia invaded Afghanistan, not because he felt sorry for the people (although he did), but because he would no longer be able to buy any decent clothes—flowing embroidered cottons—to wear. In my entire life I have only seen him wear shoes once; he rented a pair of patent-leather evening pumps for my wedding. Otherwise, rain or shine, he slips on zoris or kung-fu slippers.

Through it all, my true-heart home was the F. Suie One Company, and my grandparents, Stella and Eddy, were my emotional anchors. Sissee and Gilbert were like fairy godparents. (Because of them, I was the best-dressed child at the Salvation Army Nursery School.) Just as Choey Lon saw China City as a place filled with unique characters, so too was my Chinatown along Ord and Spring streets: Mr. Lee, who served the best custard pie; Margaret, who ran the International Grocery; Albert, called "Blackie," who eventually took over the Sam Sing Butcher Shop.

I grew up surrounded by wonderful people and hearing the stories that have filled these pages. From my grandmother I learned about her childhood in Waterville. Her stories were so vivid that when I went there, I found the town immediately familiar, for it hadn't changed much in the last hundred years. (Even the homes of Grandma Huggins and Grandma Copeland still stand.) From Sissee I heard snippets about her mother's life in Central Point. When I went there, I was lucky enough to meet Carol Harbison of the Southern Oregon Historical Society. In response to an idle question about weather on the Big Sticky, she pulled out the 1877 diary of Reverend Peterson. We both got goosebumps when we turned to the date of my great-great-grandmother's death and found that he had been present.

But there was a whole part of the story I still needed to learn. Although I knew what had happened to my relatives in the United States, I knew nothing about the family in China. Before I started the book, I didn't even know there *was* family in China; I had never heard of Fong See's first and fourth wives, or even that Uncle had had a concubine and children. I'd never *heard* the name of Dimtao—except in the form of vague anecdotes about a kidnapping in a village somewhere in China. I knew I would have to go to Dimtao, walk the alleyways, see my great-grandfather's mansion and the house where Fong Yun's children were kidnapped. More important, I knew I had to find the people who would know the stories to go along with those places.

CHAPTER 21

THE HOME VILLAGE II

Spring 1991

$\mathbf{M}$y husband is a lawyer who, in the last few years, has developed an interesting set of clients along the Pacific Rim. From 1986 to 1988 he traveled throughout Asia and Europe to find and retrieve paintings, property, and bank accounts pirated out of the Philippines by Ferdinand Marcos and return them to Corazon Aquino's new government. In the fall of 1987, on very short notice, I accompanied Dick on one of his quests to Hong Kong. On his one free day, we took a day trip to Guangzhou (the modern name for Canton) for a sightseeing excursion. At the time I had no idea that I would write this book, so we simply saw the sights and went back to Hong Kong.

In the fall of 1990 my husband accepted a case in which he was to represent the China National Coal Development Corporation in a dispute with Occidental Petroleum. In March 1991, when the Chinese government asked him to come and deal with a crisis, it seemed like the perfect opportunity for me to accompany him and do my research. We would both fly to Hong Kong. He would go on to Beijing, while I would go to Guangzhou, Foshan (the new name for Fatsan), and Dimtao. Later we would meet up again in Beijing.

But everyone says it can't be done, especially with only ten days' notice. "You can't go to the village!" Yun Fong, Fong See's second son from the second marriage, says bluntly. "You'll never find the village. To get there you have to know the right set of tire tracks through the ricefields." His brother Chuen shakes his head and warns that it took him three days just to hire a driver who could find Dimtao, and the only way he did it was by asking passing peasants the way to the *gway low,* house of ghosts. Chuen has had his own disappointments in going back to the village and discovering that the patina of childhood memory has worn away and been replaced by a grayer reality. He had remembered the house in its grandeur. When he visited a few years back, the house was in a shambles and inhabited by several families of squatters. "It was so bad," he says, "I wouldn't go inside." His wife, Teruko, adds, "The

Communists have no taste. They took the house and gave it to farmers, who didn't know how to maintain a house."

Finding the village is, for now, the least of my worries. My mother frets that I'll never find a place to pee. (I tell her I'm not going to pee.) My doctor is concerned I'll wade out into the rice paddies and get a parasite up through the soles of my feet. (I promise to wear boots.) "Don't put any mousse in your hair, because you don't want to look too American," my sister advises. "And don't go without your Ceclor." Not one but two well-meaning friends think I should hire a helicopter to airlift me to the village. They see nothing strange in this. "The Japanese do it all the time to get to golf courses," a friend assures me. People want me loaded down with a camcorder, a camera, a tape recorder, and gifts (from snap bracelets to UCLA sweatshirts).

Chuen suggests I take whiskey and cigarettes for the relatives. Teruko shakes her head and says that those Danish cookies that come in the blue tin would be better. They say I should certainly try the restaurant in Guangzhou that specializes in snake. If I don't go there, I should try the restaurant that features owl, salamander, turtle, civet cat, and dog. I laugh and smile. I know, and I think they know that I know, that they've read the same listings in the guidebooks that I have, and that I don't plan on going in for any of these delicacies, just as I bet they never did.

Between them, they settle on my gear—a raincoat ("Not a heavy one, but one you can fold up and carry in your bag"), ankle-high boots (to ward off those dreaded parasites), toilet paper, and a phrase book. Chuen promises to write a letter to Choey Ha, Uncle's daughter from the concubine Lui Ngan Fa. They hope Ha will get the letter before I get there, since what everyone is most concerned about is what the cousins will think when they see me. "I'm going to tell Ha that you are as tall as she is, slim like she is, but that you have yellow hair." (But of course my hair is red, like my grandmother's.)

I have my own anxieties. I've grown up hearing that the Chinese can't stand the smell of a *lo fan*, that they can even tell American-born Chinese by their smell. I stop eating all dairy products and beef, and hope for the best. I worry about not speaking Chinese—either Cantonese or Mandarin. I'd feel better about things if I could say *please* and *thank you*, *What a beautiful baby*, *I'm honored to meet you*. I find a phrase book and some tapes to listen to in my car. My son listens for about two minutes, shakes his head, and says simply, "No way." This isn't a language I'm going to pick up in ten days driving around town doing errands. And the phrase book is in Pinyin. . . . Let's just say that cleverer folks than I have been defeated by the intricacies of that Chinese puzzle.

I call Pauline at Lee's Travel Service in Chinatown, who says, "Oh, yes, we can take care of everything. Tell me the name of your village and we'll look it up on a map. I'll call you back this afternoon." I tell her all I know—that Dimtao has been described to me as being a half-day's walk from Fatsan. Several hours later, Pauline makes good on her promise, only this time her voice is very serious, very professional. "The proprietor of our establishment, Mr. David Lee, wishes to speak with you."

"Why do you want to go to Dimtao?" Mr. Lee asks. "Are you related to Fong See?" I'm astounded. "I knew your great-grandfather," he says.

Diplomacy now rules all travel arrangements. I wonder if, by fax, I should invite the family to dinner. "Only if you want two hundred people to show up," Mr. Lee snorts. "If you want to have dinner with them, ask them at the last minute." I'd like the China Travel Service—a mainland organization that makes travel arrangements for Chinese visitors—to call Choey Ha and ask her which day would be most convenient to meet. "You tell *her* which day *you* want to see her," Mr. Lee says. "You tell her she has to take the day off. You're going a long way, and she should be available when you want her." Mr. Lee also instructs Pauline to write a description of me in the fax. "They won't believe you if you show up looking like . . . looking like . . . you're Caucasian."

As soon as Mr. Lee is out of earshot, I plead with Pauline to amend these bossy faxes. Yes, we can let dinner drift for a while. Yes, they should know what I look like, but Choey Ha should decide whether Sunday or Monday is better. Pauline is gracious and sweet, but I don't read Mandarin. Three days before departure, my itinerary is settled. An interpreter from CTS will pick me up at ten on Monday morning, and we'll drive to Foshan to meet with Choey Ha.

The day before I leave, I visit my grandmother Stella, who gets panicky when I drive across town in the rain, but is thrilled that I'm going to China. "Maybe you'll get kidnapped by white slavers," she says hopefully, gleefully. That night—with just hours to go before our departure—we get a fax saying that the coal company has resolved its immediate problem. My husband's present trip is canceled. He will now go in another two weeks. My plans, on the other hand, would now be hard to change. I decide to go on ahead.

In Hong Kong, at the China Travel Service, I have the option of going either to the CITS side, for international visitors, or to the CTS side, for Chinese travelers. Pauline has said that my train tickets are on the CTS side, but the man whose job it is to point people in the right direction insists that I belong on the CITS side. The walls of the CITS side are plastered with travel posters featuring the Great Wall, the Forbidden City, and the mist-covered mountains of Guilin. CITS has no record of me. Against the strenuous objections of the doorman, I cross to the CTS side. No travel posters here, just a glass cabinet running the entire length of the office, chock-full of hair dryers, curling irons, batteries, radios, and ginseng. The officious man behind the counter sends me back to the CITS side, where they still haven't heard of me. Again I go back to the CTS side. A woman finally recognizes my name. They don't want to give me the ticket. I'm traveling as an "Overseas Chinese" and they can see with their own eyes that something is *very* wrong. After a check of my passport, I finally get my round-trip train ticket.

And this has been the *easy* part.

Aboard the train, the lace curtains and the antimacassars reek of mildew. At the front of the car, a clock advertises Kent cigarettes. Just beneath it, a poster proclaims "Miracle Rub—Your Family Friend." Dozens of identical fabric suitcases fill the overhead racks, and there's much bickering and teasing and general chaos about how these should be stacked. This arguing—combined with men hawking sputum in the aisle and the loudspeaker advertising duty-free products—makes for a noisy, if spirited, trip. When the women come through with the duty-free carts bearing these wares, I buy a bottle of whiskey and a tin of Danish cookies. Chuen and Teruko would be pleased.

We chug past the Hong Kong School of Motoring, Whimpey Asphalt, a soccer field. But mostly the track is edged by giant high-rise apartments looking like prehistoric porcupines. From every window, every balcony, bamboo rods extend straight out, with the week's laundry flapping in the humid air. A half hour out of Hong Kong, the detritus of the city falls away and the land becomes increasingly rural, with plowed fields and the occasional water buffalo. Along the track, tropical trees and vines are awash in lavender, yellow, pink, and white blooms.

We pass through the town of Lo Wo and cross onto the mainland. On adjacent hills in the distance, two lookout towers keep watch over the border and for a moment I glimpse rolls of razor wire sprawled up a hill. By the time I focus on this obvious barrier, it's gone. China. This border carries with it the same dramatic change as one experiences when passing from San Diego to Tijuana. We creep past shacks constructed from discarded corrugated tin siding. A rickety-looking web of bamboo scaffolding surrounds the construction of a twenty-story building. Where, in America, the precarious open sides would be fenced in with chain link, here rattan mats protect workers from danger. Workmen, dressed in blue "coolie" trousers and jackets, squat on their haunches and watch the train roll past.

In the countryside again, cultivated tracts of land appear between slight valleys carved from tentative hills. In these small plots, electric green shoots break the soil. Here and there people go about the arduous task of irrigating: A woman carries two five-gallon cans on a pole slung across her shoulders, while two men, each armed with a ladle, scoop water out of the buckets and fling it on the tender stalks. In other fields, farmers suspend primitive watering cans—the same buckets, rigged with spouts—from their bamboo sticks. This way one person can do the job. Soon we're passing rice paddies. Even on Sunday, people are out planting, sorting, thinning. All of this activity is hard, backbreaking work.

When the train pulls to a stop at the Guangzhou station, people frantically gather their bags, quickly descend the single step to the platform, then break into a run to be the first in line for passport control. Pandemonium rules the day. There are no signs in English, and no one speaks English. Eventually I make my way to the desk set up for guests of the White Swan Hotel.

Just four years before, on my day trip to Guangzhou, I had listened to the soft hum of bicycles on the streets, but now the city is one big traffic jam. It takes twenty minutes—and a lot of yelling by the White Swan driver—to exit the train station's parking lot. More shocking are the beggars. The beggar class that used to mutilate its children is supposed to be long gone. But as the White Swan van edges through this fume-filled lot, a woman knocks repeatedly on my window. Her face is covered with sores, and she holds up a sickly toddler. The mother makes the universal gesture of wanting food—bunching her fingers together and tapping at her mouth. I focus my eyes elsewhere. A man in his twenties strolls from taxi to taxi with his hands tucked up, China-style, in the capacious sleeves of his jacket. At each car he pulls out his two stumps and shoves them in the window to show the passengers.

The White Swan Hotel was the first luxury hotel in China to throw open its doors to any and all comers, including the local populace. This being the case, the lobby and public areas teem with both tourists and locals. Workers, peasants, and soldiers come through in familial parties—sometimes to have lunch, sometimes to visit guests in the hotel, but mostly to gawk and have their photographs taken in front of the lobby's "scenic waterfall."

After checking in, I have a bowl of noodles in the coffee shop. The people around me are prosperous—mostly young Chinese—with beepers and cellular phones. I go upstairs, watch "Entertainment Tonight" on cable, and fall asleep by eight-thirty. I wake up at 2:00 A.M. in a panic. What if I've come this far and the interpreter can't find me? I think that if I get everything ready for the big day, I'll be able to relax. I get out my notebook, the pictures of the family I've brought to show that I'm related, the camera, the flash, the extra batteries, and extra pens. The activity, though useful, doesn't work.

I'm not the only insomniac. People wander the halls all night. From my balcony, which overlooks the joining of two tributaries of the Pearl River, I can see boats of all sizes and shapes chugging past. Anchored in the center of the channel, a barge loads its cargo under harsh lights. Even in the middle of the night, the odor of coal smoke hangs heavy in the thick air.

Then next morning I meet Chen Mou, my interpreter, in the waiting room for tour groups. He speaks perfect English, as well as Hakka, Cantonese, Mandarin, and the Foshan dialect, which is very different from the pure Cantonese spoken only twenty-eight miles away. He carries a beeper and gets calls every few minutes, only half of which he answers. He introduces me to our driver, Xuem, a disheveled, quiet man. We have a little yellow van—more like an aluminum can laid on its side than a solid automobile. We honk our way through town and get on the Guong Fo Expressway, the first toll road of its kind in South China. Only a few years ago it took three hours to travel from Guangzhou to Foshan. Now it's barely a half hour on a highway nearly deserted except for a few vans and trucks.

Along the way, Chen Mou, who says he wants to be called "Tony," points out the sights of the countryside. He gestures to the stands of trees that mark the streams, dikes, and small dams that provide water throughout the province. "You see that small tree that looks like a mushroom?" he asks. "That's a lichee tree." When we pass a graveyard dotting a hillside, Chen Mou says, "Both businessmen and peasants wish to be buried on a hill to gain the benefits of *feng shui* in hopes of bringing prosperity to themselves and their families. I am always conscious of *feng shui*. As a tour guide I hope for smoothness and safety for my guests."

Chen Mou is originally from Shenzhen, an economic zone where families are allotted more space than in the southern capital of Guangzhou, where an entire household is lucky to get a bedroom and a sitting room. Although Chen Mou now lives in a dormitory for single men in Guangzhou, he explains that both Shenzhen and Foshan offer more beautiful settings and smaller populations. In Foshan the average family can have a sitting room and two bedrooms. Chen Mou adds that he's never wanted to leave China, but that many of his friends have escaped. "They walk or take the train to Shenzhen, then float in tubs down the Pearl River to Hong Kong."

Off the expressway, we're in bumper-to-bumper traffic bound for Foshan's city center. Billboards line the road, advertising countless capitalist products—dinette sets, washing machines, bedroom sets, nuts and bolts, power tools, face cream, portable computers, loudspeakers. Canvas-colored trucks lumber past. Flatbeds weighed down with dirt or gravel grind their gears. Bicyclists pedal through the dust and exhaust, loaded with their own wares—baskets stuffed with fresh produce, cases of Orange Crush, a side of raw meat strapped to a back wheel.

Along the shoulder lies a dirt area about twenty feet wide, stacked with sheet metal, sewer pipes, tie rods, sacks of cement, piles of gravel. Behind this, a kind of super sidewalk sale is taking place. Those dreams for sale on the billboards are a reality here, and they're all heavily influenced by western standards: western-style toilets in every conceivable color and shape, overstuffed sofas, sofa beds, pine bureaus, pots, pans, stoves, refrigerators.

In downtown Foshan, camphor trees line the wide boulevards, creating a shady oasis from the heat and humidity of the day. We stop first at the Overseas Chinese Hotel to wait for a cousin to meet us. Guan Yi Nian, my great-uncle's granddaughter and Choey Ha's daughter, arrives. Her hair is cropped short, her eyes are wide, her lips full. On this warm day, Yi Nian wears thick wool stockings and a brown wool suit hemmed well above her knees. Her lacy blouse is set off by a brooch, and she walks briskly on high heels. She's extremely nervous, but she says in English, "Hello, nice to meet you, welcome." We get in the van and she gives animated instructions to her mother's house.

We turn onto Wing On Road, named by my great-grandfather, meaning "Peace Forever." From 1966 to 1976, during the Cultural Revolution, Yi Nian explains, it was renamed Ming On—"Red Forever." One hundred years ago this was the new district of Foshan, for the most prosperous of its citizens. Today, although the buildings are old, they're well cared for and charming. We walk off the main street and down an alley where the high brick walls of the residences are whitewashed. We pass through a carved door and into a first courtyard for storing bicycles, then into a second courtyard with a few potted plants.

Choey Ha, her husband, her son, and his wife come out to greet us. Everyone has taken the day off from work. We shake hands and smile a lot. Choey Ha pulls me into the living room and orders her daughter-in-law to bring tea. A marble-topped, carved wood table sits in the center of the room. Matching straight-backed chairs are lined up against the walls in much the same way as in Fong See's home in Los Angeles. On another wall, a built-in cabinet and shelves hold about ten tins of those damned Danish cookies. Choey Ha sits next to me and pats my knee. The others stand and stare. We smile some more. Choey Ha asks through the interpreter if she looks like Choey Lon, her half-sister in Los Angeles. Of course she does, I say.

I show a photograph I've brought of Fong See, Ticie, and the five children. Pa sits in a severe suit; Ma is next to him in an elegant silk suit with ribbon trim, her hair gathered up into a bun. Ming and Ray, about fifteen and thirteen, look disaffected and bored. Bennie and my grandfather are just little kids dressed up in uncomfortable clothes. Sissee sits on her father's lap, wearing a white organza pinafore; a big white ribbon is pinned in her hair. Her face is slightly out of focus. She was the only one too young to hold still long enough for the photographer to get the shot. My relatives consider. If Fong See is their uncle, the little boy my grandfather, then I am truly a cousin. Strictly speaking, because my grandfather Eddy was Ha's first cousin, I'm her first cousin twice removed.

Having already heard Chen Mou's explanation of local housing, I'm impressed by our tour through the public rooms of Uncle's three-story town house. Outside, off the central courtyard, is a three-sided kitchen—with no window, no door—tiled in white and pink. Tin cabinets hold dishes. On the counter are two rice steamers, a metal bread box with a roll-away front, and a red thermos for tea. We go back through the main living room and upstairs to an identical sitting room above it, then up more narrow stairs to an empty room, where we pass outside to a balcony and climb another set of stairs to the roof where many years ago Uncle raised pigeons.

We troop back downstairs, out through the courtyards, and down the alley toward the house of Choey Ha's brother, Ming Tia. During this walk and others during my stay, Choey Ha either places a hand on my shoulder companionably or takes my elbow with one hand and with the other imperiously moves people out of our way. At Ming Tia's house, we go through another round of introductions. Everything is happening so fast I can't process who's who.

In some ways Ming Tia's house is primitive, in others completely modern. The first-floor anteroom is divided by a dilapidated wood-and-glass carved screen. The main room has no windows. In the dim light I see an altar table set with a vase, an artfully stacked plate of tangerines, and a ceramic azalea. Above the table hangs an exquisite mirror with a fuchsia, azure, and red phoenix painted on the glass. Nearby, two calendars dangle from nails. One of the calendars shows a beautiful Chinese girl in an off-the-shoulder sweater, vamping against a bouquet of peonies, roses, and Queen Anne's lace. The other shows a girl in a short black skirt and sleeveless top, reclining by a garden replete with flamingoes, steppingstones, and delicate bridges.

Upstairs, the main sitting room combines antiques with contemporary furnishings. The tables and chairs are antiques in the literal sense—they're *very* old—but they're not of the finest quality. Ming Tia and Choey Ha complain, as they will time and again during the next two days, that although they've been able to retrieve their property from the government since the end of the Cultural Revolution—"the Cruel Disaster" is how Ha refers to it—the family hasn't been able to recover its "good" antiques.

Out in the alley again, we briefly meet up with Uncle's surviving concubine. Lui Ngan Fa, an old woman in a padded jacket, with only a few teeth left, still suffers from headaches caused by her beating at the hands of the cadres during the Cultural Revolution. I am told she maintained a "good relationship" with Fong See's fourth wife, Si Ping, who died only a few years ago. But Ngan Fa is too old to have a conversation with a foreigner and a stranger, and I am still too ignorant to realize *who* she is.

It begins to rain, and I'm hustled off by Ha and Chen Mou. As we huddle three to an umbrella, Chen Mou comments, "Whenever you have a VIP guest, it is sure to rain. That is a saying we have in China." In a pig's eye.

We dash for the two vans that will be chauffeuring the extended family today. First stop, the ancestral temple. As we drive past the Fan River, a meandering tributary of the Pearl River, the van fills with good-natured arguing. Everyone has an opinion about the best way to get to the ancestral temple. Interspersed with this bantering, the passengers in our van—Choey Ha, her husband, and their daughter—take up a kind of chant, which Chen Mou continually translates. "You are very smart. You must be very well educated. You are very pretty. You must be very rich because you're a writer."

At the Temple of Ancestors, we pose for pictures. Guan Yi Nian stands to my right. On my left are Choey Ha, her husband, Ming Tia, his wife, "John," and his wife, "Joanie." This excursion feels like what you do when the relatives come in from out of town. We all have to go through a fair amount of *ooh*ing and *ah*ing, as they point out the 108 ancient weapons, as I comment on the bronze tripod incense burners, as Chen Mou explains the importance of the statue of the mythical Black Emperor, which was carved during the Ming Dynasty. We linger before the Ten Thousand Happiness Stage, but we pass on the hall of national treasures, the gallery of paintings and photographs of old China seen through the eyes of westerners, and the exhibit on birth control.

We gather around a low pool where people throw coins for good luck either to a statue of Kuan Yin rising out of a lotus blossom (to symbolize Buddhism), or to a statue of a turtle and a snake (the symbols of Taoism). If your coin lands on the turtle's back, Chen Mou says, you will get your wish. If your coin comes close to the turtle or the snake, then you will get something close to your wish. If you miss entirely, there goes your one desire. Chen Mou tells me that he believes in the luck brought by this wishing pond. "I came here with three friends. We didn't want to go into the army or be sent far away to work as peasants. We each threw in our coins. Mine landed on the turtle's back, and here I am. My friend's passed very near to the snake's head. He went to the countryside for two years, but is now a worker in Guangzhou." When I ask about the other friend, Chen Mou shrugs and says simply, "He missed."

We go to lunch at the Fatsan Hotel. The restaurant is so large and in so many sections of the hotel that it's more like five restaurants. As the older men scurry to different parts of the restaurant to find us a table, Choey Ha once again takes up her litany. She's been holding onto my upper arm, guiding me through this maze. Now she squeezes it, pinches it, and rattles off something to Chen Mou. "Your cousin wants you to know that you are very . . ." Here he hesitates. "You are very well kept." Then from Ha's son and daughter-in-law comes a correction. "No, slim." "She is slim." Soon all of them are saying, "Slim, slim, slim." I find myself beaming, not because they've said I'm slim, but because they're beginning to treat me like family.

We end up in the section of the restaurant that specializes in Mongolian fire pot. As we walk into a private room, the waitress turns on the television to CNN, then checks on the pot of broth in the center of the table. "Do you like this kind of food?" Chen Mou asks. "Of course," I say, but I must admit that when the waitress lifts the cover off the broth and I see how congealed and scummy it is, I have second thoughts. How many other people—complete strangers—have cooked their food in this same broth in this same container? When the pot comes to a rolling boil I'm somewhat mollified, but there's more to come.

Once we're served our drinks—either Orange Crush or the brown tea of the region—I finally have a chance to sort out who everyone is. Choey Ha is dressed today in a well-tailored off-white wool blazer, a turtleneck, and gray wool trousers. She works as a cashier at the Nam Hoi Technical School, and has an open, kind face; as Chen Mou might say, she is "very well kept" for someone who is fifty-seven. The more I look at her, the less I think she looks like her half-sister, Choey Lon, than like Sumoy—my great-half-aunt and my father's high-school flame.

To her right sits Le Chu-wa, Ha's daughter-in-law, who wants to be called "Joanie." Her hair is cropped short and she's not nearly as stylish as her sister-in-law, Yi Nian. But Joanie understands English and is generous of spirit and delightfully shy. Whenever she smiles or laughs, she covers her mouth to hide slightly crooked teeth. She would never go so far as to correct what the interpreter says, but every once in a while she'll add a few words in English to give a more subtle flavor to what's been said. She wears a white cotton blazer, a red T-shirt, a straight gray wool skirt, stockings, and heels. She works as a secretary at an import-export company, where she practices her English.

To her right is the lovely Guan Yi Nian, who works as a cashier for a construction company. When Chen Mou, unbidden, asks about her marital status, everyone teases this single man mercilessly. He has a good job. He should be able to find a wife. "Ah, but none as beautiful as your daughter," he replies. More laughter, more joshing. Yi Nian's husband works for the government and is currently stationed in Macao, where he is expected to stay for several years. It's very lonely for her. (I have already heard from Chuen about this alliance. The groom's family hosted a banquet for thirty tables—three hundred people—extravagant in any country, but astounding here. "He must be a very high official," Chuen has speculated.)

Then comes Zhumei-ying, the wife of Uncle's son Ming Tia. She is in her fifties, has the coarse features of a peasant, and works at a printing press. Her outfit is baggy, ill-fitting. Her hair style isn't as sophisticated as those of the other women in the family. Her cheeks are rosy, her hands rough and slightly swollen from her labors.

Ming Tia, Ha's younger brother, teaches electronics. His features are sharp and angular. He has high cheekbones and shrunken cheeks. His hair is receding, and little wispy tendrils curl up around his ears. He wears a starched white shirt and a gray western-style suit. Next to him sits his brother-in-law, Ha's husband, Guan Gin Hong, who has an expression of nonchalance frozen on his face. His hair is long, disheveled. He has a rumpled look about him. He chain-smokes like mad. Chen Mou explains that Guan Gin Hong is a teacher, but of what I never find out.

I don't have a clue about who the next person is. Everyone laughs because it's my driver, Xuem, whom I've only seen from the back.

Finally we come to "John," Choey Ha's son. He's the tallest in the group by several inches. He's sweet, young, earnest. He designs machines.

Everyone is more interested in asking questions than in answering them. Do I see Kuen often? When will Chuen come again? Am I sure that Choey Ha looks like Choey Lon? How am I related to them again? Even though they're all my cousins removed to various degrees, shouldn't I call Choey Ha "Auntie"? Shouldn't I call all of them either "Auntie" or "Uncle"?

All of this transpires as the waitress brings out dishes of raw vegetables, meat, seafood, tofu, and something resembling black tofu. The waitress drops much of this into the boiling broth, and soon we're using our individual wire baskets to scoop out what we want to eat. By tradition, it's proper for the host to fill the guest's dish with choice morsels. Fulfilling this function, Choey Ha drops tofu, the "black tofu," and squid into my bowl. As I chew the squid, Chen Mou turns to me and says, "Oh, so you like ox stomach." I stop in mid-chew, with the first piece of ox stomach still in my mouth. Well, I think to myself, I *thought* it was squid and it didn't bother me. It shouldn't bother me now. The waitress brings out a platter of river shrimp impaled on skewers and still twitching from their sudden death. We drop the bamboo sticks into the broth for a moment or two, burn our fingers peeling the shrimp, and manage to devour several dozen among us.

I eat my tofu and move on to the soy-bean greens and fish, but am reluctant to try the black stuff that lies reproachfully in my bowl. Finally

I break off an edge with my chopsticks. It's awful. This time I ask Chen Mou what it is. "Pig's blood," he answers. The cube of coagulated pig's blood stays at the bottom of my bowl until Ha finally reaches in with her chopsticks, removes it, and places it in a soy-sauce dish. No words are spoken about this, but Ha continues to fill my bowl without dropping in another cube of the pig's blood. No matter how many times I say I can't eat another bite, she refills my bowl. She's a good auntie.

Gradually they begin talking about themselves. "Their mother, Lui Ngan Fa, was from a very poor family from the village of Lo Hat, between Da Li and Nam Hoi," begins Chen Mou. "Her parents sold her to the Fong family when she was eight years old. She never knew what happened to her relatives—perhaps they were killed by the Japanese or died of hunger. Lui Ngan Fa worked as a servant for your great-great-grandmother. Your family raised her. Even before 1949, life was sad for Ngan Fa, since her husband was in the United States with his wife. When the Communists came, her fields were taken away and she and her children could no longer stay in their home in the village. They moved to Foshan, to the three-story house where we were this morning. Ngan Fa was thrifty and rented rooms. Si Ping, your great-grandfather's fourth wife, lived in a house behind the Fatsan Grand Hotel. Life improved."

The family wasn't bothered again until the Cultural Revolution. Uncle's family hid their valuables, including several wedding gowns, on the third floor. However, one of the tenants was made the director of the neighborhood association, and reported the hidden goods. Beginning in September 1966, the Red Guard came to the house seven times and took away the best antiques. As punishment, Si Ping and Lui Ngan Fa were sent back to Dimtao. In 1972, they were allowed to move back to Foshan, but were never able to retrieve their belongings.

After lunch, we pile back into our vans, go back to Wing On Road, park, and stroll toward what was once the Fatsan Grand Hotel. Since the civil war, the front of the hotel has housed a variety of businesses, including an herb shop, a chemical bureau, a pharmaceutical company, a radio station, and an educational company. In 1983, under the new leadership, China reevaluated its Overseas Chinese policy, and returned the hotel, as well as all other properties, to the Fong See and Fong Yun families. Cheun was paid forty years' worth of rents. This front portion of the hotel is now leased to the Chinese Industrial and Commercial Bank and an import-export company. Chuen collects rent, but he can't take the money out of China. As a result, the monies now accumulate interest in Chinese banks while Chuen tries to decide where to invest.

We pass through the courtyard—dark, dank, filled with bicycles and refuse—and go up the rickety stairs to what was once the lobby. The grand front desk is long gone, but the balustrades on the stairwells are in almost perfect condition. The tiles on the floors—now coated with years of filth—could still be brought back to a shiny gleam with a good dousing of chemicals and elbow grease. The room numbers show plainly on the glass transoms. The stained-glass windows are still in place and in perfect condition, although little light passes through because corrugated fiberglass has been mounted on the outside of them. The only illumination comes from a few fluorescent lights.

From 1949 until 1957, the hotel proper served as headquarters for the Foshan municipal government. Then it was left empty and deteriorated. In 1966 the government retook occupancy, spent 200,000 yuan on renovations, and managed the building until 1983, when it was given back to Chuen. It's currently leased by a textile company to use as a kindergarten. (By the time this book is published, all of this will probably have been demolished and a multi-use complex—with commercial, residential, and office space—built in its place. Decisions about how much square footage in the new building will revert to the Fong family are being handled thousands of miles away, in Los Angeles, by Chuen. More changes are coming. It's just a matter of time, Chuen believes, before Foshan spreads out into the countryside, either incorporating Dimtao or obliterating it entirely to make way for a Chinese version of tract housing.)

For now, the kindergarten is in place and functioning. In room 203, children rest together on wooden pallets. Some sleep under pink blankets, others raise their heads to peek at the intruders. On the third floor, another guest room has been converted to a classroom. Each wall is lined with cubbies stuffed with papers, and a jacket here and there. Yet another room is outfitted with child-sized tables and chairs. At the end of the hall a floor-to-ceiling window has been boarded up. All of the western-style toilets—luxuries back in the twenties—have been replaced by squatters.

We retrace our steps and go around the hotel to another courtyard in the back. From here my guides point to where the fourth-floor kitchen has been removed. Above and below a window on the hotel, Ming Tia shows me a stone inscription that reads, "This is the property of Fong See."

On our way to Dimtao, I see that what Yun said was true. The village would have been impossible for me to find by myself. Our two-car convoy heads out of Foshan, eventually turning onto a dirt road that passes under the expressway. We crisscross back and forth under the expressway four times before we get to the village. This is an ordeal, since at every underpass we must stop and ease the vans through without bumping their roofs. Fields spread out on either side of us. We cross a small, narrow bridge and pull to a stop in a clearing just outside Dimtao, for even today cars can't drive into the village. From the van we can see my great-grandfather's house towering over most of the buildings.

Dimtao is still home to about three hundred people, most of whom are peasants. The houses are close together, with only inches between them. We pass chickens pecking at trash lying in open lots and a pig snuffling for a tempting tidbit. We walk to Uncle's house, where the rooms are empty and swept clean. We spend a lot of time here going over the complexities of the kidnapping.

I had expected to find the records of the Fongs in the family association house, where, for centuries, villagers have kept birth and death records on stone plaques. I had especially wanted to see the names of Milton, Bennie, Ray, Sissee, and my grandfather. I had also hoped to find the true date of birth for my great-grandfather. The building still stands—cathedral-like, but desolate and abandoned. The Red Guard destroyed records in villages and cities across China during the Cultural Revolution. Dimtao was no exception.

We pass through the front gate of Fong See's compound into the preliminary courtyard, and on into the main courtyard. The whitewash has long faded; only the raw bricks remain, rendering the once-elegant house a basic gray. The front entry is still grand; on either side of it are stone panels carved with landscapes. Two small glazed ceramic elephants face each other on either side of the door, with pots of dwarf kumquat trees sitting on their backs.

The large courtyard kitchen is gone, as are many of the other outbuildings. Only a few steppingstones survive of the small pavilion that stood directly in front of the house. Most incredibly, the house has been cut in half. During the Japanese invasion, timber and metalwork were taken out of the house, and termites moved in. Then, during the Cultural Revolution, the left section of the house collapsed. Si Ping sold the majority of the bricks, keeping just enough to seal up half of the house. Now only the main entrance and everything to its right remain. The original foundation snakes through the garden as an eerie reminder of what once was. But what was once just a few shrubs and scrawny seedlings is a now a veritable jungle of banana trees, palms, and ferns. The mango tree that my great-grandfather planted with his own hands now stands fifty feet high.

I learn much about the family in Los Angeles from what I see here. For example, Sissee and Gilbert, Ming and his wife, Bennie and Bertha, my grandparents, even Ray and his wife, all had what I thought of as "Asian-flavored" gardens back in California. But they weren't "flavored" at all. They were pure Chinese. Old ginger jars and squat earthenware pots brought out of China were filled with geraniums, orchids, or cymbidiums. If a bamboo-and-straw broom was lying about, that was fine, as long as it looked artistic. If a shipping tin had been converted into a crude dustpan, so much the better—why waste money, why waste trash, use everything at hand.

An old woman, the daughter of one of Fong See's brothers and the only relative still living in Dimtao, currently serves as caretaker. She was the caretaker even before Fong See's death. She stands a little over four feet tall and wears a padded jacket. Meeting this relative, I can't help but wonder what would have happened if Fong See had never left China to search for his father. Would I—or rather a full-Chinese version of myself—still be living in the village? Would I be a peasant working in the fields, with a pole strung across my shoulders weighted down with watering cans or bundles of produce? Would I have ever seen a westerner, a bathtub, a television? There is no time for questions of this sort.

The old woman pushes us into the house and points out the little shrine she's constructed for Si Ping, just inside the entrance. When Fong See's fourth wife died, she left five hundred yuan to the old woman and asked her to take care of the house and keep a shrine in her memory. On the small table are a photo of Si Ping, a plate of kumquats, and a few sticks of incense smoldering in a pot of sand.

It's hard to imagine what the house was once like. The glass-domed skylight was removed sometime in the last decade. The spiral staircase is also gone, replaced by narrow, rickety, steep stairs—little more than a ladder, actually. The arched entry leading to the bedrooms is gone, sealed in by brick. The beautifully carved room dividers have been chipped and nicked, although the etched and painted glasswork remains intact. They are stunning enough that Chen Mou whispers, "You could sell these for a lot of money if you could ever get them out of the country. Of course, you'd never be able to get them out."

Much of the house's original grandeur is hidden under layers of dust and grime. The clay sewer pipes decorated in enameled vines, the delicate bird carvings around the windows, and the garlands over the archways are all still in good condition. However, the decorative carved and enameled landscapes that once graced the second-story veranda were destroyed during the Cultural Revolution. Shadowy traces of them, like skeletons on an X ray, still cling to the walls.

While we're upstairs on the veranda and later on the roof, the family begins recounting their version of the adventures of Fong See—things I'd never heard before, but was able to incorporate into this book: how Fong See's mother carried people from town to town; how he borrowed money to go to the States; how his first return to Dimtao, in 1901, set him on a life's mission to help the village; how he not only bought ricefields and rice seed, but also provided housing for the people of the village who needed it. From up on the roof, they point out the tile-roofed houses—really little more than shacks—that huddle next to the walls of Fong See's compound. He built those houses for his workers and their families, they tell me. It is now that Fong See becomes a three-dimensional person to me. I had always thought of him as a bit of a tyrant. But now I see that he had also helped the people of this village in ways that no one had done before or since.

It's still drizzling when we traipse through the deep, wet weeds of the village cemetery to Si Ping's grave. (Thank God I wore those boots!) Choey Ha worries about my skirt getting wet, and I have to politely bat away her hand each time she tries to lift up the hem to keep it from dragging in the muddy weeds. The grave sites—burial mounds here in China—are uncared for, with weeds almost completely covering them. "We used to build expensive tombs," Ming Tia apologizes. "I wanted to have one built for Si Ping. I sent three telegrams to Chuen to ask for money, but I received no response. I paid ten thousand yuan for her coffin in 1987. . . ." He did his best, he explains, without help from his more prosperous relatives in the United States.

Back at the vans, we say our good-byes and finalize a plan to meet at the White Swan tomorrow. Within five minutes of being back on the expressway, Chen Mou falls asleep. An hour later we beep our way back through Guangzhou and into the White Swan parking lot. Chen Mou isn't the only one who's tired. I'm exhausted and very cold after standing in the rain in wet clothes all day. When I get to my room, I climb in bed with my clothes still on, and fall straight asleep. Two hours later I wake up, grab a bag of potato chips and a Sprite from the minibar, and take a walk through the lobby. The place is hopping, but it's too much. Back in my room, I turn on the TV. Thanks to satellite technology, I watch a little of *The Right Stuff,* check the news, which is all about the upcoming Academy Awards, and watch previews for *The Witches of Eastwick* and *The Mission,* both part of the station's Academy Award Week.

The next morning we meet downstairs in the tour assembly area. Choey Ha presents me with an enameled canister of local tea. Le Chu Wa brings out a miniature wooden water buffalo with a small boy sitting on its back, as a gift for my sons. Choey Ha's husband, Guan Gin Hong, hands me a package wrapped in brown butcher paper and tied with string. Inside, he tells me, is a statue of Kuan Yin for Teruko. He hopes she will enjoy this statue, since Japanese and Chinese Buddhists worship the deity.

When Chen Mou arrives, we traverse the many terraced levels to the River Jade Canton Specialty Restaurant for breakfast. Today we are not quite as large a crowd—only Choey Ha and her husband, Le Chu-wa (Joanie), Chen Mou, Ming Tia and his wife, and me. Once we're seated in our small banquet room, young waitresses bring out steamers of *bao* stuffed with salted egg, chicken feet with honey sauce, shrimp dumplings, pork dumplings, water-chestnut cake, steamed fish mouths with bean sauce, egg tarts, sesame dumplings, and bowls of *congee* (what we have always called *jook*) with dried scallops and ginkgo fruit. We noisily sip tea, spin the lazy susan, and point out to each other the best morsels in each steamer dish or bowl.

These relatives are open, helpful, candid, whereas back in Los Angeles, brothers, sisters, and cousins were still guarded in their discussions, perhaps following the old adage "Sweep the snow in front of your own doorstep, and do not bother about the frost on top of the other's roof." (When all is said and done, I believe the main outcome of this trip was that my family in Los Angeles began to open up. Just weeks after returning, at an engagement banquet for Sumoy's son, I ran into Kuen, Fong Yun's son who went to Canton with the See family in 1919 and who avoided being kidnapped in 1927. After chatting for a few minutes about the house where he was born, he said he still felt badly about Duk, the brother who died in the kidnapping. "I didn't know he was going to die. If the kidnappers had found me, maybe that brother would be alive.")

Ming Tia has brought a notebook that he's filled with notes. He describes my great-great-grandfather, Fong Dun Shung, and his kung-fu show. The other members of the family provide the names of "lost" relatives, often consulting and arguing over dates and relationships. They chronicle what happened to Fong Guai King, Ngon Hung's mother, after 1949. Having been cataloged a landlord and hence one of the bad classes, Chen Mou translates, her life was made miserable. Over the years, she would periodically be made to kneel in the street for public confessions. Ngon Hung sent money, but even this didn't help.

In many ways Fong Guai King and Si Ping were extremely lucky. During the years of 1950, 1951, and 1952, Mao himself guessed that over 800,000 "counterrevolutionaries" were killed. A broader estimate, which includes landlords beaten to death and other civilian executions between 1948 and 1955, puts the number at closer to four million. In 1957 an Anti-Rightist Campaign was targeted against another half-million Chinese; their deaths numbered in the tens of thousands. Then, in 1958, Mao launched the Great Leap Forward. Designed to encourage China to catch up with the West, it resulted in the greatest famine known to mankind. It has been suggested that as many as thirty million people died between 1958 and 1961.

Fortunately for Fong Guai King and Si Ping, Ngon Hung sent additional funds in 1958 for the two women to move to Hong Kong. This was hardly a match made in heaven—between the fourth wife and the mother of the third wife—and Si Ping eventually abandoned the possibility of freedom to move back to Foshan. In Hong Kong, Guai King adopted several sons, who cheated her out of her house, her savings, her possessions. Ngon Hung was so mad that she refused to send any more money. In time, Guai King was placed in a nursing home. In 1971 she "broke her leg and died of complications."

Ming Tia recounts Si Ping's last years, and has brought photographs of her funeral. She died in Foshan, but wanted to be buried in the home village. In the photographs, a hundred or so mourners make their procession through Dimtao in pouring rain. Incense and personal effects were burned in her honor, Ming Tia says. Then he hands me pictures of Si Ping laid out in blue peasant slacks and a quilted jacket. She seems short, a little heavy. Her ankles are swollen; her mouth hangs open, slack.

Eventually the group turns wistful. Choey Ha went to Hong Kong once with Ngon Hung's mother to help her with some of her belongings. It had been planned that both of them would immigrate to America. But when Fong Guai King died, all plans for sponsorship ended. Ming Tia and his wife also went to Hong Kong for a visit. His wife traveled there a second time as a tourist. Even their mother, Ngan Fa, has been to Hong Kong twice, and she went to the United States in the twenties. Before Fong Yun died, five people in the family had been sponsored to leave China, but the government wouldn't let them go. They don't know what would happen if they tried again.

"Your family here is not poor and not very rich," explains Chen Mou. "Sometimes it has been a little hard, but thanks to their father they have lived comfortably. He left them some money in the United States. Each year his children here receive two hundred dollars U.S. in interest. Your aunt's son, John, has studied, has been to machinery college for four years, and has worked as a manager. He would like to go to America."

"Yeah, yeah," interrupts Joanie, John's wife. "Engineer." She adds tentatively, "I studied in a South China teaching college. Teach middle school for five years."

Choey Ha, who's been listening to this foreign exchange, rattles off some words to Chen Mou. "The older generation does not want to go America," he translates. "They are too old. But they would like the younger generation to go abroad. They would like to provide opportunities for their children. Their children are smart and hardworking. They would have more opportunities over there."

Chen Mou's eyes narrow at this turn of conversation. He's been expecting the next question for some time, as have I. "Will you sponsor this couple to help them go to America?"

"I'll try."

How about Chen Mou? Is he interested in leaving China? "Frankly, I am a rich young man in China," he says, grinning. "If I go to America,

I would have to go to middle school, then university. I would be forty before I graduate. Then I would need a girlfriend, then a wife, then one or two children, then I would die. Here, in one or two more years I'll be able to buy my own house. Yes, it's a much smaller life, but I don't want to spend my precious years in university." He shrugs. "Different people, different lives."

We gather, like countless other families before us, on a low platform in front of the White Swan's famed waterfall in the atrium. The golden characters above the gushing water proclaim, "Drink of the village of your birth." We go through another round of those impossible family group shots. Of course, the camera's batteries die and there's that universal awkwardness that always happens when someone (in this case me) wants a picture desperately and everyone else (in this case my relatives) wishes the whole thing were over. With the photographs out of the way, Chen Mou says good-bye, slings his overnight bag over his shoulder, and heads out to meet a Taiwanese tour group.

I am left alone with the family for the first time, and we struggle to communicate with a combination of Le Chu-wa's elementary English, improvised hand gestures, and drawings in my notebook. Do you like it here? What is it like in Los Angeles? What is a supermarket? How much did the airline ticket cost? With promises of letters back and forth about sponsorship (which will never get anywhere), family history, and photographs (of my children and the last two days), we shake hands, and bow our heads politely. They turn and walk away. I make my way back through the thronging tour-group lobby of the White Swan, where I overhear a slick tour guide instructing a driver on the intricacies of the English language. "Let me take a look." "Let me see." "Please take a look." "Follow me." As I walk past, the guide stops me and asks, "What does the phrase 'my heart goes out to you' mean?"

EPILOGUE (2012)

I didn't know when I wrote *On Gold Mountain* that it would change my life, and I certainly never guessed that it would have an impact on other people's lives. For me, it all started at a bookstore event I did when *On Gold Mountain* was first published, where a lot of my relatives came out to support me. It's fair to say that many of them are not what you'd call book buyers or even book readers, but they love me and they dutifully came through the line to buy a copy of the book. As I continued to sign, I could see people move away to other parts of the room, open the book, and flip through it. I started to hear exclamations: "Look, here's a photograph of my mother. I've never seen a photograph of her," or "Here's a photo of me as a baby. I thought my earliest photo was when I joined the army." I had found photos at the National Archives that no one in our family knew existed. Now those same relatives came back through the line to buy armloads of *On Gold Mountain.* It was one of my first signings and every copy was bought.

It took a while before I began to hear from readers who weren't my relatives. *On Gold Mountain* was unique. It told the story of the Chinese in America through the eyes of one family. It was adopted for use in high schools and in college courses. High school students told me they wrote essays about *On Gold Mountain* on their college applications . . . and then got in. College students wrote to inform me that the book inspired them to become Asian American Studies or American Studies majors. I also heard from people who said that in finding *my* family history, I had discovered *their* family histories, too. These were people whose parents and grandparents were gone, and their stories with them. Now, with *On Gold Mountain,* they learned about Angel Island, life in Chinatown, and discriminatory laws. In the process, the secrets their families had kept bubbled to the surface and suddenly seemed to make sense. As one woman wrote to me, "Thank you for giving language to my parents that I could truly understand and that validated all that they tried to relay to me over the years in the best way they could."

All of this was exciting and wonderful. Then one day I got a call from the Chinatown Chamber of Commerce, asking me to be a judge for the Los Angeles Miss Chinatown Pageant. This might not have meant much to other writers or even to you reading this right now, but it was a very big deal to me. When I was a little girl, Uncle Gilbert got to be a Miss Chinatown judge. Everyone in the family thought it was the most exciting honor *ever.* Now it had happened to me! My family was impressed, but I also came away knowing that the story I'd told had been fully accepted by people in Chinatown. I'd gotten the history of Chinatown right, and I hadn't embarrassed or hurt anyone in the process.

Not long after *On Gold Mountain* was published, I was invited to give a talk at the Southern Oregon Historical Society. Carol Harbison, a researcher there, had helped me a lot when I was working on the book, finding the original homesteading documents for the Pruett family and sending along newspaper clippings noting when John Milton Pruett died, when Ticie graduated from high school, when one of her brothers got married, and the like. After curiosity inspired her to drive past the old Pruett homestead, she wrote to me that the barn was still on the property and that I should come up and take a look at it too.

It was 118 degrees the day I arrived in Medford. I drove to the Pruett homestead, walked through the deserted barn (the only building on the property), and got a feel for the land and the view. Then I drove to the cemetery where Carol said Ticie's parents were buried. The weeds were up to my shoulders, but I walked up and down the rows between the burial plots until I found John Milton Pruett's headstone and next to that the one for his wife. I hadn't known her name—but then I knew almost nothing about Ticie, her parents, her siblings, or the way they lived—but now I knew that her name was Luscinda and that she had died on April 9, 1877.

Twenty minutes later, I met Carol for the first time. You never know when one question will change everything. I asked Carol if it ever snowed in Medford. (Remember, it was 118 degrees that day.) She spoke about Medford's weather—the heat, the fog, the snow. "I live pretty far from here," she said at last, "and at home I keep a Xeroxed copy of a diary written in 1877 by a man who was a farmer by day and a preacher on horseback by night. He kept the diary for just one year, and at the end of each entry he always made a notation of the weather. I use it like an almanac, so I'll know what to wear to work. Would you like to take a look at the original diary?" Absolutely!

Soon I held Reverend Peterson's diary in my hands. I had just learned that Luscinda Pruett had died on April 9, 1877. I turned to that page in the diary, and Reverend Peterson was with her when she died. It turned out that the Petersons and the Pruetts were neighbors. The entire diary was filled with anecdotes about the Pruetts—how they traded butter for lard and how much Reverend Peterson paid the Pruett boys to do hauling.

He also tracked Luscinda's illness, what passage in the Bible she asked him to read at her funeral, and even what the weather was like on the day of her burial. Carol had helped me find information about Ticie and her family that no one else knew. It's a funny thing that while everyone had stories about Fong See, very few had stories about Ticie. She was "just the mom," but I discovered her to be an extraordinary, inspiring, and ultimately tragic woman. I owed Carol for her help in giving Ticie a voice and story of her own, so off I went to give my talk.

At the end of the historical society event, a group of people approached me. Southern Oregon is still quite rural, with ranchers and orchardists. The men wore cowboy hats, cowboy boots, and big cowboy belt buckles. They introduced themselves as Ticie's brothers' descendants. (One of them had visited the historical society a few days earlier to see what he could find on his family and Carol happened to be the person who helped him. He mentioned an old family name, Pruett, and she said something along the lines of, "Boy, do I have a story to tell you.") I had been raised with the belief that Ticie's family had disowned her when she married a Chinese, and that there hadn't been any contact between the Pruett and See families for more than one hundred years. When Ticie and Sissee went to Medford in 1941, Ticie had refused to look up her relatives. Even when Sissee found them listed in the phone book, Ticie didn't want to call. She told Sissee she didn't want to see them. She was sure they wouldn't want to see her. At least that was the story I was told.

A year after my talk at the historical society, my husband, our sons, and I went to a Pruett family reunion in Medford. Zee Minear—the granddaughter of John Pruett (Ticie's youngest brother) and his wife, Effie—showed me photographs of Ticie as a baby, with the cousins she took care of as a little girl, and as a young woman. Oh, how I wish I'd had those images for the book. But what truly stunned me were the photographs Zee showed me of the See family. Ticie must have sent them when each of her children was born. But how could that be, when there had been no contact between the two families since Ticie married Fong See? Zee also recalled that she had visited Los Angeles, the store, and her great-aunt back in the early 1940s. I was convinced she was mistaken, because up until this point all archival material—letters, diaries, and the interrogations from Angel Island—had proved that the family stories I'd gathered were truthful and extremely accurate. But as a friend and scholar explained to me not long ago, "It's very difficult to accept when the historical record proves family stories wrong." So even though the evidence was right in front of me, I couldn't make myself believe what I was seeing and hearing.

The more likely story, it seemed to me, was one told to me by another Pruett cousin, who spoke about Rodelwin, Ticie's second youngest brother. When Rodelwin was on his deathbed, he kept wondering if his sister "had been happy after marrying a Chinaman." What struck me then was that

Ticie—more than a hundred years after running away from home—was like a ghost in the Pruett family. Most of the people I met at the reunion had never met Ticie, but they knew about her and wondered about her. This not only fit with *my* version of the facts, but it was also shored up by the knowledge that many families have a relative who has disappeared, for whatever reason, and lives on as a ghost in stories that are told on holidays.

It wasn't until just this past year—sixteen years after the publication of *On Gold Mountain*—that my cousin Leslee, Gilbert and Sissee's daughter, uncovered a cache of letters written by relatives in Medford and Central Point to Miss Ticie Pruett at 723 K Street in Sacramento. The letters are all written in pencil—very faded after more than a hundred years—and addressed to "Dear Sister." (I found this very touching, since Ticie wanted her daughter to be called Sister. Florence was Sister See until her brothers shortened it to Sissee.) In the early letters, Ticie's family members beg her to come home. They go on and on about how worried they are about her. The letters are also filled with comments about Medford's pesky weather, what's being planted or harvested, who's come down with consumption, who's gotten married, given birth, or died. They also have some creative spelling.

"Please think a bout coming home," one of Ticie's sisters-in-law wrote on September 2, 1897. "It been so long I think you mite come home. I hope your not distrusted with home and want to stay a way. Our home is the same as it ever was. You are always welcome . . ." She goes on to write that she's been canning and that she wishes that she and Ticie were doing this women's chore together. But there's also a line that contains a small hint of possible family gossip about Fong See: "I have never heard a word a bout you not keeping the right company."

The biggest revelation in these letters is that Ticie owned twenty acres in Oregon, which her brothers very specifically refer to as "your place." Several letters—and here the brothers seem to be quarrelling among themselves about what is a fair price—discuss whether Ticie should accept $700 or $800 from her brother, Irvin, for her land. "Do what you think is best for your self," one of the brothers wrote on December 9, 1897. "Have you anything in view that you could put your money into that you think could make more?"

So what do we make from these missives? The story has always been that Fong See and Ticie went to a lawyer to draw up their contract marriage on January 15, 1897, which means that she was no longer Miss Ticie Pruett when her family wrote to her. She was already living with Fong See at the Curiosity Bazaar at 723 K Street. And she certainly had reasons to sell her property: she was married, she was helping her husband run a business, and they were thinking about relocating to Los Angeles, where they would move by the end of the year. These letters also confirmed a lot of what I knew about Ticie. She always said that a woman should have her own money, and she did. (But I can't help wonder how much Fong See knew about her land before they married. Seven hundred dollars was a lot of money in 1897.) Last, and most important, her family didn't disown her. Her sister-in-law, Effie, even wrote to Ticie in Hong Kong during the family's first trip to Asia in 1901. "I suppose you are visiting with your husband's people, are you not? I suppose you will travel all over China before you return here. How I would like to be with you and take in some of the grand sights . . . Oh, Ticie! I wish we could be together and have a good old chat."

And then a long silence. In 1917, Ticie received a telegram and a written note about the death of one of her brothers. Then another long silence, until July 28, 1926, when Effie opens a letter with, "After so many years we haven't heard from you." By this time, Ticie and Fong See had gone their separate ways. Then jump to 1934, when Ticie received a letter from Hazel, John and Effie's daughter, saying that her father had passed away: "He talked a great deal of you of late." In 1941, Sissee took her mother to Medford. I can still visualize the scene as Sissee recounted it to me: the car parked by the side of the road, Sissee calling to her mother from the phone booth, Ticie sitting in the car, refusing to reach out to her family after days of driving and forty-seven years of separation, because she's so sure they don't want to see her. This, perhaps more than anything I've discovered about Ticie, makes me very sad. What was she feeling in that moment as she neared the end of her life? Embarrassment that she hadn't made more of an effort to stay connected to her family? Shame that her marriage to a Chinese hadn't worked out? I'll never know for sure. But what I do now know is that on January 9, 1943, both Hazel and Effie wrote to Sissee to express their condolences that Ticie had died. "I was so in hope that I might get to see her again . . ."

These letters, and my occasional visits with Zee and her family in Oregon, tell me that I was wrong—and our whole family was wrong—about Ticie never having contact with her family. (Sissee, for some unknown reason, wasn't completely forthright about all this. After all, Ticie and Sissee were very close. Sissee had to know some of these things. At the very least, she had received the condolence notes.) These letters also tell me that this story continues. I know that there are more things out there for me to discover and learn. The story will never be complete. It will grow as long as there are Sees, Fongs, and Pruetts.

On Gold Mountain has continued to nourish me, feed my fiction, and help me grow as a woman and a writer. I was asked to write the libretto for a Los Angeles Opera community production of the book. Around the same time, I was invited by the Autry Museum of Western Heritage to curate a museum exhibition based on the book. That turned into the largest exhibition ever mounted on the Chinese American experience, and it went on to be shown at the Smithsonian in Washington, D.C. An opera tells a story through the pure emotion of music, while a museum exhibition tells a story in a purely visual way. I took both of these ideas and incorporated them into my writing. Careful readers should see a difference in the quality, style, voice, and emotions of my writing before I did those two projects and all the books that came after, starting with *Snow Flower and the Secret Fan.*

Most of the things I've written about here were totally unexpected. And that's how they should be. Writers should always be surprised. Oddly enough, it wasn't until very recently that I went back and looked at the epigraph for *On Gold Mountain.* I had used the following lines from Wallace Steger's *Angles of Repose:* "Fooling around in the papers my grandparents, especially my grandmother, left behind, I get glimpses of lives close to mine, related to mine in ways I recognize but don't comprehend. I'd like to live in their clothes a while." I didn't realize when I chose those lines that they would turn out to be so profound for me. In all my novels, including the mysteries, I've written about history that has been lost, forgotten, or deliberately covered up. I've written about how history affects individual people and their families, every day, including all of us *right now.* With my writing, I've tried be in the room with my characters and to "live in their clothes a while." In fact, there is one person who has appeared in one form or another in every book I've written: In *Dreams of Joy,* she's Madame Hu; in *Shanghai Girls,* she's the mother-in-law; in *Peony in Love,* she's the grandmother; in *Snow Flower and the Secret Fan,* she's the matchmaker; in the mysteries, she's the neighborhood committee director; and in *On Gold Mountain,* she's my actual grandmother. Writing about Grandma Stella—in different times, in different countries, with different jobs, and looking so completely different than she did in real life, but with some aspect of her character that is absolutely recognizable to me—has allowed me to live in *her* clothes a while, to literally *be* with her every day, even though she has been gone now for many years. It has been one of the greatest treats and blessings of writing for me.

But nothing has been more important or precious to me than my family being proud of me. Readers sometimes tell me that Fong See was an extraordinary man. Maybe he was for his time and place, but he wasn't a Rockefeller or a Kennedy, a Gates or a Jobs. He didn't change the world or wield power outside of his own family or Los Angeles Chinatown. Uncle's and Fong See's descendants, and I include myself in this, are not extraordinary. We are quite ordinary, but I believe there's a lot to be learned from the ordinary and it's that very ordinariness that links my family to *all* American families. We *all* had someone in our families who was crazy enough, brave enough, unlucky enough, or dumb enough to leave his or her home country to come here. (Even Native Americans came from somewhere else.) We *all* share in that immigrant experience.

Maybe my family had a teapot and your family had a coffeepot, but we all—somewhere along the line—had a mother and a father. We all had people in our families who struggled and sacrificed so that we can be here today. All of us want our families to be proud of us, and they show that to us in sometimes unexpected ways.

That first time when I sat down to interview my great-aunt Sissee, I could not have imagined the wonderful things that would grow out of that day. And I certainly never could have imagined or asked for a greater honor than for my Uncle Yun (Fong See's second son from his marriage to Ngon Hung) to request that he be buried with a copy of *On Gold Mountain.* He wanted my words and our family story with him. What I learned from writing *On Gold Mountain* is that all that really matters in life is family, tradition, and love. These are the things that matter the most in all of our lives, and they continue to inspire me every day when I sit down to write.

Ticie Pruett as a baby, c. 1876

ACKNOWLEDGMENTS

I must first thank Florence Leong, who offered this story to me; and her daughter, Leslee Leong, who gave me information on the F. Suie One Company, put me in contact with old customers, and, most of all, acted as an unwavering source of support. On the See side of the family, Mary See, Marcia Norris, Pollyanne Andrews, Gilbert Leong, Margie Hee, and Bernice Leung contributed greatly to this family saga. From my great-grandfather's second family, Chuen and Teruko Fong, Yun Fong, and Sumoy Quon, as well as Mari Burr were equally frank. Fong Yun's family was also willing to speak—both here and in China. In the United States, I am indebted to Danny Ho Fong, Haw Fong, Choey Lon Fong, Choey Lau Fong, Gim Fong, and especially Kuen Fong. In China, Fong Ming Tia and Zhumei-ying, Guan Yi Nian, Le Chu-wa and Wen Xi Pin, Guan Gin Hong, and especially Fong Choey Ha were hospitable, informative, and kind. Although Tyrus Wong is not a blood relative, he might as well be. He has been a true friend to our family.

I wish to acknowledge the many customers, relatives, and friends who consented to be interviewed: Dorothy Anderson, Edward Behme, Jack Catlin, Henry Chung, Kay Copeland, Tony Duquette, Howe Fong, Peter Fong, Bernard Gelbort, Sanora Babb Howe, Dorothy Jeakins, Jackie Joseph, David Lee, Jennie Lee, Jack Levin, Herman Lew, Mary and Dill Louie, Chong Lui, Chabo Okubo, Sally Pine, Verna Plam, Procter Stafford, Sunny Stevenson, Albert Wong, Elsie Wong, George Wong, Helen and Tommy Wong, Michael Woo, and Wilbur Woo. In addition to personal interviews, many people wrote letters filled with their reminiscences: Dick Beck-Meyer, Ellin Crawford, Ron Cribbs, Betty Izant, Bettie Pycha, Leland Steinhauser, Helen Stevens, Doris Crepin Suman, William Benbow Thompson, Thomas Edward Wall, and Donald Way.

Several libraries and institutions proved extraordinarily helpful in my research. The sections on Letticie's family in Medford are present here because of the incredible persistence of Carol Harbison of the Southern Oregon Historical Society. For my Waterville research, I am grateful to Shirley Phillips, librarian of the Waterville Library; Helen Grande, librarian of the Douglas County Historical Society; and Cassie Besel, who took it upon herself to look things up out of the kindness of her heart.

I must also thank the wonderful people at UCLA Special Collections, the Asian American Studies Center at UCLA, the Asian American Studies Library at UC Berkeley, the Bancroft Library, the Los Angeles Public Library, the Chinatown Library, the Library of the Los Angeles County Museum of Art, the Sacramento History Museum, the California State Archives and Museum Collection Center, the USC Regional History Center, the California State Library, the Academy of Motion Picture Arts and Sciences, Bison Archives, and the Railroad Museum in Sacramento. My appreciation further extends to Clarence Shangra (curator of the Asian Art Museum in San Francisco) and Randall Mackinson (curator of the Gamble House in Pasadena). Suellen Cheng of the Chinese Historical Society of Southern California and El Pueblo de Los Angeles Historic Monument tirelessly answered questions, suggested people to interview, and helped sort through both the Society's and El Pueblo's large holdings—including numerous articles, dissertations, and books. She also introduced me to the wonders of the Southern California Chinese American Oral History Project, which was compiled by the Society and the Asian American Studies Center at UCLA. I consider Suellen a true friend.

My deep gratitude goes to Waverly Lowell and Neil Thomsen at the National Archives in San Bruno, and Laura McCarthy at the National Archives in Laguna Nigel, who together changed the course of *On Gold Mountain*. They unearthed close to five hundred pages of immigration documents, interrogations, and photographs of my family.

Since I am neither a historian nor an academician, I have relied heavily on the works of Sucheng Chan, Jack Chen, Alexander McLeod, Ronald Takaki, and John Weaver. Several others have unhesitatingly offered bits of knowledge: Mark Him Lai (for information on the underwear business), Judy Yung (who graciously sent me articles by Flora Belle Jan, the Chinese flapper), Mus and Stephen White (who offered their expertise in dating old photographs as well as access to their extensive photographic library), Jack Moore and Harold Hubbard (for information about Pasadena at the turn of the century), Roberta Greenwood (who shared with me her knowledge, time line, and extensive report on the archaeological excavations of Old Chinatown), Nancy Moure (for advice on the Los Angeles art scene of the 1920s and 1930s), Will South (for his research and insights into the career of Stanton MacDonald-Wright), Gretchen Kreiger (for her knowledge of Chinese herbal medicine), Russell Leong (for last-minute data on Chinese Americans in the 1990s), and, finally, Ruthanne Lum McCunn (who unwittingly set this whole project in motion and, having done so, often offered advice and leads).

Amy Schiffman and Rob Lee handled the fate of another aspect of this story with good humor and common sense. Nancy McCabe supported and pushed the project with passion and devotion. Stan Margulies and Terry Louise Fisher continue to amaze, inspire and thrill me with their visions.

A project like this could not go forward without keeping an eye to the details. For these, I am obliged to Chen Mou (in China) and Shirley Tam (in Los Angeles) for their translation services; Marian Lizzi for her attention and good words; Professor King-kok Cheung and Suellen Cheng (again) for helping me devise a modified system of Wade-Giles for the Cantonese words; Lisa Chang and Ann Britt Claesson for research, errands, and word processing. Sheila Cohn at APA Travel made my numerous trips on this side of the Pacific both adventurous and smooth, while the helpful staff at Lee's Travel Service made sure I made it to the home village.

Ultimately this book is the result of a blending of my parents—an anthropologist and a writer. My father, Richard See, has been both a critic and an enthusiast. I thank him for his insights, his papers, his hours of interviews. As for my mother, Carolyn See, I have spoken to her almost every day for the last five years about this project. She has been a constant inspiration. (For those readers who feel that her story has been given short shrift in these pages, I refer them to her book, *Dreaming: Hard Luck and Good Times in America*.) I appreciate my parents' bravery, trust, and frankness. While I'm at it, I must also thank John Espey, another "father" and old China hand; Clara Sturak, sublime sister and meticulous editor; and Stella See, wonderful grandma and tantalizing storyteller.

I'm grateful to Thomas McCormack, my editor at St. Martin's, who has shown himself to be patient, intelligent, a gentleman. Sandra Dijkstra, whose help started long before she became my agent, has balanced grace and iron, humor and commiseration, a soft heart and a hard business mind. She's the best. My husband, Richard Kendall, has gallantly encouraged me while I fretted and worried. My final thanks must go to my cousins Sian and Mara Nichols, and my sons Alexander and Christopher Kendall, whose bloodlines, youth, and sweet spirits kept me focused on the real purpose of this book.

SOURCES

CHAPTER 1. THE WONDER TIME

Author's interviews with Chuen Fong, Danny Ho Fong, Haw Fong, Kuen Fong, Gilbert Leong, Florence Leong, Leslee Leong.

Buell, Paul D., et al. *Chinese Medicine on the Golden Mountain: An Interpretive Guide*. Edited by Henry G. Schwarz. Seattle: Wing Luke Memorial Museum, 1984.

Burkhardt, V. R. *Chinese Creeds and Customs*. 3 vols. Hong Kong: Publications Division, South China Morning Post, Ltd., 1953–58.

Chan, Sucheng. *This Bitter-sweet Soil: The Chinese in California Agriculture, 1860–1910*. Berkeley: University of California Press, 1986.

Chen, Jack. *The Chinese of America*. San Francisco: Harper & Row, 1980, 23, 67–72.

George, Marian M. *A Little Journey to China and Japan*. Chicago: A. Flanagan Co., 1928.

Gunther, Barth. *Bitter Strength*. Cambridge, Mass.: Harvard University Press, 1964.

Holden, William M. *Sacramento*. Fair Oaks, Calif.: Two Rivers Publishing Co., 1987, 290.

Johnson, Paul C. *Pictorial History of California*. Garden City, N.Y.: Doubleday, 1970.

Kingston, Maxine Hong. *China Men*. New York: Vintage, 1977.

Leland, Dorothy Kupcha. *A Short History of Sacramento*. San Francisco: Lexicos Press, 1989.

McCunn, Ruthanne Lum. *An Illustrated History of the Chinese in America*. San Francisco: Design Enterprises of San Francisco, 1979.

McLeod, Alexander. *Pigtails and Gold Dust*. Caldwell, Idaho: Caxton Printers, 1947.

Mei Dai Wah and Wu Gee Chuan. *The Stories of Chinese Americans*, vol. 7. Foshan, China: Foshan Wen Shih Magazine. Department of History of the City of Foshan, 1987.

National Archives, Record Group 85: Fong See—25503/1–1.

Reid, Daniel P. *Chinese Herbal Medicine*. Boston: Shambhala Publications, 1990, 10.

Sacramento Bee. *Sacramento Guide Book*. 1940.

Southern California Chinese American Oral History Project, cosponsored by the Chinese Historical Society of Southern California and the UCLA Asian American Studies Center: Nellie Chung.

CHAPTER 2. EXCLUSION

Author's interviews with Chuen Fong, Kuen Fong, Florence Leong, Richard See.

National Archives, Record Group 85: business file, Sacramento—13542/74; Fong Quong—10157/51; Fong See—25503/1-1; Fong Yun—23852/2-15; Ray See—18889/2-2.

Beebe, Lucius, and Charles Clegg. *The American West: The Pictorial Epic of a Continent.* New York: Bonanza Books, 1955.

California State Archives and Museum Collection Center, Registry of Partnerships.

Chan. *This Bitter-sweet Soil.* (See Sources, chapter 1.)

Chen. *The Chinese of America.* (See Sources, chapter 1.)

Childers, Lida, and Ruby Lacy. *Ashland Tidings.* Self-published. Ashland, Ore., 1990.

Chiu, Ping. *Chinese Labor in California: An Economic Study.* Madison, Wisc.: State History Society of Wisconsin for the Department of History, University of Wisconsin, 1963.

Genaw, Linda Morehouse. *At the Crossroads: A History of Central Point.* Self-published. Central Point, Ore. June, 1986.

Genealogical Forum of Portland, Oregon. Genealogical Material in Oregon Donation Land Claims, vol. 1, 1957.

Gillenkirk, Jeff, and James Motlow. *Bitter Melon: Stories from the Last Rural Chinese Town in America.* Seattle: University of Washington Press, 1987.

A History of Eagle Point and Surrounding Communities, Vol I. Self-published pamphlet. Eagle Point, Oregon.

Holden. *Sacramento.* (See Sources, chapter 1.)

Jackson, Donald Dale. "Behave Like Your Actions Reflect on All Chinese." *Smithsonian,* February 1991.

James, Walter. Unpublished interview by Mark Him Lai, Laura Lai and Philip Choy on August 16, 1970. Information on Gwing Yee Hong from interview with Bing Lai, M. H. Lai's father, March–June 1967.

Leland. *A Short History.* (See Sources, chapter 1.)

Loomis, Reverend A. W. "How Our Chinamen Are Employed." *Overland Monthly,* Jan.–June 1869.

McCunn. *An Illustrated History.* (See Sources, chapter 1.)

Mei and Wu. *Stories.* (See Sources, chapter 1.)

National Archives, Record Group 85: business file, Sacramento—13542/74; Fong Quong—10157/51; Fong See—25503/1-1; Fong Yun—23852/2-15; Ray See—18889/2-2.

Peterson, Martin. Drawing courtesy of the Southern Oregon Historical Society.

Sacramento Bee. *Sacramento Guide Book,* 1940.

Sandmeyer, Elmer Clarence. *The Anti-Chinese Movement in California.* Urbana: University of Illinois, 1973.

San Francisco Bulletin, 22 February 1876; *Sacramento Record Union,* 22 June 1876; *Grass Valley National,* 11 June 1869. Bancroft Scraps. Bancroft Library, University of California Library.

See, Richard. "A Comparison of Reaction in California to the Chinese, Japanese, and Drought Refugees from 1850–1940." Unpublished paper, UCLA, circa 1956.

Takaki, Ronald. *Strangers from a Different Shore: A History of Asian Americans*. Boston: Little, Brown, 1989, 88, 103, 122, 128.

Wong, Cynthia. "The Clothing Industry." Unpublished paper, Asian American Studies Library, University of California, Berkeley, 1973.

CHAPTER 3. LOVE

Author's interview with Florence Leong.

Childers and Lacy. *Ashland Tidings*. (See Sources, chapter 2.)

Democratic Times, Jacksonville, Ore. June 1894.

Genaw. *At the Crossroads*. (See Sources, chapter 2.)

Jackson County (Ore.) marriage records, 1895.

Jackson County (Ore.) school census, 1893.

National Archives, Record Group 85: business file, Sacramento—13542/74; Fong Quong—10157/51; Fong See—25503/1–1.

CHAPTER 4. LO SANG

Asian American Studies Center, University of California, Los Angeles, and Chinese Historical Society of Southern California. *Linking Our Lives*. Los Angeles: Chinese Historical Society of Southern California, 1984. Referred to subsequently as *Linking Our Lives*.

Author's interviews with Pollyanne Andrews, Roberta Greenwood, Gretchen Kreiger, Gilbert Leong, Florence Leong, Leslee Leong, Richard See, Stella See.

Bingham, Edwin R. "The Saga of the Los Angeles Chinese." Master's thesis, Occidental College, May 1942.

De Falla, Paul M. "Lantern in the Western Sky." *Historical Society of Southern California, Annual Publication* 42, no. 1 (March 1960).

Engh, Michael E., S.J. *Frontier Faiths: Church, Temple and Synagogue in Los Angeles, 1846–1888*, Albuquerque: University of New Mexico Press, 1992.

Greenwood, Roberta S. "Cultural Resources Impact Mitigation Program Los Angeles Metro Rail Red Line Segment 1." Report submitted to the Los Angeles County Transportation Commission, December 1993.

Guinn, J. M. "The Plan of Old Los Angeles." Historical Society of Southern California, 1895.

"Indecencies in Cemetery," *Los Angeles Daily Times*. 11 December 1902.

Kwok Lo Kwai. *Useful Manual for the Use of Traders in China*. Hong Kong: Man Yu Tong, 1895.

Lee, Mabel Sam. "Recreational Interests and Participation of a Selected Group of Chinese Boys and Girls in Los Angeles, California." Master's thesis, University of Southern California, 1939.

Locklear, William R. "The Celestials and the Angels." *Historical Society of Southern California Quarterly* 42, no. 3, 239–56.

Mason, William. "The Chinese in Los Angeles." *Museum Alliance Quarterly* (publication of Los Angeles County Museum of Natural History) 6, no. 2 (1967).

McDannold, Thomas Allen. "Development of the Los Angeles Chinatown: 1850–1970." Master's thesis, California State University, Northridge, 1973.

McLeod. *Pigtails*. (See Sources, chapter 1.)

McWilliams, Carey. "Cathay in Southern California." *Common Ground*, Autumn 1945.

Mei and Wu. *Stories*. (See Sources, chapter 1.)

National Archives, Record Group 85: Fong See—25503/1–1; Fong Yun—23852/2–15; F. Suie One Company business file—13524/25.

Southern California Chinese American Oral History Project: Kenneth Ung.

Sterry, Nora. "Housing Conditions in Chinatown Los Angeles." *Journal of Applied Sociology* 7 (November–December 1922).

Workman, Boyle, with Caroline Walker. *The City that Grew*. Los Angeles: Southland Publishing Co., 1936.

Yee, George and Elsie. "The Chinese and the Los Angeles Produce Market." *Gum Saan Journal* 9, no. 2 (December 1986).

CHAPTER 5. IMMIGRATION

Author's interviews with Edward Behme, Florence Leong, Leslee Leong, Richard See, Stella See.

Chen. *The Chinese of America*, 145, 154. (See Sources, chapter 1.)

Chung Sai Yat Po (Chinese Daily Paper, San Francisco), 2, 9, 19, 23 April, 11 September, 6, 12, 15, 23 November, 12 December 1907; 8, 17, 22 May, 24 June, 31 July, 6, 20, 29 August 1908; 1 January, 12 June 1909; 3, 9 January 1913.

Jackson. "Behave Like Your Actions . . ." (See Sources, chapter 2.)

Linking Our Lives. (See Sources, chapter 4.)

Mei and Wu. *Stories*. (See Sources, chapter 1.)

National Archives, Record Group 85: Fong Lai—5522–425, 17895/17–13; Fong Quong—10157/51; Fong See—25503/1–1; Fong Yun—23852/2–15; F. Suie One Company business file—13524/25.

Southern California Chinese American Oral History Project: Betty Wong Lem, Billy Lew.

CHAPTER 6. FAMILY DAYS

Anderson, Eva G. *Pioneers of North Central Washington*. Wenatchee [Wash.] World, 1980.

Author's interviews with Pollyanne Andrews, Jack Catlin, Kuen Fong, Roberta Greenwood, Jennie Lee, Gilbert Leong, Florence Leong, Leslee Leong, Randall Mackinson, Mary See, Richard See, Stella See.

Beginnings. Wenatchee, Wash.: Commercial Printing, 1989.

Big Bend [Wash.] Empire, 2, 24 January, 7, 25 February 1901; 8 October 1914; 14 December 1916.

Burks, Arthur J. *Here Are My People*. New York: Literary Digest Books, Funk & Wagnalls, 1934.

Commission of Immigration and Housing of California. Second Annual Report, 2 January 1916.

Chung Sai Yat Po, 12, 30 October, 26 November, 16 December 1918.

Directory of Cheland & Douglas Counties. Seattle: R. L. Polk & Co., 1907.

Douglas County [Wash.] Press, 13 July 1905; 21 December 1916.

Douglas County Registry of Births, Registry of Marriages, Registry of Voters.

"Former Merchant Here." *Independent Star News* [Los Angeles], 31 March 1957.

Headland, Isaac Taylor. *Chenchu, Our Little Chinese Cousin*. Boston: L. C. Page & Co., 1903.

Larson, Louise Leung. *Sweet Bamboo*. Los Angeles: Chinese Historical Society of Southern California, 1989.

National Archives, Record Group 85: Fong Lai—5522–425 and 17895/17–13; Fong See—25503/1–1; Fong Yun—23852/2–15; Milton See—12017/39625; F. Suie One Company Business File—13524/25.

Pacific Asia Museum. "Welcome to the Pacific Asia Museum." Pamphlet.

Southern California Chinese American Oral History Project: Walter Chung.

CHAPTER 7. THE HOME VILLAGE

Author's interviews with Chuen Fong, Choey Ha Fong, Kuen Fong, Margie Hee, Gilbert Leong, Florence Leong, Leslee Leong, Marcia Norris, Mary See, Stella See.

Chen. *The Chinese of America*. (See Sources, chapter 1.)

George, Marian M. *A Little Journey to China and Japan*. Chicago: A. Flanagan Company, 1928.

Gilien, Sasha. "Profile of Ray See." *Designers West*, March 1964.

McLeod. *Pigtails*. (See Sources, chapter 1.)

Mei and Wu. *Stories*. (See Sources, chapter 1.)

Meyer, McEuen Minna. *Chinese Lanterns*. West Medford, Mass.: The Central Committee on the United Study of Foreign Missions, 1924.

Muller, Mary. *The Wretched Flea, or the Story of a Chinese Boy*. Chicago & New York: A. Flanagan Co., 1901.

National Archives, Record Group 85: Fong See—25503/1–1; Fong Yun—13524/25; Bennie See—18889/2–3; Eddy See—18889/2–4; Florence See—18889/2–5; Letticie See—8889/5–30; Milton See—12017/39625; Ray See—12017/11975.

Porter, Katherine Anne. *Mae Franking's My Chinese Marriage*. Austin: University of Texas Press, 1991.

Service, Grace. *Golden Inches: The Chinese Memoir of Grace Service*. Edited by Jack Service. Berkeley: University of California Press, 1989.

Southern California Chinese American Oral History Project: Eddie Lee.

CHAPTER 8. PLAYBOYS

Anderson. *Pioneers*. (See Sources, chapter 6.)

Author's interviews with Pollyanne Andrews, Chuen Fong, Gim Fong, Kuen Fong, Choey Ha Fong, David Lee, Jennie Lee, Gilbert Leong, Florence Leong, Leslee Leong, Dill Louie, Mary Louie, Nancy Moure, Sumoy Quon, Richard See, Stella See.

Big Bend Empire, 27 May, 30 June 1920.

Chen. *The Chinese of America*. (See Sources, chapter 1.)

Gilien. "Profile." (See Sources, chapter 7.)

Greenwood. "Cultural Resources." (See Sources, chapter 4.)

Henstell, Bruce. *Sunshine and Wealth: Los Angeles in the Twenties and Thirties*. San Francisco: Chronicle Books, 1984.

Jan, Flora Belle. "Chinatown Sheiks Are Modest Lot." *San Francisco Examiner*, 27 February 1924.

Mei and Wu. *Stories*. (See Sources, chapter 1.)

Moure, Nancy Dustin Wall. *Southern California Art*. Los Angeles: Publications in California Art, 1984.

National Archives, Record Group 85: Fong Lai—17895/17–13; Fong See—25503/1–1; Fong Yun—23852/2–15.

"Oriental Firm to Build Home." *Los Angeles Times*, 1 April 1923.

Southern California Chinese American Oral History Project: Walter Chung, Jackman Hom.

Sterry, Nora. "Social Attitudes of Chinese Immigrants." *Journal of Applied Sociology*, July 1923.

Takaki, Ronald. *Stranger*. (See Sources, chapter 2.)

Weaver, John D. *Los Angeles: The Enormous Village 1781–1981*. Santa Barbara: Capra Press, 1980.

Williams, C. A. S. *Outlines of Chinese Symbolism and Art Motives*. New York: Dover, 1976.

CHAPTER 9. THE KIDNAPPING

Author's interviews with Pollyanne Andrews, Chuen Fong, Gim Fong, Kuen Fong, Choey Ha Fong, Choey Lon Fong, Haw Fong, Howe Fong, David Lee, Florence Leong, Leslee Leong, Dill Louie, Mary Louie, Marcia Norris, Mary See, Richard See, Stella See.

Bingham. "Los Angeles Chinese." (See Sources, chapter 4.)

Greenwood. "Cultural Resources." (See Sources, chapter 4.)

Linking Our Lives. (See Sources, chapter 4.)

National Archives, Record Group 85: Fong Lai—17895/17–13; Fong See—25503/1–1; Fong Yun—23852/2–15.

Southern California Chinese American Oral History Project: Ray Lue, Bill Young.

Yee, George and Elsie. "The 1927 Chinese Baseball Team." *Gum Saan Journal* 4, no. 1.

CHAPTER 10. DEPRESSION

Author's interviews with Pollyanne Andrews, Henry Chung, Chuen Fong, Gim Fong, Roberta Greenwood, Jennie Lee, Gilbert Leong, Florence Leong, Richard See, Stella See, George Wong, Tyrus Wong.

Bingham. "Los Angeles Chinese." (See Sources, chapter 4.)

Cheng, Suellen, and Munson Kwok. "The Golden Years of Los Angeles Chinatown: The Beginning." In *The Golden Years*. Los Angeles: L.A. Corporation, 1988, 39–47.

Greenwood, Roberta S. "Rediscovering Los Angeles Chinatown." Speech given at the Institute of Archeology. UCLA, 24 May 1990.

——— . "Cultural Resources." (See Sources, chapter 4.)

"Historic Section of City to Give Way as Los Angeles Marches on." *Los Angeles Record*, 14 November 1933.

L'Allemand, Gordon. "Chinatown Passes." *Los Angeles Times Magazine*, 19 March 1933.

Larson, Louise. "Please, What Am I? Chinese or American?" *Los Angeles Times*, 4 November 1934.

Linking Our Lives. (See Sources, chapter 4.)

Los Angeles County Museum of Art artist files on Tyrus Wong.

Louis, Kit King. "A Study of American-born and American-reared Chinese in Los Angeles." Master's thesis, University of Southern California, 1931.

Lyons, James P., with Jean Bosquet. "You Are Seeing My Chinatown Pass!" *Los Angeles Times*, 2 December 1934.

Moure, Nancy Dustin Wall. *Index of Southern California Artists' Clubs and Their Exhibitions*, Los Angeles: Publications in Southern California Art, 1974.

National Archives, Record Group 85: Fong See—25503/1–1; Fong Yun—23852/2–15; Milton See—12017/39625.

Ryan, Don. "The Dragon's Shadow." *Touring Topics*, December 1926.

South, Will. "Stanton MacDonald-Wright and the Emergence of Vanguard Painting in Southern California." Lecture given at the Metropolitan Museum of Art, 10 May 1991.

Southern California Chinese American Oral History Project: James Chan, Henry Lowe, Ray Lue.

Weaver. *The Enormous Village*. (See Sources, chapter 8.)

Zeeman, Raymond. "Lugo House." *The Los Angeles Corral* 179 (Spring 1990).

CHAPTER 11. MEMORIES: TYRUS TELLS HIS STORY

Author's interviews with Gilbert Leong, Tyrus Wong.

"Dialogue with Tyrus Wong and Gilbert Leong." Chinese Historical Society of Southern California evening, 8 January 1991.

Southern California Chinese American Oral History Project: Tyrus Wong.

"Tyrus Wong." *Jade Magazine* 2, no. 1 (Winter 1976).

CHAPTER 12. DRAGON'S DEN

Author's interviews with Pollyanne Andrews, Tony Duquette, Dorothy Jeakins, Gilbert Leong, Florence Leong, Chong Lui, Richard See, Stella See, Will South, Tyrus Wong.

Scott, David W. Introduction to *The Art of Stanton MacDonald-Wright*. Washington, D.C.: Smithsonian Press, 1967.

See, Stella. Personal correspondence and miscellaneous clippings.

South. "Stanton MacDonald-Wright." (See Sources, chapter 10.)

Southern California Chinese American Oral History Project: Spencer Chan, Him Gin Quon.

"Tyrus Wong." *Jade Magazine* 2, no. 1 (Winter 1976).

CHAPTER 13. SNAPSHOTS

Academy of Motion Picture Arts and Science. "When a Little Child Fell Ill an Epic was Born." Program for the premiere of the film *The Good Earth*.

Author's interviews with Pollyanne Andrews, Henry Chung, Kay Copeland, Choey Ha Fong, Choey Lau Fong, Choey Lon Fong, Chuen Fong, Danny Ho Fong, Gim Fong, Haw Fong, Howe Fong, Kuen Fong, Ming Tia Fong, Sanora Babb Howe, Dorothy Jeakins, David Lee, Gilbert Leong, Florence Leong, Mary Louie, Chong Lui, Sumoy Quon, Mary See, Richard See, Stella See, Elsie Wong, Herman Wong, Tyrus Wong.

"Bandits Rob Dragon's Den." *Los Angeles Times*, 29 October 1937.

Chen. *The Chinese of America*. (See Sources, chapter 1.)

Cheng and Kwok. "The Golden Years." (See Sources, chapter 10.)

"The Good Earth." *Town and Sportsman*, June 1934.

Larson. *Sweet Bamboo*. (See Sources, chapter 6.)

Leung, Louise. "Night Call in Chinatown." *Los Angeles Times Magazine*, 26 July 1936.

Linking Our Lives. (See Sources, chapter 4.)

Louie, Ruby Ling. "Reliving China City." *Gum Saan Journal* 11, no. 2 (December 1988).

Mei and Wu. *Stories*. (See Sources, chapter 1.)

Meyer, Minna McEuen. *Chinese Lanterns*. West Medford, Mass.: The Central Committee on the United Study of Foreign Missions, 1924.

National Archives, Record Group 85: Fong Yun—23852/2–15.

"New Chinatown Opens." *Los Angeles Examiner*, 8 June 1938.

Okrent, Neil. "Right Place, Wong Time." *Los Angeles Magazine*, May 1990.

See, Stella. Personal correspondence and miscellaneous clippings.

Southern California Chinese Oral History Project: Eddie Lee, Lily Mu Lee, Peter Soo Hoo Jr., Maye Wong, Ruth Wong.

"Tyrus Wong." *Jade Magazine*. (See Sources, chapter 11.)

CHAPTER 14. ANNA MAY SPEAKS

Academy of Motion Picture Arts and Sciences. Anna May Wong clippings, March 1927; 20 March, 13 June 1928; 3, 11, 12 November 1930; 3 February, 2 June 1931; 29 February 1932; Paramount press releases, 28 December 1937; 9, 13 January, 7 February 1938; Paramount press release by Anna May Wong, 7 January 1938.

"Anna May Wong Is Dead at 54; Actress Won Movie Fame in '24." *New York Times*, 4 February 1961.

Author's interviews with David Lee, Verna Plam, Richard See, Stella See, Elsie Wong.

Carroll, Harrison. "Oriental Girl Crashes Footlights." *Herald Express*, 6 June 1931.

China Doll Special. "The Ultimate Anna May Wong Fanzine," 1, no. 1 (1992).

Kyle, Garland Richard. "The Legend of Anna May Wong." *Gum Saan Journal* 11, no. 2 (December 1988).

Leung, Louis. "East Meets West." *Hollywood Magazine*, January 1939.

Liu, Garding. *Inside Los Angeles Chinatown*. Self-published. Los Angeles, 1948.

Okrent. "Right Place, Wong Time." (See Sources, chapter 13.)

Palmer, Zuma. "Anna May Wong in European Stage, Movie Productions." [Hollywood] *Citizen News*, 2 May 1958.

——— . "Nickelodeon Anna May Wong's First 'School of the Drama.' " [Hollywood] *Citizen News*, 1 May 1958.

Rivers, Audrey. "Anna May Wong Sorry She Cannot Be Kissed," *Movie Classics*, November 1939.

CHAPTER 15. SECOND CHANCES

Author's interviews with Edward Behme, Tony Duquette, Choey Lau Fong, Cheun Fong, Gim Fong, Haw Fong, Margie Hee, Florence Leong, Gilbert Leong, Leslee Leong, Sumoy Quon, Richard See, Stella See, Mike Woo, Wilbur Woo.

Chen. *The Chinese of America*. (See Sources, chapter 1.)

"China City Reopens Today." *Los Angeles Examiner*, 2 August 1939.

Greenwood. "Cultural Resources." (See Sources, chapter 4.)

Lai, Him Mark, Genny Lim, and Judy Yung. *Island: Poetry and History of*

Chinese Immigrants on Angel Island 1910–1940. San Francisco: Hoc Doi, 1980.

Lee, Chingwah. "Chinese Art Through the Backdoor." *California Art and Architecture*, October 1939.

Lee. "Recreational Interests." (See Sources, chapter 4.)

Linking Our Lives. (See Sources, chapter 4.)

Liu. *Inside Los Angeles Chinatown*. (See Sources, chapter 14.)

Los Angeles Times, 26 August, 5 September 1937.

Lyons. "You Are Seeing . . ." (See Sources, chapter 10.)

"New China City Razed by Fire." *Los Angeles Examiner*, 21 February 1939.

Southern California Chinese American Oral History Project: Margaret Kwan Lee, Gilbert Leong, Bernice Leung, Him Gin Quon, Ruth Wong.

Sterry. "Social Attitudes." (See Sources, chapter 8.)

Weaver. "Enormous Village." (See Sources, chapter 8.)

Yee. "Los Angeles Produce Market." (See Sources, chapter 4.)

CHAPTER 16. THE MISSION FAMILY GETS A DAUGHTER-IN-LAW

Author's interviews with Suellen Cheng, Choey Lon Fong, Chuen Fong, Gim Fong, Haw Fong, Howe Fong, Margie Hee, David Lee, Jennie Lee, Florence Leong, Gilbert Leong, Leslee Leong, Dill Louie, Mary Louie, Marcia Norris, Chabo Okubo, Sumoy Quon, Richard See, Stella See, Albert Wong, Tyrus Wong, Wilbur Woo.

Burkhardt. *Chinese Creeds*. (See Sources, chapter 1.)

Chen. *The Chinese of America*. (See Sources, chapter 1.)

Chen, Wen-Hui Chung. "Changing Socio-Cultural Patterns of the Chinese Community in Los Angeles." Doctoral dissertation, University of Southern California, 1952.

"Chinese Want No Identity Errors." *Los Angeles Examiner*, 6 January 1942.

Engh. *Frontier Faiths*. (See Sources, chapter 4.)

——— . "A Most Excellent Field for Work: Christian Missionary Efforts in the Los Angeles Community, 1887–1900." *Gum Saan Journal* 15, no. 1 (June 1992).

"4,000 Chinese Come to Hear Madame Chiang Kai-shek." *Los Angeles Times*, 1 April 1943.

Goldberg, George. *East Meets West*. New York: Harcourt Brace Jovanovich, 1970, 117.

Jackson. "Behave Like Your Actions . . ." (See Sources, chapter 2.)

Larson. *Sweet Bamboo*. (See Sources, chapter 6.)

Lee. "Recreational Interests." (See Sources, chapter 4.)

Leong, Gilbert. Lecture on Los Angeles Chinatown Methodist Mission, Chinese Historical Society of Southern California, 6 March 1991.

Linking Our Lives. (See Sources, chapter 4.)

Louis. "A Study." (See Sources, chapter 10.)

Mason. "The Chinese in Los Angeles." (See Sources, chapter 4.)

McWilliams, Carey. *Prejudice*. Boston: Little, Brown, 1944.

See, Richard. "Chinese Economic Activities in Chinatown." Unpublished paper, UCLA, circa 1957.

——— . "A Comparison." (See Sources, chapter 2.)

Smith, Jack. "Stunning Acts of Bravery That Will Live on in Infamy." *Los Angeles Times*, 24 February 1992.

Southern California Chinese American Oral History Project: Spencer Chan, Margie Hee, Gilbert Leong, Keye Luke.

Takaki. *Strangers*, 374–75, 378. (See Sources, chapter 2.)

Weaver. "Enormous Village." (See Sources, chapter 8.)

CHAPTER 17. HOLLOW BAMBOO

Author's interviews with Pollyanne Andrews, Mari Burr, Choey Lau Fong, Choey Lon Fong, Chuen Fong, Gim Fong, Kuen Fong, Sanora Babb Howe, Dorothy Jeakins, David Lee, Leslee Leong, Marcia Norris, Sumoy Quon, Mary See, Richard See, Stella See, Albert Wong, Tyrus Wong, Wilbur Woo.

Basso, Hamilton. "Los Angeles." *Holiday*, January 1950.

"California: The Pink Oasis." *Time*, 4 July 1949.

Chen. *The Chinese of America*. (See Sources, chapter 1.)

Chen. "Socio-Cultural Patterns." (See Sources, chapter 16.)

Doerr, Conrad J. "But Most of All, I Remember Anna May Wong." *China Doll*, special edition, Spring 1992.

Gilien. "Profile of Ray See." (See Sources, chapter 7.)

"Imperturbed." *Los Angeles Times*, 8 November 1946.

Jackson. "Behave Like Your Actions . . ." (See Sources, chapter 2.)

"Last of Old Chinatown Condemned." *Los Angeles Daily News*, 7 November 1946.

Linking Our Lives. (See Sources, chapter 4.)

Liu. *Inside Los Angeles Chinatown*. (See Sources, chapter 14.)

Nee, Victor G., and Brett de Bary. *Longtime Californ': A Documentary Study of an American Chinatown*. Stanford, Calif.: Stanford University Press, 1972.

"Prevue Furniture Ensembles of Hollywood." Pamphlet prepared by the public-relations department of Prevue Furniture Ensembles, 1942.

See, Ray. Scrapbook references (dates and sources unknown): "California Market Seeks Approval, Acceptance of Modern-Minded Group" (Morris Markoff).

See, Richard. "Chinese Economic Activities." (See Sources, chapter 16.)

Smith, Jack. "A Day in the City." *Westways*, June 1970.

Southern California Chinese American Orai History Project: Gim Fong, Tyrus Wong.

Takaki. *Strangers*. (See Sources, chapter 2.)

Weaver. "Enormous Village." (See Sources, chapter 8.)

CHAPTER 18. FIRE

"The Art of Handscreen Printing." Promotional film for D. N. & E. Walter.

Author's interviews with Dell Andrews, Pollyanne Andrews, Edward Behme, Mari Burr, Kay Copeland, Choey Lon Fong, Chuen Fong, Margie Hee, Florence Leong, Gilbert Leong, Leslee Leong, Bernice Leung, Dill Louie, Mary Louie, Marcia Norris, Verna Plam, Sumoy Quon, Mary See, Richard See, Stella See, Albert Wong, Tyrus Wong, Michael Woo.

"Calinese Model Home Seen by Nearly 15,000." *Los Angeles Times*, 22 January 1950.

Chen. *The Chinese of America*. (See Sources, chapter 1.)

Chen. "Socio-Cultural Patterns." (See Sources, chapter 16.)

"Fire Razes L.A. Furniture Plant." *Los Angeles Express*, 10 October 1947.

Fong Choey Ha, letter, 6 August 1991.

Gilien. "Profile." (See Sources, chapter 7.)

"Hot Fight Rages to Save Plaza Historic Features." *The Mirror* (Los Angeles), 28 September 1950.

Mei and Wu. *Stories*. (See Sources, chapter 1.)

"One-Stop Home Show," *Los Angeles Examiner*, 27 November 1949.

See, Ray. Scrapbook references (dates and sources unknown): "Ray See Stresses Use in Designing Tables"; "See-Mar Features Hand-Carved Wood in Chinese Motifs"; "See-Mar Offers 6 Tropic Wood Tables"; "Coast Firm Presents 36 Lamps Set into Combination Tables"; "See-Mar Expands Business: Introduces Three New Items"; "City Becomes Nation's Third Furniture Center" (Mary Ann Callan).

"See-Mar Moves to Temporary Plant." *Los Angeles Times*, 19 October 1947.

Southern California Chinese American Oral History Project: Margie Leong Hee, Gilbert Leong, Bernice Leung.

Takaki. *Strangers*. (See Sources, chapter 2.)

"They Want Lugo House to Remain—But Where?" *Los Angeles Times*, 29 September 1950.

Weaver, John D. (See Sources, chapter 8.)

"Woman Dies in Fire Laid to Cigarette." *Los Angeles Times*, 22 January 1948.

CHAPTER 19. ANOTHER MARRIAGE

Author's interviews with Pollyanne Andrews, Chuen Fong, Gim Fong, Yun Fong, Jackie Joseph, Florence Leong, Gilbert Leong, Leslee Leong, Marcia Norris, Sumoy Quon, Carolyn See, Mary See, Richard See, Stella See, Albert Wong.

Chen. *The Chinese of America*. (See Sources, chapter 1.)

Chen. "Socio-Cultural Patterns." (See Sources, chapter 16.)

"Fong See, Chinatown's Oldest Resident, Dies." *Los Angeles Times*, 15 March 1957.

"Former Merchant Here." *Independent Star News*, 31 March 1957.

"Funeral Services for Fong See Conducted." *Los Angeles Times*, 24 March 1957.

Laws, George. Letter to Robert Laws, 7 October 1977.

Linking Our Lives. (See Sources, chapter 4.)

Nee and de Bary. *Longtime Californ'*. (See Sources, chapter 17.)

See, Carolyn. "Fifty Million Chinamen." Unpublished ms., 1966.

———. "Melting." In *Sex, Death and God in L.A.*, edited by David Reid. New York: Pantheon Books, 1992.

——— and John Espey. *Two Schools of Thought: Some Tales of Learning and Romance*. Santa Barbara, Calif.: John Daniel & Company, 1991.

See, Richard. "Chinese Economic Activities." (See Sources, chapter 16.)

"Services for Fong See, 99, Scheduled Here Saturday." *Los Angeles Herald Examiner*, 20 March 1957.

Takaki. *Strangers*, 416. (See Sources, chapter 2.)

Tsai, Shih-Shan Henry. *The Chinese Experience in America*. Bloomington, Indiana: Indiana University Press, 1986. 135–36.

UCLA Special Collections. Letters from George Laws, 26 May 1954, 26 March 1959; letters from Richard See (some undated; also 14 June 1951; 11, 23 December 1953; 1, 25 January, 5, 9, 13, 24 March 1954. Letters from Carolyn See, undated.

Weaver. *Enormous Village*. (See Sources, chapter 8.)

Zeeman, Raymond. "Lugo House." *Los Angeles Corral* 179 (Spring 1990).

CHAPTER 20. FAMILY MEANS EVERYTHING

Acosta, Frank, and Bong Hwan Kim. "Race-baiting in Sacramento," *Los Angeles Times*, 4 May 1993.

Author's interviews with Pollyanne Andrews, Jack Catlin, Kay Copeland, Tony Duquette, Gim Fong, Florence Leong, Gilbert Leong, Leslee Leong, Jack Levin, Herman Lew, Chong Lui, Marcia Norris, Sumoy Quon, Carolyn See, Mary See, Richard See, Stella See, Procter Stafford.

Chen. *The Chinese of America*, 228. (See Sources, chapter 1.)

Essoyan, Susan. "Concern Raised on Flow of Chinese Refugees Into U.S." *Los Angeles Times*, 11 February 1993.

Jackson. "Behave Like Your Actions . . ." (See Sources, chapter 2.)

Kristof, Nicholas D., and Sheryl Wudunn. *China Wakes*. New York: Times Books, 1994, 45.

Mann, Jim, Christine Courtney, and Susan Essoyan. "Chinese Refugees Take to High Seas." *Los Angeles Times*, 16 March 1993.

Nee and de Bary. *Longtime Californ'*. (See Sources, chapter 17.)

Smith, Jack. "Sights and Scents Celestial." *Westways*, June 1970.

The State of Asian Pacific America: Economic Diversity, Issues & Policies. LEAP Asian Pacific American Public Policy Institute and UCLA Asian American Studies Center, 1994.

The State of Asian Pacific America: Policy Issues to the Year 2020. LEAP Asian Pacific American Public Policy Institute and UCLA Asian American Studies Center, 1993.

Takaki. *Strangers*, 421–22, 425. (See Sources, chapter 2.)

CHAPTER 21. THE HOME VILLAGE II

Kristof and Wudunn. *China Wakes*, 65–66. (See Sources, chapter 20.)